Complete CL

Complete CL

The Definitive Control Language Programming Guide

Fifth Edition

Ted Holt

MC Press Online, LP
Lewisville, TX 75077

Complete CL: The Definitive Control Language Programming Guide
Ted Hold

Fifth Edition

First Printing—January 2009

Every attempt has been made to provide correct information. However, the publisher and the author do not guarantee the accuracy of the book and do not assume responsibility for information included in or omitted from it.

The following terms are trademarks of International Business Machines Corporation in the United States, other countries, or both: IBM, AS/400, OS/400, iSeries, i5, and i5/OS. All other product names are trademarked or copyrighted by their respective manufacturers.

MC Press offers excellent discounts on this book when ordered in quantity for bulk purchases or special sales, which may include custom covers and content particular to your business, training goals, marketing focus, and branding interest.

For information regarding permissions or special orders, please contact:
MC Press
Corporate Offices
125 N. Woodland Trail
Lewisville, TX 75077 USA

For information regarding sales and/or customer service, please contact:
MC Press
P.O. Box 4300
Big Sandy, TX 75755-4300 USA

ISBN: 978-158347-090-9

CONTENTS

I miss Ernie Malaga. I miss those down-to-earth, no-nonsense, just-the-facts-please technical articles he used to write. When I was in my first factory job, trying to figure my way around the S/38 after years on S/34 and S/36, Ernie taught me a lot though his articles in *Midrange Computing* and his postings on the MC bulletin board.

I wish Ernie were here to see what IBM did with the CL compiler in V5R3, V5R4, and V6R1. I'm sure he would be thrilled, because Ernie enjoyed writing CL, and I think it bothered him as much as it did me that IBM would not beef up the command language with simple structures like subroutines and while/until loops.

I wish IBM had offered Ernie a job years ago enhancing CL, and had paid him big bucks to do it.

I wish Ernie were updating this book with the new features of the most recent releases. But he's been gone for a little over four years now. As Ernie might say it, more's the pity.

I dedicate this new edition of *Complete CL* to the memory of Ernie Malaga. May those of us who knew him, and those of us who benefited from his writing, still remember him when we're old and gray.

Ted Holt
Tupelo, Mississippi
August, 2008

1

INTRODUCTION

Control Language (CL) is a programming language used primarily for control purposes with the IBM i operating system (formerly known as OS/400 and i5/OS). Originating in the early 1980s with the System/38 and continued on the AS/400 eServer iSeries, and System i, CL has undergone a series of improvements (and it still does to this day). While CL is not a general-purpose, high-level language (HLL), its flexibility does allow it to be used for much more than simple control operations. CL is based on commands. All program statements are nothing more than commands. Many of the commands are the same ones you would use manually, from the keyboard, to operate the computer.

WHO NEEDS CL?

CL is for everyone. Because commands can be included in a CL program, you can automate most i5 operations by writing a CL program that contains the necessary commands.

All i5 shops are, by necessity, at least bilingual, because they must support at least two programming languages—and CL is one of them. The other language should be a high-level language such as COBOL or RPG.

WHO HAS CL?

Because CL is part of the computer's operating system (formerly known as i5/OS, but now called IBM i), every system that runs IBM i has CL. Because every system that runs IBM i has CL, it should be the programming language of choice for any programs that do not require the higher functions provided by high-level languages like RPG. This would allow you to take the same program to another i5 with 100 percent certainty that the program will be usable. Such is not the case with other programming languages, such as RPG and COBOL, because most shops install only the compilers they need or wish to use. Yet, CL is absolutely everywhere.

CAPABILITIES OF CL

With CL you can do any of the following:

- Control system power up and power down.
- Change the configuration of the system through changes in system values or line, controller, and device descriptions.
- Manage work on the system by controlling subsystems, job queues, job priorities, memory pools, time slices, and so on.
- Start other jobs by calling programs directly or by submitting jobs to batch processing.
- Control system security by performing security checks or by actually changing user and object authorities.
- Control all forms of communications between your i5 and other systems (peers, hosts, PCs, remote controllers).
- Manage objects in libraries. Objects can be created, duplicated, changed, deleted, reorganized, cleared, renamed, and allocated with CL programs.

The preceding list is not all-inclusive. CL contains more than 1,000 commands with diverse functions.

LIMITATIONS OF CL

As previously noted, CL is not an HLL. CL cannot accomplish everything a language such as RPG can accomplish.

- Database manipulations are limited to reading files. You cannot directly update or write individual records in database files.

- CL supports only five data types: character, decimal, logical, signed integer, and unsigned integer.

2

A First Look at CL

What better way to begin a study of CL programming than by looking at a typical CL procedure?

The Parts of a CL Procedure

A procedure is a compilable set of CL commands. Dissecting and analyzing the various parts of a CL procedure serve as a good introduction to CL. Figure 2.1 shows a typical CL procedure. The lines that make up a CL procedure can be called CL statements or CL commands. The two terms are interchangeable.

```
PGM PARM(&greeting)
   COPYRIGHT  TEXT('(c) 2004, Kaiser Consulting, Inc.')
   DCL &greeting    *CHAR    5
   DCL &msg         *CHAR    80 VALUE(' ')
   DCL &terminal    *CHAR    10
   DCL &user        *CHAR    10
   MONMSG cpf0000
```

Figure 2.1: An example of typical CL procedure (part 1 of 2).

```
begin:
   RTVUSRPRF *CURRENT RTNUSRPRF(&user)
   RTVJOBA JOB(&terminal)
   CHGVAR &msg (&greeting                     *TCAT +
                ' '                            *BCAT +
                &user                          *TCAT +
                '! You''re using terminal'     *BCAT +
                &terminal                      *TCAT +
                '.')
   SNDPGMMSG MSG(&msg) MSGTYPE(*COMP)
ENDPGM
```

Figure 2.1: An example of typical CL procedure (part 2 of 2).

Figure 2.2 illustrates the structure of a typical CL procedure. The sections that follow explain each individual part of the procedure.

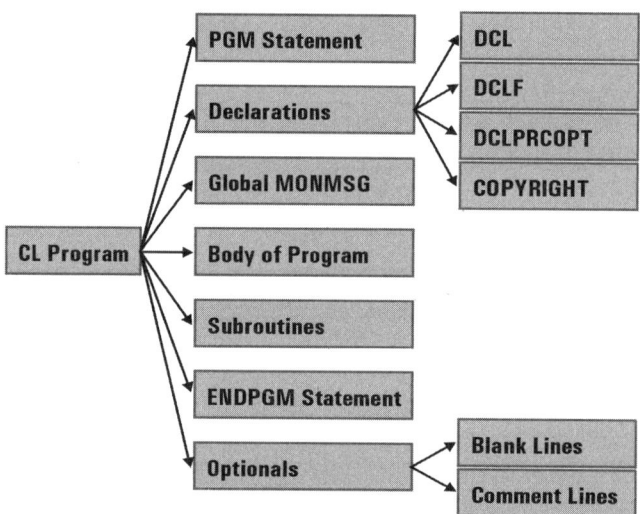

Figure 2.2: Structure of typical CL procedure.

The PGM Command

The Program (PGM) command (Figure 2.3) identifies the beginning of the procedure.

```
PGM PARM(&greeting)
```

Figure 2.3: An example of the PGM command.

The PARM parameter lists the parameters coming into (or going out of) the procedure. The example shown in Figure 2.3 contains only one parameter, called &GREETING, which is a CL variable.

The COPYRIGHT Command

The COPYRIGHT command (Figure 2.4) provides a way to embed copyright information within a CL module. It is optional. If used, the COPYRIGHT command must follow the PGM command, and it must precede the global MONMSG commands and all executable commands.

```
COPYRIGHT  TEXT('(c) 2004, Kaiser Consulting, Inc.')
```

Figure 2.4: An example of the COPYRIGHT command.

To view the copyright information, use the Display Module (DSPMOD) command.

The Declarations

Figure 2.5 shows some examples of declaration (DCL) commands.

```
DCL &greeting    *CHAR    5
DCL &msg         *CHAR    80 VALUE(' ')
DCL &terminal    *CHAR    10
DCL &user        *CHAR    10
```

Figure 2.5: Examples of the DCL command.

Each Declare (DCL) command defines a single variable to the CL procedure. All variables must be declared at the beginning of the procedure.

The DCL command has four parameters, but only the first two are required. The first parameter, VAR, names the variable being declared. The second parameter, TYPE, indicates whether it is a character, decimal, unsigned integer, signed integer, or logical variable. The third parameter, LEN, indicates the variable's length. In addition, the fourth parameter, VALUE, gives the variable its initial value.

In Figure 2.5, the parameter *keywords* VAR, TYPE, and LEN have been omitted to keep the procedure uncluttered. You could also code the DCLs as shown in Figure 2.6.

```
DCL VAR(&greeting)    TYPE(*CHAR) LEN(  5)
DCL VAR(&msg)         TYPE(*CHAR) LEN( 80) VALUE(' ')
DCL VAR(&terminal)    TYPE(*CHAR) LEN( 10)
DCL VAR(&user)        TYPE(*CHAR) LEN( 10)
```

Figure 2.6: An alternative method of coding DCL commands.

Also, notice that all variables are the *CHAR (character) type. Besides DCL, the declaration section of the procedure can contain up to five Declare File (DCLF) commands. The examples shown in Figures 2.5 and 2.6 do not include any DCLF commands.

Global MONMSG

Although the Monitor Message (MONMSG) command is described at length in Chapter 6, it deserves a brief mention now. An example is shown in Figure 2.7.

```
MONMSG cpf0000
```

Figure 2.7: An example of the MONMSG command.

The MONMSG command is used to take corrective action when an error is detected by the system after executing any command in a CL procedure. When MONMSG is coded between the declarations and the body of the procedure, it acts as a *global* error trap because it remains in effect throughout the execution of the procedure. If placed anywhere else, it applies only to the command that immediately precedes it.

The Body of a Procedure

Figure 2.8 shows an example of the body of a typical CL procedure.

```
begin:
    RTVUSRPRF *CURRENT RTNUSRPRF(&user)
    RTVJOBA JOB(&terminal)
    CHGVAR &msg (&greeting                         *TCAT +
                 ' '                               *BCAT +
                 &user                             *TCAT +
                 '! You''re using terminal' *BCAT +
                 &terminal                         *TCAT +
                 '.')
    SNDPGMMSG MSG(&msg) MSGTYPE(*COMP)
```

Figure 2.8: An example of the body of a CL procedure.

The body of the procedure is where the action takes place. It is the meat and potatoes of the CL procedure. Although the PGM and DCL commands are needed in almost all CL procedures, they perform no real function. The commands included in the body of the procedure are another matter altogether.

In the example provided (see Figure 2.8), the first command in the body of the procedure is a Retrieve User Profile (RTVUSRPRF) command, preceded by the label "**begin**:". Labels are mandatory only if they point to the destination of a GOTO, LEAVE, or ITERATE command. However, you can use them anywhere you like. In this case, "**begin**:" marks the first executable command as the beginning of the body of the procedure.

The ENDPGM Command

The End Program (ENDPGM) command indicates the end of the procedure. The CL compiler ignores source code that follows an ENDPGM command. If you choose not to use ENDPGM, your procedure stops executing when it runs out of commands in the body of the procedure. An ENDPGM command makes your source code look better and removes uncertainty about where a procedure ends. An example is shown in Figure 2.9.

```
ENDPGM
```

Figure 2.9: An example of the ENDPGM command.

The Include CL Source (INCLUDE) Command

Before IBM i 6.1, all CL source code for a procedure had to be stored in one source member. Now it is possible to store source code in two or more members. This is especially handy for reusable code, such as error-handling procedures, that are the same for many CL procedures.

One source member must be the primary source member for a procedure. This source member may use the Include CL Source (INCLUDE) command to copy other source members into the stream of source code during compilation. This feature is similar to RPG'S /COPY and /INCLUDE compiler directives, the COBOL COPY feature, and C's #include.

INCLUDE has two parameters—SRCMBR and SRCFILE, in which you provide the names of the source member and the file containing the source code to be copied. Figure 2.10 has an example of the INCLUDE command.

```
INCLUDE  SRCMBR(ERRRTNDCL) SRCFILE(TEMPLATE/QCLSRC)
```

Figure 2.10: The INCLUDE command brings source code into the compilation process.

The SRCFILE parameter may also have the special value *INCFILE. This value tells the compiler to retrieve the source file name from the INCFILE parameter of the command that was used to invoke the compiler.

ENTERING THE SOURCE CODE WITH SEU

Before you start the Source Entry Utility (SEU) to enter CL source code, choose a library in which to keep the source. Make sure the library you select has a source physical file to contain the CL source code.

The Source Physical File

CL source is stored, by IBM's default, in a source physical file called QCLSRC. You don't need to use that name. You can call your file CLSOURCE, SOURCE_CL, or even FRED. It really makes no difference. However, the commands used to compile CL source members have a default value of QCLSRC in the parameter that asks for the name of the source physical file. You save time by using QCLSRC.

If you don't have a QCLSRC file, create it by executing the command shown in Figure 2.11. MYLIB stands for the name of the library where you want to place the file.

```
CRTSRCPF FILE(MYLIB/QCLSRC) TEXT('CL source')
```

Figure 2.11: Creating a source physical file with name of QCLSRC.

Starting SEU

You must enter the source code for the procedure with SEU. You can start SEU either manually or from the Program Development Manager (PDM). To start SEU manually, type STRSEU at the command line and press F4. The panel shown in Figure 2.12 appears.

Type in the parameter values shown and press Enter.

To start SEU from PDM, go to the Work with Members Using PDM (WRKMBRPDM) panel and press F6 to create a new member.

```
Start Source Entry Utility (STRSEU)

Type choices, press Enter.

Source file  . . . . qclsrc____      Name, *PRV
  Library . . . . . mylib____        Name, *LIBL,   *CURLIB, *PRV
Source member  . . . hello____       Name, *PRV,    *SELECT
Source type  . . . . clle____        Name, *SAME,   BAS, BASP, C...
Option . . . . . . . *BLANK____      *BLANK, ' ',   2, 5, 6
Text 'description' . Example_from_Chapter_Two_____




    Bottom
F3=Exit  F4=Prompt  F5=Refresh  F12=Cancel  F13=How to use this display
F24=More keys
```

Figure 2.12: The STRSEU screen.

Formatting the Statements with F4

CL procedures consist of free-format statements. As it does with DDS or other programming languages like RPG, the meaning of the code doesn't depend upon a columnar (or linear) location. This gives you a sense of freedom to write the code the way you want it. With CL, nothing prevents you from entering the source for the HELLO procedure as shown in Figure 2.13.

```
PGM &GREETING
DCL &GREETING *CHAR 5
DCL &USER *CHAR 10
DCL &TERMINAL *CHAR 10
DCL &MSG *CHAR 80 ' '
MONMSG CPF0000
BEGIN: RTVUSRPRF *CURRENT &USER
RTVJOBA &TERMINAL
CHGVAR &MSG (&GREETING *TCAT ',' *BCAT &USER *TCAT '! You''re using +
terminal' *BCAT &TERMINAL *TCAT '.')
SNDPGMMSG MSG(&MSG) MSGTYPE(*COMP)
ENDPGM
```

Figure 2.13: An example of CL code without the benefits of formatting with indentation.

You can enter the CL code this way if you prefer. The compiler does not differentiate between easy- and hard-to-read source code. The compiler will compile the procedure just the same, and your procedure will work just as well.

Because humans have a sense of aesthetics, it is easier (and more pleasant) to work with source code that looks good and is easy to read rather than to deal with a monster like the one just presented. On the other hand, you could press the F4 key and the Enter key on each statement and end up with another style. See Figure 2.14.

```
    PGM         PARM(&GREETING)

                DCL       VAR(&GREETING) TYPE(*CHAR) LEN(5)
                DCL       VAR(&USER) TYPE(*CHAR) LEN(10)
                DCL       VAR(&TERMINAL) TYPE(*CHAR) LEN(10)
                DCL       VAR(&MSG) TYPE(*CHAR) LEN(80)

                MONMSG    MSGID(CPF0000)

    BEGIN:      RTVUSRPRF USRPRF(*CURRENT) RTNUSRPRF(&USER)
                RTVJOBA   JOB(&TERMINAL)
                CHGVAR    VAR(&MSG) VALUE(&GREETING *TCAT ',' *BCAT +
                            &USER *TCAT '! You''re using terminal' +
                            *BCAT &TERMINAL *TCAT '.')
                SNDPGMMSG MSG(&MSG) MSGTYPE(*COMP)
                ENDPGM
```

Figure 2.14: CL code formatted by prompting within SEU.

Most programmers like leaving the formatting to the command prompter (activated when you press F4 while entering the source code). The source code shown in Figure 2.14 was formatted with the command prompter.

All you need to do to activate the prompter is type the name of the command anywhere on a blank line and press the F4 key. Now you can fill in the blanks and press Enter. The F4 key works this way because you have specified a source type of CLLE, which activates the CL programming syntax checker and the command prompter. You also can type the command using free format (including parameters with or without keywords) and then press F4 followed by Enter.

For example, the command prompter will format the Change Variable (CHGVAR) command from the format shown in Figure 2.15 to the format shown in Figure 2.16.

```
CHGVAR &MSG (&GREETING *TCAT ',' *BCAT &USER *TCAT '! You''re using +
terminal' *BCAT &TERMINAL *TCAT '.')
```

Figure 2.15: An example of code formatted without using the prompter.

```
CHGVAR     VAR(&MSG) VALUE(&GREETING *TCAT ',' *BCAT +
                &USER *TCAT '! You''re using terminal' +
                *BCAT &TERMINAL *TCAT '.')
```

Figure 2.16: An example of code formatted using the prompter.

The command prompter does the following for you:

- Starts labels in column 2.
- Forces the command name in column 14.
- Starts parameters in column 25.
- Adds keywords to all parameters.
- Indents all continuation lines two positions to the right, beginning in column 27.
- Inserts or deletes lines as needed to make the command occupy as much of the display as possible, never exceeding column 71.
- Translates all labels, command names, and keywords to capital letters if entered in lowercase letters.
- Translates unquoted single-word character strings into capital letters.
- Automatically surrounds unquoted multiple-word character strings with single quotes.
- Doubles any embedded single quotes.

- Enables you to change an existing line by placing the cursor on the line and pressing F4. The command prompter shows the command with the parameters as they are coded. Now you can change some of the parameters and press Enter. The command prompter reformats the command and, if necessary, adds or deletes lines in the CL source code.

More experienced CL programmers would choose not to use the command prompter (and you might do so with time). When you stop using the prompter, the responsibility of formatting the CL source code will be entirely yours.

Uppercase or Lowercase?

The CL compiler does not interpret commands, keywords, labels, or unquote character literals differently because they are written in lowercase letters instead of uppercase. The source code compiles either way. You must decide which case to use.

Because the command prompter translates to uppercase, you might want to stick to uppercase lettering. If you don't use the prompter, then it is up to you. You can execute the SET CAPS OFF command at the SEU===> command line to enable lowercase entry or SET CAPS ON to return to all uppercase. The HELLO source code looks different in lowercase letters. See Figure 2.17.

```
    pgm         parm(&greeting)

                dcl         var(&greeting) type(*char) len(5)
                dcl         var(&user) type(*char) len(10)
                dcl         var(&terminal) type(*char) len(10)
                dcl         var(&msg) type(*char) len(80)
                monmsg      msgid(cpf0000)

    begin:      rtvusrprf   usrprf(*current) rtnusrprf(&user)
                rtvjoba     job(&terminal)

                chgvar      var(&msg) value(&greeting *tcat ',' *bcat +
                              &user *tcat '! You''re using terminal' +
                              *bcat &terminal *tcat '.')
                sndpgmmsg   msg(&msg) msgtype(*comp)
                endpgm
```

Figure 2.17: An original example of source code in lowercase.

Positional Parameters or Keywords?

Command parameters can be entered in two forms: positionally or with keywords.

Because they are easier to type, positional parameters are the method of choice when commands are executed manually. After all, no one has to read the command after it has been executed from the keyboard.

When you enter commands into a CL source member, the procedure executes just as well either with or without keywords. However, the statements might be easier to read when keywords are included. This decision is up to you; whether it's easier with or without keywords is a matter of opinion.

To give you an idea of the difference, consider the example shown in Figure 2.18. The first Create Duplicate Object (CRTDUPOBJ) command is coded without keywords (positionally); the second is coded with keywords. The second version is more readily understood.

```
CRTDUPOBJ PGM1 MYLIB *PGM YOURLIB PGM1A

CRTDUPOBJ OBJ(PGM1) FROMLIB(MYLIB) OBJTYPE(*PGM) +
          TOLIB(YOURLIB) NEWOBJ(PGM1A)
```

Figure 2.18: An example of coding the CRTDUPOBJ command positionally and with keywords.

On the other hand, some commands you'll use all the time, such as the Change Variable (CHGVAR) command, have two parameters. Figure 2.19 shows two versions (without keywords and with keywords).

```
CHGVAR &USER 'QSYSOPR'
CHGVAR VAR(&USER) VALUE('QSYSOPR')
```

Figure 2.19: An example of coding the CHGVAR command positionally and with keywords.

In this case, both versions are easy to understand. Another case is the GOTO command as shown in Figure 2.20.

```
GOTO CONTINUE
GOTO CMDLBL(CONTINUE)
```

Figure 2.20: An example of coding the GOTO command positionally and with keywords.

The inclusion of the CMDLBL keyword does little (if anything) to enhance code clarity.

The style of source code you write is a matter of personal choice or of adherence to your shop's standards. Appendix B describes the subject of code style in some detail.

Continuing on the Next Line

When a CL command has more parameters than a single line can hold, it must be continued on one or more next physical lines. This is accomplished in CL by ending a line with a plus (+) or a minus (–) sign.

If you use the command prompter (F4 key) to format your statements, these signs are entered automatically wherever they are needed. If you don't use the prompter, it is your responsibility to enter the continuation symbols yourself.

The difference between + and – is how the next line is interpreted by the compiler. If you use a + sign, the compiler ignores all leading blanks in the next line. The continuation line effectively begins with the first non-blank character. If you use a – sign, however, the compiler includes all leading blanks of the continuation line, and makes these blanks part of the statement.

This difference is important only when you separate the statement somewhere in the middle of a character constant. The example shown in Figure 2.21 clarifies this point.

```
CHGVAR VAR(&X) VALUE('AB +
        CD')
```

Figure 2.21: An example of breaking a line in the middle of a character constant using a + sign.

Variable **&x** will contain 'AB CD' (one blank between AB and CD) because there is a blank space between the B and the + sign. All leading blanks on the next line are ignored. Figure 2.22 shows the same command using a – sign as the continuation character.

```
CHGVAR VAR(&X) VALUE('AB -
        CD')
```

Figure 2.22: Example of breaking a line in the middle of a character constant using a – sign.

In this case, **&x** will contain 'AB   CD' (ten blanks between AB and CD). There is one blank between the B and the – sign, and the next line has nine leading blanks.

Indented or Unindented?

You can take advantage of CL's free-format nature to indent your code. When you indent your CL source code, the scope of DO/ENDDO groups becomes more readily apparent and source statements are much easier to understand. The more complex your procedure, the greater the benefit obtained by indenting the code.

Incidentally, using the command prompter (F4) to format your code destroys whatever indentation you create in your code. As mentioned earlier, the prompter forces the command to start at position 14 and parameters begin at position 25.

COMPILING THE PROCEDURE

CL is a compiled language. After writing the source code, you must run it through the compiler, which translates your source code into machine language and creates a program or module object.

The CRTBNDCL Command

To create a program from CL source code, use the Create Bound CL Program (CRTBNDCL) command. (CL modules and Original Program Model [OPM] CL procedures are compiled with other commands, but disregard that for now.) Refer to chapter 17 for a complete description of the command and all its parameters. For now, concern yourself with the first two parameters: PGM and SRCFILE.

The PGM parameter requires the qualified name of the program being created. Enter the name of the program (which is assumed to be the same as the source member) and the library where you want to place the compiled program.

The SRCFILE parameter must have the qualified name of the source physical file where you have entered the source code.

To compile program HELLO, execute the command shown in Figure 2.23. As in the previous examples, MYLIB represents the library of your choice.

```
CRTBNDCL PGM(MYLIB/HELLO) SRCFILE(MYLIB/QCLSRC)
```

Figure 2.23: The CRTBNDCL command to compile the CL program.

Output of CRTBNDCL

When CRTBNDCL finishes, you will have a compiled listing. This compiled listing shows the source code, lists the variables used in the program, and prints messages (information, warning, error) if necessary.

If the compile is successful, CRTBNDCL produces a program object (type *PGM with attribute CLLE) in your library. The program is now ready to be executed. If the compile is not successful, review the compiled listing's messages and correct the problems with SEU. Then try the compile again.

EXECUTING THE PROGRAM

Programs can be run in a number of ways. For now, execute the CALL command manually from the keyboard to run the HELLO program.

For this example, your user profile is PAT, and you are signed on at display station PURDSP01. Also, assume that library MYLIB is in your library list. Key in the command as shown in Figure 2.24 and press Enter.

```
CALL PGM(MYLIB/HELLO) PARM('Hello')
```

Figure 2.24: An example of a call command to run a CL program.

The CALL command immediately starts executing the program HELLO, passing the word HELLO as a parameter. As a result of the program's execution, the system sends you a message as shown in Figure 2.25.

```
Hello, PAT!  You're using terminal PURDSP01.
```

Figure 2.25: A message from the HELLO program.

OPTIONAL COMPONENTS OF A CL PROCEDURE

CL procedures can contain elements other than those described so far. These elements are optional.

Blank Lines

CL source members can contain blank lines, which help separate sections of source code that have different purposes. The blank lines create visual groups of statements. You can place blank lines almost anywhere, but they should be used wisely and never indiscriminately. Here are a few guidelines:

- Never use more than two consecutive blank lines in your source member. Two blank lines are enough to indicate a separation between two groups of statements. Actually, one blank line is usually better than two.

- Never write a CL source member without any blank lines. It looks overcrowded and cluttered, and it becomes more difficult to understand as the member gets longer and longer.

- Always leave a blank line after the PGM statement and before the ENDPGM statement.

- Leave a blank line after the declarations.

- Leave a blank line after a global MONMSG.

- Do not leave a blank line between a comment line and the statements being commented. The lack of a blank line will reinforce the idea that the comment applies to the statements that follow.

Comment Lines

CL source members should have comment lines to describe the purpose of the different sections of the procedure. By including comment lines, you make it easier for the maintenance programmer to change the source code at a later time. Even if you maintain your own source, the comments will remind you of what you did (and why) six months or a year earlier.

Comments are coded in CL by writing any text enclosed in the composite symbols /* and */. Figure 2.26 shows an example.

```
/* This is a comment line */
```

Figure 2.26: An example of a comment line.

If you have to write long comments, you can write several comment lines, one after another, each with its own /* and */ symbols. Or the entire multi-line comment can be considered a single comment line by using continuation symbols (+ or –) on all but the last line. The two methods are shown in Figures 2.27 and 2.28.

```
/* This is an example of a long comment. */
/* Each line has its own beginning and ending */
/* composite symbols. */
```

Figure 2.27: An example of coding a long comment as multiple comments on individual lines.

```
/* This is another example of a long comment. +
   Because each line ends in a plus sign, +
   all three lines are actually a single comment line. */
```

Figure 2.28: An example of coding a long comment with continuation symbols.

As shown in Figure 2.29, you can also create "boxed" comments.

```
/****************************/
/* These comments are boxed */
/* by asterisks.            */
/****************************/
```

Figure 2.29: An example of a comment boxed in by asterisks for readability.

Comments on Command Lines

Comments can be placed on the same line where you have coded a command. See Figure 2.30.

This type of comment can be entered very easily from the command prompter. When you prompt for a command (such as PGM, as illustrated), the system provides space for you to enter comments, for that command, after all parameters. You only have to type the text of the comment (you can either include or omit the /* and */) and press Enter. The prompter formats the command and adds the comment.

```
PGM PARM(&OPTION)   /* Beginning of program */
```

Figure 2.30: An example of a comment entered with a command.

Note: Do not overdo this type of comment. A CL source member with too many comments is just as bad as a CL source member without any comments. Always exercise your common sense.

3

CONSTANTS AND VARIABLES

Like other programming languages, CL can manipulate data in either constant or variable form. This chapter explains these two forms as they relate to CL programming. Variables, unlike constants, are allowed to change values. Variables have a name and are stored in memory for the duration of the procedure.

If your background involves RPG, you might already refer to variables as "fields" (even though that term is inappropriate). Like constants, variables have different types: character, decimal, integer, and logical. Because hexadecimal values are actually character strings, hexadecimal values are stored in character variables.

WHAT IS A CONSTANT?

A *constant*, also known as a *literal*, is a value that does not and cannot change. Constants are hard-coded in your source member. For example, when you code a Display Message (DSPMSG) command with MSGQ(QSYSOPR), QSYSOPR is a constant. It never changes. The DSPMSG command you have coded will always display messages from message queue QSYSOPR and no other.

Constants can be one of several types: character, decimal, integer, hexadecimal, or logical. The following sections address each type in turn.

Character Constants

Character constants can contain any number of characters, including blanks. If blanks are included, the constant must be enclosed in single quotes. If the constant contains single quotes, those must be doubled and the whole constant is then enclosed in single quotes.

If you want them to be interpreted as character constants, constants that consist of nothing but the digits 0 to 9, a plus (+) or minus (−) sign, and a decimal point or comma must be enclosed in single quotes. Table 3.1 lists examples of valid character constants and Table 3.2 lists examples of invalid character constants.

Table 3.1: Valid Character Constants	
Valid Character Constants	**Notes**
QSYSOPR	No single quotes required because the constant includes no single quotes.
'QSYSOPR'	Identical to the previous constant.
'System Operator'	A blank is included, necessitating use of single quotes.
'This is George''s report'	The single quote (apostrophe) within the constant must be doubled.
'400'	Character constant (not decimal) because it is enclosed in single quotes.
'400.'	Not equal to '400' because it has a period. '400' has three characters; '400.' has four.

Table 3.2: Invalid Character Constants	
Invalid Character Constants	**Reason for Invalidity**
ABC DEF	Quotes needed because constant contains an embedded blank.
'I didn't do it'	The embedded single quote (apostrophe) must be doubled.
400	Must be surrounded with quotes because it consists of nothing but digits. The system would treat this as a decimal constant rather than a character constant.
'QSYSOPR	Unmatched single quote; there is no single quote at the end.

Decimal Constants

Decimal constants are those that contain only the digits 0 to 9, an optional plus or minus sign, and a decimal point or comma. Commas or points to separate thousands and millions are not allowed within a decimal constant. Adding any other character forces the system to interpret the constant as character. Table 3.3 lists examples of valid decimal constants and Table 3.4 lists examples of invalid decimal constants.

Table 3.3: Valid Decimal Constants	
Valid Decimal Constants	**Notes**
2	Single-digit decimal constant.
2.	Identical to the previous constant.
+0000002.00000	Also identical to the first example.
-3,7	Comma is valid to separate the decimal portion.
-3.7	Identical to previous constant.
3.14159265	Approximation of pi to 8 decimal places.

Table 3.4: Invalid Decimal Constants	
Invalid Decimal Constants	**Reason for Invalidity**
27,935.06	Commas to separate thousands are not allowed.
46278019235682115670926354	Too long.
12.5%	Contains an invalid symbol (%).
72A	Contains a letter.

The maximum length for a decimal constant is 15 digits (of which up to 9 can be decimal places).

Integer Constants

Integer constants are like decimal constants in that they represent numeric values. However, integer constants may not contain a decimal point or decimal positions and the range of permissible integer values is more restricted. While decimal constants can include up to 15 decimal digits, integers are restricted to values from -2,147,483,648 to 4,294,967,295.

Hexadecimal Constants

Hexadecimal constants are a variation of character constants. With a hexadecimal constant, you can include characters not available from the keyboard (all 256 possible characters provided in the EBCDIC character set).

Hexadecimal constants always begin with the letter X followed by an even number of nibbles enclosed in single quotes. A *nibble* is half a byte, represented by a number from 0 to 9 or a letter from A to F. An odd number of nibbles is not allowed. No characters other than 0 to 9 or a letter from A to F are allowed inside the single quotes.

Table 3.5 lists examples of valid hexadecimal constants and Table 3.6 lists examples of invalid hexadecimal constants.

Table 3.5: Valid Hexadecimal Constants

Valid Hexadecimal Constants	Notes
X'C1'	Has one byte only: C1. Equivalent to character constant 'A'.
X'F1F2F3'	Three bytes. Equivalent to character constant '123'.
X'00'	Null character.
X'40'	Blank space.

Table 3.6: Invalid Hexadecimal Constants

Invalid Hexadecimal Constants	Reason for Invalidity
X'00F'	It contains an odd number of nibbles.
X'1G'	It contains an invalid nibble (G).
'40'X	The X is in the wrong place.
X3F	The X is in the right place, but there are no single quotes.

Hexadecimal constants also can be used to represent decimal constants in packed format when it becomes necessary to CALL a procedure that expects a decimal parameter. For more details, see the section on the SNDUSRMSG command in Chapter 6.

Logical Constants

A logical value can only have two states: true or false. Logical constants are represented either by '0' (false) or '1' (true). Logical constants must be surrounded in single quotes. No other logical constants are available in CL.

The *NULL Constant

In i 6.1, CL gained a new constant, *NULL, to represent the null value when testing or setting pointers. You may use *NULL when defining a pointer variable, in order to initialize the variable, and you may also use this constant in executable commands. See Figure 3.1 for an example.

```
DCL VAR(&Ptr) TYPE(*ptr) VALUE(*NULL)

IF COND(&Ptr *EQ *NULL) THEN(DO)
```

Figure 3.1:Use the *NULL special constant to set or test for null values.

WHAT ARE VARIABLES?

Unlike constants, variables are allowed to change values. Variables are named and are stored in memory for the duration of the procedure. Like constants, variables have different types: character, decimal, signed integer, unsigned integer, and logical. Because hexadecimal values are character strings, hexadecimal values are stored in character variables.

Declaring Variables

Before you can use a variable in a CL source member, you must first define the variable or *declare* it. Declaring variables must be done at the very beginning of the source member, after the PGM statement.

A variable name can contain up to 11 characters. The first character must be an ampersand (&), which identifies the rest as a variable name. The second character must be a letter (A to Z) or the characters @, #, or $. All characters following the second can be letters, digits (0 to 9), or the characters @, #, $, or _ ("break"). You can use the break character to improve readability. Letters are not case-sensitive. Table 3.7 lists examples of valid variable names and Table 3.8 lists examples of invalid variable names.

Variables are declared with the Declare (DCL) command. Each variable must be declared with a separate DCL command. The DCL command has eight parameters:

- VAR: Receives the name of the variable being declared. VAR is a required parameter.

- TYPE: Receives the values *CHAR, *DEC, *INT, *UINT, *LGL, or *PTR, depending on whether the variable type is character, decimal, signed integer, unsigned integer, logical, or pointer. This parameter is required, too.

- STG: Indicates the storage method; that is, the way the variable is allocated in memory. It's optional.

- LEN: Indicates the length of the variable. For character, integer, and logical variables, this value indicates the number of bytes to be allocated to the variable. For decimal variables, this value indicates the number of digits the variable can hold. This parameter is optional.

- VALUE: Indicates the initial value for the variable. It's optional too.

- BASPTR: Indicates the pointer upon which the variable is based. It's optional.

- DEFVAR: Indicates the variable with which this variable shares memory. This parameter is optional.

- ADDRESS: Indicates the initial value of a pointer. It is optional.

Table 3.7: Valid Variable Names

Valid Variable Names	Notes
&A	Short name, but valid.
&OUTQ	Suggests "output queue."
&VOL_ID	Uses the break character.
&mbr01	Uses digits. Lowercase letters are allowed.
&MBR01	Identical to the previous example (uppercase or lowercase are considered the same).
&NBRCLROUTQ	Suggests "number of cleared output queues." This example shows the maximum length of a variable name (10 characters plus the beginning ampersand).
&#SPLF	Looks strange, but it's valid.

Table 3.8: Invalid Variable Names

Invalid Variable Names	Reason for Invalidity
&NBRDLTPGMMSG	Too long.
&INV%TOTAL	Includes %, an invalid symbol.
TOTAL	Must begin with an ampersand (&).
&1TOTAL	The character following the & is invalid.

Figure 3.2 shows some examples of declarations.

```
DCL VAR(&OUTQ) TYPE(*CHAR) LEN(10)
   Declares variable &OUTQ as character, 10 bytes long.

DCL VAR(&ERRORS) TYPE(*DEC) LEN(3 0)
   Declares &ERRORS as decimal, 3 digits, 0 decimal places.

DCL VAR(&TOGGLE) TYPE(*LGL) LEN(1)
   Declares &TOGGLE as a logical var
```

Figure 3.2: Examples of variable declarations.

Note that, for decimal variables, LEN can contain two numbers: the total length of the variable (how many digits in length), and the number of decimal places. LEN(5 2), for example, could hold a number as large as 999.99.

Because logical variables are always 1 byte long, LEN(1) is optional. When the LEN parameter is omitted, the compiler assumes LEN(32) for character variables, LEN(15 5) for decimal variables, LEN(4) for integer variables, or LEN(1) for logical variables.

When you omit the LEN parameter but supply an initial value with the VALUE parameter, the VALUE parameter dictates the length of the variable that will be assumed by the compiler. For example, consider the two cases shown in Figure 3.3.

```
DCL VAR(&NAME) TYPE(*CHAR) VALUE('QSYSOPR')
DCL VAR(&PI) TYPE(*DEC) VALUE(3.14159265)
```

Figure 3.3: Examples of declaring the length of the variable based on length of data in the value parameter.

When you compile the source member that includes the variables shown in Figure 3.3, &NAME will have a length of seven (the initial value, QSYSOPR, contains seven characters). &PI will have a length of (9 8) because its initial value has nine digits (of which eight fall to the right of the decimal point).

Character variables can be as long as LEN(32767). Decimal variables are LEN(15 9). Logical variables are always LEN(1). Table 3.9 summarizes the rules for lengths for various data types.

Table 3.9: Maximum and Default Lengths for Variables		
Variable Type	**Maximum Length**	**Default Length**
TYPE(*CHAR)	LEN(32767)	LEN(32)
TYPE(*DEC)	LEN(15 9)	LEN(15 5)
TYPE(*INT)	LEN(4)	LEN(4)
TYPE(*UINT)	LEN(4)	LEN(4)
TYPE(*LGL)	LEN(1)	LEN(1)
TYPE(*PTR)	n/a	n/a

NOTE: The only acceptable values for length of both *INT and *UINT are 2 and 4.

Note: The only acceptable values for length of both *INT and *UINT are 2 and 4. Although the LEN parameter can be omitted when the default value is suitable, it does make the source member harder to read if the programmer does not know the default length. To make your source members easier to read, you should always use the LEN parameter.

CODING FOR CLARITY

You can increase the legibility of your CL source members by rearranging the DCL statements, so that they present variable names in alphabetical order. The more variables a source member uses, the more important it becomes to easily locate the correct DCL statement. Having the DCL statements sorted by variable name means more work (you will have to move statements around), but the source code will be easier to read.

Also, you can manually format DCL statements so the VAR, TYPE, and LEN parameters are aligned vertically and make up neat columns. Compare the sections of code shown in Figures 3.4, 3.5, and 3.6, which declare the same group of variables.

```
DCL        VAR(&BGNCOL)     TYPE(*DEC)   LEN(2 0)
DCL        VAR(&CVTCASE)    TYPE(*CHAR)  LEN(4)
DCL        VAR(&INDCOL)     TYPE(*DEC)   LEN(1 0)
DCL        VAR(&BGNCOL)     TYPE(*DEC)   LEN(2 0)
DCL        VAR(&CVTCASE)    TYPE(*CHAR)  LEN(4)
DCL        VAR(&INDCOL)     TYPE(*DEC)   LEN(1 0)
DCL        VAR(&INDCONT)    TYPE(*DEC)   LEN(1 0)
DCL        VAR(&MSGDTA)     TYPE(*CHAR)  LEN(80)
DCL        VAR(&MSGF)       TYPE(*CHAR)  LEN(10)
DCL        VAR(&MSGFLIB)    TYPE(*CHAR)  LEN(10)
DCL        VAR(&MSGID)      TYPE(*CHAR)  LEN(7)
DCL        VAR(&QSRCF)      TYPE(*CHAR)  LEN(20)
DCL        VAR(&RTNLIB)     TYPE(*CHAR)  LEN(10)
DCL        VAR(&SAVOLDSRC)  TYPE(*CHAR)  LEN(4)
DCL        VAR(&SRCF)       TYPE(*CHAR)  LEN(10)
DCL        VAR(&SRCFLIB)    TYPE(*CHAR)  LEN(10)
DCL        VAR(&SRCMBR)     TYPE(*CHAR)  LEN(10)
DCL        VAR(&SRCTYPE)    TYPE(*CHAR)  LEN(10)
```

Figure 3.4: Examples of DCL commands sorted by variable name and with parameters formatted into columns.

```
DCL          VAR(&BGNCOL) TYPE(*DEC) LEN(2 0)
DCL          VAR(&CVTCASE) TYPE(*CHAR) LEN(4)
DCL          VAR(&INDCOL) TYPE(*DEC) LEN(1 0)
DCL          VAR(&INDCONT) TYPE(*DEC) LEN(1 0)
DCL          VAR(&MSGDTA) TYPE(*CHAR) LEN(80)
DCL          VAR(&MSGF) TYPE(*CHAR) LEN(10)
DCL          VAR(&MSGFLIB) TYPE(*CHAR) LEN(10)
DCL          VAR(&MSGID) TYPE(*CHAR) LEN(7)
DCL          VAR(&QSRCF) TYPE(*CHAR) LEN(20)
DCL          VAR(&RTNLIB) TYPE(*CHAR) LEN(10)
DCL          VAR(&SAVOLDSRC) TYPE(*CHAR) LEN(4)
DCL          VAR(&SRCF) TYPE(*CHAR) LEN(10)
DCL          VAR(&SRCFLIB) TYPE(*CHAR) LEN(10)
DCL          VAR(&SRCMBR) TYPE(*CHAR) LEN(10)
DCL          VAR(&SRCTYPE) TYPE(*CHAR) LEN(10)
```

Figure 3.5: Examples of DCL commands sorted by variable name but with parameters specified in free-format without columns.

```
DCL &bgncol      *DEC   2
DCL &cvtcase     *CHAR  4
DCL &bgncol      *DEC   2
DCL &cvtcase     *CHAR  4
DCL &indcol      *DEC   1
DCL &indcont     *DEC   1
DCL &msgdta      *CHAR 80
DCL &msgf        *CHAR 10
DCL &msgflib     *CHAR 10
DCL &msgid       *CHAR  7
DCL &qsrcf       *CHAR 20
DCL &rtnlib      *CHAR 10
DCL &savoldsrc   *CHAR  4
DCL &srcf        *CHAR 10
DCL &srcflib     *CHAR 10
DCL &srcmbr      *CHAR 10
DCL &srctype     *CHAR 10
```

Figure 3.6: Examples of DCL commands sorted by variable name but without keywords and without LEN specified.

The block of code shown in Figure 3.6 includes DCL commands without keywords and variable names written in lowercase letters. The lack of the VAR, TYPE, and LEN keywords improves legibility because there's less repetitive clutter.

Where Variables Can Be Used

When you execute commands from the keyboard, you always enter constant values for all parameters. Consider the Display Library (DSPLIB) command shown in Figure 3.7.

```
DSPLIB LIB(QGPL) OUTPUT(*PRINT)
```

Figure 3.7: The DSPLIB command with constant values.

As shown in Figure 3.7, parameter LIB is receiving a four-character constant value (QGPL), while parameter OUTPUT is receiving a six-character constant, *PRINT.

When you code a DSPLIB command in a CL procedure, however, you have the option of using constants or variables in the parameters. Variables add flexibility when such flexibility is needed. If variable &A has a value of QGPL and variable &B has a value of *PRINT, the CL statement shown in Figure 3.8 produces the same result as the statement presented in Figure 3.7.

```
DSPLIB LIB(&A) OUTPUT(&B)
```

Figure 3.8: The DSPLIB command with variables as parameters.

Don't be fooled into believing that variables can do all sorts of magic. If variable &C has the value LIB(QGPL) and variable &D has the value OUTPUT(*PRINT), the statement shown in Figure 3.9 will not produce the same result.

```
DSPLIB &C &D
```

Figure 3.9: Invalid use of variables in a DSPLIB command.

Because it has no way of knowing what values &C and &D will have, SEU still accepts this statement as valid. The source member even compiles correctly because the compiler assumes you are entering the parameters positionally. When the procedure executes, however, it comes to a screeching halt with an error message. The statement is interpreted as shown in Figure 3.10.

```
DSPLIB LIB('LIB(QGPL)') OUTPUT('OUTPUT(*PRINT)')
```

Figure 3.10: Results of using the code as shown in Figure 3.8.

Now assume that variable &E has the value DSPLIB LIB(QGPL) OUTPUT(*PRINT). If you code Figure 3.11 as a statement, SEU's syntax checker will reject the −statement.

```
&E
```

Figure 3.11: Invalid use of a variable to code a CL command.

For the example shown in Figure 3.11, &E isn't a command; it's a variable. Only commands can be coded in CL procedures. Executing commands dynamically requires the use of the QCMDEXC API. See Chapter 13.

Another example points to an additional source of errors. Suppose you execute from the keyboard the command shown in Figure 3.12.

```
CHGJOB OUTQ(QGPL/QPRINT) RUNPTY(20) LOG(4 0 *NOLIST)
```

Figure 3.12: The CHGJOB command with constant values as parameters.

If you code this command in a CL source member, all parameters can have variables (as shown in Figure 3.13).

```
CHGJOB OUTQ(&A/&B) RUNPTY(&C) LOG(&D &E &F)
```

Figure 3.13: The CHGJOB command with variables as parameters.

A qualified name such as QGPL/QPRINT cannot be replaced by only one variable. Two variables, as in &A/&B, take the place of the qualified name. Similarly, a list must be coded with one variable per element of the list, but never with one variable for the entire list. For example, you cannot use the statement shown in Figure 3.14 to produce the same results as the example shown in Figure 3.13.

```
CHGJOB OUTQ(&G) RUNPTY(&H) LOG(&I)
```

Figure 3.14: Invalid use of variables in parameters.

The statement is incorrect if &G has the value QGPL/QPRINT and &I has the value 4 0 *NOLIST. A single variable can contain only a single value. OUTQ(&G) would be acceptable if &G had the value QPRINT only because the command would then use the library list to locate output queue QPRINT.

Parameters

In Chapter 2, the introductory program, HELLO, contains one parameter as indicated by the PGM command. Procedure parameters are always listed as variables. These variables, just like all others, must be declared with the DCL command.

When calling a CL procedure, CL allows mismatches in the declared length of parameters, but the type of parameter must always agree. For example, suppose program A calls program B and passes one parameter. In program A, the parameter variable is declared as a character variable, 8 bytes long. Program B declares the variable as a character variable, 9 bytes long. When you call program B from program A, no errors will be reported; the 8-byte value of variable **&X** will be passed to program B without trouble.

You might think of this feature as a time-saver, but it's poor programming practice. You should always take the time to ensure that parameters agree both in type and length in programs A and B.

CL procedures can have a maximum of 255 parameters. When passing parameters between procedures, remember that the names of the variables need not be the same in the two procedures.

OVERLAID VARIABLES

Overlaying variables means defining two variables so that they occupy the same memory location. Since the two variables share the same memory, changing one changes the other.

To make one variable overlay another, use the STG (storage) and DEFVAR (defined on variable) parameters of the declare command. The STG parameter takes the value *DEFINED. In the DEFVAR parameter, indicate the name of another variable and the first position of that variable that is to share memory. Look at the example in Figure 3.15.

```
DCL    &QualObj   *CHAR   LEN(20)
DCL    &Object    *CHAR   LEN(10)   STG(*DEFINED) DEFVAR(&QualObj  1)
DCL    &Library   *CHAR   LEN(10)   STG(*DEFINED) DEFVAR(&QualObj 11)
```

Figure 3.15: Examples of overlaid variables.

There is no difference between the contents of the **&Object** variable and the first ten positions of **&QualObj**, because **&Object** overlays **&QualObj** at the first postion, and overlays ten positions. In the same way, **&Library** is an alternate name for the last ten positions of **&QualObj**.

POINTER VARIABLES AND BASED VARIABLES

A pointer variable contains the address of another variable. To define a pointer variable, specify TYPE(*PTR) in the DCL command and do not code the LEN parameter. In Figure 3.16, the **&NextObj** variable is a pointer.

```
DCL     VAR(&NextObj)     TYPE(*PTR)
```

Figure 3.16: A pointer variable holds the address of another variable.

Since a pointer variable does not hold data, it is of little value until it is assigned the address of another variable. To assign an address to a pointer in a variable declaration, use the ADDRESS parameter of the DCL command. To assign an address in calculations, use the %ADDRESS function. You may shorten %ADDRESS to %ADDR. Look at the two pointer variables in Figure 3.17.

```
DCL     VAR(&TopOfList)   TYPE(*PTR)    ADDRESS(&List)
DCL     VAR(&NextObj)     TYPE(*PTR)
DCL     VAR(&Pattern)     TYPE(*CHAR)   LEN(10)
DCL     VAR(&List)        TYPE(*CHAR)   LEN(252)

CHGVAR     &NextObj       %ADDR(&Pattern)
```

Figure 3.17: Example of two pointer variables.

The **&TopOfList** variable contains the memory address of the **&List** variable. The CHGVAR command assigns the address of &Pattern to the **&nextobj** pointer variable.

To modify the value of a pointer, i.e. to do "pointer arithmetic", use the %OFFSET (or %OFS) function. In Figure 3.18, the **&NextObj** pointer is adjusted to point to the memory address ten bytes after its current position.

```
CHGVAR  VAR(%Offset(&NextObj))   VALUE(%Offset(&NextObj)+10)
```

Figure 3.18: Use the %OFFSET function for pointer arithmetic.

BASED VARIABLES

The compiler does not allocate storage to based variables. Instead, the based variable uses a pointer in order to access the storage that has been assigned to another variable. In Figure 3.19, the **&File** variable represents two other variables—**&SalesHist** and **&CurrSales**—by means of pointer **&pFile**.

```
DCL    VAR(&pFile)      TYPE(*PTR)
DCL    VAR(&File)       TYPE(*CHAR) LEN(20) STG(*BASED) BASPTR(&pFile)
DCL    VAR(&SalesHist)  TYPE(*CHAR)   LEN(20)
DCL    VAR(&CurrSales)  TYPE(*CHAR)   LEN(20)

CHGVAR   VAR(&pFile)  VALUE(%ADDR(&SalesHist))
/* ... do something using &File ... */
/* ... whatever you do will happen to &SalesHist ... */
CHGVAR   VAR(&pFile)  VALUE(%ADDR(&CurrSales))
/* ... do something using &File ... */
/* ... whatever you do will happen to &CurrSales ... */
```

Figure 3.19: A based variable indirectly accesses other variables.

4

BASIC OPERATORS AND FUNCTIONS

Chapter 3 covers the use of isolated constants and variables in a CL procedure. Chapter 4 explains the various manipulations you can perform in CL to combine two or more constant or variable values.

THE CHGVAR COMMAND

The Change Variable (CHGVAR) command is the primary means of assigning a new value to a variable. In this respect, CHGVAR is equivalent to the assignment statement found in other programming languages. Most programming languages use the equal sign (=) to this effect (Pascal uses the composite symbol := and RPG and COBOL use various verbs such as MOVE, COMPUTE, EVAL, and Z-ADD). The CHGVAR command has only two parameters, which are both mandatory:

- VAR: The name of the variable being changed.

- VALUE: The new value being assigned to the variable.

In the statement shown in Figure 4.1, variable &NUMBER is assigned the value 25. Whatever value was stored in &NUMBER is lost.

```
CHGVAR VAR(&NUMBER) VALUE(25)
```

Figure 4.1: Assigning a value of 25 to the variable &NUMBER.

VALUE can contain a single value or an expression. If it contains a single value (either a constant or another variable), the value is copied into the variable being changed. If VALUE contains an expression (such as $10 + 5$), the expression is evaluated first, and the result is assigned to the variable.

If the variable is logical, VALUE must be a logical value of '0' (FALSE) or '1' (TRUE).

If the variable is character, VALUE can be character or decimal. Either way, the variable is cleared to all blanks before the new value is assigned. If the new value is a character value, the assignment is made directly. If the new value is a decimal value, the decimal value is first converted to character. Then the result is assigned to the variable.

If the variable is decimal, VALUE can be character or decimal. In either case, the variable is cleared to zero before the new value is assigned. If it is a character value, only the digits 0 to 9, an optional sign, and a decimal point or comma may be used. If it is a decimal value, the value is assigned to the variable with the decimal mark aligned.

Figure 4.2 shows a variety of examples of the CHGVAR command:

```
DCL &name        *CHAR  10
DCL &number      *DEC   (5 1)
DCL &toggle      *LGL   1
/* Character value to a character variable */
CHGVAR &name 'ABCDEFGHIJ'
       /* &NAME now contains 'ABCDEFGHIJ' */

CHGVAR &name 'X'
       /* &NAME now contains 'X         ' */

CHGVAR &name 'AAABBBCCCDDDEEE'
       /* &NAME now contains 'AAABBBCCCD' */

/* Decimal value to a character variable */
CHGVAR &name 25
       /* &NAME now contains '0000000025' */
CHGVAR &name 123456789012345
       /* Produces error */

CHGVAR &name -32.5
       /* &NAME now contains '-0000032.5' */

/* Character value to decimal variable */
CHGVAR &number '12'
       /* &NUMBER now contains +0012.0 */

CHGVAR &number '72M'
       /* Produces error */

/* Decimal value to decimal variable */
CHGVAR &number 25.2
       /* &NUMBER now contains +0025.2 */

CHGVAR &number 3.14159265
       /* &NUMBER now contains +0003.1 */

CHGVAR &number -12
       /* &NUMBER now contains -0012.0 */

CHGVAR &number 6302931.77
       /* Produces error */

/* Logical value to logical variable */
CHGVAR &toggle '1'
       /* &TOGGLE has logical value TRUE */
```

Figure 4.2: Examples of the CHGVAR command.

ARITHMETIC OPERATORS

The CHGVAR command also accepts arithmetic operations between decimal values. When arithmetic operations are used, the system calculates the result according to the standard mathematical rules, and assigns the result to the variable. In the example shown in Figure 4.3, variable &RESULT is assigned a value of 5.

```
CHGVAR VAR(&RESULT) VALUE(2 + 3)
```

Figure 4.3: Assigning a variable the value of a result of an arithmetic operation.

If you choose to omit keywords, you still have to use the parentheses around the expression as shown in Figure 4.4.

```
CHGVAR &result (2 + 3)
```

Figure 4.4: Assigning a variable the value of a result of an arithmetic operation (no keywords).

CL recognizes the four basic operations. See Table 4.1.

Table 4.1: Valid Arithmetic Operation in CL	
+	Add
−	Subtract
*	Multiply
/	Divide

In general, the compiler does not require you to leave blank spaces around the operators. The only exception is the division operator (/). Blank spaces are required for the division operator because the slash character is also used to separate the parts of a qualified name such as QGPL/QPRINT. To avoid problems and enforce consistency, you should leave a blank space around all arithmetic operators.

The VALUE parameter of the CHGVAR command can contain more than one operation, and even include parentheses to override the natural hierarchy of the operators (see Figure 4.5).

```
CHGVAR &result (2 * 3 + 4)    /* Yields 10 */
CHGVAR &result (2 * (3 + 4))  /* Yields 14 */
```

Figure 4.5: Examples of using multiple operations and parenthesis in a CHGVAR command.

Substring Function

The substring function (coded either %SST or %SUBSTRING) can be used to extract a particular portion of a character variable. It is, therefore, equivalent to RPG's SUBST op code (RPG IV's %SUBST built-in function, too), or COBOL's reference modification. The %SST code requires three arguments:

- The name of the character variable from where a portion will be extracted.

- A decimal value representing the position, within the string, where the extraction will begin.

- Another decimal value representing the number of characters to extract.

Figure 4.6 shows two examples—one with keywords and one without.

```
CHGVAR VAR(&PORTION) VALUE(%SST(&LONG_NAME 12 5))
CHGVAR &portion %SST(&long_name 12 5)
```

Figure 4.6: Examples of using %SST to assign a value to a variable.

Variable &PORTION will be assigned a five-byte string, containing characters 12, 13, 14, 15, and 16 of &LONG_NAME. As shown in Figure 4.7, the same example would be valid using variables instead of the decimal constants 12 and 5.

```
CHGVAR &portion %SST(&long_name &start &length)
```

Figure 4.7: An example of using a variable to specify parameters for %SST.

In this example, both &START and &LENGTH must be decimal variables of whatever length is appropriate for the values they must contain. If &START is to contain a number such as 12, it could be a two-digit decimal variable or longer.

You may code the %SST function in the VAR parameter instead of in the VALUE parameter. When the function is coded this way, only a portion of the variable named in VAR will be changed. Figure 4.8 shows two examples of this.

```
CHGVAR &pattern 'XXX...XXX...'
       /* Assigns a pattern to variable &PATTERN */

CHGVAR %SST(&pattern 1 3) 'AAA'
       /* &PATTERN now contains 'AAA...XXX...' */
```

Figure 4.8: Examples of using %SST in the VAR parameter.

Instead of a variable name, you also can specify *LDA (see Figure 4.9). In that case, the local data area for the job is retrieved (with %SST in the VALUE parameter) or changed (with %SST in the VAR parameter).

```
CHGVAR &a %SST(*LDA 1 10)
       /* Assigns &A the first 10 bytes of the LDA */

CHGVAR %SST(*LDA 101 8) ' '
       /* Changes LDA positions 101-108 to blanks */
```

*Figure 4.9: Examples of *LDA with %SST.*

OVERLAID VARIABLES

Overlaying variables provides an alternative to the substring function. Look at the example in Figure 4.10.

```
DCL    &QualObj   *CHAR   LEN(20)
DCL    &Object    *CHAR   LEN(10)   STG(*DEFINED) DEFVAR(&QualObj  1)
DCL    &Library   *CHAR   LEN(10)   STG(*DEFINED) DEFVAR(&QualObj 11)
```

Figure 4.10: Examples of overlaid variables.

There is no need to use the CHGVAR command with the %SST function to copy values from **&QualObj** to **&Object** and **&Library**.

CONCATENATING STRINGS

Character strings can be combined into longer strings with three built-in concatenation operations: *CAT, *BCAT, and *TCAT. Table 4.2 explains their differences.

Table 4.2: Explanation of Concatenation Operations	
Operator	**Description**
*CAT or ‖	Joins the two strings exactly the way they are (including any trailing blanks). If the first string has three trailing blanks, the resulting string would have those three blanks in the middle.
*BCAT or ❘>	Joins the two strings in such a way that only one blank is placed between the two strings (even if trailing blanks are found in the first string). *BCAT guarantees that there will be one intervening blank only.
*TCAT or ❘<	Joins the two strings with the first string trimmed (without trailing blanks at all). *TCAT results in a string that has no embedded blanks, no matter how many trailing blanks were found in the first string.

Note: All three concatenation operators leave the second string as is. If the string contains any leading blanks, those leading blanks are always included in the resulting string.

Figure 4.11 shows some examples.

```
DCL &first      *CHAR   10
DCL &last       *CHAR   10
DCL &full       *CHAR   25

CHGVAR &first 'JOHN'
CHGVAR &last  'DOE'

CHGVAR &full (&first *CAT &last)
     /* &FULL contains 'JOHN      DOE                          ' */

CHGVAR &full (&first *BCAT &last)
     /* &FULL contains 'JOHN DOE                               ' */

CHGVAR &full (&first *TCAT &last)
     /* &FULL contains 'JOHNDOE
```

Figure 4.11: Examples of concatenation and the results.

> **Note:** You can use symbols ||, |> and |< respectively instead of *CAT, *BCAT, and *TCAT. However, using *CAT, *BCAT, and *TCAT seems the wiser choice because they are more explicit (you don't need to memorize the meaning of symbols).
>
> Also, no matter what printer you have, they are always printable. Some printers might have a problem with the | character (and even with > and <) because they might be replaced by other characters or even by blank spaces (which makes your CL source listing unreadable).
>
> Also, consider that if you download CL source code to a PC, the | character might be replaced by something totally unexpected.

As explained previously, more than two decimal variables can be combined with arithmetic operators. The same applies to the concatenation operators and the %SST function, which can be combined in many ways.

SIMULATING ARRAYS IN CL

CL does not support arrays. If you need an array in a CL procedure, you can simulate one by using a very long character string and the %SST function.

Suppose you need an array of 50 object names (each one being 10 characters long). You could declare a 500-character variable as shown in Figure 4.12.

```
DCL &obj_arr *CHAR 500
```

Figure 4.12: Defining a variable to be used as an array.

Now you can reference the first element of this pseudo-array by using **%SST(&obj_arr 1 10)**. The second element is **%SST(&obj_arr 11 10)**, and so on, all the way to the 50th element—which would be **%SST(&obj_arr &n 10)**,

If you need to reference the *n*th element (that is, where the element number is a variable), you can code something like %SST(&obj_arr &n 10), where &N has been declared as a decimal variable, and contains the number of the byte where the element should begin. Figure 4.13 shows two examples.

```
/* Changing the second element */
CHGVAR %SST(&obj_arr 11 10) 'XYZ'

/* Assigning the second element to another variable */
CHGVAR &x %SST(&obj_arr 11 10)
```

Figure 4.13: Examples of referencing portions of a variable like an array.

BINARY CONVERSION

The %BIN (or %BINARY) function extracts binary values from character variables and copies binary values to character variables. The portion of the character variable must be either 2 or 4 bytes, depending on the size of the binary number being received. The %BIN function is similar to %SST. Its use is illustrated in Figure 4.14.

```
PGM   (&counter)

    DCL &counter    *CHAR   2
    DCL &numeric    *DEC    5

    CHGVAR &numeric %BIN(&counter 1 2)
```

Figure 4.14: Using %BIN to convert binary data to numeric.

Using %BIN(&COUNTER 1 2) means to extract the first two bytes of &COUNTER (as %SST would have done), and to interpret them as a numeric value. Therefore, the result can be assigned to &NUMERIC, which is a decimal variable.

In the example shown in Figure 4.13, &COUNTER is exactly two characters long. Therefore, it feels strange to "extract its first two bytes." In this case, %BIN can be abbreviated to eliminate the second and third parameters (leaving the code shown in Figure 4.15).

```
    CHGVAR &numeric %BIN(&counter)
```

Figure 4.15: An example of an abbreviated form of the %BIN keyword.

In general, you can omit the second and third parameters of %BIN if you want to use the full length of the character variable on which %BIN is to operate (&COUNTER, in this case).

This function can be used to advantage in CL procedures that act as command processing programs (CPPs), which receive lists or varying length parameters from the command processor. The command processor passes two-byte prefixes in these cases, which need to be interpreted within the CL procedure.

You can use %BIN as a pseudo-variable in the VAR, rather than VALUE, parameter of CHGVAR (see Figure 4.16).

```
    DCL  &counter    *DEC    5
    DCL  &count_chr  *CHAR   2

    CHGVAR %BIN(&count_chr 1 2) &counter
    CALL  rpgpgm  (&count_chr)
```

Figure 4.16: An example of using %BIN in the VAR parameter.

Because the %BIN function is in the VAR parameter, the numeric value in &COUNTER is first converted to character form and then assigned to the first two characters of &COUNT_CHR. Again, because the receiving variable is only two characters long, you can omit the second and third parameters of %BIN. Figure 4.17 shows an example.

```
    CHGVAR %BIN(&count_chr) &counter
```

Figure 4.17: Coding %BIN without the second and third parameters.

Besides these uses, %BIN can be used in the COND parameter of an IF statement or in any command parameter that expects a numeric value. The statements shown in Figure 4.18 are both valid.

```
    IF  (&counter *EQ %BIN(&alpha 1 4))
        CRTPF FILE(qtemp/test) RCDLEN(%BIN(&size))
```

Figure 4.18: Other examples of %BIN usage.

Logical Operations

Logical variables also can be manipulated using the *NOT, *AND, and *OR operators. These operations can be represented by the symbols ¬, &, and |. You can use either method, but remember that some printers might have problems with the first and last symbol. Also, downloading the code to a PC could turn those symbols into something quite different.

- *NOT changes a single logical variable from TRUE to FALSE or vice versa.

- *AND combines two logical variables into a single logical value. If both variables are TRUE, the result is TRUE. Any other combination yields a FALSE result.

- *OR combines two logical variables into a single logical value. If either variable is TRUE, the result is TRUE. If both variables are FALSE, the result is FALSE.

Figure 4.19 shows some examples of the use of logical operators.

```
DCL &true        *LGL     1 VALUE('1')
DCL &false       *LGL     1 VALUE('0')
DCL &result      *LGL     1

CHGVAR &result (*NOT &true)
    /* &RESULT is FALSE */
CHGVAR &result (&true *AND &false)
    /* &RESULT is FALSE */

CHGVAR &result (&true *OR &false)
    /* &RESULT is TRUE */
```

Figure 4.19: Examples of logical operations.

EXPRESSIONS AND OPERATOR HIERARCHY

An *expression* is a combination of two or more variables or constants that use operators and can be evaluated into a single value. Like variables, expressions can be of character, decimal, or logical type.

When coding expressions, be careful not to combine values of a type not supported by an operator. For example, the *CAT operator should be used only on two character values and never on numeric or logical values.

Among the arithmetic operators, multiplication and division (* and /) take precedence over addition and subtraction (+ and -). An expression such as 2+3*4 yields 14, not 20, because the multiplication (3 times 4) is evaluated first, which gives an intermediate expression of 2+12.

If this natural order of evaluation has to be overridden, you must use parentheses to group the values that should be combined first. Therefore, the expression (2+3)*4 yields 20, not 14, because the parentheses force the system to evaluate 2+3 first, and then multiply the result by 4.

Because they have the same hierarchy, all character operators (*CAT, *BCAT, and *TCAT) are evaluated from left to right without exception.

Among the logical operators, *NOT is evaluated first, followed by *, and then *OR. Again, you can circumvent this natural order by using parentheses.

THE CVTDAT COMMAND

Out of the hundreds of commands available, Convert Date (CVTDAT) stands out because it performs an often-needed function. With it, you can convert a date value from any format to any other (with the option of placing date-separator characters in the result or omitting them). CVTDAT has five parameters:

- DATE: The date being converted. This must be a character value (either variable or constant).

- TOVAR: Name of the CL variable that will receive the converted date. This must be a character variable that is from 5 to 10 bytes long, depending on the format desired.

- FROMFMT: Indicates what format DATE is in. You can enter any of the values listed in Table 4.3.

- TOFMT: The format you want TOVAR to be in. TOFMT accepts the same values as FROMFMT (listed in Table 4.3).

- TOSEP: The date separator character that is desired for TOVAR. Valid values are listed in Table 4.4.

Table 4.3: Valid Formats for the FROMFMT Parameter

Valid Formats	Description
*SYSVAL	Use if DATE is in the default date format indicated by system value QDATFMT.
*JOB	Use if DATE is in the default date format specified for this job. The job's date format defaults to system value QDATFMT, but can be changed with the Change Job (CHGJOB) command.
*MDY	Use if DATE is in the format MMDDYY.
*MDYY	Use if DATE is in the format MMDDYYYY.
*YMD	Use if DATE is in the format YYMMDD.
*YYMD	Use if DATE is in the format YYYYMMDD.
*DMY	Use if DATE is in the format DDMMYY.
*DMYY	Use if DATE is in the format DDMMYYYY.
*CYMD	Use if DATE is in the format CYYMMDD.
*JUL	Use if DATE is in the format (YYYYDDD).
*LONGJUL	Use if DATE is in the format (YYYYDDD).
*ISO	Use if DATE is in the International Standards Organization format YYYY-MM-DD.
*JIS	Use if DATE is in the Japanese Industrial Standards format YYYY-MM-DD.
*USA	Use if DATE is in the United States format MM/DD/YYYY.
*EUR	Use if DATE is in the European format DD.MM.YYYY.

Table 4.4: Valid Date Separator Characters for the FROMFMT Parameter

Valid Formats	Description
*NONE	Use if no separator characters are desired.
*SYSVAL	Use if TOVAR is to be formatted with the default date separator character, as retrieved from system value QDATSEP.

Table 4.4: Valid Date Separator Characters for the FROMFMT Parameter, continued

Valid Formats	Description
*JOB	Use if TOVAR is to be formatted with the default date separator character for the job. The job's date separator character defaults to system value QDATFMT, but can be changed with CHGJOB.
*BLANK	Use blanks as separators.
'/'	Use slashes as separators.
'-'	Use dashes as separators.
'.'	Use periods as separators.
','	Use commas as separators.

Figure 4.20 shows an example of the CVTDAT command.

```
DCL  &filedate   *CHAR    6
DCL  &dspdate    *CHAR    6

CVTDAT DATE(&filedate) TOVAR(&dspdate) +
       FROMFMT(*YMD) TOFMT(*MDY) TOSEP('/')
```

Figure 4.20: An example of the CVTDAT command.

A file contains a date in the YYMMDD format. This date is stored in variable &FILEDATE. The same date must be shown on the display in the MMDDYY format using slashes as separator characters.

When you use CVTDAT, keep in mind that all fields must have valid date values. For instance, you cannot convert a date of 02/29/99 to some other format.

Date formats that express the year as a two-digit number (*MDY, *DMY, *YDM, *JUL) can contain dates between January 1, 1940 and December 31, 2039. Date formats that express the year as a four-digit number can contain dates between August 24, 1928 and May 9, 2071.

5

CONTROL STATEMENTS

The preceding chapters cover only straightforward CL programming in which the statements are executed sequentially. Most programs (in any language) do not run that way. They perform decisions, execute loops, and so on. CL also has commands to control execution of the program.

THE IF COMMAND

First and foremost is the IF command. You use the IF command to perform a decision based on the result of a test. The nature of this test is always a logical expression.

Simple Logical Expressions

A simple logical expression has one comparison operator between two expressions of any other type. For example, if you say, "the option number is equal to 5," you have a comparison operator ("is equal to") and two other expressions ("the option number" and "5"). In CL, this could be coded as shown in Figure 5.1.

```
DCL &option     *DEC    2
IF (&option *EQ 5) CHGVAR &x 'A'
```

Figure 5.1: Expression with comparison operator.

There are several points worth noting:

- The IF command has two parameters: COND (condition) and THEN (what to do if the condition is true). The example shown in Figure 5.1 has been given without keywords. With keywords, it would look like the example shown in Figure 5.2.

```
IF COND(&OPTION *EQ 5) THEN(CHGVAR VAR(&X) VALUE('A'))
```

Figure 5.2: Comparison expression with keywords.

As you can see, CHGVAR VAR(&X) VALUE('A') is executed if the condition is true.

- The comparison operator in the example is *EQ (equal). Actually, *EQ is just one of the comparison operators you can use in a logical expression. See Table 5.1.

You are probably better off using the *XX notation instead of the symbols, especially because some printers might not print the ¬, <, and > symbols correctly (or might not print them at all). You risk making your CL program listings more difficult to understand.

- The two expressions being compared must be of the same type. In the example, both have decimal values.

- The COND parameter must have a logical expression that can be evaluated to either TRUE or FALSE.

Table 5.1: Logical operators	
Comparison	Description
*EQ or =	Equal to
*NE or ¬=	Not equal to
*LT or <	Less than
*LE or <=	Less than or equal to
*NL or ¬<	Not less than
*GT or >	Greater than
*GE or >=	Greater than or equal to
*NG or ¬>	Not greater than

Once in a while, you will have to test a logical variable. Because the variable being tested already has a logical value of TRUE or FALSE, you can take a shortcut when you code the IF statement. Figure 5.3 shows an example.

```
    /* Declare indicators 03 and 12 from a display file    */
    /* These indicators turn on when F3 or F12 is pressed */
    DCL &in03       *LGL     1
    DCL &in12       *LGL     1

    /* The two IFs that follow are equivalent */
    /* Use either style in your programs.      */
    IF (&in03 *EQ '1' *OR &in12 *EQ '1') ...

    IF (&in03 *OR &in12) ...
```

Figure 5.3: Using a comparison operator with logical variables.

To test whether or not &IN03 is FALSE, you can code the expression as shown in Figure 5.4.

```
    IF (&in03 *EQ '0') ...

    /* Or the shortcut: */
    IF (*NOT &in03) ...
```

Figure 5.4: An example of testing for FALSE.

Complex Logical Expressions

The COND parameter can contain a complex logical expression that consists of several simple expressions connected with the logical operations *AND, *OR, or *NOT. Table 5.2 summarizes the logical value (T=TRUE, F=FALSE) of these logical operators. For example, a TRUE value and a FALSE value combined with an *AND operator yields a false value.

Table 5.2: Results of Complex Logical Expressions							
*AND			***NOT**			***OR**	
First Value	Second Value	Result	First Value	Second Value	Result	Value	Result
T	T	T	T	T	T	T	F
T	F	F	T	F	T	F	T
F	T	F	F	T	T		
F	F	F	F	F	F		

For example, you can say, "Send a warning message to the system operator if the option number is 2 or 3." In CL, this is coded as shown in Figure 5.5.

The COND parameter can contain extremely complicated logical expressions with many *ANDS, *ORS, and *NOTS, even using parentheses to group subexpressions when it becomes necessary to alter the natural order of evaluation. However, in all cases, the condition must evaluate to either TRUE or FALSE.

```
DCL &option     *DEC    2

IF (&option *EQ 2 *OR +
    &option *EQ 3     ) +
   SNDPGMMSG MSG('Warning') TOMSGQ(qsysopr)
```

Figure 5.5: Example of complex logical expression using *OR.

Remember that:

- *NOT is evaluated first, whenever present.

- *AND is evaluated next, if present.

- *OR is evaluated last, if present.>

- *NOT reverses the TRUE or FALSE value of the expression.

- *AND yields a TRUE result if both expressions are TRUE. In all other cases, it yields FALSE.

- *OR yields a FALSE result if both expressions are FALSE. In all other cases, it yields TRUE.

THE DO AND ENDDO COMMANDS

An IF statement can be used to execute one command if the condition is met. With the DO and ENDDO commands, you can change the function of the IF command so that a group of statements is executed if the condition is met. This group of statements must be enclosed between a DO and an ENDDO command pair.

Single-Level DO Groups

Suppose you want to execute four commands when an option number is equal to three. You would need to code a CL routine like the one shown in Figure 5.6.

```
    DCL &option        *CHAR    1

    IF (&option *EQ '3') DO
        SNDPGMMSG MSGID(cpf9898) MSGF(qcpfmsg) +
                MSGDTA('You''ve taken option 3') +
                TOPGMQ(*EXT) MSGTYPE(*STATUS)
        CHGVAR &option ' '
        CALL abc (&this &that)
        GOTO again
    ENDDO
```

Figure 5.6: An example of single-level DO group.

The four commands enclosed in the box (SNDPGMMSG, CHGVAR, CALL, and GOTO) are executed if &OPTION equals '3'. Note that the DO is placed in the IF statement's THEN parameter and the ENDDO is isolated.

Nesting DO Groups

Now that you know how to create a DO group, you should also know that you can code an IF statement inside the DO group. As shown in Figure 5.7, this second IF statement can open another DO group completely nested within the first one.

```
IF (&a *EQ '1') DO
        *
        *
        *
        IF (&b *EQ '2') DO
            *
            *
            *
        ENDDO
        *
        *
        *
    ENDDO
```

Figure 5.7: An example of a nested DO group with indenting for easier reading.

You can take nested DO groups to a maximum of 10 levels. The source code shown in Figure 5.7 takes advantage of CL's free-format nature to indent the code (thus revealing the levels of nested DOs). If you let the command prompter format the code for you, however, all commands are aligned the same. The result, as shown in Figure 5.8, is less readable code.

```
IF          COND(&A *EQ '1') THEN(DO)
*
*
*
IF          COND(&B *EQ '2') THEN(DO)
*
*
*
ENDDO
*
*
*
ENDDO
```

Figure 5.8: An example of a nested DO group without benefit of indenting.

Nesting IF Commands

CL lets you nest IF commands up to 10 levels deep. You can code an IF statement within the THEN parameter of another IF, as shown in Figures 5.9 and 5.10.

```
IF (&a *EQ &b) IF (&c *EQ &d) CALL xyz
```

Figure 5.9: An example of nested IF commands (no keywords).

```
IF          COND(&A *EQ &B) THEN(IF COND(&C *EQ &D) +
                            THEN(CALL PGM(XYZ)))
```

Figure 5.10: Example of nested IF commands with keywords.

In this example, the CALL command runs only if &A equals &B and &C equals &D. This particular case could be coded more clearly with the *AND logical operator in a single IF statement, as shown in Figure 5.11.

```
IF (&a *EQ &b) IF (&c *EQ &d) CALL xyz
```

Figure 5.11: Alternative method of coding nested IFs using *AND.

65

There are cases, however, when nesting the conditions separately is perfectly valid and is the only way to code what you want. In this case you should consider using the DO command for the outer IF statement, as shown in Figure 5.12.

```
IF (&a *EQ &b) DO
      IF (&c *EQ &d) CALL xyz
      *
      *
      *
    ENDDO
```

Figure 5.12: An example of using DO command for nested IF statements.

THE ELSE COMMAND

The ELSE command works with the IF command. It provides instructions about what to do when the condition in the IF command tests FALSE. ELSE is optional.

For example, suppose that a user enters a 'Y' or an 'N' to a question presented by a display file (the variable name is &ANSWER). The CL program will use the response, but it first must be translated to '*YES' or '*NO'. The IF and ELSE pair shown in Figure 5.13 will take care of this problem.

```
DCL &answer     *CHAR    1
DCL &yesno      *CHAR    4

IF (&answer *EQ 'Y') +
    CHGVAR &yesno '*YES'
ELSE +
    CHGVAR &yesno '*NO'
```

Figure 5.13: An example of translating input variables to different values using IF and ELSE.

The IF command evaluates the condition in the COND parameter. If true, it executes the command found in the THEN parameter (which is a CHGVAR command to assign '*YES' to variable &YESNO).

The ELSE command follows. If the condition previously tested is true, the ELSE command is skipped altogether. If the condition is not true, the system runs the command found in the CMD parameter (which is another CHGVAR command).

Using DO with ELSE

You also can use the DO/ENDDO pair with the ELSE command when you need to execute more than one command with an ELSE. See Figure 5.14.

```
IF (&a *EQ &b) DO
     *
     *
     *
    ENDDO
    ELSE DO
     *
     *
     *
    ENDDO
```

Figure 5.14: An example of using ELSE with DO/ENDDO.

What you code inside each DO/ENDDO pair is up to you. Except to limit you to 10 levels of nested DO groups, CL places no restrictions on you. It is possible to have another IF. See the example shown in Figure 5.15.

```
    IF (&a *EQ &b) DO
     IF (&c *EQ &d) DO
          *
          *
          *
        ENDDO
        ELSE DO
          *
          *
          *
        ENDDO
    ENDDO
    ELSE DO
        IF (&e *EQ &f) DO
          *
          *
          *
        ENDDO
         ELSE DO
          *
          *
          *
        ENDDO
    ENDDO
```

Figure 5.15: An example of IF commands within the ELSE construct.

Note how indenting the code makes it much easier to follow the hierarchy of the various IFs and ELSEs.

THE SELECT COMMAND

The SELECT, WHEN, OTHERWISE, and ENDSELECT commands implement a case structure in CL procedures. Case structures are suited for situations in which only one of several alternatives is to be executed.

A SELECT group begins with the SELECT command and ends with the ENDSELECT command. Neither of these commands has parameters.

Each condition that must be tested is coded in the COND parameter of a WHEN command. The command to be executed is coded in the THEN parameter. You can see that WHEN is like IF in structure.

You may use the optional OTHERWISE command to execute a command when none of the conditions proves true. OTHERWISE accepts only a single parameter—CMD—which makes it similar in structure and function to ELSE.

In the example in Figure 5.16, a variable named &OPTION is tested for values of 1 through 4. If &OPTION has any of those values, one or two programs will be executed. If &OPTION has any other value, the SIGNOFF command will execute, ending the session.

```
DCL         VAR(&option) TYPE(*CHAR) LEN(1)

  SELECT
      WHEN      COND(&option *EQ '1') THEN(CALL PGM(pgm1))
      WHEN      COND(&option *EQ '2') THEN(CALL PGM(pgm2))
      WHEN      COND(&option *EQ '3') THEN(CALL PGM(pgm3))
      WHEN      COND(&option *EQ '4') THEN(DO)
          CALL      PGM(pgm4)
          CALL      PGM(pgm5)
      ENDDO
      OTHERWISE CMD(SIGNOFF)
  ENDSELECT
```

Figure 5.16: Case structures are implemented with SELECT and its associated commands.

THE DOWHILE COMMAND

Use the DOWHILE command to implement a top-tested loop. That is, the condition that controls the loop is tested before each iteration of the loop. If the condition is false when control reaches the DOWHILE command, the commands in the body of the loop will not be executed at all.

The DOWHILE takes one parameter—COND—which defines the condition that must be true for the loop to continue to execute. The end of the loop structure is indicated with the ENDDO command. The commands that make up the body of the loop follow DOWHILE and precede ENDDO.

In the example in Figure 5.17, three commands—two CALL commands and one CHGVAR—are governed by the DOWHILE command. If the &STATUS variable has a value of five zeros when control reaches the DOWHILE, the three inner commands will not execute. If &STATUS has a non-zero value, the loop will begin execution and continue until program PGM3 changes the value of &STATUS to a value of zeros.

```
DOWHILE    COND(&STATUS *NE '00000')
    CALL       PGM(pgm2)
    CALL       PGM(pgm3) PARM(&STATUS)
    CHGVAR     VAR(&COUNT) VALUE(&COUNT + 1)
ENDDO
```

Figure 5.17: DOWHILE defines a top-tested loop.

THE DOUNTIL COMMAND

The DOUNTIL command defines a bottom-tested loop. That is, the condition that controls the loop is tested after each iteration of the loop. The commands in the body of the loop will be executed at least once. In Figure 5.18, the loop continues to execute until program PGM3 returns a status value of five zeros.

```
DOUNTIL    COND(&STATUS *EQ '00000')
   CALL       PGM(pgm2)
   CALL       PGM(pgm3) PARM(&STATUS)
ENDDO
```

Figure 5.18: DOUNTIL defines a bottom-tested loop.

THE DOFOR COMMAND

Most programming languages have some form of the counted loop. This type of loop has a control variable, which is given an initial value and incremented or decremented with each iteration, until the control variable falls outside some acceptable range. The counted loop is defined with the DOFOR command.

DOFOR has three required parameters and one optional one. All four parameters require integer values. In the VAR parameter, provide the name of a signed or unsigned integer variable to be used for the control variable. The FROM parameter allows you to specify the value to which the control variable is to be initialized. In the TO parameter, specify the terminal value of the control variable. The last parameter, BY, is the quantity to be added to the control variable after each iteration. Specify a negative value for a descending loop.

The loop in Figure 5.19 executes four times. Variable &OFFSET assumes the following values: 3, 13, 23, and 33.

```
DCL    VAR(&OFFSET) TYPE(*INT) LEN(2)

DOFOR    VAR(&OFFSET) FROM(3) TO(33) BY(10)
   (CL commands)
ENDDO
```

Figure 5.19: DOFOR defines a counted loop.

THE LEAVE AND ITERATE COMMANDS

The LEAVE and ITERATE commands provide further control over DOWHILE, DOUNTIL, and DOFOR looping structures. LEAVE causes an immediate exit from a loop. ITERATE passes control the bottom of a loop.

You may specify an optional CMDLBL parameter with LEAVE and ITERATE. If you do not use the CMDLBL parameter, the LEAVE or ITERATE command applies to the innermost loop. To exit or continue an outer loop, provide a label for a DOWHILE, DOUNTIL, or DOFOR command, and refer to this label in the LEAVE or ITERATE command.

The example code segment in Figure 5.20 contains two loops, one within the other. The first two IF commands refer to the inner loop, referred to with label NEXT. The last IF refers to the outer loop, named PROMPT.

```
prompt: DOWHILE COND(*NOT &IN03)
        ...
        CHGVAR  VAR(&pos) VALUE(1)
next:   DOWHILE COND(&pos *LT 120)
        ...
        IF COND(&fname *EQ ' ') THEN(LEAVE)
        ...
        IF COND(&error *EQ '1') THEN(ITERATE)
        IF COND(&error *EQ '2') THEN(LEAVE CMDLBL(prompt))
        ...
        ENDDO
        ...
        ENDDO
```

Figure 5.20: LEAVE and ITERATE alter the normal behavior of loops.

THE GOTO COMMAND

Many programmers (especially those who have adopted structured programming techniques) dread the thought of using the GOTO command. After all, modern languages offer structured operations such as DO WHILE, DO UNTIL, iterative DO, CASE groups, calling subroutines, and premature leave of a loop. As of V5R3, CL also has such structures. In previous releases, it was necessary to use GOTO to control looping and branching.

The GOTO command has only one parameter (which is required): CMDLBL. The CMDLBL parameter must contain the label where the GOTO is to continue execution of the program. Figure 5.21 shows an example.

```
loop:
    *
    *
    *
    GOTO end_loop

    *
    *
    *
    GOTO loop

end_loop:
```

Figure 5.21: An example of a GOTO command.

In the example shown in Figure 5.21, the first GOTO transfers control to label END_LOOP (at the bottom). The second GOTO transfers control to label LOOP, which is at the top. The only limitation of the GOTO command is that the labels cannot be repeated. You can go to the same label from many different GOTOs, but you cannot use the same label name for more than one label. The code shown in Figure 5.22 is incorrect.

```
prompt:
    SNDRCVF

    *
    *
    *
    GOTO prompt
    *
    *
    *

prompt:
```

Figure 5.22: Incorrect use of multiple labels with the same name.

This program won't compile because the name PROMPT is assigned to two labels.

Subroutines

As of V5R4, CL supports internal subroutines. As with other languages, you can use CL subroutines to divide a large task into two or more smaller tasks, or to group calculations that must be repeated during execution of the procedure.

Subroutines follow the main body of executable statements, and immediately precede the ENDPGM command. The general format of a CL procedure, then, is the following:

- PGM

- Declarations (DCL, DCLF, DCLPRCOPT, COPYRIGHT)

- Global MONMSG

- Main body of procedural code

- Subroutines

- ENDPGM

The Syntax of Subroutines

A subroutine begins with the SUBR command and ends with the ENDSUBR command. The SUBR command accepts one parameter, the SUBR parameter, which names the subroutine.

You may precede the SUBR and ENDSUBR commands with labels. Branching to the label of a SUBR command, or to a null label preceding a SUBR command, is equivalent to branching to the first command within a subroutine. You may also use labels within the subroutine. Two or more labels may have the same name if they are not in the same routine (i.e. the main routine or a subroutine).

To invoke a subroutine, use the CALLSUBR command. In the first parameter, SUBR, indicate the name of the subroutine to be called. Figure 5.23 shows the pattern for subroutines.

```
        PGM
        DCL        &SomeVar      *char   2

        CALLSUBR   SUBR(DoATask)
        CALL       PGM(DoAPgm)
        CALLSUBR   SUBR(DoATask)


        SUBR       SUBR(DoATask)

        CALL       PGM(pgm1)
        DOUNTIL    COND(&SomeVar *NE ' ')
          CALL     PGM(pgm2) PARM(&SomeVar)
          CALL     PGM(pgm3) PARM(&SomeVar)
        ENDDO
        IF         COND(&SomeVar *EQ 'XX') THEN(GOTO End)
        CALL       PGM(pgm4)
        CALL       PGM(pgm5)

End:    ENDSUBR

        ENDPGM
```

Figure 5.23: An example of calling a program with a list of parameters.

CALLSUBR has a second, optional parameter, RTNVAL, which must be a four-byte integer variable. It is used to receive a return value from the subroutine. To make a subroutine return a value, use the RTNVAL parameter on the ENDSUBR command or the Return from Subroutine (RTNSUBR) command. See Figure 5.24 for a subroutine that includes a return value.

```
          PGM
          DCL        &SomeVar     *char    2
          DCL        &Error       *int     4

          CALLSUBR   SUBR(DoATask) RTNVAL(&Error)
          IF         COND(&ERROR *GT 100) THEN(RETURN)
          IF         COND(&ERROR *GE 2) THEN(DO)
             CALL    PGM(DoAPgm)
          ENDDO
          CALLSUBR   SUBR(DoATask)


          SUBR       SUBR(DoATask)

          CALL       PGM(pgm1)
          CALL       PGM(pgm2) PARM(&SomeVar)
          IF         COND(&SomeVar *EQ '01') THEN(RTNSUBR RTNVAL(1))
          IF         COND(&SomeVar *EQ '02') THEN(RTNSUBR RTNVAL(2))
          IF         COND(&SomeVar *EQ '03') THEN(RTNSUBR RTNVAL(3))
          CALL       PGM(pgm3) PARM(&SomeVar)
          IF         COND(&SomeVar *EQ 'ZZ') THEN(RTNSUBR RTNVAL(101))
          CALL       PGM(pgm4)
          CALL       PGM(pgm5)

  End:    ENDSUBR    RTNVAL(0)

          ENDPGM
```

Figure 5.24: The general pattern of a procedure with subroutines.

Notice that the subroutine has five commands that return a value to the caller. If a RTNSUBR command is executed, control immediately returns to the calling routine, and the returned value is placed into the **&Error** variable. The RTNVAL parameter of the ENDSUBR is not necessary in this example, because ENDSUBR returns a zero by default.

The Subroutine Stack

Subroutines cannot contain other subroutines, but subroutines can call subroutines. A subroutine can even call itself. Every time a subroutine is called, CL pushes an entry onto a stack. By default, you may have 99 levels of subroutines active at once, but you can use the SUBRSTACK parameter of the Declare Processing Option (DCLPRCOPT) command, as Figure 5.25 demonstrates, to change the stack depth to any value from 20 to 9,999.

```
DCLPRCOPT    SUBRSTACK(24)
```

Figure 5.25: Use DCLPRCOPT to control the number of subroutine stack levels.

A CL procedure may include only one DCLPRCOPT command.

If a program-level MONMSG traps an error that occurs during execution of a subroutine, and the MONMSG contains a GOTO that transfers control to a statement in the main routine, CL must exit all subroutines. The subroutine stack remains intact, so that a Dump CL Program (DMPCLPGM) command can display its contents. However, the system clears the subroutine stack when CALLSUBR is next executed.

THE CALL AND CALLPRC COMMANDS

You can code the CALL command in a CL procedure to start execution of another program or code the CALLPRC (Call Procedure) command to start execution of a bound procedure. CALLPRC is not valid in OPM programs. Program execution continues at the statement following the CALL or CALLPRC. The CALL command has only two parameters:

- PGM: The qualified name of the program to execute. If the library name is not given, the system uses the library list to locate it.

- PARM: The list of parameters to be passed to the other program.

```
CALL mylib/abc (&a 'I' &b 2.5)
```

Figure 5.26: An example of calling a program with a list of parameters.

The statement in Figure 5.26 illustrates a CALL to another program.

The CL statement shown in Figure 5.26 causes program ABC in library MYLIB to start executing. It passes four parameters from the calling program to program ABC. The first parameter is variable &A, the second is character constant 'I', the third is variable &B and the fourth is decimal constant 2.5.

The CALLPRC command has three parameters:

- PRC: Identifies the bound procedure to be called. The name can be fully qualified with a library and name if the procedure being called is in a service program; otherwise, the name must be of a module contained in the same ILE program as the calling module. You cannot use a variable to identify the procedure.

- PARM: See the preceding description of the PARM parameter for the CALL command.

- RTNVAL: You can place a CL variable in this parameter in order to receive a returned value from the procedure you have called, provided, of course, that the called procedure returns one. You can use either a character or a decimal CL variable. If you do not want to receive a value, use the default value of *NONE in this parameter.

Passing Variables as Parameters

When you pass variables as parameters (such as &A and &B in the preceding example), it is your responsibility to make sure that the parameters match in both programs. In most cases, the variables must match both in type and in length. The only exception is with character variables. Character variables can have different lengths in the calling and called programs. Be aware that even in this case the results cannot always be predicted. The variable names don't have to match. Parameters are passed in sequential order—not by name. Figure 5.27 maps out the process.

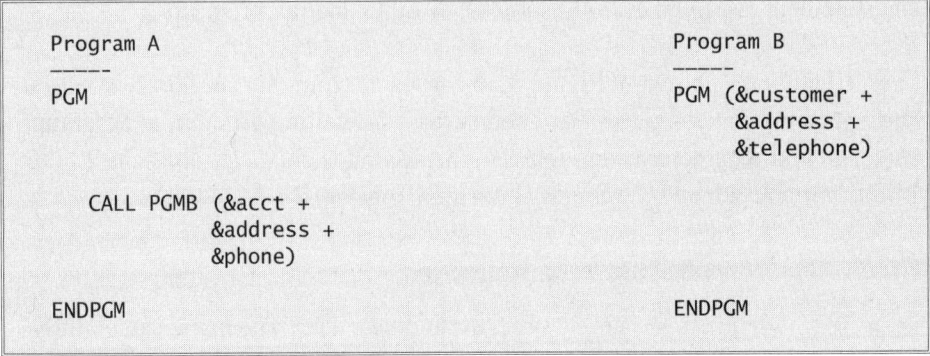

Figure 5.27: Set up of variables when one program calls another.

Variables &ACCT and &CUSTOMER must be declared identically in both programs. For example, they could both be TYPE(*DEC) LEN(6 0). Variable &ADDRESS must have the same type and length in both programs. Variables &PHONE and &TELE-PHONE should be declared with the same type and length. Note that, except for &ADDRESS, the names don't match.

Note: CL programs cannot process floating-point data because variables cannot be declared as TYPE(*float). Still, you can call a CL program and pass floating-point variables (or constants) to it. The CL program must receive these variables or constants in character variables (8 bytes long). Then the CL program can call another program that supports floating point and can pass these character variables to it.

Passing Constants as Parameters

You can pass a constant to another program. Passing constants is a little trickier than passing variables because you must adhere to more rules. For simplicity, consider the case of program A calling program B.

Character constants passed to program B must have the same length as the parameter variable declared in program B, unless program B expects a character value of 32 bytes or less. In this case, the lengths do not have to match. The system pads the string with blanks (if characters are missing) or chops off the right end to the size required by program B.

Decimal constants passed to program B are always passed as if they were of LEN(15 5). Therefore, program B must receive them in a variable declared as TYPE(*DEC) LEN(15 5), or errors will occur. If program B expects a decimal value of any other length, use a hexadecimal constant instead.

Hexadecimal constants passed to program B must have the correct length. If program B expects a character value of 4 bytes, or a decimal value of six or seven digits (regardless of the number of decimal places), you must pass a hexadecimal constant of 8 nibbles, such as X'0000067F'. This value would be received by program B as decimal value 67 or 6.7 or .67, depending on its definition.

Logical constants passed to program B must be either '1' or '0', the only valid values for logical constants.

Although floating-point constants such as 2.5E+73 can be passed to a CL program, the CL program won't be able to use them. The constant must be received into TYPE(*CHAR) LEN(8) variables, which the CL program can pass to a third program without trouble. Special values *NAN (not a number), *INF (infinity), and *NEGINF (negative infinity) can be passed to CL programs the same way.

THE ENDPGM AND RETURN COMMANDS

Chapter 2 briefly describes the End Program (ENDPGM) command used to mark the physical end of a CL source member. When the ENDPGM command is reached, execution continues in the caller at the statement following the CALL command.

You can think of the RETURN command as another ENDPGM with the added flexibility that it doesn't have to appear at the end of the source member. The RETURN command also ends execution and returns control to the caller. Figure 5.28 helps to illustrate the use of RETURN and ENDPGM.

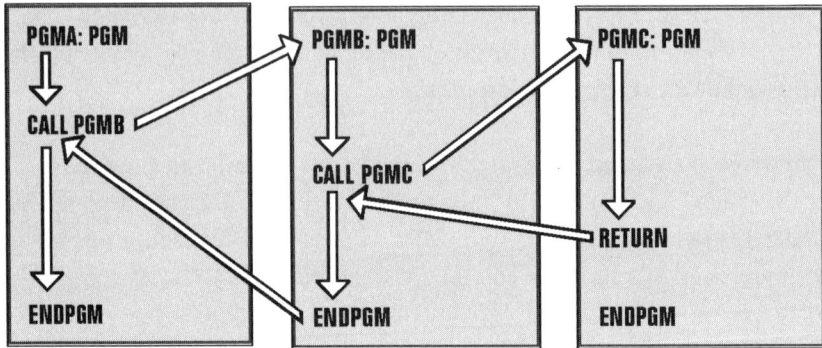

Figure 5.28: The RETURN and ENDPGM commands.

THE TFRCTL COMMAND

The Transfer Control (TFRCTL) command works like the CALL command in that they both stop executing one program and start another. The main difference between the two is what is done when the second program ends.

Figure 5.29 helps to clarify the workings of CALL and TFRCTL. Program PGMA issues a CALL to PGMB, and then issues a TFRCTL to PGMC. When PGMC ends, the system returns control not to PGMB, but to PGMA. In other words, the program that issued the TFRCTL is skipped.

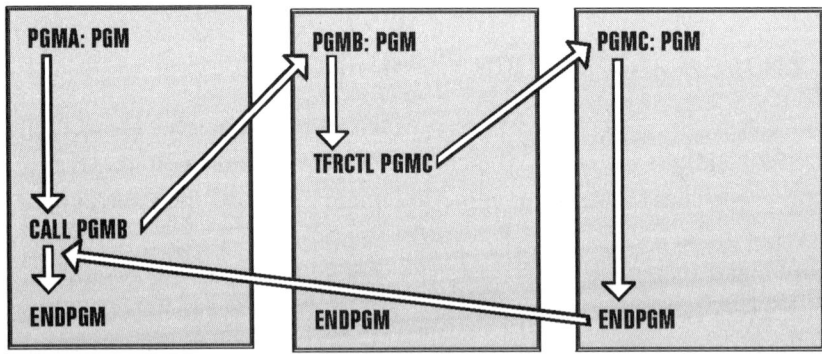

Figure 5.29: The CALL and TFRCTL commands.

If you had called PGMB from the keyboard instead of from another program, control would have returned to the keyboard when PGMC ended. TFRCTL has rather severe limitations.

- TFRCTL is not supported in ILE programs.

- When PGMB issues a TFRCTL to PGMC, it can pass parameters to PGMC, but only if those parameters were received from PGMA. PGMB cannot pass any parameters it didn't receive from its caller.

Nevertheless, TFRCTL is a good alternative to CALL when there is no need to return to the original program. For example, you could have an initial program in your user profile. When you sign on, this program runs in order to set some initial job attributes not otherwise available through job descriptions. Once the attributes are set, you need to run another program. Rather than calling the second program, use TFRCTL.

6

MESSAGE MANAGEMENT

The i5 is a message-based machine. Because messages seem to be everywhere, controlling practically all aspects of the i5, the omnipresence of messages makes it important to understand what they are and how to manage them.

WHAT IS A MESSAGE?

A message is a free-format communication between two entities. These entities can be two users, two programs, or one user and one program. More often than not, the purpose of the communication is to call attention to a possible problem or to report a special condition such as "Job completed normally."

Messages are always spoken of as being sent somewhere. The entity at the other end is said to receive the message. Messages can be predefined (as message descriptions in message files) or impromptu (composed on the fly).

Messages are not always received the instant they are sent. On the contrary, they usually accumulate at the receiving end until the recipient has a chance to look at them—the way voice messages accumulate in your answering machine when you're out. This accumulation takes place in a message queue.

MESSAGE QUEUES

A message queue is a place where messages accumulate in the order in which they are sent. Message queues can be actual, permanent objects (type *MSGQ) or temporary entities (job message queues). The following sections examine each type in turn.

Permanent Message Queues

A permanent message queue is an object of type *MSGQ contained in a library. You must create it yourself before you can use it. In most cases, this creation must be done manually with the Create Message Queue (CRTMSGQ) command. However, the system creates message queues automatically when you create user profiles or device descriptions for displays.

i5/OS has several predefined message queues. The most notable is QSYSOPR (the system operator's message queue).

Although permanent message queues can be used for any type of work involving messages, they are most often used for communication between two users or when a program needs to send a message to a user.

Job Message Queues

The system creates a temporary message queue for each job when the job starts. This is the external message queue (*EXT), which is the display station of the requester if the job runs interactively. If the job runs in batch, *EXT is the system operator's message queue, QSYSOPR.

In addition, the system automatically creates a temporary message queue—as soon as a message is sent to the program or procedure—for each program or procedure that enters the job's call stack. This type of message queue, called a *program message queue,* exists for as long as the program or procedure remains in your call stack. The program message queue has the same name as the program or procedure it serves.

Program message queues are used for communications between two programs or procedures. The external (*EXT) message queue is used for direct communication between the requester and the various programs that run in a job.

TYPES OF MESSAGES

Message queues differ from other queues (such as data queues) because entries are not automatically removed when received; they remain in the message queue as old messages. In contrast, messages not yet received are considered new messages. This distinction will become important as you examine the Receive Message (RCVMSG) command later in this chapter.

New versus Old

Sometimes it is necessary to change all messages back to "new" status. The Change Message Queue (CHGMSGQ) command handles the task easily. See Figure 6.1.

```
CHGMSGQ MSGQ(...) RESET(*YES)
```

Figure 6.1: An example of the CHGMSGQ command.

Only those messages contained in permanent message queues can revert to "new" status. You cannot change the status of messages in job-message queues.

Purpose of the Message

A message can be categorized according to its purpose. It is very important for you to learn the nine types of messages. Table 6.1 lists these types.

Table 6.1: Types of Messages

Message Type	Description
Request (*RQS)	Request messages are, quite literally, an order you issue to execute a command. You actually send a *RQS message each time you key in a command at the command entry panel and press the Enter key. Your request-handling program (usually QSYS/QCMD) receives the messages and carries out the order. Request messages can be sent only to job message queues (program or *EXT).
Inquiry (*INQ)	Inquiry messages are messages that prompt the receiver for a reply. The receiver gets the message and an input field where the reply can be typed in. Entering the reply sends the original user a *RPY message. Inquiry messages can be sent to permanent message queues or to *EXT.
Reply (*RPY)	Reply messages are sent automatically when the receiver of an *INQ message types a reply. Reply messages cannot be sent manually anywhere; the mechanism for sending them is built in.
Completion (*COMP)	Completion messages inform the receiver that the previous request or command has been carried out without trouble (it has completed normally). Completion messages can be sent anywhere.
Diagnostic (*DIAG)	Diagnostic messages inform the receiver of errors encountered during the execution of a request or command. Diagnostic messages can be sent anywhere.
Escape (*ESCAPE)	Escape messages inform the receiver that the previous request or command ended abnormally. Escape messages can be sent to program message queues only. The program that sends the escape message ends immediately. The receiving program issues a function check (causing its termination) unless it is monitoring for the arrival of the escape message using the Monitor Message (MONMSG) command.

Message Type	Description
	Table 6.1: Types of Messages, continued
Notify (*NOTIFY)	A notify message informs the receiver of a recoverable error condition and, like an *INQ message, prompts for a reply. Notify messages can only be sent to a program message queue or to *EXT. When a program sends a notify message to its caller, the sending program stops processing. Processing of the sending program does not resume unless the receiving program is monitoring for the notify message or if the notify message was sent to *EXT and the user entered a reply.
Informational (*INFO)	Informational messages are used to send some piece of information to another program or user. They do not describe success or failure, and they do not require a reply. Informational messages can be sent anywhere.
Status (*STATUS)	Status messages are used to report progress of an ongoing task (usually one consisting of many steps). Although status messages can be sent to program message queues or *EXT, they are mostly sent to *EXT. When *EXT receives a status message, the message appears at the bottom of the display while the program runs. If the status message is sent to another program, the receiving program might or might not be monitoring for the status message. If the receiving program is not monitoring, the sending program continues processing.

Impromptu and Predefined Messages

While you write CL procedures, you can hard-code the text of messages in the source code as you compose your messages. This type of message, called the *impromptu message,* can be used for all message types except *ESCAPE, *STATUS, and *NOTIFY.

If you standardize your messages, most of their contents can be fixed by pre-defining the messages in message files. Defining messages involves assigning them a seven-character message ID and fixing their text (which might or might not contain embedded variables).

USING PREDEFINED MESSAGES

If you compose fixed text and store it in a message file, messages frequently sent by you or your programs can be predefined. *Predefining* a message involves assigning it a unique seven-character message identifier and adding all the message characteristics to the message file.

You can then send the message by referencing the message identification and the name of the message file, and then adding any variable message data to be inserted into the message text.

For example, you could predefine a message with the identification LIB0001 and text "Library &1 not found." When you send message LIB0001 and supply message data "MYLIB," the system issues the message "Library MYLIB not found."

Message Files

The first step to predefining messages is to create a message file. You do this by running the Create Message File (CRTMSGF) command, as shown in Figure 6.2.

```
CRTMSGF mylib/mymsgf TEXT('Sample message file')
```

Figure 6.2: An example of defining a message to create a message file.

Running the command creates message file MYMSGF in library MYLIB. Every time you send a message you have predefined in this message file, you will have to reference the message file name, MYMSGF, and the library where it resides, MYLIB (unless MYLIB can be located in the library list).

Message Descriptions

Each predefined message is stored in a message file by adding a message description. Use the Add Message Description (ADDMSGD) command. Later, you can change the predefined message with the Change Message Description (CHGMSGD) command or remove it with the Remove Message Description (RM-VMSGD) command.

You can view message descriptions with the Display Message Description (DSPMSGD) or Work with Message Descriptions (WRKMSGD) command.

The code for adding a couple of predefined messages to the message file just created is shown in Figure 6.3.

```
ADDMSGD MSGID(lib0001) MSGF(mylib/mymsgf) +
        MSG('Library &1 not found.') +
        SECLVL('The library you specified, &1, does not exist on this +
               system.  Either create library &1 with the CRTLIB +
               command, or specify a different library name.') +
        SEV(99) FMT((*CHAR 10))
```

Figure 6.3: An example of adding messages to a message file.

The message identification is LIB0001. No two messages in the same message file can have the same identification. IBM recommends that no two messages on the entire system have the same identification. The message ID always has three letters followed by four nibbles. Remember that a nibble is a hexadecimal digit; that is, 0-9 or A-F.

Note: Never use letters such as CPF, CPD, or CPI as the three-letter prefix to your own messages; such letter combinations are reserved for IBM's use. IBM recommends that all your message IDs begin with the letter U. IBM has vowed not to employ the letter U in its own messages.

The qualified name of the message file that will store the predefined message you are adding is MYLIB/MYMSGF.

The MSG parameter contains the text of the message. The **&1** indicates the presence of a variable insertion point; you can have more than one. The FMT parameter is a list that indicates the format of the variables. In the example (Figure 6.3), there's only one message. Therefore, FMT describes only one variable (which turns out to be character, 10 bytes long).

The SECLVL parameter provides second-level text for the message. This additional text is displayed if a user presses the Help key while the cursor is positioned on the message. Second-level text is very helpful because it can contain anything you want; it can even reference the same variables as the actual message text, such as **&1**. You should consider including second-level text for all your predefined messages.

The SEV parameter indicates the severity of the message. Severity 99 is the highest. IBM uses the severity levels listed in Table 6.2.

Table 6.2: Message Severity Levels	
Severity	**Description**
00	Information message.
10	Warning.
20	Error.
30	Severe error.
40	Abnormal end of program.
50	Abnormal end of job.
60	System warning.
70	Device malfunction.
80	System alert.
90	System/subsystem integrity.
99	Operator action required.

The following section includes an example of using predefined messages with embedded substitution variables.

THE SNDPGMMSG COMMAND

i5/OS provides several ways to send messages. By far the most versatile (although also the most complicated) is the Send Program Message (SNDPGMMSG) command. SNDPGMMSG cannot be executed interactively; you cannot run it from the command line. SNDPGMMSG must be included in a CL procedure or in a REXX procedure in order to execute.

With SNDPGMMSG, you can send messages to message queues or temporary program- message queues within the same job. Even though the SNDPGMMSG command looks intimidating at first, it is not all that difficult to figure out. It contains many parameters, but certain pairs of parameters are mutually exclusive.

What to Say in the Message

SNDPGMMSG can send either an impromptu or a predefined message. Impromptu messages can be explicitly coded in the MSG parameter. Predefined messages require the MSGID and MSGF parameters for the message ID and qualified message file name, respectively. MSG and MSGID/MSGF are mutually exclusive.

- If you want to send a *NOTIFY, *ESCAPE, or *STATUS message, you must use MSGID and MSGF.

- If you want to send a *RQS message, you are required to use the MSG parameter.

- All other types of messages allow either the MSG parameter or the MSGID/MSGF parameter pair.

The MSGDTA parameter can be used with MSGID/MSGF if the predefined message contains variables (such as **&1, &2**). MSGDTA is not allowed when the MSG parameter is used.

Figure 6.4 shows two examples of using SNDPGMMSG. The first example uses the MSG parameter; the second example uses MSGID.

```
SNDPGMMSG MSG('Library MYLIB saved successfully.')
SNDPGMMSG MSGID(usr0001) MSGF(yourmsgf) MSGDTA('MYLIB')
```

Figure 6.4: Examples of SNDPGMMSG without and with MSGID.

Message USR0001 must be in message file YOURMSGF. In order for the two examples to yield the same result, USR0001 should be added to YOURMSGF as shown in Figure 6.5.

```
ADDMSGD MSGID(usr0001) MSGF(yourmsgf) +
        MSG('Library &1 saved successfully.') +
        FMT((*CHAR 10))
```

Figure 6.5: Adding message USR0001 to YOURMSG.

USR0001 contains one substitution variable, **&1**, defined as 10 characters. The message data indicated in the MSGDTA parameter is placed in **&1**.

Who Should Get the Message

There are three methods to identify the message recipient. You can send the message to a program message queue, to a permanent message queue object, or to a user. A review of each method follows.

Use the TOPGMQ parameter to send the message to a program message queue. The TOPGMQ parameter is a mixed list of two elements. The first element indicates the relationship of the message queue to the call stack entry named in element two. Element two is further divided into three items—a program or procedure name, an ILE module name, and an OPM or ILE program name.

Some common combinations of the two elements are listed in Table 6.3.

Table 6.3: Valid TOPGMQ Parameters

TOPGMQ Values

First	Second	Purpose
*PRV	*	Default combination. Sends the message to the program or procedure that called the current program.
*PRV	name	Sends the message to the program or procedure that called the named program or procedure.
*SAME	*	Sends the message to the current program or procedure.
*SAME	name	Sends the message to the named program or procedure.
*EXT	*	Sends the message to *EXT (external message queue). The second value (*) can be omitted.
*EXT	name	Illegal combination.

Note: The value "name" stands for the name of the program or procedure to which the message is being sent. If it is a program, you can enter a name of up to 10 characters. If it is a procedure, you can qualify it with the name of the program and module as shown in Figure 6.6.

```
TOPGMQ(*SAME (procedure module program))
```

Figure 6.6: An example of sending a message to a procedure.

When you specify a program or procedure name in the second value, the most recent program or procedure of that name in your call stack is the one that receives the message.

Several programs have been called, making a chain; program PGM1 calls PGM2, which in turn calls PGM3. PGM3 calls PGM1 again, which this time calls PGM4. The arrows shown in Figure 6.7 indicate the destination of the messages being sent by each program.

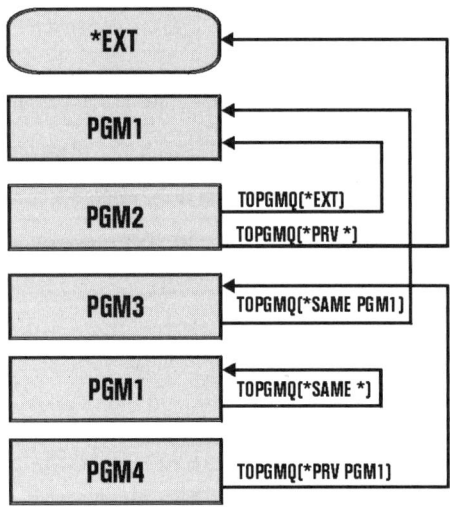

Figure 6.7: Message destinations.

Use the TOMSGQ parameter to send the message to a permanent (or regular) message- queue object. You can use TOMSGQ in addition to TOPGMQ.

TOMSGQ defaults to *TOPGMQ, which means that the message is sent to the program queue specified in the TOPGMQ parameter. You can change this to *SYSOPR to send the message to QSYS/QSYSOPR (the system operator's message queue) or change it to any other message queue you care to mention. Indicate the qualified name of the message queue.

Because the system log (QHST) is actually a special *MSGQ object, you can write information directly into QHST by sending *INFO or *DIAG messages TOMSGQ (QSYS/QHST). Do so only to record important events. You don't want to clutter QHST with noise.

Use the TOUSR parameter to send the message to a specific user. TOUSR is mutually exclusive with both TOPGMQ and TOMSGQ; you cannot use TOUSR in combination with either. TOUSR can have:

- *SYSOPR (to send the message to the system operator).

- *REQUESTER (to send the message to the current user if the job is interactive or to QSYSOPR in case of a batch job).

- *ALLACT (to send the message to all users currently signed on).

- A specific user whose user profile name you provide. Note that *ALLACT cannot be used for *INQ messages.

Type of Message

The MSGTYPE parameter indicates what type will be assigned to the message you're sending. It defaults to *INFO, but you can change it to *INQ (inquiry), *COMP (completion), *DIAG (diagnostic), *NOTIFY, *ESCAPE, *RQS (request), or *STATUS. You cannot send *INQ messages to program message queues. On the other hand, only program message queues can receive *COMP, *DIAG, *ESCAPE, *NOTIFY, and *STATUS messages.

Note: The combination TOPGMQ(*EXT) MSGTYPE(*STATUS) sends a real-time message to the requesting workstation while the program is running. The message appears at the bottom line of the screen in high intensity (white color).

Because *STATUS messages require usage of MSGID/MSGF/MSGDTA, you cannot use impromptu messages. Use MSGID(CPF9898) MSGF(QCPFMSG) and supply the text of the message in the MSGDTA parameter as shown in Figure 6.8. When the message is sent, it will be followed by a period automatically.

```
SNDPGMMSG MSGID(cpf9898) MSGF(qcpfmsg) +
          MSGDTA('One moment, please..') +
          TOPGMQ(*EXT) MSGTYPE(*STATUS)
```

Figure 6.8: Setting up a *status message with MSGID, MSGF, and MSGDTA.

The system sends the message as "One moment, please..." (with three dots at the end, even though only two were specified).

Note: If you do not want the system to add a period at the end of the message, use CPF9897 instead of CPF9898.

Getting the Reply

If you send an *INQ message, the user receiving it eventually will send you a reply. The reply must be received somewhere; the RPYMSGQ parameter of SNDPGMMSG indicates who gets the reply.

The default value is *PGMQ. The current program receives the message directly into its own program message queue. You would then use the RCVMSG command to receive it.

RPYMSGQ also can indicate a qualified message queue name if you would rather receive the reply into a permanent message-queue object. Again, you would use the RCVMSG command to receive it.

Figure 6.9 shows an example of using the RPYMSGQ parameter.

```
SNDPGMMSG MSG('Enter name of file to be created') +
          TOPGMQ(*EXT) MSGTYPE(*INQ) RPYMSGQ(*PGMQ)

RCVMSG MSGTYPE(*RPY) WAIT(*MAX) MSG(&file)
```

Figure 6.9: Receiving a message with RCVMSG.

SNDPGMMSG sends the inquiry message to *EXT because it needs to communicate with the user. Your CL program's job-message queue receives the reply because RPYMSGQ (*PGMQ) is indicated.

The RCVMSG command that follows receives a reply message after waiting indefinitely for it [WAIT(*MAX)]. The text of the reply message (the name of the file) is assigned to CL variable &FILE.

Message Key

As each message is sent, the system assigns it a unique 4-byte key. You can use the key to reference this message when you work with other commands such as RCVMSG and RMVMSG. SNDPGMMSG's KEYVAR parameter lets you code a CL variable name where the system is to place the key of the message being sent. You can then use the CL variable like any other.

Note: The CL variable used to store the message key must be declared as TYPE(*CHAR) LEN(4).

The example shown in Figure 6.9 has one problem. The RCVMSG command might find another reply message in the CL program's message queue and could assign &FILE to the wrong value. To ensure that the RCVMSG command gets the correct reply, use message keys. Message keys allow you to process message queues randomly instead of sequentially. Figure 6.10 shows the corrected code segment (new items are shown in boldface).

```
DCL &msgkey     *CHAR    4

   SNDPGMMSG MSG('Enter name of file to be created') +
             TOPGMQ(*EXT) MSGTYPE(*INQ) RPYMSGQ(*PGMQ) +
             KEYVAR(&msgkey)

   RCVMSG MSGTYPE(*RPY) MSGKEY(&msgkey) WAIT(*MAX) +
          MSG(&file)
```

Figure 6.10: Using a message key to retrieve a message.

Using message keys works because the system assigns the same key to both the *INQ message and its reply. The SNDPGMMSG command sends the program message and shows you the key to the message just sent (in the &MSGKEY variable). The RCVMSG command that follows reads the message queue randomly, by key, and thereby picks up the correct message.

THE SNDUSRMSG COMMAND

The Send User Message (SNDUSRMSG) command provides a different way to send messages from CL procedures or REXX procedures. SNDUSRMSG is not as complex (or versatile) as SNDPGMMSG, and the two commands consequently are not always interchangeable.

Basically, SNDUSRMSG can be used to send *INFO or *INQ messages only. Further, the message can go only to user or permanent message queues—not to program message queues. You can use either impromptu or predefined messages. On the positive side, SNDUSRMSG gives you simplicity, especially when you want to send an *INQ message and capture the reply.

Sending Impromptu Messages

Use the MSG parameter to code the message text. You can enter up to 512 characters. If you are sending an *INQ message, use the VALUES parameter to list up to 20 valid replies for the message. Each value can be up to 32 characters in length. Also, use the DFT parameter for *INQ messages. With DFT, indicate what reply to send if the receiving user presses the Enter key without typing in a reply.

Sending Predefined Messages

Use the MSGID parameter to specify the message ID of the predefined message you wish to send. The MSGF parameter holds the qualified name of the message file, and the MSGDTA parameter can be used to list the message data if the predefined message has embedded variables.

Because predefined messages already indicate what replies they can receive, you cannot use the VALUES or DFT parameters to define valid replies.

Type of Message

Use the MSGTYPE parameter to indicate whether the message is to be issued as informational (*INFO) or inquiry (*INQ). If you send the message as *INFO, your CL procedure continues executing past the SNDUSRMSG command. If the message type is *INQ, however, your CL procedure automatically pauses after SNDUSRMSG until the recipient sends back the reply.

Who Gets the Message

Use either the TOUSR or TOMSGQ parameter to indicate who will receive the message. These parameters are mutually exclusive. TOUSR can be:

- SYSOPR (to send the message to the system operator).

- *REQUESTER (to send it to the current user if the job is run interactively or to the system operator in the case of a batch job).

- Or an actual user profile name.

TOMSGQ can be:

- * (to send the message to *EXT, if the program runs interactively, or to the system operator in the case of a batch job).

- *EXT (to send the message to the external message queue).

- *SYSOPR (to send it to the system operator).

- Or an actual message queue name (qualified).

Receiving the Reply

Inquiry messages can take advantage of the MSGRPY parameter. In MSGRPY, you enter the name of a CL variable that will receive the user's reply to the inquiry message. This CL variable must be declared as TYPE(*CHAR), with a length between 1 and 32 characters.

Note: You also can use the TRNTBL parameter to specify the name of a translation table to translate special values in the reply. For example, you can translate all lowercase letters into uppercase. This simplifies coding in your CL program. If your user enters a 'C' or a 'c' as reply, your program would need to check only for 'C'.

The TRNTBL parameter defaults to QSYSTRNTBL (an IBM-supplied translation table in QSYS). The table translates lowercase letters to uppercase; other characters are left unchanged. You can specify a qualified name here if you would rather use one of your own translation tables (created with the CRTTBL command) or you can even use *NONE If you do not want any translation to occur.

Figure 6.11 illustrates the use of the TRNTBL parameter in processing a reply to an inquiry message. During the execution of a CL program that initializes many tapes, you might want to prompt the user to insert the next tape into the tape drive.

```
PGM

    DCL &option      *CHAR    1

loop:
    SNDUSRMSG MSG('Insert the next tape.') +
              VALUES(C G) DFT(C) MSGTYPE(*INQ) +
              TOMSGQ(*EXT) +
              MSGRPY(&option) TRNTBL(qsystrntbl)

    IF (&option *EQ 'G') DO
        INZDKT DEV(tap01) NEWVOL(volid) +
               CHECK(*NO) DENSITY(*QIC2GB) ENDOPT(*UNLOAD)

        GOTO loop
    ENDDO

ENDPGM
```

Figure 6.11: Using a translation table in processing a reply to an inquiry message.

The SNDUSRMSG command interrupts the program with the request to insert the next tape. If the user enters a reply that is not C or G, the system rejects it. If the user enters no reply value but presses Enter, DFT(C) ensures that a reply of C is assumed. Whatever reply is given, it goes to variable &OPTION TRNTBL (QSYS-TRNTBL) to ensure that the user's reply is converted to uppercase before being assigned to &OPTION. In this way, TRNTBL eliminates the need to compare both the uppercase and lowercase values in the IF command.

MESSAGES THAT CAN BE MONITORED

CL procedures can contain almost all the available commands. Most commands issue error messages when they fail. If you include one such command in your CL procedure, and the command fails, your CL procedure is interrupted.

If your CL procedure is run interactively, the user receives the Program Messages panel (where the error message appears). The user must then reply to the message to resume execution of the CL procedure. If the CL procedure runs in batch, the message is received by QSYSOPR. The system operator must reply to the message from the Display Messages (DSPMSG) panel.

Yet, most error situations can be corrected by the CL procedure itself (if only the procedure were somehow allowed to continue). For example, if you want to delete a file in the middle of your CL procedure, you would code the Delete File (DLTF) command to get rid of the file. If the file doesn't exist, however, the CL procedure should be allowed to ignore the error condition and continue. After all, you want the file not to exist. If the file doesn't exist in the first place, that shouldn't be considered an error situation!

The Monitor Message (MONMSG) command takes care of the error situation described in the preceding section. MONMSG acts like an error trap in CL procedures. Suppose you code a command such as DLTF in your CL procedure even though you suspect that sometimes the file might not be there to be deleted. As Figure 6.12 shows, you can follow the DLTF command with MONMSG and monitor for message CPF2105 (the message that DLTF issues when the file to be deleted does not exist).

```
DLTF workfile
MONMSG cpf2105
```

Figure 6.12: An example of using MONMSG to keep a failing command from abnormally ending a program.

Because the CL procedure now monitors for CPF2105, the error message's arrival doesn't interrupt the procedure.

Note: Of course, you might be wondering how it's possible to know that DLTF would issue CPF2105 if the file didn't exist. One way is by running DLTF from the command line, against a file you know that doesn't exist, and see what message you get. You can also check the online help (by pressing the F1 key while prompting the DLTF command) or IBM's manual Programming: Reference Summary.

PARAMETERS

The MSGID parameter can hold up to 50 message IDs as a list. When more than one message ID is coded in the MSGID parameter, all the messages listed are treated the same way.

Although rarely used, the CMPDTA parameter refines the message-monitoring process. Predefined messages sometimes contain embedded variables. If you want to monitor for only those messages that contain certain message data, you can code that message data in the CMPDTA parameter. Up to 28 characters can be compared (always beginning with the first byte of message data).

For example, CPF3347 reads "Device &1 not found" (&1 is an embedded variable). You might want to monitor for CPF3347, but only if it was issued because device PRT01 was not found. If the message applies to any other device, you will not want to trap the error message. To accomplish this, use code like that shown in Figure 6.13.

```
MONMSG cpf3347 CMPDTA('PRT01')
```

Figure 6.13: An example of using the CMPDTA parameter to restrict a monitored message.

If the CL program receives message CPF3347 because PRT02 was not found, the CL program will act as if there were no MONMSG.

In addition, the EXEC parameter indicates what to do upon receipt of the message or messages you have monitored. The EXEC parameter is optional. If you don't include it, errors are ignored and program execution continues with the next command.

You can code almost any valid command in the EXEC parameter, including a DO if you wish to execute more than one command. For a discussion of the only restriction, see the next heading, Program-Level (Global) MONMSG.

If source physical file SOURCE doesn't exist in QGPL, you'll want to create it, and then add a member named SCRATCH as type CLP. Figure 6.14 shows you what to do.

```
CHKOBJ qgpl/source *FILE
MONMSG cpf9801 EXEC(DO)
    CRTSRCPF qgpl/source RCDLEN(92) TEXT('Programming source')
    ADDPFM qgpl/source MBR(scratch) SRCTYPE(clp)
ENDDO
```

Figure 6.14: Using CHKOBJ to determine whether or not to create a file.

Check Object (CHKOBJ) tests the existence of file QGPL/SOURCE. If it doesn't exist, CHKOBJ issues CPF9801, which you monitor and execute CRTSRCPF and ADDPFM in that case. Notice how the DO and ENDDO pair bracket the commands to be executed if CPF9801 is received.

Program-Level (Global) MONMSG

If MONMSG is coded at the beginning of your CL procedure, the entire procedure benefits from this MONMSG command. To work this way, MONMSG must be coded right after the declarations (DCL and DCLF). If there are no declarations, MONMSG must be coded right after the PGM statement. In other words, global MONMSG commands must fall before any executable commands. See Figure 6.15.

```
PGM

    DCL &this       *CHAR    10
    DCL &that       *CHAR    10

    MONMSG cpf2105 EXEC(GOTO error)

    /* Program begins */
```

Figure 6.15: An example of the global MONMSG command.

As shown in Figure 6.15, MONMSG has been coded immediately after the last DCL statement. For the duration of the procedure, all CPF2105 messages are monitored. If CPF2105 is issued at any time, the procedure automatically carries out the GOTO ERROR instruction.

Note: Program-level MONMSGS can only have GOTO in the EXEC parameter. No other commands are allowed.

Command-Level MONMSG

When the MONMSG command is coded immediately after another command, the MONMSG applies to that command only. For example, the MONMSG in Figure 6.16 applies only to the first DLTF command.

```
DLTF work1
MONMSG cpf2105
DLTF work2
```

Figure 6.16: Example of a command-level MONMSG.

The first DLTF has a command-level MONMSG. If file WORK1 doesn't exist, the procedure continues. Because the MONMSG statement has no EXEC parameter, the procedure takes no special action.

The second DLTF command has no MONMSG after it. If file WORK2 doesn't exist, the CL procedure is interrupted unless there's a program-level MONMSG overseeing the entire procedure.

Unlike the program-level MONMSG, the command-level MONMSG can have any valid command in the EXEC parameter.

Note: If both program-level and command-level MONMSGS are coded, the procedure uses first the command-level MONMSG. If the error condition is not covered by the command-level MONMSG, the procedure then refers to the program-level MONMSG.

Specific and Generic Monitoring

So far the examples illustrate specific monitoring. All the messages that have been monitored have unique meanings. You can use MONMSG to monitor for *generic messages* just as well. To make this happen you must replace the last two or the last four characters of the message ID with zeros. For example, monitoring for CPF1200 means "trap all error messages between CPF1201 and CPF12FF, both inclusive."

The most generic you can get is by monitoring for CPF0000. All error messages beginning with CPF will be trapped. No matter what happens during the execution of the program, the program will not be interrupted—unless, of course, the message ID begins with letters other than CPF (such as MCH).

If you want to send the error message back to the caller of your CL procedure, as the code shown in Figure 6.17 does, using CPF0000 is convenient at the program level.

```
PGM

    DCL &msgid      *CHAR    7
    DCL &msgf       *CHAR   10
    DCL &msgflib    *CHAR   10
    DCL &msgdta     *CHAR  132

    MONMSG cpf0000 EXEC(GOTO snderrmsg)

    /* Program begins */
    *
    *
    *
    /* Program ends */

    RETURN

snderrmsg:
    RCVMSG MSGTYPE(*EXCP) MSGDTA(&msgdta) MSGID(&msgid) MSGF(&msgf) +
           SNDMSGFLIB(&msgflib)
    MONMSG cpf0000
    SNDPGMMSG MSGID(&msgid) MSGF(&msgflib/&msgf) MSGDTA(&msgdta) +
              MSGTYPE(*ESCAPE)
    MONMSG cpf0000

ENDPGM
```

Figure 6.17: Returning unexpected error messages to the caller.

The sort of coding shown in Figure 6.17 is common in CL procedures, and it is usually called "forwarding error messages." The MONMSG at the top traps any error messages serious enough to abort the program. Instead of aborting, it transfers control to label SNDERRMSG near the bottom of the program.

First, RCVMSG is used to receive the exception message (retrieving the message data, message ID, and message file name). SNDPGMMSG then forwards the same message to the program that called this CL program or forwards it to the requester (who sees the error message).

Notice that both RCVMSG and SNDPGMMSG are followed by MONMSG. Omitting these MONMSGs is a common mistake. To see why omitting the MONMSGs is a mistake, consider what would happen if, for example, RCVMSG failed for whatever reason.

If RCVMSG fails, it issues some kind of CPFXXXX message—which is trapped by the program-level MONMSG (since there's no command-level MONMSG in this hypothetical scenario). But the program-level MONMSG directs the program to branch to SNDERRMSG, which, again, attempts to run RCVMSG—which would fail again.

The program then enters a tightly knit infinite loop, and the result is a runaway job that consumes CPU resources and does nothing else.

THE RCVMSG COMMAND

As the preceding section explains, you can send messages to a CL program's message queue with the SNDPGMMSG command. The receiving program must execute a Receive Message (RCVMSG) command to become aware of the message sent to it.

RCVMSG can be executed by CL procedures or REXX procedures. The program or procedure receives a message from either a program message queue or a permanent message- queue object. You can code RCVMSG to pick and choose which messages to receive. When a message is received, the message ID, text, and data are placed in CL variables.

Get the Message from Where?

First, you must indicate whether RCVMSG should receive the message from a program message queue or from a permanent message-queue object. You do this by using either the PGMQ or the MSGQ parameters. The two are mutually exclusive.

Use PGMQ to name the program message queue from which to obtain the message. The PGMQ parameter is identical to SNDPGMMSG's TOPGMQ parameter: it is a list containing two elements. Table 6.4 lists all possible combinations and their meanings.

Table 6.4: Valid PGMQ Combinations		
PGMQ Values		
First	**Second**	**Purpose**
*SAME	*	Default combination. Gets the message from the message queue of the current program or procedure.
*SAME	name	Gets the message from the message queue of the named program or procedure.
*PRV	*	Gets the message from the message queue of the program or procedure that called the current program.
*PRV	name	Gets the message from the message queue of the program or procedure that called the named program or procedure.
*EXT	*	Gets the message from the external message queue. The second value (*) can be omitted.
*EXT	name	Illegal combination.

Note: The value "name" stands for the name of the program or procedure from which the message is being received. If it is a program, you can enter a name of up to 10 characters. If it is an ILE procedure, you can qualify it with the name of the program and module, as in PGMQ(*SAME (procedure module program)).

Use the MSGQ parameter to specify the qualified name of the permanent message queue object from which to receive the message.

Which Message to Receive?

Left to itself, RCVMSG receives any message sent to the program message queue or permanent message queue indicated. With the correct combination of MSGTYPE and MSGKEY parameters, however, you can select which messages to receive. MSGTYPE and MSGKEY do work together, but in a rather intricate fashion. Use Table 6.5 to find the combination that meets your requirements.

MSGTYPE	MSGKEY	Result of Combination
		Table 6.5: Valid MSGTYPE and MSGKEY Combinations
(unused)	(CL variable)	Receives the message whose key is specified in the CL variable, if that message exists. If the message does not exist, the CL program receives an escape message. Because both the reply and the sender's copy of the original message have the same key, the reply to the message is received if existent. If not, no message is received.
*ANY	*NONE	Default combination. Any message is received, except a sender's copy. RCVMSG will get the first new message in first-in, first-out order.
*ANY	(CL variable)	If the first message found is a reply message, the CL variable will have the message key of the sender's copy message. Otherwise, the CL variable will have the message key of the message received.
*COPY	*NONE	Receives a new sender's copy message in first-in, first-out order.
*COPY	(CL variable)	Receives the sender's copy of an inquiry message whose key is referenced in the CL variable.
*COMP	*NONE	Receives a new completion message in first-in, first-out order.
*COMP	(CL variable)	Receives the completion message referenced by the key in the CL variable.
*DIAG	*NONE	Receives a new diagnostic message in first-in, first-out order
*EXCP	*NONE	Receives a new exception message (escape or notify) in last-in, first-out order.

Table 6.5: Valid MSGTYPE and MSGKEY Combinations, continued

MSGTYPE	MSGKEY	Result of Combination
*EXCP	(CL variable)	Receives the exception message (escape or notify) referenced by the key in the CL variable.
*FIRST	*NONE	Receives the first (oldest) message in the message queue or program message queue indicated.
*INFO	*NONE	Receives a new informational message in first-in, first-out order.
*INFO	(CL variable)	Receives the informational message referenced by the key in the CL variable.
*INQ	*NONE	Receives a new inquiry message in first-in, first-out order.
*INQ	(CL variable)	Receives the inquiry message referenced by the key in the CL variable.
*LAST	*NONE	Receives the last (most recent) message in the message queue.
*NEXT	*TOP	Receives the first message in the message queue. If using a program message queue, it receives the first message that follows the last request (*RQS) message.
*NEXT	(CL variable)	Receives the first message following the message referenced by the key in the CL variable.
*PRV	(CL variable)	Receives the message prior to the message referenced by the key in the CL variable.
*RPY	*NONE	Receives a new reply message in first-in, first-out order.
*RPY	(CL variable)	If the key in the CL variable refers to either a sender's copy or an inquiry message, it receives any reply to the sender's copy or to the inquiry message. If there is no reply to that sender's copy or inquiry message, it receives no message.
*RQS	*NONE	Receives a new request message in first-in, first-out order.
*RQS	(CL variable)	Receives the request message referenced by the key in the CL variable.
*DIAG	(CL variable)	Receives the diagnostic message referenced by the key in the CL variable.

The following are important notes regarding message keys:

- The message key CL variable, if used, must be declared as TYPE(*CHAR) LEN(4). MSGKEY acts like the key to an indexed file, which allows you to receive messages in random order.

- MSGKEY defaults to *NONE. You can leave it blank if *NONE is appropriate.

- If you code a RCVMSG command to receive request messages from *EXT, the Command Entry panel is presented if *EXT has no request messages at that moment. This peculiarity could pose a security risk by providing a command line.

- A number of MSGTYPE/MSGKEY combinations receive new messages only. If you need to receive an old message from a permanent message queue-object, run the CHGMSGQ command against the message queue. CHGMSGQ makes all messages new again. When receiving messages by key (using MSGKEY), you can receive either new or old messages.

Message Received—Now What?

When a message is received, information about the message is placed in the CL variables you have indicated in a number of optional parameters. These parameters are listed as follows:

- KEYVAR is the CL variable that will contain the message key of the message received. The CL variable must be of TYPE(*CHAR) LEN(4).

- MSG is the CL variable that will contain the first-level text of the message after all embedded variables are replaced with data in predefined messages. The CL variable must be TYPE(*CHAR) of any length. Most messages have a first-level text of 132 characters or fewer.

- MSGLEN is the CL variable that will contain the length (in bytes) of the first-level text. The CL variable must be TYPE(*DEC) LEN(5 0).

■ SECLVL is the CL variable that will contain the second-level text (help text) of the message, after all embedded variables are replaced with data in predefined messages. The CL variable must be TYPE(*CHAR) of any length. Most messages have second-level text of 3000 characters or fewer.

■ SECLVLLEN is the CL variable that will contain the length (in bytes) of the second-level text. The CL variable must be TYPE(*DEC) LEN(5 0).

■ MSGDTA is the CL variable that will contain the message data for the embedded variables in predefined messages. The CL variable must be TYPE(*CHAR) of any length.

■ MSGDTALEN is the CL variable that will contain the length (in bytes) of the message data. The CL variable must be TYPE(*DEC) LEN(5 0).

■ MSGID is the CL variable that will contain the message ID of the message received. The CL variable must be TYPE(*CHAR) LEN(7). If an impromptu message is received, MSGID is set to blanks.

■ SEV is the CL variable that will contain the severity code of the message received. The CL variable must be TYPE(*DEC) LEN(2 0). If an impromptu message is received, SEV is set to zero.

■ SENDER is the CL variable that will contain an identification of the sender and receiver of the message received. The CL variable must be of TYPE(*CHAR). If SENDERFMT(*SHORT) is specified (which is the default), the CL variable must be at least 80 bytes long. If SENDERFMT(*LONG) is specified, however, the CL variable must be at least 720 bytes long. The only difference between the *SHORT and *LONG formats is how much information is obtained. Tables 6.6 and 6.7 list both formats of the SENDER variable.

Table 6.6: Received Message Information (Short Format)

Locations

To	From	Description
Identification of sending job:		
1	10	Job name
11	20	User name
21	26	Job number
Identification of sending progrqam:		
27	38	Program name. For ILE procedures, this is the bound program name.
39	42	Instruction number. Blanks for ILE procedures.
Time stamp:		
43	49	Date in CYYMMDD format.
50	55	Time in HHMMSS format.
Identification of receiving program:		
56	65	Receiving program name. For an ILE procedure, this is the bound program name.
66	69	Instruction number. Blanks for ILE procedure.
Sender and receiver types:		
70	70	"0": Sender is a program. "1": Sender is an ILE procedure
71	71	"0": Receiver is a program. "1": Receiver is an ILE procedure.
72	80	Reserved for future use.

Table 6.7: Received Message Information (Long Format)

Locations

From	To	Description
Identification of sending job:		
1	10	Job name
11	20	User name
21	26	Job number
Time stamp:		
27	33	Date in CYYMMDD format.
34	39	Time in HHMMSS format.
Sender and receiver types:		
40	40	"0": Sender is a program '1': Sender is an ILE procedure..
41	41	'0': Receiver is a program. '1': Receiver is an ILE procedure.
Identification of sending program:		
42	53	Program name. For ILE procedure, this is the bound program name.
54	63	Module name. Blanks for OPM programs.
64	319	Procedure name. Blanks for OPM programs.
320	320	Reserved.
321	324	Number of statements available. It is the point in the sending program from which the message was sent.
325	354	These positions contain a maximum of three statement numbers, each 10 characters long.

Table 6.7: Received Message Information (Long Format), continued

Locations

From	To	Description
Identification of receiving program:		
355	364	Receiving program name. For an ILE procedure, this is the bound program name.
365	374	Module name. Blanks for OPM programs.
375	630	Procedure name. Blanks for OPM programs.
631	640	Reserved.
641	644	Number of statements available.
645	674	These positions contain a maximum of three statement numbers, each 10 characters long.
675	720	Reserved.

RTNTYPE is the CL variable that will contain the code for the type of message received. The CL variable must be TYPE(*CHAR) LEN(2). Table 6.8 lists the type codes.

Table 6.8: Message Return Types

Message Type Code	Description
01	Completion
02	Diagnostic
04	Informational
05	Inquiry
08	Request

Table 6.8: Message Return Types, continued	
Message Type Code	**Description**
10	Request with prompting
14	Notify (exception already handled at time of RCVMSG)
15	Escape (exception already handled at time of RCVMSG)
16	Notify (exception not handled at time of RCVMSG)
17	Escape (exception not handled at time of RCVMSG)
21	Reply, not checked for validity
22	Reply, checked for validity
23	Reply, message default used
24	Reply, system default used
25	Reply, from System Reply List

- ALROPT is the CL variable that will contain the alert option of the message received. The CL variable must be TYPE(*CHAR) LEN(9).

- MSGF is the CL variable that will contain the name of the message file containing the predefined message that was received. If an impromptu message is received, MSGF is set to blanks. The CL variable must be TYPE(*CHAR) LEN(10).

- MSGFLIB is the CL variable that will contain the name of the library that contains the message file identified in the MSGF parameter. If an impromptu message is received, MSGFLIB is set to blanks. The CL variable must be TYPE(*CHAR) LEN(10). If *LIBL is used when the message is sent, MSGFLIB returns *LIBL instead of the actual library name.

- SNDMSGFLIB is similar to MSGFLIB; an exception is that, if *LIBL is used, the actual message file library is returned. The CL variable must be TYPE(*CHAR) LEN(10).

How Long to Wait?

The RCVMSG command can be executed prematurely when no message is available to be received. The WAIT parameter lets you indicate how long the CL procedure should wait for a message and continue executing.

The WAIT parameter defaults to zero. If no messages are available, none are received, and the CL variables listed in the preceding heading are set to blanks (or zeros).

You also can specify a number of seconds to wait for the message. The CL procedure stops executing at the RCVMSG command for that length of time or until the message is received—whichever is shorter. If, at the end of that period of time, no message is received, the CL variables used to retrieve the message information are set to blanks or zeros.

WAIT(*NOMAX) also can be specified. In this case, the CL procedure stops executing, for as long as necessary, until a message is received. Except when you are receiving a reply message, your CL procedure cannot wait for messages sent to program-message queues.

Remove the Message Received?

Use the RMV parameter to indicate whether the message received should be removed from the message queue. The only valid values are *YES (remove the message), *NO (do not remove it), and *KEEPEXCP (keep exception messages).

The default is *YES, and it causes the message to be removed from the message queue. Unhandled exception messages are automatically handled by the mere fact that RCVMSG is being executed.

If you choose *NO, the message stays in the message queue as an old message. As in the case of *YES, unhandled exception messages are automatically handled by the RCVMSG command.

*KEEPEXCP is a bit more obscure, and it differs from *NO only when the message being received is an exception message. *KEEPEXCP keeps the message in the message queue (like *NO does), but unhandled exception messages are left unhandled as new messages. Handled exception messages also are left in the message queue, but as old messages.

Examples of RCVMSG

Appendix A contains a utility command with code that includes examples of RCVMSG. This utility command is named Display Program Messages (DSPPGMMSG).

OTHER MESSAGE MANAGEMENT COMMANDS

A few more commands can help you manage messages on the system. Except for RMVMSG and SNDRPY, these commands are better suited for manual execution. However, they can be included in CL procedures just as well.

Remove Messages (RMVMSG)

The RMVMSG command must be executed from a CL procedure or REXX procedure. Its purpose is to remove messages from a program message queue or a permanent message queue object.

The PGMQ and MSGQ parameters identify the message queue from which to remove messages. These two parameters are mutually exclusive. MSGQ contains the qualified name of the permanent message queue. PGMQ is more complicated because it lists two values. Use Table 6.9 to select the combination that best suits the situation.

Table 6.9: Valid PGMQ Combinations

PGMQ Values

First	Second	Description of Values
*SAME	*	Default combination. Remove messages from the current program message queue.
*SAME	(name)	Remove messages from the named program message queue.
*PRV	*	Remove messages from the program message queue of the program or procedure that called the current program or procedure.
*PRV	(name)	Remove messages from the program message queue of the program or procedure that called the named program or procedure.
*ALLINACT	(blank)	Remove all messages from all the program message queues of programs or procedures that have ended. CLEAR(*ALL) must be specified.
*EXT	(blank)	Remove messages from the external program message queue.

Note: The value "(name)" stands for the name of the program or procedure from which the message is being removed. If it is a program, you can enter a name of up to 10 characters. If it is an ILE procedure, you can qualify it with the name of the program and module, as in: pgmq(*same (procedure module program)).

The CLEAR parameter indicates which messages to remove. The default, *BYKEY, removes only the message that corresponds with the key referenced in the MSGKEY parameter (see below). CLEAR also can have the following values:

- *ALL (all messages are removed).

- *OLD (all old messages are removed).

- *NEW (all new messages are removed).

- *KEEPUNANS (all messages are removed, except unanswered inquiry messages).

You cannot remove messages from a program message queue if CLEAR (*KEEPUNANS) is specified.

The RMVEXCP parameter complements the CLEAR parameter, providing additional information about how to process exception messages. It applies only when the RMVMSG command is used on the program message queue of a called ILE procedure. It is ignored otherwise. The default value of *YES causes RMVMSG to remove unhandled exception messages from the specified program message queue, resulting in the exception being handled. The *NO value preserves the unhandled exception message.

The MSGKEY parameter is used only if CLEAR(*BYKEY) is specified or if CLEAR is not specified at all because it defaults to *BYKEY. In these cases, MSGKEY must have the 4-byte character key that identifies the message targeted for removal.

If you receive many messages in your *EXT program message queue, the Program Messages panel fills up quickly and can become a source of confusion. You can clear the Program Messages panel by executing the command (shown in Figure 6.18) from within a CL procedure.

```
RMVMSG PGMQ(*EXT) CLEAR(*ALL)
```

Figure 6.18: Clearing the Program Messages panel.

Send Reply (SNDRPY)

The SNDRPY command is very limited in what it can do, and can only be used in a CL or REXX procedure. You cannot execute the command from the keyboard. SNDRPY sends a reply to an inquiry message that was sent to a permanent message queue. SNDRPY must know the key to the message in order to work. Figure 6.19 contains an example of SNDRPY.

```
SNDRPY MSGKEY(&msgk) MSGQ(qsysopr) RPY('R') RMV(*YES)
```

Figure 6.19: Using the SNDRPG command.

As shown in Figure 6.19, this command sends a reply of 'R' (retry) to a message in QSYSOPR (identified by message key &MSGK). After the reply is sent, both the original message and the reply are removed from the message queue.

Send Message (SNDMSG)

The SNDMSG command lets you send impromptu informational or inquiry messages to users or specific message queues. SNDMSG is better suited for manual execution, but you can include it in a CL procedure. The MSG parameter can contain up to 512 characters that comprise the message you are sending.

Next, you must identify who will receive the message. You can do so with either the TOUSR or TOMSGQ parameter (but not both). TOUSR can contain a specific user profile name:

- *SYSOPR (to send the message to the system operator).

- *REQUESTER (to send the message to oneself).

- *ALLACT (to send the same message to all users currently signed on).

If you send an inquiry message, you cannot use *ALLACT.

TOMSGQ can be used instead of TOUSR if you would rather send the message to a message queue. Because TOMSGQ can accept a list of up to 50 values, you could also use TOMSGQ to send the same message to several specific users. Each value can have the qualified name of a message queue object or *SYSOPR.

The MSGTYPE parameter defaults to *INFO, which means that the message is just informational. You can change it to *INQ (inquiry) unless you are sending the message to more than one recipient. In other words, MSGTYPE(*INQ) is invalid if TOUSR(*ALLACT) is specified or if TOMSGQ contains more than one message queue name.

If you are sending an inquiry message, the RPYMSGQ parameter names the message queue that is to receive the reply. It defaults to *WRKSTN; your workstation's message queue receives the reply. You can change this default to the qualified name of the message queue of your choice.

> *Note:* Because the system log (QHST) is a message-queue object, you can use SNDMSG to write directly to the system log.

Send Break Message (SNDBRKMSG)

SNDBRKMSG works more or less like SNDMSG, except that the message is sent in *BREAK mode. Unless the message queue has been altered with a program that intercepts and handles break messages, the message interrupts the recipient's interactive job. Under normal circumstances, the messages you send with SNDBRKMSG are displayed immediately and replace anything the user has on the screen at the time.

The MSG parameter contains the text of the impromptu message you send. It can have up to 512 characters.

The TOMSGQ parameter identifies the names of the workstation message queues that are to receive the break message. Only workstation message queues (message queues named after display-station devices) can be entered. You can enter one or more workstation message-queue names or *ALLWS. If you enter *ALLWS, the break message is sent to all workstation message queues whether or not they are signed on. Further, *ALLWS is allowed for informational messages only.

The MSGTYPE parameter defaults to *INFO (send informational message), but you can change the value to *INQ (inquiry message) if you want a reply from the recipient.

If MSGTYPE(*INQ) is specified, the RPYMSGQ parameter identifies the message queue that should receive the reply. It defaults to QSYSOPR, but you can change this to the qualified name of any user or workstation message queue.

DSPMSG AND WRKMSG

The Display Messages (DSPMSG) and Work with Messages (WRKMSG) commands are nearly identical. Both commands are used to display the contents of a message queue object and, optionally, to reply to inquiry messages and to remove messages.

The MSGQ parameter identifies the message queue to be displayed. You can use the *WRKUSR default or choose among *SYSOPR, *USRPRF, *WRKSTN, or a qualified name.

*WRKUSR first displays the current workstation's message queue (but only if any messages exist there). Then it displays the current user's message queue (whether or not it contains messages). *USRPRF and *WRKSTN display the current user's or the current workstation's message queue. *SYSOPR displays the system operator's message queue.

The OUTPUT parameter determines whether to display or print the messages. It defaults to * (display if DSPMSG is run interactively or print if it runs in batch). It also can have the value *PRINT to send the output to the printer.

The MSGTYPE parameter indicates what types of messages should be displayed. Although it defaults to *ALL, you can specify *INFO, *INQ, or *COPY.

The START parameter (on the DSPMSG command only) indicates whether to start displaying the messages from the oldest message (*FIRST) or the newest message (*LAST). The default is *LAST. The messages always appear in chronological order.

The SEV parameter is a filter used to avoid displaying unimportant messages. With the default at 0, the SEV parameter allows all messages to be displayed regardless of their severity code. You can enter any valid value between 0 and 99. If changed to 40, for example, the DSPMSG or WRKMSG command would only display messages with a severity of 40 or higher. You can also enter *MSGQ to display messages that have a severity equal or greater than that of the message queue.

The ASTLVL parameter indicates how much assistance to get from Operational Assistant. The default value, *PRV, means that Operational Assistant will give the same assistance level it gave you the last time you used Operational Assistant. Other values are *USRPRF (pick up the assistance level from the user profile), *BASIC (give lots of assistance), and *INTERMED (no assistance).

Once the messages are displayed, you can press function keys to remove one message at a time (F11), all messages at once (F13), or all unanswered messages (F16).

Replying to messages is as simple as moving the cursor to the correct input field, typing a reply value, and pressing Enter.

Note: Avoid using F13. If any inquiry messages are unanswered, F13 makes the computer reply to unanswered inquiry messages with the default reply (which might be inappropriate). Then the messages and their replies are removed, and that leaves you no way of knowing what happened. F16 is much safer because unanswered inquiry messages remain intact.

You can display second-level text (help text) for any message by moving the cursor to the line containing the message and pressing the Help key. If the message is an inquiry message, you can reply to it from the help information panel or from the normal panel.

Messages stay in the message queue until you manually remove them. If you press F3 or F12 (or even Enter) from the DSPMSG or WRKMSG panel, the messages are not removed. You must get into the habit of removing the messages manually once you display them and no longer need them for reference. Be sure to use F16 (never use F13).

Clear Message Queue (CLRMSGQ)

The CLRMSGQ command is another way to remove messages from a message queue object. The MSGQ parameter identifies the message queue object to be cleared of messages. Enter the qualified name of the message queue or *WRKSTN to clear the current workstation's message queue.

The CLEAR parameter indicates what messages to remove. It defaults to *ALL for the removal of all messages. Because it keeps the unanswered inquiry messages after removing all the rest, *KEEPUNANS is a safer approach. Because the system first replies to the unanswered inquiry messages with the default reply (which might not be adequate) and then removes both the message and its reply, *ALL can be dangerous. You will have no clue about what happened.

THE SYSTEM REPLY LIST

i5/OS has an internal object called the system reply list. Although you will find no commands to create, change, or delete this object, there are commands to add, change, and remove its entries. You can add entries with the Add Reply List Entry (ADDRPYLE) command, change entries with CHGRPYLE, remove entries with RMVRPYLE, or work with entries with WRKRPYLE. Each entry in the system reply list contains the following items:

- A four-digit sequence number that can be any number between 1 and 9999.

- A seven-character message identifier such as CPF1234.

- A comparison string up to 28 characters long.

- A comparison starting position (which can be any number between 1 and 999).

- An automatic reply to the message (up to 32 characters long).

- An option (*YES or *NO) to print a dump of the job that sent the message.

Purpose of the System Reply List

The system reply list is a handy object. With it you can run your system unattended (without several around-the-clock system operators). If an expected error condition appears during off-hours, the system reply list takes care of the error message by replying to it in the manner you specify.

The operative words here are "expected error condition." You must anticipate the specific error message and add an entry to the system reply list to accommodate the error.

Using the System Reply List

In order to use the system reply list in your job, you must ensure that the job description under which it runs has INQMSGRPY(*SYSRPYL). If this parameter contains some other value, you can still use the system reply list if you use the CHGJOB command with INQMSGRPY(*SYSRPYL). Until you do this, the system reply list is ignored.

This important step is easily forgotten because the INQMSGRPY parameter defaults to *RQD for both the job and the job description.

Pitfalls

Using the system reply list is not without trouble. Keep in mind that the system reply list is system wide: whatever entries you place there are used by all jobs in the system—not just yours. What you believe is an innocent reply to an innocent message might be the cause of serious errors in other jobs that are issued the same message.

MESSAGE SUBFILES

CL supports only one type of subfile in display files: message subfiles. Message subfiles give you the capability to display informational, diagnostic, and other kinds of messages in a subfile. These messages could be the result of activity requested from a panel presented by the CL program. For example, the panel shown in Figure 6.20 contains a menu with several options to control printers.

```
MCR                    Printer Control Menu
1/01/99
MALERN
20:27:59

Select one of the following:

       1. Display printer messages
       2. Work with spooled files
       3. Work with output queues
       4. Work with printer writers
       5. Start printer writer
       6. End writer
       7. Hold writer
       8. Release writer
       9. Change writer

      90. Sign off


Your option:                            Last option taken was 1
   __


   F3=Exit   F5=Refresh   F12=Cancel
```

Figure 6.20: A typical i5-style menu.

The bottom line (line 24) will provide a subfile for messages generated when any of the options are taken.

The Display File

The specifications for display file PRTCTLMNUD are shown in Figure 6.21.

```
*******************************************************************
*
* To compile:
*
*     CRTDSPF FILE(xxx/PRTCTLMNUD) SRCFILE(xxx/QDDSSRC)
*
*******************************************************************
```

Figure 6.21: Source code for the printer control menu display file. (part 1 of 3.)

```
*..1....+....2....+....3....+....4....+....5....+....6....+....7....+....8
A                                       DSPSIZ(24 80 *DS3)
A                                       PRINT
A                                       CA03(03 'Exit')
A                                       CA05(05 'Refresh')
A                                       CA12(12 'Cancel')
   *=================================================================
A          R MSGRCD                     SFL
A                                       SFLMSGRCD(24)
A            MSGKEY                      SFLMSGKEY
A            PGMQ                        SFLPGMQ
   *=================================================================
A          R MSGCTL                     SFLCTL(MSGRCD)
A                                       SFLDSP
A                                       SFLDSPCTL
A                                       SFLINZ
A N98                                    SFLEND
A                                       SFLSIZ(20)
A                                       SFLPAG(1)
A          R MENU
A                                       OVERLAY
A                                       BLINK
A                                 1  2SYSNAME
A                                 1 31'Printer Control Menu'
A                                       DSPATR(HI)
A                                 1 73DATE
A                                       EDTCDE(Y)
A                                 2  2USER
A                                 2 73TIME
A                                 4  2'Select one of the following:'
A                                       COLOR(BLU)
A                                 6  7'1. Display printer messages'
A                                 7  7'2. Work with spooled files'
A                                 8  7'3. Work with output queues'
A                                 9  7'4. Work with printer writers'
A                                10  7'5. Start printer writer'
A                                11  7'6. End writer'
A                                12  7'7. Hold writer'
A                                13  7'8. Release writer'
A                                14  7'9. Change writer'
A                                16  6'90. Sign off'
A                                19  2'Your option:'
```

Figure 6.21: Source code for the printer control menu display file. (part 2 of 3.)

```
A              OPTION      2A  B 20  6VALUES(' '1 ' '2 ' '3 ' '4 ' '5 -
A                                    ' '6 ' '7 ' '8 ' '9 ' ' 1' ' 2' ' 3-
A                                    ' ' 4' ' 5' ' 6' ' 7' ' 8' ' 9' '90-
A                                    ')
A  99                            20 41'Last option taken was'
A  99          LASTOPTION   2A  O 20 63
A                                    23  2'F3=Exit   F5=Refresh   F12=Cancel'
A                                    COLOR(BLU)
*..1....+....2....+....3....+....4....+....5....+....6....+....7....+....8
```

Figure 6.21: Source code for the printer control menu display file. (part 3 of 3.)

As with any subfile, you must define two record formats: one for the subfile record (named MSGRCD in the example) and one for the subfile control record (named MSGCTL).

MSGRCD uses the SFLMSGRCD(24) keyword to specify that messages are to appear on line 24 of the screen. Two other specifications are required:

- An A-spec defining a variable that will hold the four-character message key of the messages to be displayed. You can give this variable any name you want, and you don't have to indicate its length or data type. Be certain to use the SFLMSGKEY keyword.

- An A-spec defining a variable that will contain the program message queue name. Of course, this name will be the same as the CL program or procedure that presents the display file. Again, you don't have to declare its length or type, but you must use the SFLPGMQ keyword.

The subfile control record, MSGCTL, must reference the subfile record (MSGRCD) in the SFLCTL keyword. Then it must have the following:

- Unconditioned SFLDSP, SFLDSPCTL, and SFLINZ keywords.

- SFLSIZ and SFLPAG to indicate the size of the subfile and of the subfile page— just like any other subfile. Because the subfile begins on line 24, SFLPAG cannot be greater than 1. If you choose a different starting-line number (with the SFLMSGRCD keyword in the previous record format), you can specify a different number in the SFLPAG keyword. For example, specifying SFLMSGRCD(21) means you can use SFLPAG(1), SFLPA G(2), SFLPAG(3), or SFLPAG(4).

- An A-spec that references the same variable used in the subfile record to describe the program message queue name. Copy it from the subfile record. It must have the same variable name and use the SFLPGMQ keyword as well.

Because the other record format, MENU, will be written on the screen after the subfile, MENU must include the OVERLAY keyword to avoid wiping out the message subfile.

The CL Program

The source code for CL program PRTCTLMNU, which drives the menu, is shown in Figure 6.22.

```
/*******************************************************************
/*                                                                 */
/* To compile:                                                     */
/*                                                                 */
/*    CRTCLPGM PGM(xxx/PRTCTLMNU) SRCFILE(xxx/QCLSRC)              */
/*                                                                 */
/*******************************************************************/
PGM

   DCLF prtctlmnud
   DCL &blank    *CHAR   1  ' '
   DCL &off      *LGL    1  '0'
   DCL &on       *LGL    1  '1'

   MONMSG cpf0000

   CHGVAR &in98 &off
   CHGVAR &pgmq 'PRTCTLMNU'

again:
   SNDF RCDFMT(msgctl)
   SNDRCVF RCDFMT(menu)
```

Figure 6.22: CL source code to drive the printer control menu (part 1 of 3).

```
RMVMSG CLEAR(*ALL)

IF (&in03 *OR &in12) +
   GOTO normal_end
IF (&in05) +
   GOTO again

/* Option 90:  Sign off */
IF (&option *EQ '90') +
   SIGNOFF

/* Option 1:  Display messages */
IF (&option *EQ '1 ' *OR &option *EQ ' 1') DO
   DSPMSG printers
   CHGVAR &lastoption '1'
ENDDO

/* Option 2:  Work with spooled files */
ELSE IF (&option *EQ '2 ' *OR &option *EQ ' 2') DO
   ? WRKSPLF
   MONMSG cpf6801 EXEC(GOTO again)
   CHGVAR &lastoption '2'
ENDDO

/* Option 3:  Work with output queues */
ELSE IF (&option *EQ '3 ' *OR &option *EQ ' 3') DO
   ? WRKOUTQ
   MONMSG cpf6801 EXEC(GOTO again)
   CHGVAR &lastoption '3'
ENDDO

/* Option 4:  Work with writers */
ELSE IF (&option *EQ '4 ' *OR &option *EQ ' 4') DO
   ? WRKWTR
   MONMSG cpf6801 EXEC(GOTO again)
   CHGVAR &lastoption '4'
ENDDO

/* Option 5:  Start printer writer */
ELSE IF (&option *EQ '5 ' *OR &option *EQ ' 5') DO
   ? STRPRTWTR
   MONMSG cpf6801 EXEC(GOTO again)
   CHGVAR &lastoption '5'
ENDDO

/* Option 6:  End writer */
ELSE IF (&option *EQ '6 ' *OR &option *EQ ' 6') DO
   ? ENDWTR
```

Figure 6.22: CL source code to drive the printer control menu (part 2 of 3).

```
            MONMSG cpf6801 EXEC(GOTO again)
            CHGVAR &lastoption '6'
      ENDDO

      /* Option 7:  Hold writer */
      ELSE IF (&option *EQ '7 ' *OR &option *EQ ' 7') DO
            ? HLDWTR
            MONMSG cpf6801 EXEC(GOTO again)
            CHGVAR &lastoption '7'
      ENDDO

      /* Option 8:  Release writer */
      ELSE IF (&option *EQ '8 ' *OR &option *EQ ' 8') DO
            ? RLSWTR
            MONMSG cpf6801 EXEC(GOTO again)
            CHGVAR &lastoption '8'
      ENDDO

      /* Option 9:  Change writer */
      ELSE IF (&option *EQ '9 ' *OR &option *EQ ' 9') DO
            ? CHGWTR
            MONMSG cpf6801 EXEC(GOTO again)
            CHGVAR &lastoption '9'
      ENDDO

      CHGVAR &in99    &on
      CHGVAR &option &blank

      GOTO again
normal_end:
      RETURN

ENDPGM
```

Figure 6.22: CL source code to drive the printer control menu (part 3 of 3).

This program is fully functional; you can actually use it to control your printers. Take note of the following points:

- DCLF is used to declare the display file, PRTCTLMNUD.

- Three DCLs are used to declare constants often used throughout the program.

- The MONMSG command is used at the program level so that escape messages issued by any of the options do not abort the program. Instead, the messages will appear on the message subfile.

- Variable &IN98 (indicator 98) controls the display file's SFLEND keyword. It is initialized to '0' (off).

- Variable &PGMQ is initialized to the program name, PRTCTLMNU. This variable is used twice in the display file (as you saw before).

- With each request for input, the program writes the subfile control record with the Send File (SNDF) command, then writes/reads the input-capable record with the Send Receive File (SNDRCVF) command. SNDF RCDFMT(MSGCTL) causes the message subfile to appear on the screen. SNDRCVF RCDFMT(MENU) causes the menu to appear (overlaying the message subfile).

- After the SNDRCVF command and before anything else, the RMVMSG command removes all messages from the program message queue. Without this instruction, the messages would keep showing up even after the error condition they describe has been corrected. Keep in mind that the message subfile will present on the screen not just the new messages, but all the messages contained in the program-message queue.

- Although variable MSGKEY is not referenced in the CL program, it is used in the display file with the SFLMSGKEY keyword.

- No manual write of the subfile records is necessary; the system does this automatically. However, you do need to write the subfile control record.

- The program assumes that messages for all printers are sent to a message queue named PRINTERS. To use this program on your system, you must change this name (it is in the DSPMSG command) or make it a variable (such as &MSGQ) that the program receives as a parameter.

7

INTERPROGRAM AND
INTERMODULE COMMUNICATIONS

The program object is the only type of object that actually performs work on the system. If you want to run a complicated application such as Materials Requirements Planning (MRP), you are likely to code many, many programs. By following the guidelines for modular programming, you make program maintenance easier than if you had a single, mammoth program to handle everything. When you spread the work among several programs or procedures, however, you quickly realize that you need a method to pass information between them. One program must be able to communicate with others. Information can be passed between programs using any of the following:

- Database files (This method is not discussed here because CL procedures cannot write to database files.)
- Parameters
- Data areas, including the local data area (LDA)
- Switches
- Messages
- Data queues

This chapter discusses each of these methods in separate sections.

USING PARAMETERS

Chapter 5 presents the CALL and Transfer Control (TFRCTL) commands as the two means to activate one program from another, and the Call Bound Procedure (CALLPRC) command as the method one procedure uses to invoke another one. When you use one of these commands, you can pass information to the called program or procedure through parameters.

CALL and TFRCTL require parameters to be passed by reference only. As of V5R3, CALLPRC allows parameters to be passed by reference or by value. To pass a parameter by value means that a copy of the parameter, not the parameter's address, is passed to the caller. The result is that the caller cannot change the value of a parameter that is passed by value. In the following example, parameters &RTNCD and &PRINTER are passed by reference, but &OPTION is passed by value.

```
CALLPRCPRC(P) PARM((&RTNCD*BYREF)(&OPTION*BYVAL) &PRINTER)
```

The advantages parameters offer are that they are very easy to use, require no external objects, and can pass a considerable amount of information. They also happen to be the fastest medium to pass that information.

The disadvantage with parameters is that the data can be passed to the another program or module only when the second program or module is initiated. For example, you cannot pass parameter data to a program that is already running in batch mode.

Parameter Variables

CL supports character, decimal, integer, and logical variables. You can pass parameter data using any of these variable types if the second program supports them.

IBM likes the phrase "unpredictable results may occur," which is exactly what happens if both programs do not declare the parameter variables identically. The second program might or might not perform as expected.

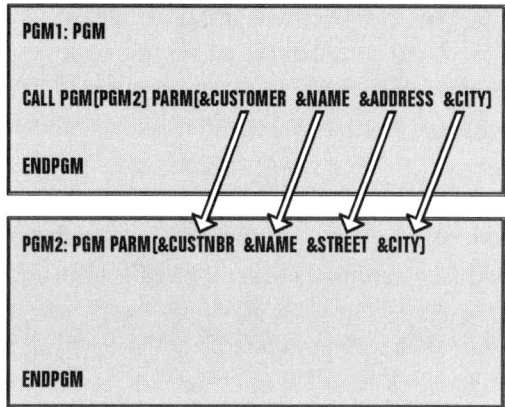

Figure 7.1: How parameters are passed.

Figure 7.1 illustrates how parameters are passed. Note that the variables don't need to have the same name in both programs. For example, PGM1 passes &CUSTOMER, which is received by PGM2 into variable &CUSTNBR.

> *Note:* Take care to match the parameter variables in both programs, not only in type (*CHAR variable to *CHAR variable, *DEC to *DEC, etc.) but also in length. If the first program sends a parameter variable declared as type(*DEC) LEN(9 2), make sure the second program receives it in a variable declared the same way. Otherwise, unpredictable results may occur.

Parameter Constants

Passing constants as parameters is somewhat riskier. If the second program expects a character variable of 32 characters or less, you can code the character constant directly in the CALL command. Enclose it in single quotes.

If the second program expects a character variable of more than 32 characters, however, you must code the character constant in the CALL command using the exact number of characters expected. You must include trailing blanks in the character constant (as many as needed) to make up the required length.

If the second program expects a decimal variable of LEN(15 5), you can code the decimal constant in the CALL command (without quotes, of course). The system takes care of converting it to decimal form for you; it places the decimal point at the proper spot.

If the expected decimal variable is of any other length (or number of decimal places), you must code the decimal constant in hexadecimal format. This process is so cumbersome and error-prone that you are better off using a variable.

Because they always have the same implied length of 1 byte, logical constants present no obstacles. Code them as '0' or '1' in the CALL command.

Limitations

You already encountered one limitation of interprogram communication by parameters: the information passes to the second program only when the program is activated. The information passes back to the first program when the second program ends. Communication does not happen at any other time.

Another limitation is the number of parameters. CL procedures can have a maximum of 255 parameters.

Additionally, the TFRCTL command has a rather serious limitation. You can pass only variables as parameters, and only those variables that the first program received as parameters itself.

If program A received parameters &P1, &P2, and &P3, it cannot TFRCTL to program B passing parameter &Q1 or constant 'X'. Both are invalid. Only &P1, &P2, and &P3 could be passed to program B with the TFRCTL command.

USING DATA AREAS

Data areas are objects of type *DTAARA that you can create and delete at will. A data area is an area of storage with a name, but without any structure. You cannot define fields within data areas the way you can with files.

You can use data areas to store information. One program can write information to a data area, and another program can read that information at a later time (thus accomplishing asynchronous communication).

Data areas allow you to establish communication between two or more programs that may be running in different jobs. This communication is possible because data areas are permanent objects that do not depend on one job or another except for two special data areas (described in the subheading, Special Data Areas, that follows).

The CRTDTAARA and DLTDTAARA Commands

Data areas are created with the Create Data Area (CRTDTAARA) command. When you create a data area, you must supply a qualified name, an optional 50-character text description, a type (*CHAR, *DEC, or *LGL), a length of up to 2000 for *CHAR or up to (24 9) for *DEC, and an optional initial value.

You can delete a data area with the Delete Data Area (DLTDTAARA) command, which just requires the qualified name of the data area to be deleted. Both CRTDTAARA and DLTDTAARA can be placed in CL programs or executed manually.

The CHGDTAARA, RTVDTAARA, and DSPDTAARA Commands

Once a data area is created, you can change its contents with the Change Data Area (CHGDTAARA) command. CHGDTAARA requires the qualified name of the data area, the position within the data area to be changed, the length of the data to be changed, and the new data to be placed.

Suppose you create data area DA1 in library QGPL and supply an initial value of 'ABCDEF' (as shown in Figure 7.2).

```
CRTDTAARA DTAARA(qgpl/da1) TYPE(*CHAR) LEN(20) VALUE('ABCDEF')
```

Figure 7.2: Creating a data area with the initial value of ABCDEF.

Now you want to replace the fourth and fifth characters with the numbers 1 and 2. You would use the code shown in Figure 7.3 to accomplish that.

```
CHGDTAARA DTAARA(qgpl/da1 (4 2)) VALUE('12')
```

Figure 7.3: An example of replacing the fourth and fifth characters in data area QGPL.

The Retrieve Data Area (RTVDTAARA) command can be used in a CL program to place the contents of a data area (or a portion thereof) into a CL variable. For example, you can retrieve the second, third, and fourth characters of data area DA1 into variable &PART (as shown in Figure 7.4).

```
DCL &part        *CHAR   10

RTVDTAARA DTAARA(qgpl/da1 (2 3)) RTNVAR(&part)
```

Figure 7.4: An example of retrieving a portion of a data area with the RTVDTAARA command.

Notice that, because data area da1 is *CHAR, &PART has been declared as type *CHAR. Because &PART is longer than the 3 bytes RTVDTAARA is extracting, the rest of the variable is erased.

You can use the Display Data Area (DSPDTAARA) command anytime you want to see the contents of a data area. The output can be directed to the display or to a printer, depending on the value given to the OUTPUT parameter.

Only RTVDTAARA must be executed in a CL procedure. CHGDTAARA and DSPDTAARA can be executed either manually or in a CL procedure.

Special Data Areas

For each job, the system automatically creates a 1024-byte local data area (named *LDA). With the exception that you cannot delete it, this local data area can be treated like any other data area of type *CHAR. The local data area is always available until the job ends. Furthermore, because it cannot be accessed from other jobs, you can think of *LDA as a data area that has been created in library QTEMP (although that is not the case).

In addition, the system automatically creates a 512-byte group data area (named *GDA) for each group job. It also can be treated like any other data area of type *CHAR, with the same restriction that prevents you from deleting it. When the job stops being a group job (or when it ends), the *GDA is deleted by the system.

"Prestart" jobs can use the special program initialization parameter (PIP) data area, which is referenced by the name *PDA. The system automatically creates this data area (which is 2000 characters long).

All of the data area commands presented before, except CRTDTAARA and DLTDTAARA, apply to the special data areas as well. Just use special values *LDA, *GDA, or *PDA as the data-area name.

The %SST function accepts special values *LDA, *GDA, and *PDA instead of a variable name (which makes it easier to retrieve or change the local, group, and "prestart" data areas). The CL statement shown in Figure 7.5 places the first 10 characters of the GDA into the last 10 characters of the LDA.

```
CHGVAR %SST(*LDA 1015 10) %SST(*GDA 1 10)
```

Figure 7.5: An example of using special values *LDA and *GDA with %SST.

USING SWITCHES

In addition to the local data area (LDA), each job has eight switches that are logical variables. CL procedures can turn these switches on and off and make decisions based on their status.

When a job starts, the switches are set to the values indicated by the job description. Because the job description probably specifies an initial status of 00000000, all switches start with an off status. However, this is by no means certain; you should verify it by checking the job description or by running the Display Job (DSPJOB) command.

Turning Switches On and Off

You can turn the switches on and off with the Change Job (CHGJOB) command, specifying the new status of the switches in the SWS parameter. The SWS parameter must receive an eight-character string with the characters '0' (to turn off), '1' (to turn on), or 'X' (to leave the switch as is). For example, the command shown in Figure 7.6 turns on the first three switches, turns off the next three, and leaves the last two unchanged.

```
CHGJOB SWS('111000XX')
```

Figure 7.6: Example of turning switches on and off in the CHGJOB command.

If all you want to do is turn on switch number 4, execute the command shown in Figure 7.7.

```
CHGJOB SWS('XXX1XXXX')
```

Figure 7.7: Changing switch 4 while leaving all other switches at current value.

All other switches remain unchanged.

Testing the Switches

Of course, the switches would not be of much use if you could not determine their status in a CL procedure. You can go about it in two ways: with the Retrieve Job Attributes (RTVJOBA) command or with the %SWITCH function in an IF statement. The first method is a bit laborious and requires you to declare an eight-character variable, but it gets the job done. It works as shown in Figure 7.8.

```
    DCL &switches    *CHAR    8
    RTVJOBA SWS(&switches)
  a:
    IF (&switches *EQ '00011100') ...
  b:
    IF (%SST(&switches 1 1) *EQ '1') ...
```

Figure 7.8: Using RTVJOBA to determine the value of switches.

There are two IF statements; one is labeled A, the other B. The first IF checks that the eight switches have a certain combination of values and no other: 00011100. The second IF checks that the first switch is turned on.

You might prefer using the %SWITCH function instead of the RTVJOBA approach. With the %SWITCH function, the same two IF statements could be coded as shown in Figure 7.9.

```
  a:
    IF %SWITCH(00011100) ...
  b:
    IF %SWITCH(1XXXXXXX) ...
```

Figure 7.9: Using the %SWITCH function to determine the value of switches.

Three things are worth mentioning. First, this approach requires no variables. Second, the status of the switches is not enclosed in single quotes. Third, the IF command—having nothing but the %SWITCH function—becomes much less complicated.

Using the Switches

Switches, like data areas, are good for passing data asynchronously to another program in the same job. Because there are only eight switches, however, you are severely limited in the amount of information you can pass.

If you need more than eight switches, perhaps you should consider using part of the LDA for switches or creating a data area in QTEMP for that specific purpose. Switches are not accessible in all high-level languages. Only CL, RPG, and COBOL offer support for them.

USING MESSAGES

Messages can be used to pass information between two programs. The two communicating programs can be in the same or different jobs.

Another Look at SNDPGMMSG

Chapter 6 explains the workings of the Send Program Message (SNDPGMMSG) command in detail. It is mentioned here because it is the command you need to send information to another program. As Chapter 6 explains, you can send a message to a program message queue or to a permanent message queue. You can use program message queues only if the two programs that communicate are active in the call stack of the same job. If they are not, you must use message queue objects (*MSGQ). For example, you can pass the value 'COMPLETE' to program PGM1 as shown in Figure 7.10.

```
SNDPGMMSG MSG('COMPLETE') TOPGMQ(*SAME pgm1) MSGTYPE(*INFO)
```

Figure 7.10: Passing a value to a program through a program message queue.

Again, the receiving program (PGM1) must be in your job's call stack. If PGM1 is not there, the SNDPGMMSG command will fail. To overcome this limitation, use a message queue as shown in Figure 7.11.

```
SNDPGMMSG MSG('COMPLETE') TOMSGQ(qsysopr) MSGTYPE(*INFO)
```

Figure 7.11: Passing a value to a message queue with SNDPGMMSG.

This example uses the system operator's message queue (QSYSOPR). You should consider using a different message queue, preferably one you have created specifically for this case.

Another Look at RCVMSG

If SNDPGMMSG is used to send the message, RCVMSG is used to receive it. Figure 7.12 shows how PGM1 can be coded to receive the message of the example shown in Figure 7.10.

```
DCL &msg        *CHAR   50
RCVMSG MSGTYPE(*INFO) WAIT(*MAX) MSG(&msg)
```

Figure 7.12: Receiving a message from a program message queue.

As indicated by WAIT(*MAX), the program will wait indefinitely for an *INFO message. When a message is received, its text is placed in variable &MSG, which was declared as a 50-byte *CHAR. In reality, this variable could be shorter or longer. While the length doesn't matter, the variable should be long enough to hold the entire message.

By changing the WAIT parameter to something more realistic (any number of seconds, 0 inclusive), you can control how long the program would wait for the incoming message. Specifying 0 causes the program not to wait for the message. If the message is there, &MSG will contain the message text. If no message is there to be received, &MSG will be blank.

The RCVMSG command, as coded in Figure 7.12, receives the message from the current program's message queue. If the other program didn't send the message to a program message queue, but sent it to a message queue object, you will have to change the coding of the RCVMSG command as shown in Figure 7.13.

```
DCL &msg          *CHAR    50
RCVMSG MSGQ(qsysopr) MSGTYPE(*INFO) WAIT(*MAX) MSG(&msg)
```

Figure 7.13: Receiving a message from a message queue object.

Once again, QSYSOPR has been used for illustration only. You should use a different message queue for practical purposes.

USING DATA QUEUES

Data queues are permanent objects (type *DTAQ) that can be used for asynchronously communicating a stream of values between programs or jobs.

You are already familiar with the concept of a queue. The system supports other queue objects: job queues (*JOBQ), message queues (*MSGQ), output queues (*OUTQ), and user queues (*USRQ). Except that you can control what goes into a queue, and when it is flushed, data queues are no different.

Types of Data Queues

There are three types of data queues: *FIFO, *LIFO, and *KEYED.

- *FIFO (first-in, first-out) is the typical queue object that works like a line of people waiting for the next available teller in a bank. Customers arrive at the queue on one end and exit the queue on the other end. The customer arriving first gets to leave first.

- *LIFO (last-in, first-out) is a stack object that is like a pile of trays at a cafeteria. The staff puts trays on the stack, which piles higher and higher. The next person who comes in picks up a tray from the top of the stack. The tray that was placed on the stack last is the first tray to be used. The first tray to enter the stack could remain in the stack forever.

- *KEYED is a special type of data queue. Essentially, entries are placed in the queue haphazardly, but leave it randomly in the order you want.

Entries can even leave in an alphabetized (i.e., sorted) order. Think of keyed data queues as data queues that have a built-in index. Therefore, you can retrieve entries by key.

The CRTDTAQ and DLTDTAQ Commands

Data queues can be created and deleted at will with the Create Data Queue (CRTDTAQ) and Delete Data Queue (DLTDTAQ) commands. CRTDTAQ has eight parameters:

- DTAQ: Where you enter the qualified name of the data queue you want to create.

- MAXLEN: Where you must enter a number that represents the length of the longest entry you will place in the data queue. This parameter is not unlike the record length of a database file. You can enter any number between 1 and 64512.

  SEQ: Can be *FIFO, *LIFO, or *KEYED. These options are explained in the preceding section on the types of queues. The default is *FIFO.

- TEXT: Where you enter a brief (50-character) description of the data queue.

- FORCE: Indicates whether the data queue should be written to DASD each time an entry arrives or leaves the data queue. The default is *NO.

- SENDERID: Indicates whether to identify each entry with the name of the job, the library, and the user profile name of the user who sent the entry to the data queue.

- AUT: Indicates what authority the public has to the data queue.

- KEYLEN: If the data queue is to be *KEYED, indicates the length of the key to the data queue. The key length can be anywhere from 1 to 256.

The DLTDTAQ command, with only one parameter, is much simpler. The parameter indicates the qualified name of the data queue to be deleted.

Sending, Receiving, and Clearing Data Queues

Just as you can send and receive messages when you use message queues, you can send and receive data entries when you use data queues. The difference is that commands such as Send to Data Queue (SNDDTAQ) and Receive from Data Queue (RCVDTAQ) don't exist. You must use a CALL to an API in each case. (APIs are IBM-supplied programs; the acronym stands for Application Program Interface.)

Most of the time, you probably will be sending or receiving data from programs written in languages (such as RPG or COBOL) other than CL. Similarly, you must call another API to clear a data queue. No Clear Data Queue (CLRDTAQ) command exists. Appendix A contains the source code for a version of the SNDDTAQ, RCVDTAQ, and CLROUTQ commands that will make it easier for you to use data queues in CL procedures. To send data to a data queue, call program QSNDDTAQ as shown in Figure 7.14.

```
DCL  &dtaq      *CHAR   10
DCL  &lib       *CHAR   10
DCL  &len       *DEC     5
DCL  &data      *CHAR   20

CALL qsnddtaq (&dtaq &lib &len &data)
```

Figure 7.14: Sending data to a data queue using QSNDDTAQ.

The variable &DTAQ must be 10 characters long and contain the name of the data queue to which you are sending the data. Also, the variable &LIB must be 10 characters long and contain the name of the library where the data queue resides. You can, of course, make use of the library list by specifying *LIBL instead of a library name.

The variable &LEN must be decimal (5 0) and contain the length of the data being sent. You must ensure that the length does not exceed the maximum data length with which you created the data queue. The variable &DATA is the actual data, and it must be a character variable of any length. If the data queue is keyed, you must add two parameters to program QSNDDTAQ. Figure 7.15 shows an example.

```
DCL &dtaq        *CHAR   10
DCL &lib         *CHAR   10
DCL &len         *DEC     5
DCL &data        *CHAR   20
DCL &keylen      *DEC     3
DCL &key         *CHAR   16

CALL qsnddtaq (&dtaq &lib &len &data &keylen &key)
```

Figure 7.15: Sending data to a keyed data queue using QSNDDTAQ.

The &KEYLEN variable must always be a decimal variable of three digits. It must not have decimals, and it must contain the length of the key specified when the data queue was created (which also must match the length of the &KEY variable).

The &KEY variable is a character variable that matches the length of the key of the data queue. In other words, if the data queue was created with a key length of 16, &KEYLEN must have a value of 16 and &KEY must be a 16-character variable.

To receive data from a data queue, call program QRCVDTAQ or QMHRDQM. QRCVDTAQ is the easier API to use and it's the one you would usually use. QMHRDQM is discussed later in this chapter, under the subheading Receiving from Data Queue without Deletion.

Figure 7.16 shows an example of a CL program that calls QRCVDTAQ.

```
DCL &dtaq        *CHAR   10
DCL &lib         *CHAR   10
DCL &len         *DEC     5
DCL &data        *CHAR   20
DCL &wait        *DEC     5

CALL qrcvdtaq (&dtaq &lib &len &data &wait)
```

Figure 7.16: An example of a CL program to call QRCVDTAQ.

As shown in Figure 7.16, the first four parameters are the same as for program QSNDDTAQ. The variable &WAIT must be a decimal (5 0) variable that indicates how many seconds to wait for data to become available. Zero (0) means not to wait; any negative number means to wait indefinitely. A positive number indicates the number of seconds you want the program to pause.

If the data queue is keyed or if you intend to receive the sender's ID, you must include five additional parameters to program QRCVDTAQ. See Figure 7.17.

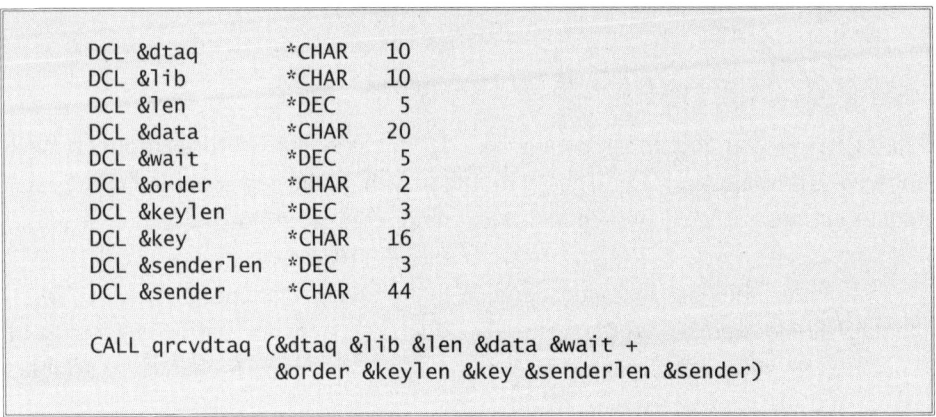

```
DCL &dtaq        *CHAR   10
DCL &lib         *CHAR   10
DCL &len         *DEC     5
DCL &data        *CHAR   20
DCL &wait        *DEC     5
DCL &order       *CHAR    2
DCL &keylen      *DEC     3
DCL &key         *CHAR   16
DCL &senderlen   *DEC     3
DCL &sender      *CHAR   44

CALL qrcvdtaq (&dtaq &lib &len &data &wait +
               &order &keylen &key &senderlen &sender)
```

Figure 7.17: An example of a CL program to call QRCVDTAQ when the data queue is keyed.

- &ORDER: A two-character variable that indicates in what order to receive entries from the keyed data queue. It can have the values EQ, NE, LT, LE, GT, or GE (which should be self-explanatory).

- &KEYLEN: Indicates the length of the key to the data queue.

- &KEY: A character variable that matches the key of the data queue and the value of &KEYLEN in length. For example, if the keyed data queue was created with a key length of 16, &KEYLEN must have the value 16 and &KEY must be a 16-character variable.

- &SENDERLEN: A decimal variable that indicates the length of the &SENDER parameter. Because the sender ID fits in a 44-character variable, &SENDERLEN could always have a value of 44.

- &SENDER: A character variable that will receive the sender ID of the data queue entry being received. Because this identification is 44 characters long, you might want to declare &SENDER as a 44-character variable. The variable &SENDER contains eight characters of garbage followed by the complete qualified name of the sender and the user profile name of the sender. See Table 7.1.

Table 7.1: Contents of Field &SENDER		
Sender Locations:		
From	To	Description
1	8	Garbage
9	18	Job name
19	28	Job user
29	34	Job number
35	44	User profile name

Note: If you need to retrieve the sender ID of a non-keyed data queue, you must still include the &order, &keylen, and &key parameters. Because they have no meaning for non-keyed data queues, they can be left blank or zero.

The code shown in Figure 7.18 uses command QCLRDTAQ to clear a data queue.

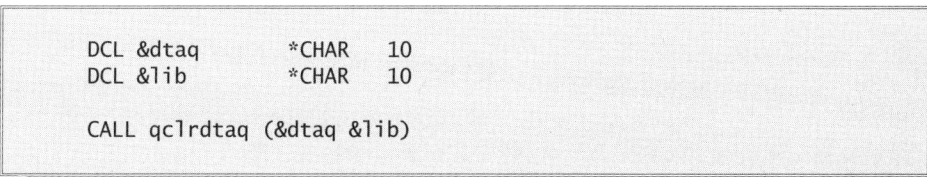

```
DCL &dtaq      *CHAR   10
DCL &lib       *CHAR   10

CALL qclrdtaq (&dtaq &lib)
```

Figure 7.18: Clearing a data queue with QCLRDTAQ.

Retrieving Data Queue Description

The API named QMHQRDQD lets you retrieve the data queue description to variables. The API gives you all the bits of information you need to create the data queue again—such as maximum entry length, sequence, and text description. To call QMHQRDQD, you must— as shown in Figure 7.19—pass four parameters.

```
      /* &DATADS is a data structure.  Its subfields follow. */
      DCL &datads          *CHAR   80
           /* Subfields */
           DCL &bytrtn     *CHAR    4  /* Binary,  1 to  4 */
           DCL &bytavl     *CHAR    4  /* Binary,  5 to  8 */
           DCL &maxlen     *CHAR    4  /* Binary,  9 to 12 */
           DCL &keylen     *CHAR    4  /* Binary, 13 to 16 */
           DCL &seq        *CHAR    1  /* Char,   17 to 17 */
           DCL &senderid   *CHAR    1  /* Char,   18 to 18 */
           DCL &force      *CHAR    1  /* Char,   19 to 19 */
           DCL &text       *CHAR   50  /* Char,   20 to 69 */
           DCL &filler     *CHAR    3  /* Char,   70 to 72 */
           DCL &nbrent     *CHAR    4  /* Binary, 73 to 76 */
           DCL &maxent     *CHAR    4  /* Binary, 77 to 80 */

      DCL &dslen           *CHAR    4  /* Binary */
      DCL &format          *CHAR    8
      DCL &qual_dtaq       *CHAR   20

      DCL &dtaq            *CHAR   10
      DCL &lib             *CHAR   10

      CHGVAR %BIN(&dslen)  80
      CHGVAR &format       'RDQD0100'
      CHGVAR &qual_dtaq    (&dtaq *CAT &lib)

      CALL qmhqrdqd (&datads &dslen &format &qual_dtaq)
```

Figure 7.19: Correct parameters for command QMHQRDQD.

The first parameter is a data structure, 80 bytes long, that will receive all the information about the data queue. Notice how the indentation helps identify the data structure subfields. Of course, data structures are not supported in CL. Therefore, you'll have to fake them. Figure 7.20 shows you how.

```
CHGVAR &maxlen    %BIN(&datads  9  4)
CHGVAR &keylen    %BIN(&datads 13  4)
CHGVAR &seq       %SST(&datads 17  1)
CHGVAR &senderid  %SST(&datads 18  1)
CHGVAR &force     %SST(&datads 19  1)
CHGVAR &text      %SST(&datads 20 50)
CHGVAR &nbrent    %BIN(&datads 73  4)
CHGVAR &maxent    %BIN(&datads 77  4)
```

Figure 7.20: Building a pseudo data structure in CL.

So that you can place the correct values in each subfield, code the sequence of CHGVARS immediately after the CALL.

The first two subfields are inconsequential; they tell you how many bytes were received (it will always be 80) and how many are available (always zero). The next two binary subfields contain the maximum length of a data queue entry (&MAXLEN) and the key length (&KEYLEN). The key length is zero if the data queue is not keyed.

The variable &SEQ indicates the sequence of the data queue: L = *LIFO, F = *FIFO, K = *KEYED. The variables &SENDERID and &FORCE contain Y = *YES or N = *NO to indicate whether the data queue includes the sender ID and whether entries are forced to auxiliary storage. The variable &TEXT contains the 50-character text description of the data queue object.

The variable &FILLER is a 3-byte filler that currently isn't used. The variable &NBRENT is the number of entries that currently occupy the data queue, and &MAXENT tells you how many entries you can place in the data queue without causing it to overflow (i.e., without causing the system to extend the data queue).

The second parameter, QMHQRDQD, &DSLEN, is a 4-byte binary number that represents the length of the previous parameter (the data structure). Because the variable &DADADS is an 80-byte data structure, you must pass a number 80 expressed in binary.

The third parameter, &FORMAT, is an eight-character variable that contains the constant RDQD0100. This is not unlike API format names, and it is possible that IBM will define other formats in the future to retrieve additional data-queue information.

The fourth parameter, &QUAL_DTAQ, is the qualified name of the data queue. The variable &QUAL_DTAQ must contain the name of the data queue (in the first 10 characters) followed by the name of the library (in the second 10 characters). No slash is accepted. You can use special values *LIBL or *CURLIB instead of a library name.

Receiving from Data Queue without Deletion

Under normal circumstances, you want QRCVDTAQ to delete messages from a data queue as it receives them. This ensures that the same data queue entry is not received and processed twice.

However, if it suits your purposes, you may also retrieve a data queue message without deleting it. There are two ways to retrieve a message from a data queue without deleting it. In V4R3 of i5/OS and above, QRCVDTAQ includes an optional eleventh parameter. If this parameter has a value of *YES, the message is deleted when retrieved. This is the default value. To leave the message on the data queue, specify *NO.

Under older releases of i5/OS, the programmer must use the Retrieve Data Queue Message (QMHRDQM) API.

Using QMHRDQM lets you retrieve multiple entries at once, but it has a serious disadvantage that sometimes makes it practically useless in CL procedures. There is no mechanism to let you select which data queue entry to receive, other than "the first *n* entries" or "the last *n* entries." The only time you are allowed to retrieve a particular entry is when you retrieve from a *KEYED data queue and each entry is long.

Because QMHRDQM places all entries retrieved in a single CL character variable, the entries retrieved can easily account for more than 9999 bytes, which is the maximum length of *CHAR variables. In this case, you should call QMHRDQM from an RPG IV, COBOL, or C program. Although calling QMHRDQM from CL can be cumbersome, it can be done. There will be many cases when it will be useful because the 9999-byte limit won't be reached. Figure 7.21 shows how to call this API.

```
CALL qmhrdqm (&data        /* OUT: Entries retrieved       */ +
              &datalen     /* IN:  Length of &DATA         */ +
              &datafmt     /* IN:  Always 'RDQM0100'       */ +
              &qual_dtaq   /* IN:  Qualified data queue name */ +
              &dtaslt      /* IN:  Selection of entries    */ +
              &dtasltlen   /* IN:  Length of &DTASLT        */ +
              &dtasltfmt   /* IN:  'RDQS0100' or 'RDQS0200' */ +
              &errcode     /* I/O: API error code structure */ +
```

Figure 7.21: Calling API QMHRDQM with the proper parameters.

In the following discussion of QMHRDQM parameters, remember that the variable names listed here are arbitrary. The names reflect the choices for variable names made for the CALL statement shown in Figure 7.21.

The variable &DATA (Output) is a *CHAR variable that contains the data-queue entries received in the format indicated by the &DATAFMT parameter. Currently, the only format allowed is RDQM0100. The &DATA variable must be at least 8 bytes long. If the variable is too short to hold all of the entries received, QMHRDQM will put in as many whole entries as it can.

The variable &DATALEN (Input) indicates the length of the &DATA variable in a 4-byte binary format. Use a *CHAR variable and the %BIN function.

The variable &DATAFMT (Input) currently is allowed only to have the value RDQM0100. It must be in an 8-byte character variable.

The variable &QUAL_DTAQ (Input) is a 20-byte *CHAR variable that contains the name of the data queue and the library in which it resides (in that order, left-justified in 10-byte buckets) as shown in Figure 7.22.

```
....+....1....+....2
 'DTAQ      DTAQLIB   '
```

Figure 7.22: Correct placement of data in &QUAL_DTAQ.

The variable &DTASLT (Input) is a *CHAR variable (its length is indicated by &DTASLTLEN) that indicates which entries to retrieve from the data queue. Depending on &DTASLTFMT, it can have one or two formats.

The variable &DTASLTLEN (Input) indicates the length of &DTASLT, which is a 4-byte binary value.

The variable &DTASLTFMT (Input) specifies in which format &DTASLT is provided. Only two values are valid: RDQS0100 and RDQS0200. The variable &DTASLTFMT must be an 8-byte character variable.

The variable &ERRCODE (Input/Output) is the standard API error structure. It needs to be a *CHAR variable of at least 8 bytes.

Additional information about QMHRDQM can be obtained from the *System Programmer's Interface Reference* manual.

Utility Commands

Data queues are very useful, but IBM did not provide a very intuitive or user-friendly interface. Having to call the programs shown in the previous sections is not easy to do. Program QMHQRDQD in particular has what seems to be an arbitrary name and its parameters aren't easy to remember.

Appendix A contains several useful utility commands to manipulate data queues. SNDDTAQ, RCVDTAQ, and CLRDTAQ are self-explanatory and support all types of data queues, including *KEYED. RTVDTAQ lets you retrieve the data queue's description to CL variables. RGZDTAQ deletes and recreates a data queue automatically.

Advantages of Data Queues

Data queues are most useful in applications that require asynchronous communication between two jobs running in parallel (when one job can send data at a different rate than the other receives it). While message queues also could be used, data queues provide much better performance. Another advantage in using data queues is that RPG and COBOL programs can process them more easily than they can process message queues.

Output queues can be compared to data queues if you stretch the similarities and disregard the differences. For example, suppose you have two jobs: one that writes information to a printer file, and another that takes that information and feeds it to the actual printer device. The second job is usually the slower of the two. The first job sends data much faster than the second job can process it. But because the data is accumulating in the output queue, it does not really matter. It would be inefficient if the first job had to do everything. The first job would have to wait for the printer to become available before it could process more data.

Data queues can be used by any two jobs under similar circumstances. Picture the following scenario:

> Inventory transactions are entered throughout the day in a busy manufacturing shop. Some inventory transactions don't require much processing. For example, an inventory adjustment only needs to change the on-hand quantity. Other transactions, such as a move between locations, need to check the existence of the two locations, then decrease supply on-hand at the first location, and increase goods on-hand at the second location at the same time.

Interactive transaction entry can have slow response time if many inventory control clerks are entering transactions simultaneously. To speed up data entry, your inventory transaction entry program could perform minimal data verification and then send the transaction to a data queue.

Another job, running in batch (with low priority), can receive data from the data queue all day long and update the master files. When writing transactions to a transaction history file that has several logical views built over it, updating the master files is especially resource-intensive.

Accumulation of transactions in the data queue does not matter much; the batch program will process them one at a time. As soon as there is a pause in data entry (such as an employee coffee break), the program will catch up with the data-entry clerks.

Another advantage of data queues is that any number of jobs can be sending to, and receiving from, the same data queue.

Disadvantages of Data Queues

Data queues are not without problems, however. The most severe problem is that, once an entry is received from a data queue, the data queue forgets the entry forever. If the program that received the entry ends abnormally, before it has a chance to process the entry, the entry is lost and cannot be recovered.

Another disadvantage is that, when many entries are sent to a data queue, the data queue object increases in size. Later, when the entries are received (and therefore removed from the data queue), the data queue object *does not decrease* in size. Data queues must be deleted and recreated periodically to avoid having empty data queues of enormous size. Use the Reorganize Data Queue (RGZDTAQ) command, provided in Appendix A, to automate this process.

8

JOB AND SYSTEM INTERFACE

CL programmers can easily obtain information about running jobs and about their system. And you can change that information with equal ease.

LIBRARY LIST SUPPORT

The job's library list can be modified with the following commands:

- Add Library List Entry (ADDLIBLE)

- Remove Library List Entry (RMVLIBLE)

- Change Library List (CHGLIBL)

- Change Current Library (CHGCURLIB)

- Change System Library List (CHGSYSLIBL)

The command ADDLIBLE lets you add a library to the user portion of the library list. Using the POSITION parameter, you can even specify where in the library list to insert the new library. Figure 8.1 shows some examples.

```
/* Place MYLIB at the top of the user portion of the library list */
ADDLIBLE mylib POSITION(*FIRST)

/* Place MYLIB at the bottom of the library list */
ADDLIBLE mylib POSITION(*LAST)

/* Place MYLIB right after YOURLIB in the library list */
ADDLIBLE mylib POSITION(*AFTER yourlib)

/* Place MYLIB right before YOURLIB in the library list */
ADDLIBLE mylib POSITION(*BEFORE yourlib)

/* Place MYLIB instead of YOURLIB in the library list */
ADDLIBLE mylib POSITION(*REPLACE yourlib)
```

Figure 8.1: Examples of adding libraries to your library list with ADDLIBLE.

The command RMVLIBLE lets you remove a library from the user portion of the library list. Figure 8.2 shows an example.

```
RMVLIBLE mylib
```

Figure 8.2: An example of removing a library from your library list with RMVLIBLE.

With a single command, CHGLIBL lets you change the user portion of the library list entirely and optionally assign a current library. See Figure 8.3.

```
CHGLIBL LIBL(lib1 lib2 lib3) CURLIB(lib4)
```

Figure 8.3: An example of changing your library list and assigning a current library with CHGLIBL.

The command CHGSYSLIBL lets you change your copy of the system portion of the library list. It only affects your job; it doesn't affect other jobs on the system. All you can do is add a library to the top of the system portion of the library list or remove a library from it. Unless you have changed system value QSYSLIBL, QSYS is the first library in the system portion of the library list. The command shown in Figure 8.4 places library ALTQSYS ahead of QSYS for the current job.

The command CHGCURLIB lets you change the current library for your job. You can indicate that you don't want any current library by specifying special value *CRTDFT as the current library name.

```
CHGSYSLIBL altqsys OPTION(*ADD)
```

Figure 8.4: Adding library ALTQSYS to the front of your library list.

RETRIEVING SYSTEM VALUES

System values have such an impact in the control of system operations that CL procedures often need to obtain these values. With the Retrieve System Value (RTVSYSVAL) command, you can copy a given system value to a CL variable. Once it is in a CL variable, you can use the variable just like any other.

The variable you use to retrieve the system value must be of the same type as the system value you are retrieving. For example, system value QCONSOLE contains the name of the system console used during attended IPLs. Device names are character strings 10 bytes long. Therefore, you would retrieve QCONSOLE into a CL variable that was declared as TYPE(*CHAR) LEN(10).

The rudimentary job scheduler program shown in Figure 8.5 is an example of what you can do with the RTVSYSVAL command. The program goes to sleep for five minutes, checks the time (hours only), depending on the hour retrieved, then processes the appropriate section of code. You can use it by changing the logic to suit your needs.

```
PGM

    DCL &hour          *CHAR      2

loop:
    DLYJOB DLY(300) /* Wait 5 minutes */
    RTVSYSVAL qhour &hour

    IF (&hour *EQ '07') DO
        *
        * /* Processing for 07:00 */
        *
    ENDDO

    ELSE IF (&hour *EQ '12') DO
        *
        * /* Processing for 12:00 */
        *
    ENDDO

    ELSE IF (&hour *EQ '18') DO
        *
        * /* Processing for 18:00 */
        *
    ENDDO

    ELSE IF (&hour *EQ '23') DO
        *
        * /* Processing for 23:00 */
        *
    ENDDO

    GOTO loop

ENDPGM
```

Figure 8.5: A job scheduler program.

Table 8.1 contains a partial listing of system values. The list shows the name of the system value, a brief description, and the TYPE and LEN of the CL variable you need to use in the RTVSYSVAL command.

Table 8.1: System Values		
Name	**Description**	
QASTLVL	Assistance level. Can be *BASIC, *INTERMED, or *ADVANCED.	CHAR 10
QATNPGM	Name of Attention key handling program.	CHAR 20
QCONSOLE	Name of system console device.	CHAR 10
QCRTAUT	Default create authority.	CHAR 10
QCTLSBSD	Name of controlling subsystem.	CHAR 20
QCURSYM	Currency symbol.	CHAR 1
QDATE	System date. It is in the format indicated by system value QDATFMT. Use LEN(5) to retrieve system date in Julian format.	CHAR 5 or 6
QDATFMT	Date format. Can have values YMD, MDY, DMY, or JUL.	CHAR 3
QDATSEP	Date separator character.	CHAR 1
QDAY	Day portion of the system date.	CHAR 2
QDEVNAMING	Device naming convention. Can be *NORMAL, *S36, or *DEVADR.	CHAR 10
QHOUR	Hour portion of system time.	CHAR 2
QIPLDATTIM	Next IPL date and time.	CHAR 20
QMINUTE	Minute portion of system time.	CHAR 2
QMODEL	AS/400, iSeries, or i5 model.	CHAR 4
QMONTH	Month portion of system date.	CHAR 2
QPRTDEV	Name of system printer device.	CHAR 10
QPRTKEYFMT	Print key format. Can be *PRTHDR, *PRTBDR, *PRTALL, or *NONE.	CHAR 10
QPRTTXT	Print text at bottom of pages.	CHAR 30
QSECOND	Second portion of system time.	CHAR 2

Table 8.1: System Values, continued		
Name	**Description**	
QSECURITY	Security level. Can be 10, 20, 30, 40, or 50.	CHAR 2
QSRLNBR	Serial number.	CHAR 8
QSTRPRTWTR	Whether to start printer writers at IPL. Can be 1 or 0.	CHAR 1
QSTRUPPGM	Name of the start-up program.	CHAR 20
QSTSMSG	Whether to display status messages. Can be *NORMAL or *NONE.	CHAR 10
QSYSLIBL	System portion of library list.	CHAR 175
QTIME	System time. Use LEN(9) to retrieve it with millisecond accuracy.	CHAR 6 or 9
QUSRLIBL	User portion of library list.	CHAR 275
QYEAR	Year portion of system date.	CHAR 2

CHANGING SYSTEM VALUES

Using the Change System Value (CHGSYSVAL) command, CL procedures can change system values just as easily as they can retrieve their contents. To use the CHGSYSVAL command, you need the name of the system value you want to change and the new value (either as a constant or in a CL variable). Figure 8.6 shows an example of how you can change QCURSYM to the letter L.

```
CHGSYSVAL qcursym 'L'
```

Figure 8.6: An example of changing system value QCURSYM to a value of L.

THE RTVJOBA AND CHGJOB COMMANDS

Jobs have many settings. Because these settings (also known as *attributes*) control the behavior of the job, it can become important to know what values they have. The Retrieve Job Attributes (RTVJOBA) command can be used to obtain the job settings and make them known to a CL procedure using a CL variable.

For example, interactive jobs use the name of the display station device as the name of the job. A CL procedure running interactively can obtain the name of the display station by performing the steps shown in Figure 8.7.

```
DCL &dspnam     *CHAR   10
RTVJOBA JOB(&dspnam)
```

Figure 8.7: An example of using RTVJOBA to retrieve the name of the display station.

The CL variable you use to retrieve the job attribute must have the correct data type and length. The prompter for the RTVJOBA command shows what type and length is correct for each attribute. For example, the prompter shows (10) to indicate that a 10-byte character variable is required or (5 0) to ask for a decimal variable of five digits and no decimals.

Once you have retrieved the job attribute in a CL variable, you can use the variable as you would any other. For example, suppose you have created a CL program that you do not want the user to run from the system console. You may use the code shown in Figure 8.8 in the program to preclude the program from running from the system console.

```
RTVSYSVAL qconsole &console
RTVJOBA JOB(&dspnam)

IF (&dspnam *EQ &console) DO
   SNDPGMMSG MSGID(cpf9898) MSGF(qcpfmsg) +
            MSGDTA('You cannot run this program from the system +
                  console') +
            MSGTYPE(*ESCAPE)
ENDDO
```

Figure 8.8: An example of blocking a program from the system console.

The code shown in Figure 8.8 illustrates the use of the RTVSYSVAL and RTVJOBA commands. Both &CONSOLE and &DSPNAM are character variables of a length of 10 bytes.

The code works because RTVSYSVAL retrieves the name of the system console and RTVJOBA retrieves the name of the current display station. The IF command compares the two; if equal, SNDPGMMSG sends an *ESCAPE message (aborting the program automatically). You also can change some of the job attributes with the Change Job (CHGJOB) command. While RTVJOBA can retrieve the attributes of the current job only, CHGJOB can change any job on the system (although it defaults to the current job).

To illustrate the RTVJOBA and CHGJOB commands, imagine you have a program that you run in batch mode. Part of the program has a resource-intensive section. Batch jobs normally run at priority 50. Because this resource-intensive section can be run at priority 75 (which is lower), it does not interfere with the rest of the system as much.

First, use RTVJOBA to obtain the value of the run priority, which will be stored in a CL variable. Then use CHGJOB to change the run priority to 75. When the resource-intensive portion is finished, use CHGJOB again to change the run priority back to its original value (see Figure 8.9).

```
DCL &runpty      *DEC    2

/* Resource-intensive portion begins */
RTVJOBA RUNPTY(&runpty)
CHGJOB  RUNPTY(75)
*
*
*
CHGJOB  RUNPTY(&runpty)
/* Resource-intensive portion ends */
```

Figure 8.9: Using the CHGJOB command to modify the job's priority while it is running.

THE RTVUSRPRF, CHGUSRPRF, AND CHGPRF COMMANDS

CL procedures can become aware of the settings of user profiles with the Retrieve User Profile (RTVUSRPRF) command. This command passes the settings to CL variables.

The first parameter is the name of the user profile that you want to retrieve. Because the parameter defaults to *CURRENT, the command will retrieve the settings of the user running the CL procedure. The rest of the parameters can be specified to retrieve certain settings and to ignore all others. For example, the section of code shown in Figure 8.10 could be included for your users in the initial program that begins running automatically when they sign on.

```
DCL &text        *CHAR    50
DCL &hour        *CHAR     2
DCL &greeting    *CHAR    20

RTVUSRPRF USRPRF(*CURRENT) TEXT(&text)
RTVSYSVAL qhour &hour

IF (&hour *LT '12') +
   CHGVAR &greeting 'Good morning'

ELSE IF (&hour *LT '18') +
   CHGVAR &greeting 'Good afternoon'

ELSE +
   CHGVAR &greeting 'Good evening'

SNDPGMMSG MSGID(cpf9898) MSGF(qcpfmsg) +
          MSGDTA(&greeting *TCAT ',' *BCAT &text) +
          TOPGMQ(*EXT) MSGTYPE(*STATUS)
```

Figure 8.10: An example of code to personalize a message with user name and time.

First, RTVUSRPRF retrieves the text description of the user profile, where the program assumes it will find the complete name of the user profile (an assumption we are making for the sake of illustration). Then, RTVSYSVAL is used to retrieve the hour of the day.

Depending on the hour, variable &GREETING is set to the proper value of "Good morning" (before 12:00), "Good afternoon" (before 18:00), or "Good evening" (anytime at or after 18:00). Also, the SNDPGMMSG command is used to send a status message to *EXT (the external program message queue; i.e., the display station), which concatenates the greeting (variable &GREETING), a comma, and the user's full name (&TEXT). If the user's name is Woody and he signs on at 14:00, he will receive the message shown in Figure 8.11.

```
Good afternoon, Woody.
```

Figure 8.11: An example of output from the program shown in Figure 8.10.

CL procedures also can change user profiles with either the Change User Profile (CHGUSRPRF) command or the Change Profile (CHGPRF) command. The only difference between the two is in scope. While CHGUSRPRF can change any setting in any user profile—provided you are authorized to do so—CHGPRF can change only certain settings in the current user profile (i.e., your own).

THE RTVNETA COMMAND

The Retrieve Network Attributes (RTVNETA) command is rarely used outside of communications applications, but it can provide the system name (something you cannot obtain using any other command). i5/OS displays show the system name at the top-right corner of system menus. If you want to pass the system name to another program, use RTVNETA as shown in Figure 8.12.

```
DCL &sysname    *CHAR    8
RTVNETA SYSNAME(&sysname)
CALL pgma (&sysname)
```

Figure 8.12: Retrieving the system name using RTVNETA.

SUMMARY OF THE RETRIEVE (RTV) COMMANDS

You probably noticed some similarities between RTVSYSVAL, RTVJOBA, RTVUSRPRF, and the RTVNETA commands. Most Retrieve (RTVXXX) commands perform similarly; they extract some information from an object or event and place that information in CL variables.

The command prompter tells you what type and length of variable you must use to retrieve a particular piece of information. For example, the command prompter shows (10) for the OUTQ parameter in the RTVJOBA command's prompt. You need a variable declared as TYPE(*CHAR) LEN(10). In contrast, the TIMESLICE parameter shows (7 0), which indicates you must receive the information in a TYPE(*DEC) LEN(7 0) variable.

Table 8.2 lists most RTVXXX commands that return information to CL variables.

Table 8.2: Retrieve Commands	
Retrieve (RTV) Command	**Description**
RTVAUTLE	Retrieve Authorization List Entry. For a given combination of authorization list and user name, RTVAUTLE retrieves the status (granted or revoked) for each specific authority, such as *ALL, *CHANGE, *OBJOPR, and *READ.
RTVBCKUP	Retrieve Backup. Retrieves the current settings of the automatic backup function to CL variables. You get information such as what device to use and whether to submit it to batch.
RTVCLNUP	Retrieve Cleanup. Retrieves the current settings for Operational Assistant's automatic cleanup function.
RTVCFGSTS	Retrieve Configuration Status. For a given configuration object (device, controller, or line description), it returns a status code that indicates whether the object is active, available, on line.
RTVDTAARA	Retrieve Data Area. Retrieves the contents of a data area into a CL variable.

Table 8.2: Retrieve Commands, continued

Retrieve (RTV) Command	Description
RTVJOBA	Retrieve Job Attributes. Retrieves many job attributes to CL variables, including (but not limited to) the job name, output queue name, accounting code, runtime priority, library list, and date format.
RTVLIBD	Retrieve Library Description. Retrieves the type of the library (*TEST or *PROD), its create authority, ASP, and text.
RTVMBRD	Retrieve Member Description. For a given file member, it returns to CL variables an indication of whether it comes from a source or data file, its source type, number of records, number of deleted records, and much statistical information such as date of creation, date of last change, total size, and so on.
RTVMSG	Retrieve Message. This command should have been named Retrieve Message Description (RTVMSGD) because it retrieves the description of a predefined message from a message file.
RTVNETA	Retrieve Network Attributes. As shown before, it retrieves the system name among other things.
RTVOBJD	Retrieve Object Description. The system keeps much information for each object; the RTVOBJD command lets you have, in CL variables, the name of the library where it resides, text description, object attribute, name of the owner, ASP, date of creation, date of last change, and date last saved.
RTVPWRSCDE	Retrieve Power Schedule Entry. Retrieves an entry from Operational Assistant's automatic power schedule and places its information into CL variables.
RTVS36A	Retrieve System/36 Attributes. Retrieves the current configuration of the S/36 Environment into CL variables.
RTVSYSVAL	Retrieve System Value. Returns in a CL variable the contents of any system value.
RTVUSRPRF	Retrieve User Profile. Retrieves practically any attribute of a user profile (notable exception: the password) into CL variables. For example, it retrieves text description, special authorities, total storage used by objects created, default output queue, and so on.

9

USING FILES

By definition, CL is a control language. Because control languages rarely need to process files, processing files is usually left to more advanced programming languages. However, CL can process files in a limited way, and it can read and write to display files. Therefore, you can present prompt screens from a CL procedure and have user interaction with complete function key support.

While CL procedures also can read database files, writing database files is not supported. Files can be processed in two different ways. First, they can be processed record by record, the same way RPG programs can. Second, they can be processed as a whole—like other objects.

RECORD-BY-RECORD PROCESSING OF A FILE

CL procedures can process database and display files. Before a file can be processed record by record, however, it must be declared to the CL procedure using the Declare File (DCLF) command. A CL procedure can have up to five DCLF commands.

The DCLF Command

The DCLF command has three parameters. The first parameter, FILE, identifies the file being declared. You must enter the name of the file (which can be qualified with a library name). The second parameter, RCDFMT, lists the record formats that will be known to the CL procedure. It defaults to *ALL to give you a shortcut. If you are going to use a file (such as a display file) that has many record formats, but you will use only one or two in your procedure, it is to your advantage to list only those record formats you will use in the procedure in the RCDFMT parameter. Your program object will become smaller when compiled, and your compile listing will be less cluttered. The third parameter, OPNID, is optional, and defaults to *NONE, if only one file is declared. This value is used to distinguish one file from another. The OPNID must be referenced in all operations that pertain to the file, such as RCVF, SNDRCVF, SNDF, ENDRCV, and WAIT.

If your file was created from DDS, the CL procedure will know all the fields contained in the file because the CL compiler grabs the external-file definition. The CL procedure can use any of the fields as CL variables. For a file whose OPNID is *NONE (the default value), the variable name is the field name prefixed with an ampersand. For example, if a file has a field named TYPE, you can expect to find variable &TYPE in your procedure. This definition of variables is automatic, and you can use &TYPE as you would any other variable. If the OPNID parameter has some other value, each variable name consists of the leading ampersand, the OPNID value (without trailing blanks), an underscore character, and the field name. For example, if a file is declared with OPNID(F1) and has two fields named FILE and LIB, the CL compiler would automatically declare two variables named &F1_FILE and &F1_LIB.

If the file you are reading was created without DDS, the CL procedure has no way of knowing what fields you are using in the file. Therefore, the compiler creates only one variable, that has the same name as the file, and declares it as type (*CHAR). The variable's length is the same as the length of the record. For example, suppose you created FILE2 by running the command shown in Figure 9.1.

```
CRTPF mylib/file2 RCDLEN(256)
```

Figure 9.1: An example of creating a file with the CRTPF command.

When you declare the file in a CL procedure with the DCLF command, remember that you must use variable &FILE2, which will be a 256-byte character string. Use the %SST function to extract the parts you need.

The RCVF, WAIT, and ENDRCV Commands

The Receive File (RCVF) command is what CL procedures use to read the file declared with the DCLF command. RCVF always reads one record. If you process several RCVF commands, the file will be read sequentially. If the file member contains no more records, RCVF issues the escape message CPF0864 (end of file was detected).

Four parameters are defined to RCVF, and all of them are optional. The first, DEV, allows you to specify the name of a display device from which data is read. By using a variable in this parameter, you can retrieve data from different devices by changing the value of the variable. The default value for the DEV parameter is *FILE, which indicates that data is to be received from the display file declared with DCLF.

The second parameter, RCDFMT, is necessary when there are two or more record formats in a file. You may use the default value, *FILE, when there is only one record format in the file.

The OPNID parameter specifies which declared file is to be accessed. This value must match the OPNID parameter of the DCLF command.

The last parameter, WAIT, applies only to display files. WAIT accepts two values—*YES (the default) and *NO. WAIT(*YES) causes the system to suspend execution of the CL procedure until the input operation is complete. WAIT(*NO) causes the system to continue to execute CL commands until it encounters a corresponding WAIT command.

The WAIT command accepts two, both optional, parameters. The first, DEV, may contain a CL variable that contains the name of a display device from which input is expected. A value of *NONE means that no device need be specified.

The second parameter, OPNID, must match the OPNID for the DCLF command and the corresponding RCVF command in order to link WAIT with the appropriate RCVF command.

To cancel a wait state, use the End Receive (ENDRCV) command. Like WAIT, EN-DRCV has DEV and OPNID parameters. However, the DEV parameter differs in that it requires a literal device name rather than a CL variable.

RCVF and Random Input

In combination with the Override with Database File (OVRDBF) command, RCVF can read a database file randomly by record number, by key, or in reverse sequential order. All you need to do is use OVRDBF for the file being read and indicate the desired record in the POSITION parameter. Then use RCVF to read the record. For instance, suppose you want to read record number 725 of FILE1. You could use the code as shown in Figure 9.2.

```
OVRDBF file1 POSITION(*RRN 725)
RCVF
```

Figure 9.2: Reading a specific record in a database file.

Suppose you need to read the record immediately before the record that has a key value of 'ABC' in a keyed file with three key fields. You would use code as shown in Figure 9.3.

```
OVRDBF file1 POSITION(*KEYB 1 FILE1R 'ABC')
RCVF
```

Figure 9.3: Reading the record prior to key 'ABC'.

*KEYB indicates that the next RCVF will read a record by key. The "B" means that a "key before" type of read is requested. The "1" indicates that you are using only one key field in the file. FILE1R is the name of the record format that has the key. "ABC" is the key value.

RPG programmers can think of OVRDBF as SETGT or SETLL, and RCVF as a READ or READP. In the preceding example, OVRDBF acts like SETLL and RCVF acts like READP.

The technique just presented (using OVRDBF and RCVF) to emulate random reads by key fails in one particular case. If the last key field of the database file is of type character and is not full (this field's last byte is blank), RCVF cannot read the file randomly by key. For example, if the key to the file is 4 bytes long and there is record with a key "ABC " (ABC plus a blank), OVRDBF and RCVF won't be able to find this record using *KEY. Use *KEYBE and repeat RCVF until you find the record you want.

Note: Another technique is to use a character variable that is 1 byte longer than the key field, and place any non-blank character in the last position. Then you can issue an OVRDBF with *KEY (Figure 9.4) and it will work okay.

```
DCL &key_plus_1 *CHAR     5 /* Key plus one byte: The key length is 4 */

CHGVAR &key_plus_1 (&key *CAT 'X')
OVRDBF file1 POSITION(*KEY 0 *N &key_plus_1)
RCVF
```

Figure 9.4: Positioning a file read using a key that is 1 byte longer than the file key.

Note: Variable &KEY is the file key (4 bytes long). You can build variable &KEY_PLUS_1 using the key value plus the letter X so the last byte is not blank. Then use OVRDBF just like before.

Notice the use of 0 and *n in the position parameter. These are shortcuts. If you want to use the full key (all key fields), use zero instead of the actual number of fields. And if there is only one record format, you can use *n instead of its name.

The SNDF and SNDRCVF Commands

The Send File (SNDF) command cannot be used on database files because CL procedures are not allowed to write into them. You can use the SNDF command to write a display file record, which means an output-only operation to present a panel to the interactive user.

If you follow the SNDF command with the RCVF command, you are actually displaying a panel and waiting for user input. You also can use the Send Receive File (SNDRCVF) command, which combines the two operations in a single command. In RPG terms, this command would be an EXFMT operation.

If the panel uses any indicators, they become &INXX logical variables to your CL procedure. For example, the panel may allow F3=Exit and F12=Cancel. You can use the code shown in Figure 9.5 to terminate the procedure.

```
DCLF dspfile

SNDRCVF RCDFMT(options)

IF (&in03 *OR &in12) +
    RETURN
```

Figure 9.5: An example of allowing F3 or F12 to terminate your procedure.

Another way to code the procedure is shown in Figure 9.6.

```
DCLF dspfile

SNDRCVF RCDFMT(options)

IF (&in03 *EQ '1' *OR &in12 *EQ '1') +
    RETURN
```

Figure 9.6: An alternative method for coding F3 or F12 to terminate your procedure.

The *EQ '1' business is not required because both &IN03 and &IN12 are logical variables. You can use whichever method you like. (You also can test if an indicator is off with the *NOT logical operator. An example would be IF (*NOT &IN05) to check whether indicator 05 is off. Using the other coding method, you can compare &IN05 against '0'.)

Similarly, you can turn indicators on or off before or after you present the panel. For example, you can highlight fields that have conditioning indicators in the DDS of the display file for such display attributes as high intensity or underline. Remember that any indicators used in the DDS of the display file become known to the CL procedure as logical variables &IN01 to &IN99. The command shown in Figure 9.7 turns on indicator 21.

```
CHGVAR &in21 '1'
```

Figure 9.7: Using CHGVAR command to turn on indicator 21.

The CLOSE Command

The CLOSE command closes a file that was defined with the DCLF command. Once the file is closed, it is available for processing again. The first RCVF after a close of that same file re-opens the file. CLOSE accepts one parameter—the open identifier. For an example, see Figure 9.8.

```
PGM

DCLF    FILE(TempList)  OPNID(Temp)
... omitted lines ...
DOWHILE '1'
   RCVF   OPNID(Temp)
   MONMSG  CPF0864  EXEC(LEAVE)   /* end of file */
... omitted lines ...
ENDDO
CLOSE   OPNID(Temp)
/* the file may be re-opened by issuing another RCVF */
```

Figure 9.8: As of V6R1, you may close a file manually.

PROCESSING A FILE AS A WHOLE

CL procedures also can process files as another type of object. In this case, the entire file is processed as a whole and you are not limited to one file per CL procedure. Furthermore, you don't use the DCLF command to declare the file.

Creating and Deleting Files

CL procedures can be used to create and delete files by coding the appropriate commands in the CL procedure. For example, you can create a physical file with the Create Physical File (CRTPF) command and later delete it with the Delete File (DLTF) command.

Remember that you don't need DDS to create a physical file if you are willing to give up the benefits of external file definition. Keep in mind that creating and deleting files is a somewhat resource-intensive process that should be kept to a minimum. It is more efficient to create the files once and leave them in the libraries.

Processing Database File Members

Database files can be processed at the member level with the following commands:

- Add Physical File Member (ADDPFM) and Add Logical File Member (ADDLFM).

- Change Physical File Member (CHGPFM) and Change Logical File Member (CHGLFM).

- Remove Member (RMVM).

- Clear Physical File Member (CLRPFM).

- Reorganize Physical File Member (RGZPFM).

For example, suppose you have created a work file (WORKFILE) for a job. This work file is not created and deleted each time the procedure runs. To improve performance, the work file is left in the library between job runs.

Because it exists all the time, the job must ensure that there is no data from previous runs left over. The easiest way to make sure is to run the CLRPFM command to erase all data that exists. If no data exists, CLRPFM will do nothing.

This technique works when the procedure is run by only one person at a time. An example would be a program that is always submitted to the same single-threaded job queue. Because the job queue is single-threaded, it runs only one job at once. But what if the programmer cannot guarantee that two or more people won't attempt to run the same program at the same time?

One solution is to use different *members* and assign each job a separate member. This member must be added (ADDPFM command) at the beginning of the job and removed (RMVM command) at the end. Each member must have a different name. To assign unique names, you can use the six-digit job number (as shown in Figure 9.8).

```
DCL &jobnbr      *CHAR    6
DCL &mbr         *CHAR    10

RTVJOBA NBR(&jobnbr)
CHGVAR &mbr ('JOB' *CAT &jobnbr)
ADDPFM FILE(...) MBR(&mbr)

/* Processing */

RMVM FILE(...) MBR(&mbr)
```

Figure 9.8: Assigning a unique name to a member using the six-digit job number.

This method for using temporary files is not foolproof; use it with care. The program is provided only as an example of using ADDPFM and RMVM. One of the problems with this method is that the job might be canceled before it has a chance to run RMVM, and that leaves unwanted data in the database file.

The OVRXXXF and DLTOVR Commands

Files can be overridden for a number of reasons. Database files, in particular, can be overridden for three important reasons:

- They are not in any library of the library list. Rather than change the library list, the programmer can issue an Override with Database File (OVRDBF) command (Figure 9.9), which indicates that file FILE1 must be obtained from MYLIB.

```
OVRDBF file1 TOFILE(mylib/file1)
```

Figure 9.9: Telling the procedure to obtain a file that is not in the library list.

- The HLL program to be called refers to the file by a different name. Again, the OVRDBF solves this problem. In Figure 9.10, the HLL program uses file SOURCE, but the CL programmer wants to process QRPGSRC in library QGPL.

```
OVRDBF source TOFILE(QGPL/QRGPSRC)
CALL ...
```

Figure 9.10: Telling a program to use a file of another name.

- The CL programmer wants the HLL program being called to process a particular member of the database file—not the first one.

```
OVRDBF source TOFILE(QGPL/QRGPSRC)
CALL ...
```

Figure 9.11: Telling a program to use member WORKMBR of database file FILE1.

In this case, the program being called will process member WORKMBR. Left to itself, the system would have processed the first member by default.

Printer and display files also can be overridden with the Override with Printer File (OVRPRTF) and Override with Display File (OVRDSPF) commands. For example, suppose you created file INVPRT to print invoices on form INVOICE, which has a form size of 25 lines by 80 columns. Now you need to print invoice images on regular stock paper. Run the OVRPRTF command in Figure 9.12 before you call the HLL program that prints them.

```
OVRPRTF invprt FORMTYPE(*STD) PAGESIZE(66 132) OVRFLW(60)
```

Figure 9.12: Using the OVRPRTF command to change form attributes for the job.

When you use any of the override commands (OVRXXXF), remember the following rules:

- The override applies only to the current and following levels in the call stack. If you CALL a program that performs an override, the override will no longer be effective when control returns to your program.

- The system will activate only one override at each call level. If you override a database file with the TOFILE parameter now, and a few statements later perform another override with the MBR parameter, the file will be overridden only in member. If you suspect the file has been overridden and want to start over, run the Delete Overrides (DLTOVR) command first to delete any overrides currently in effect before you issue new ones.

Note: You can always use the Display Overrides (DSPOVR) command to check out what overrides a file might have at any moment.

Sorting with OPNQRYF

The Open Query File (OPNQRYF) command probably is the best method to sort files for later use. With OPNQRYF, you can specify what file or files to use, perform calculations on the fields from the files used, and select and sort the records based on the original fields or the calculated results. Because a detailed discussion of OPNQRYF fills a book by itself, OPNQRYF is described briefly here. For additional information, see MC Press' *Open Query File Magic!* by Ted Holt.

OPNQRYF uses the external file definition; the record layout DDS is provided when the file is created. You can reference the fields by their names (instead of by their absolute beginning and ending positions). Doing so gives you flexibility because you don't have to worry about changing the parameters of OPNQRYF if your file changes at some future date. The steps to use OPNQRYF for one file are as follows:

- Override the database file with SHARE(*YES) using the Override with Database File (OVRDBF) command. This command makes the HLL program that reads the query file use a shared open data path (ODP) for the file in question, rather than creating a new ODP when it opens the file.

- Run OPNQRYF. OPNQRYF creates an open data path over the data file(s) being queried.

- Run your HLL program to make use of the sorted file. Your HLL program must reference the file by its original name and can be coded as keyed or sequential access (it makes no difference). Again, because you created an open data path, the HLL program will use that data path and not open another. The HLL uses the sorted file (not the original file).

- Close the file with the Close File (CLOF) command.

- Delete the override with the Delete Override (DLTOVR) command.

The following CL program illustrates the entire procedure. An inventory master file (INVMST) is defined in Figure 9.13.

```
....+....1....+....2....+....3....+....4....+....5....+....6....+....7
       A            R IMREC
       A              IMITEM    15A       COLHDG('Item Number')
       A              IMTYPE    1A        COLHDG('Item' 'Type')
       A              IMCLAS    2A        COLHDG('Item' 'Class')
       A              IMCOST    7P  2      COLHDG('Standard' 'Cost')
       A                                 EDTCDE(1)
       A              IMPRCE    9P  2      COLHDG('Sell' 'Price')
       A                                 EDTCDE(1)
       A              IMDESC    30A       COLHDG('Item Description')
       A              IMDRAW    15A       COLHDG('Engineering' 'Drawing')
       A              IMLVL     3P  0      COLHDG('Level' 'Number')
       A                                 EDTCDE(3)
       A            K IMITEM
```

Figure 9.13: Inventory master file (INVMST).

Now suppose you need to write an HLL program—to list the inventory master file by item number and class code—that includes only the records that have "1" in the item type field. You can code the CL program as shown in Figure 9.14.

```
OVRDBF invmst SHARE(*YES)

   OPNQRYF invmst QRYSLT('imtype *EQ ''1''') +
           KEYFLD((imclas) (imitem))
   CALL ...
   CLOF invmst
   DLTOVR invmst
```

Figure 9.14: Using OPNQRYF to pre-select the items to be included in a report.

The OPNQRYF command creates the shared data path. OPNQRYF sorts the file by item by class (which means that the records will be sorted by item number for each item class) and selects only those records that have an item type equal to "1". Your HLL program is executed and the report prints. The CLOF command closes the open data path and DLTOVR removes the override. Remember that your HLL program must reference the file as INVMST.

> *Note:* When OPNQRYF is processing very large files and/or selecting more than 80 percent of the records in a file member, you can improve performance by allowing OPNQRYF to use a sort routine instead of access paths. To permit the use of a sort, specify ALWCPYDTA(*OPTIMIZE). This does not guarantee that OPNQRYF will use a sort routine. The query engine may choose to use an access path instead.

CAPTURING OUTPUT USING QTEMP

QTEMP is a temporary library that exists only between the beginning and the end of a job. The system creates a QTEMP library (a different QTEMP library) for each job when the job begins, and it deletes the job's QTEMP library when the job ends. Each job has a different QTEMP. If you create an object in your job's QTEMP, no other job in the system can use that object.

QTEMP is the ideal place to put all the objects you create that are needed for the duration of the job only. For example, some commands or programs could create work files that contain data extracted from several files, which will be used to print a report. The work file has no further use after printing the report. Work files are by no means the only example and *FILE is not the only type of object you can put in QTEMP.

Because QTEMP is deleted when the job ends (either normally or abnormally), all objects placed in QTEMP will be lost at that time. If you create many objects in QTEMP in your interactive session, the SIGNOFF command will take a while to sign you off and present the sign-on screen again. During this time, the system will be busy deleting the many objects in QTEMP and then QTEMP itself.

Using Permanent Work Files

Frequently, you will need to create work files for temporary use. For example, you might have to design a report that gathers information from several files and performs many selections before it prints the report. Resist the temptation to create a "flat" file without DDS to describe the fields. It might be faster, but you lose the capability to use external file definitions in your procedures. Also, program maintenance becomes more difficult. Get into the habit of creating permanent work files in your production libraries. You should put work files in the same library where you create the programs that use them. For example, you can create the file MYLIB/WORKFILE after you write the DDS for the file.

Each time you need to use the permanent file, create a duplicate in QTEMP (as in Figure 9.17). The copy in QTEMP will automatically share the complete record definition you provided with the DDS. In order to use the file, all you need to do is override it so the QTEMP copy is used instead of the original.

```
PGM

    CRTDUPOBJ workfile mylib *file qtemp

    OVRDBF workfile TOFILE(qtemp/workfile)

    /* Rest of the CL procedure goes here.  All references to WORKFILE */
    /* automatically apply to the copy in QTEMP, not to the original.*/

ENDPGM
```

Figure 9.17: Example of using permanent work files.

To simplify the task of creating these copies in QTEMP, appendix A includes the Create Work File (CRTWRKF) command. Figure 9.18 shows an example of using CRTWRKF instead of CRTDUPOBJ.

```
PGM

    CRTWRKF MODEL(mylib/workfile)

    OVRDBF workfile TOFILE(qtemp/workfile)

    /* Rest of the CL procedure goes here.  All references to WORKFILE */
    /* automatically apply to the copy in QTEMP, not to the original.*/

ENDPGM
```

Figure 9.18: Example of using the CRTWRKF utility.

Because it resides in QTEMP, the system automatically deletes the file when the job ends.

Using Outfiles

i5/OS commands that begin with the verb Display (DSP) are meant to produce output to the display station or to the printer. For example, the Display Program (DSPPGM) command shows information about a particular program. Its OUTPUT parameter determines where the information is presented. If the user selects * (the default value for the OUTPUT parameter), output goes to the display (if the command runs interactively) or to the printer (if the command runs in batch). If the user selects *PRINT, the output goes to the printer.

Other commands have a third option named *OUTFILE. In this case, output is directed to a database file you specify. For example, consider the command shown in Figure 9.19.

```
DSPOBJD OBJ(qgpl/*ALL) OBJTYPE(*ALL) OUTPUT(*OUTFILE) +
        OUTFILE(qtemp/objects) OUTMBR(*FIRST *REPLACE)
```

Figure 9.19: Using an OUTFILE with DSPOBJD.

The system will run the Display Object Description (DSPOBJD) command but, instead of displaying or printing the information gathered, the information goes to the first member of file QTEMP/OBJECTS and replaces whatever records might have been there. If file QTEMP/OBJECTS doesn't exist, it is automatically created.

The command executed (DSPOBJD) contains help text for all parameters. If you press the Help key while the cursor is on the OUTFILE parameter, the help text will tell you the name of the QSYS file that is used as a "model" for the file created.

In the case of the DSPOBJD command, the model outfile is QSYS/QADSPOBJ. You can use the Display File Field Description (DSPFFD) command to get the layout of QADSPOBJ's record. The layout will show you what information you are getting in the outfile, and where it is within the record.

Outfiles can be processed in CL procedures. For example, suppose you have approximately 200 user profiles on your system. For administrative purposes, you must change every profile that belongs to group profile GRP_A so it belongs to group profile GRP_B. If you performed this task manually, it would be an extremely tiresome, time-consuming, and error-prone job. Instead, you can write a CL procedure (let's name it CHGGRPPRF) as shown in Figure 9.20.

```
PGM (&oldgrpprf &newgrpprf)

    DCL &newgrpprf  *CHAR  10
    DCL &oldgrpprf  *CHAR  10

    DCLF qadspupb

    DSPUSRPRF *ALL TYPE(*BASIC) OUTPUT(*OUTFILE) +
              OUTFILE(qtemp/qadspupb)
    OVRDBF qadspupb TOFILE(qtemp/qadspupb)

loop:
    RCVF
    MONMSG cpf0864 EXEC(RETURN)
    IF (&upgrpf *EQ &oldgrpprf) DO
        CHGUSRPRF USRPRF(&upuprf) GRPPRF(&newgrpprf)
    ENDDO

    GOTO loop

ENDPGM
```

Figure 9.20: A CL procedure to automatically change the group profile in every user profile.

Now, execute the program and supply the old and new group profiles. All user profiles that had the old user profile will automatically be changed to the new group profile as shown in Figure 9.21.

```
CALL chggrpprf ('GRP_A' 'GRP_B')
```

Figure 9.21: Calling the program shown in Figure 9.19 and supplying old and new group profile names.

If you encounter this sort of situation often, you might consider creating a command so that you don't have to remember what parameters to pass and in what order. The program works by running the Display User Profile (DSPUSRPRF) command to an outfile. Because the outfile has the same name as the QSYS model (QADSPUPB), OVRDBF runs to make sure that the program uses the file in QTEMP instead of the empty QSYS model file.

The RCVF command is processed and reads a record from QTEMP/QADSPUPB. If the end of file is detected, CPF0864 is issued (which is trapped by the MONMSG command, resulting in an end of the program). Otherwise, the program compares the group profile name in the user profile just read (field &UPGRPF from the outfile) against &OLDGRPPRF. If they are equal, it changes the user profile (&UPUPRF) to the new group profile. Variables &UPGRPF and &UPUPRF come from the external definition of the outfile.

Capturing OUTPUT(*PRINT)

For those commands that don't offer the *OUTFILE option in the OUTPUT parameter, you can still process the output in a CL procedure if you direct the output to *PRINT and then read the printed report in the CL procedure. Here's what you need to do:

- Override the printer file to HOLD(*YES). You need to know the name of the printer file that is used by the command whose output you want to process. By holding the file, you ensure that it is not printed.

- Execute the command that has the output you want to process. Specify OUTPUT(*PRINT).

- Copy the spooled output to a physical file. The physical file must already exist without an external file definition. Use the Copy Spooled File (CPYSPLF) command to copy the spooled output to the physical file.

- Now you can process the physical file one record at a time. Remember that the file will contain the report headings, column headings, and footers of the normal printed output. These records will have to be recognized and ignored by the procedure.

■ Finally, delete the spooled file with the Delete Spooled File (DLTSPLF) command and remove the override to the printer file with the Delete Override (DLTOVR) command.

■ This process is automated by using the Convert Print to Physical File (CVTPRTF) command provided in appendix A.

10

USING QUOTES

Quotes are very important characters in CL procedures. In discussing this topic, it helps to first define the terms single quote, double quote, and apostrophe.

Single quote is the character ' when used to enclose a word or group of words such as 'this is a phrase.'

Double quote is the character " when used to enclose a word or group of words such as "this is what he said." Note that the double quote is one character (not two characters). Two single quotes in succession are, of course, two characters. The results do look the same, but to the computer the characters are represented differently.

Apostrophe is the character ' when used to indicate the omission of one or more letters such as in the word *ma'am*. In this case, the apostrophe takes the place of the letter *d*.

Programmers often use the terms single quote and apostrophe interchangeably. This chapter deals primarily with single quotes and there are a few references to double quotes. The term *apostrophe* isn't used. The term *quote* (without the single or double qualification) is used to mean single quote.

USING QUOTES IN CL

Quotes are used in CL to delimit character strings. For additional information, see the Chapter 3 description of constants.

In many cases, CL assumes the quotes. For example, you can code the CHGVAR command shown in Figure 10.1 in a CL procedure without causing errors during compile or execution time.

```
CHGVAR &endopt *REWIND
```

*Figure 10.1: Coding a CHGVAR command without quotes around the *REWIND constant.*

To be theoretically correct, this command should have been coded with quotes around *REWIND because *REWIND is a character constant that is being assigned to the &ENDOPT variable. See Figure 10.2.

```
CHGVAR &endopt '*REWIND'
```

*Figure 10.2: Coding a CHGVAR command with quotes around the *REWIND constant.*

Actually, both variations execute normally. The quotes can be omitted when the character constant contains no embedded blanks, quotes, special symbols, or lowercase letters.

EMBEDDED QUOTES

When a character string has a single quote character somewhere in the middle, you must double the single quote. For example, suppose you want to assign variable &SENTENCE the value "quick 'n' easy." This character string contains two occurrences of embedded single quotes. Figure 10.3 shows how to code the CHGVAR command in this example.

```
CHGVAR &sentence 'Quick ''n'' easy'
```

Figure 10.3: Coding embedded single quotes with two single quote characters.

As you can see, each embedded single quote became two single quotes in succession.

Expressions, Character Strings, and Command Strings

Some command parameters require an expression (logical or arithmetic), others require a character string, and others require command strings. Differentiating between them is important because only character strings require quotes around them.

Expression is a string of values separated by operands, such as A + B. You code an expression in the CHGVAR command (VALUE parameter) and in the IF and WHEN commands (COND parameter).

A *command string* is a string made up of a command name and parameter values, with or without keywords, separated by blanks—such as DSPMSG MSGQ (QSYSOPR). You code a command string in the IF and WHEN commands (THEN parameter), ELSE command (CMD parameter), MONMSG command (EXEC parameter), and SBMJOB command (CMD parameter).

A *character string* is a string of characters with no particular meaning except that it is a value that can be assigned to a character variable. Character strings have no syntax (unlike expressions and command strings). Character strings cannot be "wrong."

Some command parameters require that you enter a character string even though you might think that an expression or command string would be required. For example, the SBMJOB command's RQSDTA parameter can accept a command with parameters (but contained in a character string). Or consider the OPNQRYF command's QRYSLT parameter, which describes a condition similar to the IF command's COND parameter (except that the condition in the OPNQRYF command must be expressed in a character string). In both cases, you must enclose the string in single quotes—and double embedded single quotes, if any are found.

Multiple Quotes

Quotes sometimes have to be quadrupled or multiplied even further in certain cases. For example, suppose you want to code a SNDMSG command in a CL procedure, to send the message "I'm here" to the system operator. See Figure 10.5.

```
SNDMSG MSG('I''m here') TOMSGQ(qsysopr)
```

Figure 10.5: Coding quotes within quotes.

Suppose you now want to execute this command in batch mode. You need to use the SBMJOB command to place it in a job queue. Figure 10.6 shows how you can use the RQSDTA parameter, instead of the CMD parameter, to indicate which message to send.

```
SBMJOB RQSDTA('SNDPGMMSG MSG(''I''''m here'') TOMSGQ(qsysopr)')
```

Figure 10.6: Example of three levels of embedded quotes.

Using an &QUOTE Variable

When you start getting creative in your string manipulations in CL, you probably will have to concatenate several strings together, and you possibly will have to concatenate single quotes to longer strings. Figure 10.7 shows how a constant that contains just a single quote character is represented in CL.

```
''''
```

Figure 10.7: Representing an embedded single quote.

As you can imagine, a long expression that contains many *CAT operators and many single quotes can quickly become confusing. Rather than use single quote constants, it is better to declare a variable named &QUOTE at the beginning of the procedure. See Figure 10.8.

```
DCL &quote       *CHAR    1  VALUE('''')
```

Figure 10.8: Defining a variable with quotes.

From then on, you can use variable &QUOTE instead of the single quote literal. To appreciate the use of this variable, consider the OPNQRYF example shown in Figure 10.9. OPNQRYF will be used to select all records that have a state code equal to CA from a customer file.

```
OPNQRYF FILE((customer)) QRYSLT('state *EQ ''CA''')
```

Figure 10.9: An example of using the OPNQRYF command with hard-coded quote characters.

To add flexibility, however, you might want to replace the hard-coded value of CA with a two-character variable named &STCODE. See Figure 10.10. This way the same OPNQRYF command could be used to select records from NY, KS, FL, or any other state.

```
OPNQRYF FILE((customer)) QRYSLT('state *EQ ''' *CAT &stcode *CAT '''')
```

Figure 10.10: A more complex example of hard-coded quote characters.

Instead of the command shown in Figure 10.10, you can use the &QUOTE variable, as shown in Figure 10.11.

```
OPNQRYF FILE((customer)) +
        QRYSLT('state *EQ ' *CAT &quote *CAT &stcode *CAT &quote)
```

Figure 10.11: Using a variable instead of hard-coded quote characters.

193

11

MANAGING OBJECTS

Objects can be managed in CL procedures just as easily as they are managed manually from the command line. Depending on what type of object is being created, objects are created with different CRTXXX commands. For example, you create an output queue with the Create Output Queue (CRTOUTQ) command.

CREATING OBJECTS: THE CRTXXX COMMANDS

Most CRTXXX commands assume that the object doesn't exist when the CRTXXX command is executed. CRTXXX commands that have a REPLACE parameter such as CRTRPGPGM are an exception. Executing a CRTXXX command manually is not difficult because, if an error message is received, the user can analyze the problem. However, CL procedures are not that smart. If a CL procedure encounters a CRTXXX command, it will try to execute it. If the CRTXXX command fails because the object is already there, the CL procedure will stop with an inquiry message.

Of course, this is not the only reason why a CRTXXX command might fail. Specifying an invalid value in a parameter or a nonexistent library as the place to put the object will also cause a CRTXXX command to fail. If there is any chance that your CRTXXX commands will fail, you should make sure you trap error messages with the MONMSG command, either at the program level or at the command level.

For instance, the code shown in Figure 11.1 attempts to create a data area named INVOICE in library QGPL. If that data area already exists, i5/OS will send escape message CPF1023 (Data area INVOICE exists in QGPL). Because the programmer cannot be sure whether this data area is already in QGPL when the CL procedure runs, the CRTDTAARA command is immediately followed by a MONMSG command.

```
CRTDTAARA qgpl/invoice *CHAR 10
MONMSG cpf102
```

Figure 11.1: Creating a data area and using MONMSG to trap an error condition.

The approach shown in Figure 11.2 is better because the message CPF1023 is removed from the job log.

```
CRTDTAARA qgpl/invoice *CHAR 10
MONMSG cpf1023 EXEC(DO)
   RCVMSG MSGTYPE(*EXCP) RMV(*YES)
ENDDO
```

Figure 11.2: Creating a data area, trapping a potential error message with MONMSG, and then removing it from the job log.

DELETING OBJECTS: THE DLTXXX COMMANDS

Depending on the type of object being deleted, deleting objects also requires different commands. For example, you can delete a program with the DLTPGM command.

Deleting objects can produce error messages, too. Because the object could be in use at the time the DLTXXX command is carried out or you might not have enough authority to the object to delete it (it takes *OBJEXIST authority), error messages are more likely to be issued when you delete than when you create objects. The code shown in Figure 11.3 attempts to delete a file. Note that there are three MONMSG commands following it; each one traps a different problem.

```
DLTF datafile

MONMSG cpf2105 EXEC(DO)
   /* File does not exist */
   RCVMSG MSGTYPE(*EXCP) RMV(*YES)
   CHGVAR &error 'F'
ENDDO

MONMSG cpf3202 EXEC(DO)
   /* File is in use */
   RCVMSG MSGTYPE(*EXCP) RMV(*YES)
   CHGVAR &error 'U'
ENDDO

MONMSG cpf3219 EXEC(DO)
   /* Logical file exists */
   RCVMSG MSGTYPE(*EXCP) RMV(*YES)
   CHGVAR &error 'L'
ENDDO
```

Figure 11.3: An example of deleting an object and checking for potential error messages.

After this code runs, variable &ERROR will contain different codes (depending on the reason why DLTF failed). Your CL procedure then can take corrective actions appropriate to each case.

CHECKING EXISTENCE: THE CHKOBJ COMMAND

Depending on whether or not an object exists, CL procedures often need to perform one action or another. You can use the Check Object (CHKOBJ) command in a CL procedure, REXX procedure, from the keyboard, or QCMDEXC. CHKOBJ accepts two parameters that identify the object:

1. OBJ, where you enter the qualified name of the object.

2. OBJTYPE, where you enter the code that indicates what type of object you are checking for (such as *MSGQ for message queue).

If the object type is *FILE, you have the option to use the MBR parameter to enter a member's name to check its existence. If you don't want to check for a specific member, leave the MBR parameter at its default value of *NONE and no checking will occur.

Also, CHKOBJ can check that the user who runs the CL procedure has the proper authority to the object. For example, Figure 11.4 shows how you can check that the user has *USE authority by coding AUT(*USE). Again, you should leave the AUT parameter at its default value of *NONE if you are not interested in checking authorities.

```
CHKOBJ mylib/myfile *FILE MBR(abc) AUT(*USE)
```

Figure 11.4: An example of using the CHKOBJ command to check for existence of an object.

When CHKOBJ runs, it issues different *escape messages* if any of the conditions being checked are not met. If all conditions are met, CHKOBJ issues no messages. Table 11.1 lists the messages that are available.

Table 11.1: Escape Messages for the CHKOBJ Command	
Message ID	**Error Condition**
CPF9801	Object not found. The system could not find file MYFILE in library MYLIB.
CPF9802	User not authorized to the object. The user does not have *USE authority to file MYFILE.
CPF9803	Cannot allocate the object. Someone has allocated file MYFILE for exclusive use.
CPF9804	Object is damaged. File MYFILE is damaged. You should have a backup.
CPF9805	Object is destroyed. Now you definitely need a backup.

Table 11.1: Escape Messages for the CHKOBJ Command, continued

Message ID	Error Condition
CPF9810	Library not found. Library MYLIB does not exist.
CPF9815	Member not found. File MYFILE does not have a member by the name of ABC.
CPF9820	Not authorized to use library. User does not have the authority to use library MYLIB.
CPF9830	Cannot assign library &1.
CPF9899	Error occurred during processing of command.

RETRIEVING DESCRIPTION: THE RTVOBJD COMMAND

With the Retrieve Object Description (RTVOBJD) command, you can gain access to basic information about objects and pass the information to CL variables. For example, one of the parameters, RTNLIB, tells you which library (among all libraries of your library list) is the one that contains the object. You can create the program shown in Figure 11.5 to make the system find an object for you.

```
/******************************************************************/
/*                                                                */
/* To compile:                                                    */
/*                                                                */
/*    Install utility command FWDPGMMSG (see Appendix A)          */
/*                                                                */
/*    CRTCLPGM PGM(xxx/FNDOBJ) SRCFILE(xxx/QCLSRC)                */
/*                                                                */
/******************************************************************/
PGM (&obj &objtype)

    DCL &obj        *CHAR   10
    DCL &objtype    *CHAR   10
    DCL &rtnlib     *CHAR   10
```

Figure 11.5: A program to identify the library that contains a specified object (part 1 of 2).

```
        /* Program-level MONMSG to trap any errors that may */
        /* be produced by RTVOBJD command */
        MONMSG cpf0000 EXEC(GOTO error)

        /* Retrieve the object's library */
        RTVOBJD &obj &objtype RTNLIB(&rtnlib)

        SNDPGMMSG MSG(&objtype *BCAT &obj *BCAT 'found in library' +
                     *BCAT &rtnlib) MSGTYPE(*INFO)

        RETURN

    error:
        FWDPGMMSG
        MONMSG cpf0000

    ENDPGM
```

Figure 11.5: A program to identify the library that contains a specified object (part 2 of 2).

Notice that the program makes use of utility command Forward Program Messages (FWDPGMMSG), which is provided in appendix A. To use the program, run the CALL command and supply the following parameters to program FNDOBJ:

- The name of the object to be found (no library qualifier).

- The type of object, such as *PGM or *FILE.

- For example, Figure 11.6 finds program PGM001.

```
    CALL fndobj (pgm001 *PGM)
```

Figure 11.6: Calling the FNDOBJ program to locate a program named PGM001.

If program PGM001 is found, you'll get an informational message that tells you where it was found. If the program is not found or, if the object type isn't correct, you will get an escape message.

RETRIEVING DESCRIPTION: THE RTVMBRD COMMAND

Just as RTVOBJD lets you retrieve information about an object, the Retrieve Member Description (RTVMBRD) command allows you to retrieve important information about file members, and to place this information in CL variables. For example, you can determine in a CL procedure how many records exist in a member, how many are deleted, whether the member is in a source or data file, source type (if in a source file), and text. You also can find out other important statistics such as date of last use, date of last change, date of last save, and date of last restore.

Two parameters identify the member to be retrieved. The FILE parameter receives the qualified name of the file.

The MBR parameter can contain two values. The first value receives the name of the member or *FIRST (the default value), *LAST, *FIRSTMBR, or *LASTMBR. The second value is optional and can contain *SAME, *NEXT, or *PRV.

Note: The difference between *FIRSTMBR and *FIRST is that *FIRST-MBR processes the first member in an alphabetic list of members (the member whose name has the lowest collating sequence), while *FIRST processes the member that was added first to the file (the oldest member). *LASTMBR and *LAST have a similar difference.

For example, you can retrieve the second member by specifying MBR(*FIRSTMBR *NEXT). If the file contains a member named ABC, you can retrieve the member prior to that by specifying MBR('ABC' *PRV).

The program skeleton shown in Figure 11.7 illustrates a mechanism so that you can process all members in a file.

```
    DCL &file      *CHAR   10
    DCL &lib       *CHAR   10
    DCL &mbr       *CHAR   10

    /* Retrieve name of first member */
    RTVMBRD &lib/&file MBR(*FIRSTMBR) RTNMBR(&mbr)
    MONMSG cpf0000 EXEC(GOTO end_mbrs)

    /* Process the member named &MBR */
process:
    /* Place here any commands you want to run on every member. */
    /* The name of the "current" member is contained in &MBR.   */

    /* Retrieve name of next member */
    RTVMBRD &lib/&file MBR(&mbr *NEXT) RTNMBR(&mbr)
    MONMSG cpf0000 EXEC(GOTO end_mbrs)

    GOTO process

end_mbrs:
    /* End */
```

Figure 11.7: A CL program that loops to process all members in a file.

CREATING DUPLICATES: THE CRTDUPOBJ COMMAND

The Create Duplicate Object (CRTDUPOBJ) command is an oddity. It could have been more appropriately named Copy Object (CPYOBJ). Also, its parameters don't conform to those of other commands. IBM did not use a qualified name to identify the object to be duplicated, but decided to use two separate parameters for the object (OBJ) and its library (FROMLIB). This difference poses a difficulty because before V4R5, the FROMLIB parameter did not allow the use of *LIBL, which forced the programmer to hard code the library in the FROMLIB parameter.

As an example, suppose you want to assign your department's workstations to a different interactive subsystem, which is to be called PGMRQINTER. Rather than using the Create Subsystem Description (CRTSBSD) command to create a new subsystem from scratch, you can use CRTDUPOBJ to create a duplicate ("clone") of QINTER (see Figure 11.8).

```
CRTDUPOBJ OBJ(qinter) FROMLIB(qsys) OBJTYPE(*SBSD) +
          TOLIB(mylib) NEWOBJ(pgmrqinter)
```

Figure 11.8: Using CRTDUPOBJ instead of CRTSBSD to create a new subsystem.

As of V4R5, you may use the special values *LIBL and *CURLIB in the FROMLIB parameter. In a CL procedure under a prior release, you can avoid hard coding the name of the library in the FROMLIB parameter by using the technique shown in Figure 11.9.

```
DCL &lib        *CHAR   10

RTVOBJD *LIBL/qinter *SBSD RTNLIB(&lib)

CRTDUPOBJ OBJ(qinter) FROMLIB(&lib) OBJTYPE(*SBSD) +
          TOLIB(mylib) NEWOBJ(pgmrqinter)
```

Figure 11.9: The technique to avoid hard coding a library name in the FROMLIB parameter.

Because the RTVOBJD command does allow *LIBL, it will locate QINTER for you, and put the name of its library in variable &LIB. You can then run the CRTDUPOBJ command using &LIB in the FROMLIB parameter. If the object being duplicated is a physical file, CRTDUPOBJ creates a duplicate file with the same members. The DATA parameter indicates whether the data should be duplicated, too. It defaults to *NO.

MANIPULATING OBJECTS: MOVOBJ, CHGOBJD, AND RNMOBJ

The Move Object (MOVOBJ), Change Object Description (CHGOBJD), and Rename Object (RNMOBJ) commands can be used either manually or in CL procedures. They perform different manipulations on objectss. MOVOBJ lets you take an object from one library into another. MOVOBJ is useful after objects have been thoroughly tested in one library and are ready to be placed into a production library.

The difference between MOVOBJ and CRTDUPOBJ is that MOVOBJ doesn't create a copy of the object. The object itself is transferred to another library. For example, if you use CRTDUPOBJ to copy a program from one library to another, the new program might not have the right owner (which means that adopted authority won't work as it should). Because CRTDUPOBJ creates a new object, you won't have to edit authorities for the new object all over again. MOVOBJ solves these problems as well as others.

CHGOBJD lets you change the text description of the object without recreating it. It also lets you reset the days-used counter to zero (which is maintained by the system). To do this, specify USECOUNT(*RESET).

RNMOBJ lets you change the name of an object. Again, you could use CRTDUPOBJ to do almost the same thing, but you would be creating a new object. RNMOBJ is more direct; it preserves all the authorities and statistics (such as date of last use) while it changes the name of the object. RNMOBJ also can be used to rename an entire library.

ALLOCATING: THE ALCOBJ COMMAND

If your job opens a file for input, the system automatically allocates the file to your job in such a way that other jobs also can read or update the file, but not rename or delete it. Because the system takes care of it, this feature is called *automatic allocation.*

Occasionally, however, you might want to allocate an object to your job before it is actually used. For example, suppose you design a CL program that is meant to execute in batch mode to produce a mass update on a database file. To guarantee that no one else is updating the file, you can easily allocate the file to the job even before the first HLL program opens the file.

This manual allocation is performed with the Allocate Object (ALCOBJ) command. The allocation (or "lock") remains in effect until the job ends or until you cancel the lock with the Deallocate Object (DLCOBJ) command.

Table 11.2 lists the different lock states and the limitations they impose on your job and other jobs on the system.

Table 11.2: Lock States and Job Attributes					
	Other Job's Attributes			**Your Job's Attributes**	
Lock State	Obj Mgt	Read	Update	Obj Mgt	Read	Update
*EXCL	Yes	Yes	Yes	No	No	No
*EXCLRD	No	Yes	Yes	No	Yes	No
*SHRUPD	No	Yes	Yes	No	Yes	Yes
*SHRNUP	No	Yes	No	No	Yes	No
*SHRRD	No	Yes	No	No	Yes	Yes

Almost all object types that can be allocated accept any of the five lock states listed above (*EXCL, *EXCLRD, *SHRUPD, *SHRNUP, and *SHRRD), with the following exceptions:

- *DEVD accepts *EXCLRD only.

- *LIB doesn't accept *EXCL. Also, locking a library doesn't lock the objects contained within.

- *MSGQ accepts *EXCL and *SHRRD only.

- *PNLGRP accepts *EXCL and *EXCLRD only.

- *PGM accepts *EXCL, *EXCLRD, and *SHRRD only. To prevent a program from running in more than one job, allocate it with *EXCL in the first job before it is called.

- *SBSD accepts *EXCL only.

The CL code shown in Figure 11.10 illustrates the use of the ALCOBJ command. This program calls several HLL programs that perform mass updates in various ways, and then does a member reorganization. Because the CL program does so much on a single file, it is allocated for exclusive use at first.

```
PGM

    /* Attempt to allocate FILEA. */
    /* If not successful, abort program. */

    ALCOBJ OBJ((filea *FILE *EXCL)) WAIT(0)
    MONMSG cpf0000 EXEC(DO)
        SNDPGMMSG MSGID(cpf9898) MSGF(qcpfmsg) +
                    MSGDTA('FILEA could not be allocated') +
                    MSGTYPE(*ESCAPE)
    ENDDO

    /* Processing begins */
    CALL pgm1   /* Some mass-update */
    CALL pgm2   /* More mass-update */
    CALL pgm3   /* Still more mass-update */
    CALL pgm4   /* Even more */

    RGZPFM filea   /* Remove deleted records */

    /* Deallocate FILEA */
    DLCOBJ OBJ((filea *FILE *EXCL))

ENDPGM
```

Figure 11.10: An example of the ALCOBJ command to allocate an object for exclusive use.

Because the ALCOBJ command is specified with WAIT(0), this program shouldn't wait any time at all if an exclusive lock cannot be acquired. The MONMSG that follows takes care of this failure (if it happens) by issuing an *ESCAPE message and ending the program. Otherwise, processing begins and programs PGM1 through PGM4 are executed.

The last program performs a mass delete (which deletes possibly hundreds of records from the file). In addition, the RGZPFM command removes the deleted records, and DLCOBJ is used to release the exclusive lock obtained at the start of the program.

If this program runs in batch mode, the DLCOBJ command could be omitted because all objects allocated are released when the job ends. If the program is run interactively, on the other hand, locks would remain in place until the user signs off (which might be a long time after this program ended).

When you are not sure which objects are allocated to a job, you can run the Work with Object Locks (WRKOBJLCK) command, which presents panels that list all the objects allocated to a job and the lock states requested. You also can use the Display Record Locks (DSPRCDLCK) command to display a list of jobs that have locks on database file records.

12

BATCH JOB PROCESSING

When you sign onto a display station, you start an *interactive processing* job in the system. The job is called interactive because there is interaction between you and the computer. You type in a command and the system responds. It asks a question, you answer the question, and then the system presents more information.

THE CONCEPT OF BATCH PROCESSING

Jobs also can run in a batch environment. The term *batch processing* probably comes from the early days of punched-card systems, such as the System/360, that didn't support interactive jobs. On a System/360, a job was a deck of punched cards that contained both the program and the data to be processed. This deck (or batch) of cards was submitted to the system for processing.

Computers have come a long way, but batch processing is still with us. In many cases, batch processing performs better than interactive processing. Because a batch job has no interaction with the user, a user's terminal is not tied up while the job is running. The job begins and, if it runs smoothly, it produces the expected result. Batch jobs are ideal for long-running tasks such as file updates, producing reports, and any activity—such as deleting a large library—that doesn't require input from the user once it is started.

JOB QUEUES

Batch jobs begin when they are submitted to a job queue. A job queue is another object in a library (type *JOBQ) that you can create, change, and delete yourself. The i5 supports any number of job queues.

In order to work, job queues must be attached to a subsystem (object type *SBSD). The subsystem also must be started (or "active") and the job queue must be released. If the job queue is held or the subsystem is ended, jobs submitted to the job queue will not run.

If you are not familiar with the concept of job queues, think of a job queue as the line that forms when you go to the supermarket. Each checkout counter is a job queue. If a cashier is there, the job queue is released. Each customer passes through and pays for groceries just as jobs submitted to a job queue are released for execution one at a time.

THE SBMJOB COMMAND

Submitting a job for batch processing is easy; all you need to do is run the Submit Job (SBMJOB) command. The command has two parameters that allow you to enter the command you want to execute in batch mode: CMD and RQSDTA. The CMD parameter is recommended.

Suppose you want to save a file to tape. This is an example of an activity that should be performed in batch mode. Begin by prompting for the SBMJOB command by keying in SBMJOB and pressing the F4 key.

Note that the first input field is the CMD parameter. Key in SAVOBJ and press the F4 key again. The system now prompts for the SAVOBJ command (which you can fill out at your leisure). When you press Enter, the system takes you back one level to the SBMJOB command prompter, where you will see the SAVOBJ command properly formatted. Now you can complete the rest of the SBMJOB prompts and press Enter. The CMD parameter can contain a command string of up to 3000 characters. The SBMJOB command has three other important parameters:

- The JOB parameter gives the batch job a name. You might not think naming a job is important, but it is. You don't have to come up with unique names for all your batch jobs, but the name should be descriptive. That way, when you look up which batch jobs are running, you will be able to quickly identify them. If you don't supply a name for the job, the system uses the name of the job description (in the JOBD parameter) as the job's name.

- The JOBQ parameter identifies the job queue where the job is submitted. It defaults to *JOBD, which means that the name of the job queue will be picked up from the job description.

- The JOBD parameter identifies the job description that contains all the settings and attributes of the job being submitted. It defaults to *USRPRF, which means that the name of the job description will be picked up from the requester's user profile.

All other parameters are overrides of one type or another and are optional. The RQSDTA parameter, however, deserves some explanation. You can use the RQSDTA parameter instead of the CMD parameter to enter the command you want to run in batch mode. Like the CMD parameter, RQSDTA can contain a maximum of 3000 characters. The RQSDTA parameter, however, has two disadvantages:

- The entire command string must be enclosed in single quotes. Therefore, embedded single quotes must be doubled, which can lead to mismatched quotes if you aren't careful.

- You cannot use the command prompter as you can when you use the CMD parameter. Therefore, you must know in advance the syntax of the command you are submitting to batch.

The RQSDTA parameter has one advantage over CMD, however. You can use CL variables instead of hard coding the command as a constant in your CL procedure. For example, the statement shown in Figure 12.1 is invalid.

```
        SBMJOB CMD(&cmdstr) JOBQ(qbatch)
```

Figure 12.1: Invalid use of the CMD parameter in a SBMJOB command.

The statement shown in Figure 12.1 is invalid even if &CMDSTR were a character variable that contained a syntactically correct command string. The CMD parameter cannot accept a variable for a command name. To use a variable, you must use the RQSDTA parameter as shown in Figure 12.2.

```
        SBMJOB RQSDTA(&cmdstr) JOBQ(qbatch)
```

Figure 12.2: Correctly using the RQSDTA parameter to pass a variable to the SBMJOB command.

AN UNEXPECTED PROBLEM WITH SBMJOB

The command in the CMD or RQSDTA parameter is passed to the new job as a request message. Any CL variables in the CMD parameter are resolved to the values they contain, before the message is built, because the new job won't be able to reference the submitting job's variables. For example, suppose a CL procedure submits a CLRPFM member command, as shown in Figure 12.3, and that variables &FILE, &LIB, and &MBR have the values "APXACTS", "MYLIB", and "BATCH00002", respectively.

```
    DCL        &file   *CHAR   10
    DCL        &lib    *CHAR   10
    DCL        &mbr    *CHAR   10
 ...
    SBMJOB     CMD(CLRPFM FILE(&lib/&file) MBR(&mbr)) +
                  JOB(clearmbr) JOBQ(qbatch)
```

Figure 12.3: Submitting a command with CL variables for batch processing.

When job CLEARMBR begins to run in batch mode, it retrieves the request message passed to it and sees the CLRPFM command (Figure 12.4). Notice that the new job sees the values that were in the CL variables (not the names of the variables).

```
CLRPFM FILE(MYLIB/APXACTS) MBR(BATCH00002)
```

Figure 12.4: The submitted job sees the values, not the names, of the submitting job's variables.

The submitted job, now running in batch, interprets the request message in the same way commands are interpreted when typed from a command line. (These rules are discussed in Chapter 5, under the topic Passing Constants as Parameters.)

This means that the SBMJOB command causes problems when you code a CALL in the CMD parameter (or RQSDTA parameter) and the command being called expects a character parameter longer than 32 characters or a decimal parameter that is not defined as 15 digits with five decimal places. In order to keep these problems from occurring, you should understand the following points:

- Character parameters are passed to the submitted job without trailing blanks.

- If the new batch job expects a character parameter longer than 32 bytes, but the value of the variable passed into that parameter—without trailing blanks—is shorter than the expected value, the new batch job reads garbage instead of the trailing blanks.

- The new batch job interprets all decimal parameters as 15-digit numbers with five decimal positions.

- For example, suppose that PGM1 expects a 64-character variable and you submit it with the command shown in Figure 12.5.

```
SBMJOB CMD(CALL pgm1 (&string))
```

Figure 12.5: An example of a potential problem where &STRING may contain garbage.

If &STRING is full (the last character is not a blank space), PGM1 will run fine. If &STRING ends in one or more blanks, however, you can almost bet that some of the trailing blanks will be replaced with garbage. To circumvent the problem, design PGM1 so that it expects a character string that is 1 byte longer than it needs to be, and use all but the last character. Your main CL program should then look like Figure 12.6.

```
DCL &string     *CHAR   64
DCL &stringx    *CHAR   65

CHGVAR &stringx (&string *CAT 'X')
SBMJOB CMD(CALL pgm1 (&stringx))
```

Figure 12.6: Circumventing the potential problem of garbage in a string passed with a CALL command.

PGM1 receives a 65-character string that ends in an X. Because the X is a non-blank character, it forces the SBMJOB command to send the string without the garbage. Figure 12.7 shows the results in PGM1.

```
PGM (&stringx)

DCL &stringx    *CHAR   65
DCL &string     *CHAR   64

CHGVAR &string %SST(&stringx 1 64)
```

Figure 12.7: The code in PGM1 needed to receive the 64-byte parameter.

A similar problem exists with decimal parameters. If your SBMJOB command shows a CALL command that passes a decimal literal or a decimal variable, the submitted program will fail if the parameter is not received into a decimal variable 15 digits long with 5 decimal places.

Assume a program passes two decimal parameters—one a three-digit variable and one a literal, as in Figure 12.8—to a submitted program.

```
    DCL         &batch   *DEC    3
    ...
    SBMJOB      CMD(CALL apbatch03 PARM(&batch 2)) +
                JOB(apb99001) JOBQ(qbatch)
```

Figure 12.8: An example of passing decimal values to a submitted program.

If variable &BATCH has the value 45, job APB99001 sees the request message in Figure 12.9.

```
    CALL PGM(APBATCH03) PARM(45 2)
```

Figure 12.9: The submitted job receives all decimal values as if they were literals.

Program APBATCH03 should define two 15-digit decimal parameters—each one with five decimal positions—to correctly receive the data.

WORKING WITH SUBMITTED JOBS

Once submitted to a job queue, you can display the job with the Work with Submitted Jobs (WRKSBMJOB) command. The WRKSBMJOB command presents a panel that lists all the jobs you have submitted to batch, whether they are still waiting in the job queue (status = JOBQ), currently running (status = ACTIVE), or complete with output waiting in an output queue (status = OUTQ). WRKSBMJOB has the disadvantage of not allowing you to display anyone else's jobs (even if you are the security officer). Plus, if you submit many jobs to batch, the WRKSBMJOB panel fills up rather quickly.

The Work with Job Queue (WRKJOBQ) command lets you work with the jobs that have been submitted to a given job queue, but have not yet started executing. As soon as a job begins executing, it no longer shows up in the WRKJOBQ panel.

Remember that you can always use the Work with User Jobs (WRKUSRJOB) command to segregate a particular user's jobs, no matter what status they have, or use the Work with Subsystem Jobs (WRKSBSJOB) command to segregate the jobs that are running in a particular subsystem. Because most batch jobs are likely to run in subsystem QBATCH, WRKSBSJOB can be used effectively to work with jobs that are running in batch mode.

THE QSYSOPR MESSAGE QUEUE

A batch job has no interaction with the user. The job begins and, if it runs smoothly, it produces the expected result. However, batch jobs can run into trouble and might require user intervention.

When problems occur, the job issues an inquiry (*INQ) message to the System Operator's message queue (QSYSOPR). The system operator must monitor this message queue for incoming messages and take corrective action. Anyone with the appropriate authority can display messages in QSYSOPR and reply to them. You don't have to display the message from the system console.

When a batch job issues an inquiry message to QSYSOPR, you can use the Display Messages (DSPMSG) command, as shown in Figure 12.10, to display message queue QSYSOPR.

```
DSPMSG MSGQ(qsysopr) MSGTYPE(*INQ)
```

Figure 12.10: An example of code to display message queue QSYSOPR for *INQ messages from a batch job.

Depending on your configuration, QSYSOPR might contain anywhere from a few to many messages. By specifying MSGTYPE(*INQ), you don't have to be bothered with hundreds of unimportant messages that could require a lot of browsing to find the one you need.

Move the cursor to the input field of the message in question and press the Help key. The system responds by describing the meaning of the message and even suggests corrective actions. Sometimes this Help information does not give you the whole picture. In that case, you will have to display the job log for the batch job that ran into trouble.

You can work with the batch job, using any of the methods—WRKSBMJOB, WRKS-BSJOB, WRKUSRJOB, or even WRKACTJOB—presented in the preceding section. Place a 5 next to the job, press Enter, and then select option 10 from the menu that appears. Press F10 to display all messages in the job log.

The job log gives you a history of the job. Near the bottom (which you can reach quickly by pressing F18), you should be able to see the message that explains what went wrong. Move the cursor to that line and press Help to display additional information.

When you are done with the job log, press F3 several times until you return to the command line, display QSYSOPR messages again, and reply to the inquiry message. In many cases, you will have to resubmit the job if there is no recovery for the problem.

SELF-SUBMITTING PROGRAMS

If submitting the CALL command, a CL program can submit another CL program for execution using the SBMJOB command. For example, the program PGM1 shown in Figure 12.11 submits program PGM2 for batch execution.

```
PGM

    SBMJOB CMD(CALL pgm2 (&a &b &c))

ENDPGM
```

Figure 12.11: Submitting a program from within another program for batch execution.

Nothing prevents a program from submitting itself for batch execution. In many cases, this feature could even be desirable. For example, a menu option (to request printing a report) could call program PGM1, which performs some checking and then submits program PGM2 to batch processing. Program PGM2 then sorts data and calls an HLL program that produces the printed output.

If this scenario is repeated 100 times in your menus, you have 100 CL programs too many. Program PGM1 could submit itself and perform all the functions, including sorting and calling the HLL program, as shown in Figure 12.12.

```
PGM

    DCL &jobtype    *CHAR    1

    RTVJOBA TYPE(&jobtype)
    IF (&jobtype *EQ '0') +
       GOTO exec

    /* Perform checking and submit to batch */
    *
    *   /* Checking, validating, whatever */
    *
    SBMJOB CMD(CALL pgm1) JOBQ(qbatch)

    RETURN

    /* Sort data and produce report */
exec:
    OVRDBF filea SHARE(*YES)
    OPNQRYF FILE((filea)) QRYSLT(...) KEYFLD(...)
    *
    *
    *
    CALL hll_pgm
    CLOF filea
    DLTOVR filea

ENDPGM
```

Figure 12.12: An example of a program that submits itself.

The trick is in the use of the &JOBTYPE variable. Retrieve Job Attribute (RTVJOBA) can retrieve information about a job, including whether the job is an interactive job or a batch job. RTVJOBA sets the variable specified in the TYPE parameter to '0' for batch jobs and '1' for interactive jobs.

The first time through program PGM1 runs interactively (it starts from a menu option). Because the program is run interactively, RTVJOBA sets &JOBTYPE to '1', which means that the:

- IF command fails.

- Program execution falls through.

- Program performs its checking and validation.

- Program runs the SBMJOB command.

SBMJOB submits a call to PGM1 (the same program), and then ends because of the RETURN command.

Job queue QBATCH now has a job waiting. The job is to call program PGM1, but this time in batch mode. When the program starts, RTVJOBA assigns '0' to &JOBTYPE because it is running in batch mode. The condition of the IF command is then true, which causes the program to branch to label EXEC. The program then starts sorting and number crunching for the printed report.

One program took care of both functions.

13

ADVANCED TOPICS

Selective prompting is one example of an advanced technique. With selective prompting, you activate the prompter for a command from within a CL procedure. In other words, a CL procedure can contain an instruction that causes the procedure to stop, display the command prompter for a particular command, and wait for the user to enter parameter values and press the Enter key. When the user presses Enter, the CL procedure continues to execute.

HOW TO CODE SELECTIVE PROMPTING

The key to selective prompting is a question mark (?) placed immediately before the command name. See Figure 13.1.

```
PGM

    DCL  &a            *CHAR    2
    ?SNDMSG
    CALL  pgm1  (&a)

ENDPGM
```

Figure 13.1: An example of selective prompting.

The procedure shown in Figure 13.1 stops at the SNDMSG command and prompts for it as if you had keyed in SNDMSG at the command line and pressed the F4 key. The operator is prompted for the DSPMSG command (Figure 13.2). The difference is that when the operator presses Enter, the system not only executes the SNDMSG command, but executes the rest of the procedure as well.

```
Send Message (SNDMSG)

  Type choices, press Enter.

  Message text . . . . . . . . . . _____
      _____
      _____
      _____
      _____
      _____
      _____

  To user profile . . . . . . . _____       Name, *SYSOPR,
    *ALLACT...




  Bottom
  F3=Exit    F4=Prompt    F5=Refresh    F10=Additional parameters
  F12=Cancel
    F13=How to use this display        F24=More keys
```

Figure 13.2: The SNDMSG command was prompted from a CL procedure.

A Common Mistake

When using selective prompting in your CL procedures, you must remember that the CL procedure stops and the command prompter appears. All function keys supported by the command prompter are active, including F3 (Exit) and F12 (Cancel). When the user presses F3 or F12, the command prompter issues an *ESCAPE message (CPF6801) to your CL procedure. Your CL procedure must always monitor for this message immediately following selective prompting.

The section of code shown in Figure 13.2 is incorrect because it has no provision for the F3/F12 keys. Figure 13.3 shows how this procedure should be coded.

```
PGM

   DCL  &a            *CHAR    2

   ?SNDMSG
   MONMSG cpf6801 EXEC(RETURN) .

   CALL pgm1 (&a)

ENDPGM
```

Figure 13.3: An example of selective prompting with correct provision for F3/F12.

Now the procedure ends (executes RETURN) if the user presses F3 or F12 from the command prompter.

Message CPF6801 includes the name of the key pressed (F3 or F12) as message data. Therefore, your CL procedure can tell the difference. In other words, you can take one action or another depending on what key the user presses to remove the command prompter.

For example, Figure 13.4 shows how to code the procedure so that, if the user presses F12, the procedure skips the CALL to the program; if the user presses F3, the entire CL procedure ends.

```
PGM

   DCL  &a            *CHAR    2

   ?SNDMSG

   /* If user presses F3, abort program */
   MONMSG cpf6801 CMPDTA('F3') EXEC(RETURN)
```

Figure 13.4: Processing an F3 or F12 request when using selective prompting (part 1 of 2).

```
    /* If user presses F12, skip CALL to PGM1 */
    MONMSG cpf6801 EXEC(GOTO skip)

    CALL pgm1 (&a)
skip:
    *
    *
    *

ENDPGM
```

Figure 13.4: Processing an F3 or F12 request when using selective prompting (part 2 of 2).

MONMSG compares the message data (either 'F3' or 'F12') against constant 'F3'. If they are equal, MONMSG performs a RETURN. Otherwise, it continues. The next MONMSG monitors again for CPF6801, but transfers control to label SKIP.

Making the Prompt Selective

In the preceding example, the system prompts for the SNDMSG command without asking for any particular parameter (which is the normal way). All parameters normally prompted for will be prompted for.

Selective prompting derives its name from the fact that you can control (or select) which parameters are prompted for and how. You perform selective prompting by putting special control character prefixes on the command's parameter keywords. Table 13.1 lists the valid control characters.

NOTES

- You can enter one or more spaces between the question mark and the name of the command.

- You cannot enter any spaces between the selective prompt control characters (??, ?*, ?-) and the parameter keyword.

- You must use keywords for the parameters you want to prompt selectively. Positional parameters cannot be used.

- There are two other control character sets, which are used only by IBM in IBM-supplied commands.

Table 13.1: Selective Prompting Control Characters		
Control	**Example**	**Description**
??	?SNDMSG ??MSG()	The MSG parameter appears on the prompter, showing its default value.
	?SNDMSG ??MSG('Hello')	The MSG parameter appears on the prompter, showing the value 'Hello' as the suggested value. The user can change this value.
?*	?SNDMSG ?*TOMSGQ()	The TOMSGQ parameter appears on the prompter with its default value. The user cannot change this default value.
	?SNDMSG ?*TOMSGQ(QSYSOPR)	The TOMSGQ parameter appears on the prompter with the value 'QSYSOPR' as mandatory. The user cannot change it.
?-	?SNDMSG ?-MSGTYPE()	The MSGTYPE parameter does not appear on the prompter, therefore the user cannot give it a value. Because no value is given, the system will use the default value.
	?SNDMSG ?-MSGTYPE(*INQ)	The MSGTYPE parameter does not appear on the prompter. It has the value '*INQ' and cannot be changed.

- If you press F3 or F12 from the prompter presented by selective prompting, the system sends escape message CPF6801. Your CL procedure must monitor for the message, using the MONMSG command, and must take appropriate action (such as canceling the procedure).

■ You can use variables to supply values to the parameters being prompted for. When the prompter appears, the parameter will have the value of the variable by default. If the user changes this value and presses Enter, the command is carried out using the new value, but the CL variable doesn't change.

USING QCMDCHK

QCMDCHK is an IBM-supplied API in library QSYS. QCMDCHK checks that a command string you provide follows proper syntax. If it does, nothing happens. If there is a syntax error, QCMDCHK sends one or more diagnostic messages followed by escape message CPF0006. QCMDCHK can be used in programs written in any language, but it is most useful in CL.

Calling QCMDCHK

QCMDCHK requires two parameters. The first parameter is the command string being checked for accuracy. This parameter can be given as a constant, but doing so certainly decreases the usefulness of QCMDCHK. In most cases, you will want to use a *CHAR variable of an adequate length.

The second parameter is the length of the command string. Again, this length can be passed as a constant, but a variable might be more useful. If you use a variable, make sure it is declared as TYPE(*DEC) LEN(15 5). Figure 13.5 shows an example.

```
DCL &cmd       *CHAR   256
DCL &len       *DEC    (15 5)
DCL &msgid     *CHAR   7
DCL &msgf      *CHAR   10
DCL &msgflib   *CHAR   10
DCL &msgdta    *CHAR   80

CHGVAR &cmd 'SIGNOFF LOG(*OFCOURSE)'
CHGVAR &len 256
CALL qcmdchk (&cmd &len)
```

Figure 13.5: An example of calling QCMDCHK to validate a command (part 1 of 2).

```
MONMSG cpf0006 EXEC(DO)
   RCVMSG MSGTYPE(*DIAG) MSGID(&msgid) MSGF(&msgf) +
      MSGFLIB(&msgflib) MSGDTA(&msgdta)
ENDDO
```

Figure 13.5: An example of calling QCMDCHK to validate a command (part 1 of 2).

QCMDCHK is sure to find a syntax error. The command string is SIGNOFF LOG(*OFCOURSE), but the LOG parameter of the SIGNOFF command doesn't accept special value *OFCOURSE. It does, however, accept *YES.

Because QCMDCHK issues CPF0006 (the command string that contains a syntax error), the procedure executes the RCVMSG command. In addition, the RCVMSG command reads a diagnostic message, also sent by QCMDCHK, along with CPF0006. This diagnostic message contains the reason the command failed the syntax check.

Selective Prompting and QCMDCHK

Nothing prevents you from passing to QCMDCHK a command string containing selective prompting. Figure 13.6 shows an example.

```
DCL &cmd          *CHAR 3000

CHGVAR &cmd '?CRTPRTF'

CALL qcmdchk (&cmd 3000)
MONMSG cpf6801 EXEC(GOTO cancel)
```

Figure 13.6: Passing a command string containing selective prompting to QCMDCHK.

In this case, the command string, ?CRTPRTF, causes QCMDCHK to invoke the prompter for the CRTPRTF command.

Note: The 3000 bytes are allocated for variable &CMD because &CMD will contain the entire command string (including parameter keywords and values) when the user presses Enter from the prompter. Variable &CMD will actually change from '?CRTPRTF'

227

to something like 'CRTPRTF FILE(PRTF1)' after the call to QCMDCHK. The question mark will be removed automatically.

CPF0006 is not being monitored for. Because the command prompter is invoked, it is unlikely that it will return a command string with a syntax error. CPF6801 is being monitored because the user may press F3 or F12 from the CRTPRTF command prompter. If this happens, the CL procedure branches to label CANCEL.

USING QCMDEXC

QCMDEXC is an API in QSYS you can use to execute a single command from within a program or procedure. QCMDEXC works like QCMDCHK. The main difference is that QCMDEXC not only checks the command for syntax accuracy, but also executes the command. QCMDEXC can be used in programs written in any language.

Why Bother with QCMDEXC in CL?

CL procedures can execute virtually all commands by coding them directly in the source code. It might seem that you would have no use for QCMDEXC in a CL procedure, but nothing could be farther from the truth. QCMDEXC lets you execute a command that you have built within the CL procedure.

For example, suppose your CL procedure is used to run OPNQRYF to sort a file in one of three different ways. If the user gives parameter &SORT a value of 'A' you must sort by item number; if &SORT equals 'B' you must sort by class code and item number; if it is 'C' you must sort by price.

With QCMDEXC, you can run OPNQRYF by first composing the command string in a CL variable, splicing pieces together with the concatenation operators, and finally submitting it to QCMDEXC for execution. See Figure 13.7.

```
   DCL &sort        *CHAR   1
   DCL &cmd         *CHAR   256

   /* Initialize &CMD to the portion of the     */
   /* OPNQRYF command that is common in all cases */
   CHGVAR &cmd 'OPNQRYF FILE((filea)) QRYSLT(*ALL)'

   /* Sort by item number */
   IF (&sort *EQ 'A') DO
      CHGVAR &cmd (&cmd *BCAT 'KEYFLD((item))')
   ENDDO

   /* Sort by class code */
   ELSE IF (&sort *EQ 'B') DO
      CHGVAR &cmd (&cmd *BCAT 'KEYFLD((class)(item))')
   ENDDO

   /* Sort by price */
   ELSE IF (&sort *EQ 'C') DO
      CHGVAR &cmd (&cmd *BCAT 'KEYFLD((price))')
   ENDDO

   /* Execute the OPNQRYF command */
   CALL qcmdexc (&cmd 256)

   /* Monitor for errors during OPNQRYF */
   MONMSG cpf0000 EXEC(DO)
      *
      * /* Take corrective action if OPNQRYF fails */
      *
   ENDDO

   /* Call your HLL program to print the report */

ENDPGM
```

Figure 13.7: Using QCMDEXC to execute a command that you have built within the CL procedure.

As you can imagine, all three possibilities have 'OPNQRYF FILE((FILEA)) QRYSLT(*ALL)' in common; what makes the three cases different is the sort sequence, which is specified in OPNQRYF's KEYFLD parameter. For this reason, initialize &CMD to this common portion of OPNQRYF. Then, append the proper KEYFLD value depending on the value of &SORT.

Notice that the *BCAT concatenation operator is used in order to insert a blank space between 'OPNQRYF FILE((FILEA)) QRYSLT(*ALL)' and the KEYFLD parameter.

Note: If QCMDEXC detects a syntax error in the command string passed to it, it sends escape message CPF0006 to your CL procedure (the same thing QCMDCHK does).

Note: If the command passes the syntax check, but nonetheless ends in error (for example, you run a CRTPF command but the file already exists), the command issues its own escape message. This escape message is received by QCMDEXC and sent back to your CL procedure, which should monitor for it. The procedure shown in Figure 13.7 does this with a MONMSG command immediately following the call to QCMDEXC.

Commands Not Allowed

Not all commands are allowed to run by way of QCMDEXC. When you use QCMD-EXC to execute a command, the command runs as if you had executed it manually from the command line. Almost no RTVXXX commands can be run with QCMD-EXC because most RTVXXX commands return data to CL variables and must, therefore, run directly from a CL procedure.

To make sure a command can be executed with QCMDEXC, run a Display Command (DSPCMD) command for the command in question. The "Where allowed to run" (parameter ALLOW) must include the value *EXEC. If it doesn't, the command cannot be run with QCMDEXC.

USING QCLSCAN

QCLSCAN is an API in QSYS you can use to scan a CL variable and see if it contains a certain pattern. For example, you might want to find all customers in a customer file that have COMPUTER in their names. Your procedure could then read one record at a time, scan for the string COMPUTER, and present only those records on the screen.

Most languages have built-in functions to perform this sort of scan. RPG III, for example, has the SCAN op code. RPG IV also has SCAN, plus the %SCAN built-in function. COBOL has the INSPECT verb. Yet, QCLSCAN has the advantage of providing support for wild cards.

Calling QCLSCAN

Table 13.2 lists a complete description of QCLSCAN's eight parameters.

Table 13.2: Parameters for QCLSCAN.		
Parameter	**Description**	**Attributes**
&STRING	Character string where you want to search for a pattern.	Up to 999 characters
&STRLEN	Must be equal to the length of variable &STRING and no greater.	3 digits, 0 decimals
&STRPOS	Position in &STRING where the scan begins. You may scan &STRING more than once to see if the pattern appears more than once.	3 digits, 0 decimals
&PATTERN	Pattern you are looking for.	Up to 999 characters
&PATLEN	Length of the &PATTERN variable and no greater.	3 digits, 0 decimals
&XLATE	Must contain '1' if you want alphabetic characters in &STRING to be translated to uppercase letters. Give it a value of '0' if you do not wish to translate.	1 character

Table 13.2: Parameters for QCLSCAN, continued

Parameter	Description	Attributes
&TRIM	Must contain '1' if you want QCLSCAN to ignore trailing blanks in &pattern. If you give it a value of '0' those trailing blanks will be included in the scan, which means that the scan is more likely to fail.	1 character
&WILD	Can contain a blank (if no wild card is desired) or a character that has been used in &PATTERN to indicate a wild card. A wild card is a character position that matches any character. A wild card is equal to any character.	1 character

Four of QCLSCAN's parameters are decimal with 3 digits and 0 decimal places. These parameters must be passed as variables, never as literals, because decimal literals would be received with a precision of (15 5), which is incorrect. (You might use hexadecimal literals, however.) All other parameters can be passed as either literals or variables. Figure 13.8 shows an example of calling this API.

```
         DCL &string      *CHAR    30
         DCL &strlen      *DEC      3
         DCL &strpos      *DEC      3
         DCL &pattern     *CHAR    10
         DCL &patlen      *DEC      3
         DCL &xlate       *CHAR     1
         DCL &trim        *CHAR     1
         DCL &wild        *CHAR     1
         DCL &result      *DEC      3

         CHGVAR &string   'CL character string'
         CHGVAR &strlen   19

         CHGVAR &strpos   2         /* start scanning in position 2 */

         CHGVAR &pattern  'R*C'
         CHGVAR &patlen   3
```

Figure 13.8: An example of calling API QCLSCAN (part 1 of 2).

```
      CHGVAR &xlate    '1'    /* translate to uppercase */
      CHGVAR &trim     '1'    /* ignore trailing blanks in pattern */
      CHGVAR &wild     '*'

      CALL qclscan (&string &strlen &strpos +
                    &pattern &patlen +
                    &xlate &trim &wild +
                    &result)
```

Figure 13.8: An example of calling API QCLSCAN (part 2 of 2).

In this example, QCLSCAN looks for the pattern "R*C" within "CL character string", using * as a wildcard (any character matches it). The scan is to start at position 2. After execution of QCLSCAN, variable &RESULT has a value of 7 to indicate that the pattern was found at position 7 of the string.

USING QDCXLATE

Using IBM-supplied program QDCXLATE, you can perform translations on character variables. For example, the i5 uses the EBCDIC character set while most other computer manufacturers use the ASCII character set. QDCXLATE Lets you convert a character string from EBCDIC to ASCII. You also can use QDCXLATE to convert all lowercase letters in a character string to uppercase. Calling QDCXLATE is easy. As shown in Figure 13.9, you supply four parameters to it.

&DATALEN contains the length of the data to be translated and must be expressed in a decimal variable (five digits and no decimals).

&DATA is the actual character to be translated. This data can be in a variable of any length. When QDCXLATE completes the translation, &DATA will have the translated data.

&TBL and &TBLLIB together identify the translation table to be used.

```
DCL &datalen    *DEC    5
DCL &data       *CHAR   132
DCL &tbl        *CHAR   10
DCL &tbllib     *CHAR   10

CALL qdcxlate (&datalen &data &tbl &tbllib)
```

Figure 13.9: An example of calling QDCXLATE.

Standard Translations

To convert from EBCDIC to ASCII, use translation table QASCII in library QSYS. To convert from ASCII to EBCDIC, use translation table QEBCDIC in QSYS.

To convert from lowercase to uppercase letters, you have two choices. First, translation table QSYSTRNTBL in QSYS translates only the unaccented lowercase "a" to "z" to their uppercase counterparts. Translation table QCASE256 in QUSR-SYS, on the other hand, translates all accented lowercase letters (such as "á" and "ñ") to uppercase.

In addition, you can create your own translation tables with the Create Table (CRTTBL) command.

Using DLYJOB

The Delay Job (DLYJOB) command can be included in any CL procedure to force the system to wait. While waiting, the CL procedure uses no system resources. The procedure, so to speak, goes to sleep.

DLYJOB can be used in two different ways. You can indicate a time of the day when the procedure should resume or you can indicate a length of time to wait. Consider the CL code shown in Figure 13.10.

```
start:
   /* Start processing */
   *
   *
   *

loop:
   ALCOBJ ((abc *DTAQ *EXCL 0))
   MONMSG cpf0000 EXEC(DO)
      DLYJOB DLY(30)
      GOTO loop
   ENDDO

   *
   *
   *

   DLYJOB RSMTIME(000000)
   GOTO start
```

Figure 13.10: Two examples of the DLYJOB command.

The skeleton procedure shown in Figure 13.10 performs some initial processing before it attempts to allocate data queue ABC for exclusive use. If the data queue cannot be allocated, the DLYJOB command delays the procedure for 30 seconds, and then goes back to "loop" to try again. This loop is repeated until the data queue is allocated.

More processing takes place and, at the end of the procedure, the DLYJOB command puts the procedure to sleep until midnight. The procedure then goes back to "start" to begin executing the code all over again.

DLYJOB with DLY

When the DLYJOB command is used with the DLY parameter, you must specify how many seconds to wait. It can be any value up to 999,999 seconds (which is more than 11 days). If you use a CL variable to hold the value of the DLY parameter, be sure to use a *CHAR variable. The RSMTIME parameter cannot be used when using DLY.

DLYJOB with RSMTIME

DLYJOB can be told to wait until a certain time of the day by using the RSMTIME parameter instead of DLY. The RSMTIME parameter must contain a six-digit number that represents the time of the day in the HHMMSS format. If you use a CL variable, use a TYPE(*CHAR) LEN(6) variable.

If the time indicated in RSMTIME has already passed when the procedure executes DLYJOB, the procedure will wait until the time indicated of the next day. For example, DLYJOB RSMTIME(120000) is specified (wait until noon), but the procedure encounters DLYJOB at 12:00:01. The procedure would then wait until noon tomorrow.

USING RCLRSC AND RCLACTGRP

The Reclaim Resources (RCLRSC) command is used primarily in first-level OPM CL programs that control applications to perform the following:

- Free static storage used by the application.
- Close any files left open.
- Terminate any programs left running.
- Reclaim active CPI communication conversations.
- Disable links that were enabled by user-defined communication programs.
- Reclaim DDM conversations with no active users.

In most cases, however, you will be using the RCLRSC command to terminate programs you've left running in the background. For example, you might have created an RPG program that opens a series of files and then returns without setting the last record indicator (LR) on. This type of program often is used to leave files with shared open data paths open to speed up processing.

Rather than calling the program again to terminate it by turning on LR, you can run the RCLRSC command before ending the CL program. RCLRSC will automatically take care of the open files and will terminate the RPG program.

If you run an ILE CL program, however, you shouldn't use RCLRSC. Use Reclaim Activation Group (RCLACTGRP) instead.

RETRIEVING CL SOURCE

OPM CL programs are unusual in that you can easily decompile them to obtain the source code when all you have is the compiled *PGM object. This feature can be invaluable in cases when you have lost the source code or when you receive a CL program from someone, without source, but you need to make some changes.

In order for decompilation to work, however, the CL program must have been compiled with ALWRTVRSC(*YES), which is the default when you run CRTCLPGM. If the program is compiled with ALWRTVRSC(*NO), you won't be able to retrieve the source code. To retrieve the source, use the Retrieve CL Source (RTVCLSRC) command.

The RTVCLSRC Command

The RTVCLSRC command has three parameters:

1. PGM (where you enter the qualified name of the CL program whose source you want to obtain).

2. SRCFILE (where you enter the qualified name of the source physical file where you want to put the retrieve source code).

3. SRCMBR (where you enter the name of the source member that will contain the code).

The SRCMBR parameter defaults to *PGM, which means that (unless you enter a value) the source code will go to a member named after the program object. This member doesn't have to exist when RTVCLSRC is executed.

RTVCLSRC produces source code in a very ugly format. It begins with 20 lines of comments that list the program source statistics.

The source code follows immediately under this header. All commands begin on column 6. RTVCLSRC doesn't produce any blank lines to separate CL statements into logical groups (as you probably would if you wrote the program). RTVCLSRC also doesn't retrieve any comments.

14

SECURITY CONSIDERATIONS

No book about CL would be complete without some discussion of system security concepts. CL progra mmers must be aware of security issues to keep a secure system. Most of the security considerations discussed in this chapter are applicable only to systems that have a security level of 30 or higher. If your system is at security level 20 or 10, refer to the section that discusses the command line.

SECURING THE *PGM OBJECT

i5/OS provides a comprehensive security system that allows you to secure objects so that only some users (whom you specify) can perform certain functions (which you also specify). For example, you can indicate that user JANE will be allowed to read the employee master file, but not change it in any way.

When you design an application, you will probably want to create commands to let users start any of the application activities without bothering with menus. Or you might prefer to stick with menus. Either way, the user is actually running programs (probably CL programs) to run the application.

Don't forget to secure the program objects, especially in sensitive areas of applications, that require the most protection from tampering or sabotage.

An Example

Suppose you have created a CL program, PGM1, to perform such month-end tasks as closing the General Ledger and purging the General Ledger master file of old journal entries. Now suppose one of your users runs PGM1 at the wrong time.

In this disastrous situation, you would have to restore the master files from your last backup and lose a lot of time to return the system to the state it was in before this unfortunate program call.

Perhaps PGM1 is executed by the command Close General Ledger (CLSGL), which you have created. You probably thought that securing the CLSGL command was enough. It isn't. Secure the program object, too.

Securing an Object

To secure an object, run the Edit Object Authority (EDTOBJAUT) command. This command provides a convenient interactive maintenance program and requires two parameters:

- OBJ, in which you must supply the qualified name of the object to be secured.

- OBJTYPE, which is the type of object. Use *PGM for programs, *FILE for files, *CMD for commands, and so on.

Once you obtain the EDTOBJAUT panel, you enter the names of the user profiles that should be authorized to the object and the level of authority you want to give them. You can simplify the maintenance of these authorities by using group profiles or authorization lists. Press Enter and the object's authorities are immediately updated.

You also can use the Grant Object Authority (GRTOBJAUT) and Revoke Object Authority (RVKOBJAUT) commands to change the authority a user holds to an object.

Take Care of *PUBLIC

When working with EDTOBJAUT, GRTOBJAUT, and RVKOBJAUT, you will come across a fictitious user profile named *PUBLIC. *PUBLIC means "everyone else."

For example, if running EDTOBJAUT for program A shows two user profiles (FRED and WILMA) that have *USE and *CHANGE authority, respectively, user BARNEY may still be authorized to run the program through *PUBLIC.

It works as follows: If *PUBLIC has *USE authority, every user except FRED and WILMA will enjoy *USE authority. Therefore, BARNEY can run program A, too. If you want to prevent other users from running the program, give *PUBLIC the *EXCLUDE authority.

ADOPTING AUTHORITY

Whoever creates an object is automatically the owner of the object. Because the system gives the creator complete control and access to the object, the user, as owner, can perform any function on the object. However, don't assume that the owner has all authority to an object. Authorities can be taken away from the user by use of the EDTOBJAUT and RVKOBJAUT commands.

Ownership

You can change the ownership of an object with the Change Object Owner (CHGOBJOWN) command. Supply the qualified name of the object, the object type, and the user profile name of the person who is to become the new owner.

Adopting Authority

Because the program can, upon request, adopt the authority of its owner no matter who runs the program, it is important to know who owns a program object. The system will merge the authorities granted to the user running the program and the user who owns the program before checking for authority to an object.

For example, let's say you create a program that reorganizes a physical file before it uses it. This program is going to be used by a number of people who are not authorized to reorganize the file.

Instead of granting these users the *OBJMGT authority needed to reorganize the file, you can change the program so that it adopts the authority of its owner (who should be authorized to reorganize the file). Any user can run the program and it will execute normally. When the RGZPFM command is encountered, the physical file member will be reorganized because the program is using its owner's authority in addition to the authority of the user who is running it.

To make a program adopt its owner's authority, specify USRPRF(*OWNER) in the CRTCLPGM, CRTBNDCL, CRTSRVPGM, CRTPGM, or CHGPGM command.

Another Example

If your CL program adopts the authority of the owner, any Check Object (CHKOBJ) command within the CL program will merge the authority of the owner with that of the current user to the objects indicated.

Suppose user ABLE owns a physical file, CUSTOMER, in library MYLIB. Another user, BAKER, owns a program that adopts authority, and contains the statement shown in Figure 14.1.

```
CHKOBJ mylib/customer *FILE AUT(*ALL)
```

Figure 14.1: An example that adopts authority from the owner of the object and then checks authority.

Table 14.1 lists which authorities these users have to the CUSTOMER file.

Table 14.1: Authority Granted for the CUSTOMER File.									
	Object Authorities				Data Authorities				
User	Opr	Mgt	Exist	Alter	Ref	Read	Add	Update	Delete	Execute
ABLE		X	X	X	X	X		X	X	X
BAKER	X				X		X			

As you can see from Table 14.1, neither user has complete authority to the file. If either user runs the program under one user's authority only, the CHKOBJ command fails with escape message CPF9802 (Not authorized to object CUSTOMER in MYLIB.).

However, if the CL program adopts authority from the owner, the CHKOBJ succeeds if ABLE runs the program, but fails if BAKER runs it. When ABLE runs the program, i5/OS merges the authorities of the two users and the result satisfies *ALL authority.

Adopted Authority from Other Programs in the Call Stack

If program PGM1, which adopts the authority of the owner, calls program PGM2, PGM2 may or may not use the authority of the owner of PGM1. This depends on the setting of the "Use adopted authority" attribute of PGM2.

Suppose PGM1's owner is QSECOFR and PGM2 (which has the "Use adopted authority" attribute set to *YES) presents a command line. The user who runs PGM1 will be able to run any command and control the entire system from the command line just presented. This situation is certainly a security risk.

To allow a program to use adopted authority from programs already in the call stack, use the Change Program (CHGPGM) command; specify USEADPAUT(*YES).

Other Risks of Adopted Authority

Adopting authorities can be risky.

Security can be compromised—if the program that adopts authority calls the QCMDEXC, QCAPCMD, or QCMD programs—because these programs can carry out any command given them. A program that adopts authority from a powerful user (such as QSECOFR) and calls QCMDEXC, QCAPCMD, or QCMD can become a "Trojan horse" rather easily.

Consider using fully qualified object names whenever you adopt authority in a program. This will ensure that the objects that you meant to reference will indeed be those that are ultimately referenced. For instance, if you call an RPG program named UPDEMP that updates your EMPLOYEE file (both the program and the file are in library PAYROLL), be sure to code it as shown in Figure 14.2.

```
OVRDBF employee TOFILE(payroll/employee)
CALL payroll/updemp
DLTOVR employee
```

Figure 14.2: An example of code to call a program named UPDEMP.

COMMAND LINES

Command lines are input fields presented on the screen, by the system, where the user can type any command and have it executed. Command lines can appear in menus (either IBM-supplied or user-defined) and in most WRKXXX commands such as WRKSPLF and WRKSBMJOB.

Presenting a command line is not necessarily a security risk. Nevertheless, many i5 administrators go out of their way to ensure that no program run by a user ever presents a command line. These administrators feel that command lines should be only for programmers and system administrators.

Limited Capabilities

One way to remove the security risk from command lines is to give regular users limited capabilities. You can change their user profiles to LMTCPB(*YES) with the Change User Profile (CHGUSRPRF) command.

A user assigned limited capabilities cannot execute most QSYS commands from the command line (although they can be executed when included in a CL program). Harmless commands—such as DSPMSG, SNDMSG, DSPJOB, DSPJOBLOG, and SIGNOFF—are always available even for limited-capabilities users. A user with limited capabilities cannot delete files or libraries, change user profiles, or do almost anything else.

Each command has an attribute controlled by the ALWLMTUSR parameter of the Create Command (CRTCMD) and Change Command (CHGCMD) commands. If this attribute is set to *YES, limited-capabilities users will be allowed to execute the command from the command line. If the attribute is *NO (as is the case in the vast majority of QSYS commands), the limited-capabilities user cannot run the command from the command line.

To see the ALWLMTUSR attribute of a particular command, use the Display Command (DSPCMD) command. Although changing this attribute reduces security risks enormously, it doesn't eliminate them.

Note: The Command Entry panel (which appears when you call QCMD) pays absolutely no attention to the limited-capabilities setting in the user profile. Therefore, you must not present the Command Entry panel to any limited-capabilities user.

Pros and Cons of Command Lines

The experienced user can benefit from a command line. You can execute commands directly instead of having to navigate through several menus before reaching the needed activity. Think of command lines as shortcuts. If a user remembers a command and knows how to use it, why forbid command usage?

If you use command lines, however, you will have to keep security tighter than if you do not use them. The decision is entirely up to you.

Appearing Command Lines

Command lines appear in the following cases:

- By calling program QSYS/QCMD. This program presents the Command Entry panel, which is the ultimate command line.

- By calling program QSYS/QCL. This program presents a different version of the Command Entry panel that is suitable for entering System/38 commands.

- Running most WRKXXX commands.

- Calling program QUSCMDLN, which is an API. This program opens up a small window with a command line.

- Running the RCVMSG command in a CL program for PGMQ(*EXT) with MSGTYPE(*RQS).

- Displaying menus that include command lines.

15

Sign-on Programs

So-called sign-on programs (more accurately called *initial programs*) are special programs that run when a user signs on to the system. The sign-on program is indicated in the user profile's initial program (INLPGM) attribute. With INLPGM (*NONE) in a user's profile, the system doesn't run any program at sign-on and shows the initial menu immediately. If the user has a value other than *NONE in the INLPGM attribute, the system runs the indicated program before it presents the initial menu. With INLMNU(*SIGNOFF) in a user's profile, the user is signed off when the user's sign-on program ends.

You can write sign-on programs in any language, but they are commonly written in CL because they usually need to manipulate objects, set user environments, and interact with the system. This chapter presents a typical sign-on program that you can tailor to your own requirements.

> *Note:* Sign-on programs cannot have any parameters.

USING JOB DESCRIPTIONS

Although you can use sign-on programs to set up user environments, most of the attributes in the user environment can be set up with a job description. For example, you can define the user's library list in the INLLIBL parameter of the Create Job Description (CRTJOBD) or Change Job Description (CHGJOBD) command.

Using job descriptions is simple. Managing job descriptions is not difficult either. When you create a job description for a user, you attach the job description to the user by changing the user profile (as shown in Figure 15.1).

```
CHGUSRPRF myself JOBD(mylib/myjobd)
```

Figure 15.1: Attaching a job description to a user profile.

This command changes user profile MYSELF. Each time MYSELF signs on, the user will use job description MYJOBD in library MYLIB. This job description will set up the job attributes.

WHAT JOB DESCRIPTIONS CANNOT DO

Many things cannot be done with job descriptions. For example, using only sign-on programs you can:

- Alter the system portion of the library list. You could have several libraries that can go above QSYS in the library list, and use one or another depending on who signs on. In these libraries you could have duplicated QSYS commands or other objects that have been customized to the person who is using the system.

- Add a "scratch" or project library to your programmer's library list that is named after the programmer's user profile. Although you could do this with job descriptions, you would need a separate job description for each programmer. By delegating this task to the sign-on program, you can use a single job description for all programmers.

- Create work files and other objects in QTEMP so that they are ready for repeated use.

- Run the Display Message (DSPMSG) command if there are messages in the user's message queue.

- Run an RPG program that writes a record to a database file, which logs the user's sign-on for historical purposes. The record could include the user profile name, display station name, and a time stamp.

SAMPLE SIGN-ON PROGRAM

The sign-on program shown in Figure 15.2 is an illustration only. You should customize it to your own needs by removing or adding sections. Instead of showing the entire program in one continuous listing, you will see text inserted when an explanation is necessary. The complete program is provided in Appendix C.

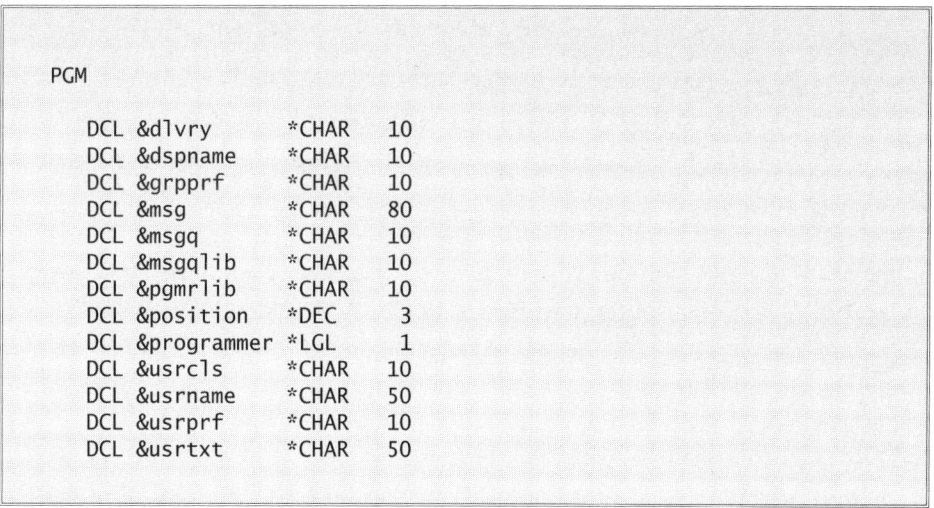

```
PGM
        DCL &dlvry      *CHAR   10
        DCL &dspname    *CHAR   10
        DCL &grpprf     *CHAR   10
        DCL &msg        *CHAR   80
        DCL &msgq       *CHAR   10
        DCL &msgqlib    *CHAR   10
        DCL &pgmrlib    *CHAR   10
        DCL &position   *DEC     3
        DCL &programmer *LGL     1
        DCL &usrcls     *CHAR   10
        DCL &usrname    *CHAR   50
        DCL &usrprf     *CHAR   10
        DCL &usrtxt     *CHAR   50
```

Figure 15.2: An example of a generic sign-on program.

The program shown in Figure 15.2 can generate many *ESCAPE messages. Because none of the *ESCAPE messages should interrupt the program, you should ignore them all.

Figure 15.3 shows the MONMSG command to do this.

```
MONMSG cpf0000
```

Figure 15.3: The MONMSG command to ignore all error messages.

First, retrieve some of the attributes of the user profile with the Retrieve User Profile (RTVUSRPRF) command, and the name of the display station with the Retrieve Job Attributes (RTVJOBA) command (shown in Figure 15.4). This information is necessary in later parts of the program.

```
/* Retrieve the user profile attributes */
   RTVUSRPRF *CURRENT RTNUSRPRF(&usrprf) GRPPRF(&grpprf) +
           MSGQ(&msgq) MSGQLIB(&msgqlib) +
           TEXT(&usrtxt) USRCLS(&usrcls) DLVRY(&dlvry)

   RTVJOBA JOB(&dspnam)
```

Figure 15.4: Retrieving attributes from the user profile and name of the display station.

In the job where this sign-on program is used, the security administrator uses the user profile's text description (retrieved with RTVUSRPRF to &USRTXT) to store important user information. The text description always begins with the user's complete name, followed by a colon (:) and the name of the department in which the user works.

You can also have the system send a status message (to line 24) saying "Signing on John Smith" (or other names) when a user signs on. To do this, you must extract the complete name from the user profile's text description. The complete name is everything contained up to, but excluding, the colon.

You can use QCLSCAN to look for this colon. If QCLSCAN finds the colon, its exact position is reported to variable &POSITION, which was declared as *DEC 3.

If the position is greater than zero (colon found), the user name is everything prior to it. Therefore, subtract one from &POSITION and then use the %SST function to extract the user's full name from &USRTXT. Otherwise, you can conclude that the security administrator forgot to place the colon in the text description, and you can presume that the text description contains nothing but the user's full name.

Either way, variable &USRNAME contains the user's full name. Now you can use the Send Program Message (SNDPGMMSG) command to present the *STATUS message. In order to show, it must go to *EXT. Note that message CPF9898 is used (which already contains an ending period in its definition). In the MSGDTA parameter, you place "Signing on" concatenated with the user name, the word "at," the display station name, and two periods. These two periods, combined with the built-in period of CPF9898, make up an ellipsis (...) and the message appears as "Signing on John Smith at SYSDSP01..." This code is shown in Figure 15.5.

```
/* Display "Signing on..." message */
   CALL qclscan (&usrtxt X'050F' X'001F' +
                 ':' X'001F' +
                 '0' '0' ' ' &position)

   IF (&position *GT 0) DO
      CHGVAR &position (&position - 1)
      CHGVAR &usrname  %SST(&usrtxt 1 &position)
   ENDDO
   ELSE DO
      CHGVAR &usrname &usrtxt
   ENDDO

   SNDPGMMSG MSGID(cpf9898) MSGF(qcpfmsg) +
             MSGDTA('Signing on' *BCAT &usrname *BCAT 'at' +
                    &dspname *TCAT '..') +
             TOPGMQ(*EXT) MSGTYPE(*STATUS)
```

Figure 15.5: Displaying a message with user name and display station.

Suppose everyone in your Accounting Department uses Client Access to sign on to the i5 from their PCs. Their display stations are named ACGDSPNN, where NN is a two-digit number, and they all have PC printers configured as i5 printers connected to them. These emulated printers are named ACGDSPNNP1.

The code shown in Figure 15.6 makes it possible for your Accounting Department users to print everything they request, at their PC printers, reformatted so that 132 columns can be printed on letter-size paper in portrait mode and placed on hold.

```
/* If signing on with Client Access, override printer files */
IF (%SST(&dspname 1 6) *EQ 'ACGDSP') DO
   OVRPRTF *PRTF DEV(&dspname *TCAT 'P1') +
           PAGESIZE(82 132) LPI(8) CPI(16.7) OVRFLW(80) +
           FOLD(*NO) PAGRTT(0) OUTQ(*DEV) HOLD(*YES)
ENDDO
```

Figure 15.6: Setting up override printer and attributes for a group of users.

The users of this sign-on program want to have borders and headers in their Print key images (overriding system value QPRTKEYFMT). The code shown in Figure 15.7 will accomplish this task.

```
/* Ensure print key formats output */
CHGJOB PRTKEYFMT(*PRTALL)
```

Figure 15.7: Overriding the print key output format.

All your programmers have either QPGMR or GRP_PGMR as their group profile (GRP_PGMR is a user profile you created). Because you want to set up a special environment for your programmers, begin by determining if the user is a programmer.

Earlier in the program, you used RTVUSRPRF to retrieve the user profile's attributes, including the group profile name, which is in &GRPPRF. Therefore, determining if the user is a programmer and placing the result of this test in logical variable &PROGRAMMER is a simple matter. See Figure 15.8.

```
/* Determine if user is a programmer */
IF (&grpprf *EQ 'QPGMR'     *OR +
    &grpprf *EQ 'GRP_PGMR'     ) DO
   CHGVAR &programmer '1'
ENDDO
ELSE DO
   CHGVAR &programmer '0'
ENDDO
```

Figure 15.8: Setting up a logical variable to identify the user as a programmer or normal user.

Suppose that programmers and system operators need to have library ALTQSYS at the top of the system portion of the library list. No other users require this library. The Change System Library List (CHGSYSLIBL) command is run, but only if &PROGRAMMER is true or if the user profile has a user class equal to *SYSOPR. (See Figure 15.9.) You retrieved the user class earlier and placed it in &USRCLS.

```
/* Place ALTQSYS at top of library list */
/* for programmers and system operators */
IF (&programmer         *OR +
    &usrcls *EQ '*SYSOPR'     ) DO
   CHGSYSLIBL altqsys OPTION(*ADD)
ENDDO
```

Figure 15.9: Code to place ALTQSYS at the top of the library list for programmers and system operators.

Your programmers need a "scratch" or project library of their own, which has a name equal to a dollar sign ($) followed by the first nine characters of their user-profile name. You don't want to be bothered creating this library. You want the sign-on program to create the library, if the programmer has deleted it, and prepare it by creating the standard source physical files the programmer is likely to need. The code shown in Figure 15.10 will accomplish this task.

```
/* If user is programmer, create programming library */
   IF (&programmer) DO
      CHGVAR &pgmrlib ('$' *CAT %SST(&usrprf 1 9))
      CRTLIB &pgmrlib TEXT('Project library for' *BCAT &usrprf)
      CRTSRCPF &pgmrlib/source TEXT('Main source file')
      ADDLIBLE &pgmrlib POSITION(*FIRST)
   ENDDO
```

Figure 15.10: Code to create a project library for each programmer.

If the user's message queue is not set to *BREAK mode and has any messages at all, run DSPMSG to show them. The message queue delivery mode is in &DLVRY, and the name of the message queue is in &MSGQ and &MSGQLIB. This information was retrieved with the RTVUSRPRF at the beginning of the program.

Figure 15.11 shows how you can use the Receive Message (RCVMSG) command to receive the first message without removing it and placing its text in &MSG. If there are no messages, &MSG will be blank. If it is not blank, DSPMSG is run to display the user profile's message queue.

RCVMSG is then used again to see if the display station's message queue (which is always named after the display station itself) has any pending messages. If so, DSPMSG displays them.

```
/* If any messages are found in the user's message queue, */
   /* display those messages before proceeding */
   IF (&dlvry *NE '*BREAK') DO
      RCVMSG MSGQ(&msgqlib/&msgq) MSGTYPE(*NEXT) MSGKEY(*TOP) +
            RMV(*NO) MSG(&msg)
      IF (&msg *NE ' ') DO
         DSPMSG MSGQ(&msgqlib/&msgq)
      ENDDO

      RCVMSG MSGQ(&dspname) MSGTYPE(*NEXT) MSGKEY(*TOP) +
            RMV(*NO) MSG(&msg)
      IF (&msg *NE ' ') DO
         DSPMSG MSGQ(&dspname)
      ENDDO
   ENDDO
```

Figure 15.11: Code to check for messages and display them.

Each user in your installation can have another program, named after the user profile, where the user can include personalized touches. For example, the user might want to create objects in QTEMP that only the user needs. All these programs are contained in library MGTLIB (which is one of your libraries). If there is no personalizing program for the current user, this program—because of the global MONMSG command—will not cancel. This section of the code is shown in Figure 15.12.

```
/* Call personalizing program */
   CALL mgtlib/&usrprf
```

Figure 15.12: Calling a program to personalize the environment for an individual user.

Because of the convenience of entering commands directly and having useful feedback from the system, programmers and system operators like to use the Command Entry panel all the time. Therefore, the code shown in Figure 15.13 can be added.

```
MONMSG cpf0000
```

Figure 15.3: The MONMSG command to ignore all error messages.

This is the end of the program. When this program ends, users are presented with their initial menu.

16

DEBUGGING

The Start Debug (STRDBG) command can be used for debugging OPM programs, ILE programs, and Java classes. This chapter discusses debugging ILE programs and OPM programs with the full-screen ILE debugger. For information about debugging OPM programs with the line-oriented debugger, see appendix D.

THE STRDBG COMMAND

The Start Debug (STRDBG) command starts the ILE interactive debugger. STRDBG has many parameters, but only some of them apply to ILE.

- PGM (Program): The qualified names of the program objects you want to debug. You can enter up to 10 program names. If your CL program calls another program, both programs can be debugged simultaneously. If you need to add a program to the debugging session after you have run STRDBG, you can run the Add Program (ADDPGM) command; conversely, you can run Remove Program (RMVPGM) if you want to remove a program from the debugging session.

- UPDPROD (Update Production Files): Whether to allow files in production libraries to be updated, by specifying *YES or *NO. If you specify *NO (default value) and the program being debugged attempts to write a record or change a record in a database file of a production library, an error message is issued. If the program being debugged has write or update statements to database files, you should enter the value *YES to avoid these error messages or leave it as *NO but move the file to a test library.

- SRVPGM (Service Program): The qualified names of up to 20 service programs to be debugged.

The following additional parameters are applicable to ILE, but are less likely to be needed.

- CLASS: The names of up to 20 class files to be debugged.

- DSPMODSRC (Display Module Source): Whether or not the source debug program display is shown when debugging begins. In ILE programs, the source debug program is always shown.

- SRCDBGPGM (Source Debug Program): The name of the program to be used as the source debugger. The default value, *SYSDFT, means that IBM's debugger program is to be used.

THE ENDDBG COMMAND

The ENDDBG command is the counterpart to STRDBG. It ends the debugging session. Breaks and watches are cleared. Signing off the system also ends debug.

DEBUGGING VIEWS

When you create a program, you specify how much debugging information you want to include with the program object. This is specified in the Debugging View (DBGVIEW) parameter of the CRTBNDCL and CRTCLMOD commands.

- SOURCE: The interactive debugger will display the source code for the module.

- *LIST: The interactive debugger will display the compiler listing for the module.

- *STMT: The interactive debugger will not display source code. However, you may still debug using statement numbers and identifiers (variable names).

- *ALL: The source debugger can use any of the viewing options.

- *NONE: The source debugger cannot be used with the generated module.

The following example illustrates how the debugger works with these different views.

AN EXAMPLE INTERACTIVE DEBUGGING SESSION

Suppose you have written a short program that prompts for certain information and produces a report. The DDS for the display file is shown in Figure 16.1. Notice that it defines one indicator and eight fields, which will be included in the CL program as variables.

```
     A                                   DSPSIZ(24 80 *DS3)
     A           R PROMPT
     A                                   CF03(91 'Cancel')
     A                                   CF12(91)
     A                                   PRINT
     A             PANELID    10A  O  1  2
     A                                 1 29'Open Receivables Report'
     A                                   DSPATR(HI)
     A                                 1 73DATE
     A                                   EDTCDE(Y)
     A                                 2 73TIME
     A                                 6  7'Company . . . . . . . . :'
     A             COMPANY    3S OB  6 33
     A                                 7  7'Customer(s) . . . . . . :'
     A             CUST1      5S OB  7 33
     A             CUST2      5S OB  7 40
     A             CUST3      5S OB  7 47
```

Figure 16.1: Display file AR155DF (part 1 of 2).

```
A            CUST4        5S 0B  7 54
A            CUST5        5S 0B  7 61
A            CUST6        5S 0B  7 68
A                             8  7'Printer . . . . . . . . :'
A            OUTQ        10A B   8 33
A                             9  7'Copies . . . . . . . :'
A            COPIES       1S 0B  9 33
A                            23  8'F3=Exit    F12=Cancel'
```

Figure 16.1: Display file AR155DF (part 2 of 2).

Figure 16.2 shows the CL program source (complete with source-sequence numbers).

```
0001.00        PGM
0002.00
0003.00        DCLF      FILE(AR155DF)
0004.00
0005.00        DCL       VAR(&CHARWORK) TYPE(*CHAR) LEN(5)
0006.00        DCL       VAR(&QRYSLT) TYPE(*CHAR) LEN(256)
0007.00
0008.00        DCL       VAR(&ERRBYTES) TYPE(*CHAR) LEN(4) +
0009.00                    VALUE(X'00000000')
0010.00        DCL       VAR(&ERROR) TYPE(*LGL) VALUE('0')
0011.00        DCL       VAR(&MSGKEY) TYPE(*CHAR) LEN(4)
0012.00        DCL       VAR(&MSGTYP) TYPE(*CHAR) LEN(10)
                           VALUE('*DIAG')
0013.00        DCL       VAR(&MSGTYPCTR) TYPE(*CHAR) LEN(4) +
0014.00                    VALUE(X'00000001')
0015.00        DCL       VAR(&PGMMSGQ) TYPE(*CHAR) LEN(10) VALUE('*')
0016.00        DCL       VAR(&STKCTR) TYPE(*CHAR) LEN(4) +
0017.00                    VALUE(X'00000001')
0018.00
0019.00        MONMSG    MSGID(CPF0000) EXEC(GOTO    CMDLBL(ERRPROC))
0020.00
0021.00        CHGVAR    VAR(&PANELID) VALUE(AR155)
0022.00        SNDRCVF
0023.00        IF        COND(&IN91) THEN(RETURN)
0024.00
0025.00        CHGVAR    VAR(&CHARWORK) VALUE(&COMPANY)
0026.00        CHGVAR     VAR(&QRYSLT) VALUE('HXCOMP =' *CAT +
0027.00                    %SST(&CHARWORK 3 3))
0028.00        CHGVAR    VAR(&QRYSLT) VALUE(&QRYSLT *CAT +
0029.00                    'HXCUST=%VALUES(')
0030.00        IF        COND(&CUST1 *NE 0) THEN(DO)
0031.00        CHGVAR    VAR(&CHARWORK) VALUE(&CUST1)
```

Figure 16.2: CL program AR155CL (part 1 of 2).

```
0032.00                CHGVAR     VAR(&QRYSLT) VALUE(&QRYSLT *CAT    &CHARWORK)
0033.00                ENDDO
0034.00                IF         COND(&CUST2 *NE 0) THEN(DO)
0035.00                CHGVAR     VAR(&CHARWORK) VALUE(&CUST2)
0036.00                CHGVAR     VAR(&QRYSLT) VALUE(&QRYSLT *CAT    &CHARWORK)
0037.00                ENDDO
0038.00                IF         COND(&CUST3 *NE 0) THEN(DO)
0039.00                CHGVAR     VAR(&CHARWORK) VALUE(&CUST3)
0040.00                CHGVAR     VAR(&QRYSLT) VALUE(&QRYSLT *CAT    &CHARWORK)
0041.00                ENDDO
0042.00                IF         COND(&CUST4 *NE 0) THEN(DO)
0043.00                CHGVAR     VAR(&CHARWORK) VALUE(&CUST4)
0044.00                CHGVAR     VAR(&QRYSLT) VALUE(&QRYSLT *CAT    &CHARWORK)
0045.00                ENDDO
0046.00                IF         COND(&CUST5 *NE 0) THEN(DO)
0047.00                CHGVAR     VAR(&CHARWORK) VALUE(&CUST5)
0048.00                CHGVAR     VAR(&QRYSLT) VALUE(&QRYSLT *CAT    &CHARWORK)
0049.00                ENDDO
0050.00                CHGVAR     VAR(&QRYSLT) VALUE(&QRYSLT *CAT ')')
0051.00
0052.00                IF         COND(&OUTQ *EQ ' ') THEN(RTVUSRPRF OUTQ(&OUTQ))
0053.00                IF         COND(&COPIES *LE 0) THEN(CHGVAR   VAR(&COPIES) +
0054.00                           VALUE(1))
0055.00                OVRPRTF    FILE(AR155P1) OUTQ(&OUTQ) COPIES(&COPIES)
0056.00                OVRDBF     FILE(ARHISTPF) SHARE(*YES)
0057.00                OPNQRYF    FILE((ARHISTPF)) QRYSLT(&QRYSLT) +
0058.00                           KEYFLD((HXDATE *DESCEND))
0059.00                CALL       PGM(AR155RG)
0060.00                CLOF       OPNID(ARHISTPF)
0061.00                DLTOVR     FILE(ARHISTPF)
0062.00                DLTOVR     FILE(AR155P1)
0063.00                RETURN
0064.00
0065.00 ERRPROC:       IF         COND(&ERROR) THEN(GOTO CMDLBL(ERRDONE))
0066.00                ELSE       CMD(CHGVAR VAR(&ERROR) VALUE('1'))
0067.00
0068.00    /* Move all *DIAG messages to previous program queue */
0069.00                CALL       PGM(QMHMOVPM) PARM(&MSGKEY &MSGTYP +
0070.00                           &MSGTYPCTR &PGMMSGQ &STKCTR    &ERRBYTES)
0071.00
0072.00    /* Resend last *ESCAPE message */
0073.00 ERRDONE:       CALL       PGM(QMHRSNEM) PARM(&MSGKEY
          &ERRBYTES)
0074.00                MONMSG     MSGID(CPF0000) EXEC(DO)
0075.00                SNDPGMMSG  MSGID(CPF3CF2) MSGF(QCPFMSG) +
0076.00                           MSGDTA('QMHRSNEM') MSGTYPE(*ESCAPE)
0077.00                MONMSG     MSGID(CPF0000)
0078.00                ENDDO
0079.00
0080.00                ENDPGM
```

Figure 16.2: CL program AR155CL (part 2 of 2).

Suppose you're developing and testing this program. So far the program is not working right. It is retrieving records for customers other than the ones selected at the prompt screen. Here's how you could use the debugger to find the problem.

DEBUGGING IN SOURCE VIEW

The first case to consider is when you've compiled with DBGVIEW(*SOURCE). Type "STRDBG AR155CL" and press Enter. The first page of the source code is shown in a debug window. Page down until you see the OPNQRYF command. In this program, it's on lines 57 and 58. Place the cursor on line 57 and press Enter, or type "BR 57" on the debugger command line and press Enter. The system responds that a breakpoint has been added on line 58. See Figure 16.3.

Press F12 to return to the command line. Type "CALL AR155CL" and press Enter. The program begins execution and prompts the operator for data. See Figure 16.4.

```
  Display Module Source

  Program:    AR155CL        Library:    JLIB          Module:    AR155CL
     46                  IF         COND(&CUST5 *NE 0) THEN(DO)
     47                  CHGVAR     VAR(&CHARWORK) VALUE(&CUST5)
     48                  CHGVAR     VAR(&QRYSLT) VALUE(&QRYSLT *CAT &CHARWORK)
     49                  ENDDO
     50                  CHGVAR     VAR(&QRYSLT) VALUE(&QRYSLT *CAT ')')
     51
     52                  IF         COND(&OUTQ *EQ ' ') THEN(RTVUSRPRF OUTQ(&OUTQ)
     53                  IF         COND(&COPIES *LE 0) THEN(CHGVAR VAR(&COPIES) +
     54                               VALUE(1))
     55                  OVRPRTF    FILE(AR155P1) OUTQ(&OUTQ) COPIES(&COPIES)
     56                  OVRDBF     FILE(ARHISTPF) SHARE(*YES)
     57                  OPNQRYF    FILE((ARHISTPF)) QRYSLT(&QRYSLT) +
     58                               KEYFLD((HXDATE *DESCEND))
     59                  CALL ·     PGM(AR155RG)
     60                  CLOF       OPNID(ARHISTPF)

  More...
  Debug . . . _____

  F3=End program    F6=Add/Clear breakpoint    F10=Step    F11=Display variable
  F12=Resume        F17=Watch variable   F18=Work with watch    F24=More keys
  Breakpoint added to line 58.
```

Figure 16.3: A breakpoint has been added before execution of the OPNQRYF command.

```
    AR155                        Open Receivables Report
    12/16/98

           21:07:50




           Company . . . . . . . . : 1__
           Customer(s) . . . . . . : 101    200___ _____ _____ _____
           Printer . . . . . . . . : QPRINT_____
           Copies  . . . . . . . . : 3__




           F3=Exit   F12=Cancel
```

Figure 16.4: The program prompts for runtime information.

Press Enter. The program continues running and halts at the breakpoint. This is shown in Figure 16.5. On the debugger command line, type "EVAL &QRYSLT" to see the value of the &QRYSLT variable.

Press Enter. The system responds with the "Evaluate Expression" display, showing the value of &QRYSLT (Figure 16.6). Notice that the only field being tested is HXCOMP.

Press Enter to return to the source display, then F12 to resume execution, or F3 to cancel debugging. At the CL command line, enter "ENDDBG" to leave debug mode.

Now it's time to determine why the query selection string didn't test the HXCUST field for the list of customer numbers. The problem turns out to be that the *CAT operator was used in lines 28, 32, 36, 40, 44, 48, and 50. The proper operator is *BCAT, which strips off trailing blanks before concatenating one blank and the second operand.

```
Display Module Source
Program:    AR155CL        Library:    JLIB         Module:    AR155CL
    54                          VALUE(1))
    55                OVRPRTF   FILE(AR155P1) OUTQ(&OUTQ) COPIES(&COPIES)
    56                OVRDBF    FILE(ARHISTPF) SHARE(*YES)
    57                OPNQRYF   FILE((ARHISTPF)) QRYSLT(&QRYSLT) +
    58                          KEYFLD((HXDATE *DESCEND))
    59                CALL      PGM(AR155RG)
    60                CLOF      OPNID(ARHISTPF)
    61                DLTOVR    FILE(ARHISTPF)
    62                DLTOVR    FILE(AR155P1)
    63                RETURN
    64
    65   ERRPROC:     IF        COND(&ERROR) THEN(GOTO CMDLBL(ERRDONE))
    66                ELSE      CMD(CHGVAR VAR(&ERROR) VALUE('1'))
    67
    68       /* Move all *DIAG messages to previous program queue */

More...
Debug . . .    eval &qryslt_____
_____
F3=End program   F6=Add/Clear breakpoint   F10=Step   F11=Display variable
F12=Resume        F17=Watch variable   F18=Work with watch   F24=More keys
Breakpoint at line 58
```

Figure 16.5: The program continues running and halts at the breakpoint.

```
Evaluate Expression

 Previous debug expressions

 > EVAL &qryslt
   &QRYSLT =
               ....5...10...15...20...25...30...35...40...45...50...55...60
  '        1   'HXCOMP =001
  '       61   '
  '      121   '
  '      181   '
         241   '                        '



 Bottom
 Debug . . .    _____

  F3=Exit    F9=Retrieve    F12=Cancel    F16=Repeat find    F19=Left
 F20=Right
  F21=Command entry        F23=Display output
```

Figure 16.6: The value of &QRYSLT.

Once those changes are made, the program can again be tested. Enter "CALL AR155CL", press Enter, and the program cancels again. The job log tells the reason: "Missing operator in expression on QRYSLT parameter." It's time for the debugger again. This time the EVAL command provides the display shown in Figure 16.7.

```
  Evaluate Expression

  Previous debug expressions

> EVAL &qryslt
  &QRYSLT =
            ....5...10...15...20...25...30...35...40...45...50...55...60
       1    'HXCOMP =001 HXCUST=%VALUES( 00101 00200 )                 '
      61    '
         '
     121    '
         '
     181    '
         '
     241    '                         '




                                                                    Bottom
  Debug . . . _____

  F3=Exit    F9=Retrieve    F12=Cancel    F16=Repeat find    F19=Left    F20=Right
  F21=Command entry    F23=Display output
```

Figure 16.7: Using the debugger again.

The problem is that there is no *AND operator between the two logical expressions. The solution is to change line 29, as shown in Figure 16.8, to include the missing operator.

```
  0028.00              CHGVAR       VAR(&QRYSLT) VALUE(&QRYSLT *BCAT +
  0029.00                             '*AND HXCUST=%VALUES(')
```

Figure 16.8: Line 29 includes the missing operator.

Now the program runs to a normal end of job and you place it into production.

A few weeks later, a user calls to say that this program canceled. You look at the user's job log and see the same error: "Missing operator in expression on QRYSLT parameter." It's time for the debugger once again.

You go to the user's office, place the program into debug as before, set the breakpoint at line 57 (or 58, if you prefer), and ask the user to rerun the program. This time the EVAL command results in the display shown in Figure 16.9.

```
   Evaluate Expression

   Previous debug expressions

 > BREAK 58
 > EVAL &qryslt
   &QRYSLT =
                ....5...10...15...20...25...30...35...40...45...50...55...60
        1     'HXCOMP =003 *AND HXCUST=%VALUES( )
        '
       61     '
        '
      121     '
        '
      181     '
        '
      241     '                          '




   Bottom
   Debug . . . _____

   F3=Exit  F9=Retrieve  F12=Cancel  F16=Repeat find  F19=Left  F20=Right
   F21=Command entry      F23=Display output
```

Figure 16.9: Results from rerunning the program.

The user, wanting a listing for all company 3 customers, didn't enter any customer numbers. Again, debugging has shown you the problem. The solution is not to select by customer if all customer numbers are zero.

OTHER IMPORTANT DEBUGGER COMMANDS

So far, you have seen how the BREAK and EVAL commands are used. This section briefly explains two other commands that you will probably want to use frequently.

The STEP command allows you to execute a procedure one line at a time. Each time you enter the STEP command (or press the F10 key), the next line of code is executed and the debugger stops, as if you had set a breakpoint on the following line.

You can step over calls to other processes (by pressing F10) or you can step into them (by pressing F22). Stepping over is the default. If you step over, the other process is executed and the debugger stops at the command following the call. If you step into a process, the debugger enters the other module and you can debug it.

You also might want to become familiar with the WATCH command. It allows you to stop execution each time a variable is changed. For instance, suppose a variable is being corrupted, but you can't determine where. When you use the WATCH command, the debugger will inform you each time the variable's value changes.

SUMMARY OF DEBUGGER COMMANDS

Table 16.1 lists interactive debugger commands and gives a brief description of each one. For more information, see the online Help for an explanation of each command in more depth and for examples of debugging programs in several languages—including CL.

Table 16.1: ILE Source Debugger Commands

Command[1]	Abbreviation	Function Key[2]	Description
attr	att		Display a variable's size and data type (attributes).
bottom	bo		Position to the last line.
break	br	F6	Specify a breakpoint.
break ine-number when	br		Specify a conditional breakpoint.

Table 16.1: ILE Source Debugger Commands, continued

Command[1]	Abbreviation	Function Key[2]	Description
clear	c	F6	Remove breakpoints and watch conditions.
display	di	.	Display definitions created with the EQUATE command or display a different source module.
down	do		Window source toward the end of the view.
equate	eq		Create a shorthand name for an expression, variable, or debug command.
eval	ev	F11	Display or change the value of a variable, or display the value of an expression.
find	f		Search for a line number or specific text.
help	h	F1	Display online help information for debugger commands.
left	l		Window source to the left.
next	n		Position to the next breakpoint.
previous	p		Position to the previous breakpoint.
qual	q		Define the scope of variables in EVAL and WATCH commands.
right	r		Window source to the right.
set	se		Change debug options.
step	s	F10	Run one or more statements of the procedure being debugged.
top	t		Positions source to the first line.
up	u		Window source towards the beginning of the view.
watch	w	F17	Causes a breakpoint when the value of a variable changes.

1 You may enter commands in either uppercase or lowercase.

2 The function keys are not exact equivalents. For example, F11 can be used to display the value of a variable, but not to change its value.

DEBUGGING IN LIST VIEW

Debugging in list view is similar to debugging in source view. The difference is that the source debugger displays the compiler listing rather than the source code. The compiler listing begins with a summary of compilation parameters, and then continues with a listing of the source code. In this example, the compiler listing also includes the list of all fields in the display file following the DCLF command (as shown in Figure 16.10).

```
Display Module Source

Program:   AR155CL      Library:   JLIB      Module:   AR155CL_V1
    19   Compiler  . . . . . . . . . . :   IBM AS/400 Control
    20                              Control Language Source
    21   SEQNBR  *...+... 1 ...+... 2 ...+... 3 ...+... 4 ...+... 5 ...+... 6
    22    100-            PGM
    23    200-
    24    300-            DCLF        FILE(AR155DF)
    25
    26          QUALIFIED FILE NAME - JLIB/AR155DF
    27
    28             RECORD FORMAT NAME - PROMPT
    29
    30             CL VARIABLE    TYPE     LENGTH     PRECISION    TEXT
    31             &IN91         *LGL      1                       Cancel
    32             &PANELID      *CHAR     10
    33             &COMPANY      *DEC      3           0
                                                          More...
 Debug . . . _____

 F3=End program   F6=Add/Clear breakpoint   F10=Step   F11=Display variable
 F12=Resume       F17=Watch variable   F18=Work with watch   F24=More keys
```

Figure 16.10: An example of debugging in list view.

You will have to debug with compiler listing line numbers rather than with the line numbers stored in the source code. In this example, the OPNQRYF command is on lines 96 and 97, in list view, instead of lines 57 and 58, as in the source view.

DEBUGGING IN STATEMENT VIEW

If you compile with DBGVIEW(*STMT), the debugger won't display source code. However, you can still debug using statement numbers. When you enter "STRDBG AR155CL" and press Enter, you see a display like the one shown in Figure 16.11.

```
  Display Module Source

    Program:   AR155CL      Library:   JLIB        Module:   AR155CL

      (Source not available.)








        Bottom
   Debug . . . br ar155cl/5700_____
  _____
    F3=End program  F6=Add/Clear breakpoint  F10=Step  F11=Display variable
    F12=Resume       F17=Watch variable    F18=Work with watch
  F24=More keys
```

Figure 16.11: The *STMT view doesn't show source code.

As shown in Figure 16.11, enter "BR AR155CL/5700" and press Enter to add the breakpoint. Notice that the break command requires you to specify the module name before the line number, and that the two are separated by a slash.

From this point, debugging proceeds as before. Press F12 to return to the CL command line, type "CALL AR155CL" and press Enter. The system halts at the breakpoint and you can enter the EVAL command, as before.

OPM PROGRAMS AND THE ILE DEBUGGER

You can use the ILE debugger to debug OPM programs but you must remember to do two important things.

- When you compile the CL program, you must specify OPTION(*SRCDBG) on the Create CL Program (CRTCLPGM) command.

- You must use OPMSRC(*YES) on the STRDBG command.

DEBUGGING ANOTHER JOB

You can debug a program running in another job. This is especially helpful when you must debug a program that always runs in batch mode and cannot run interactively.

Figure 16.12 contains such a program. It is the same accounts receivable program used in the illustration, but has been modified to run twice each time a report is requested. The first time, it runs interactively to prompt the user for company number, up to six customer numbers, output queue, and number of copies. The program submits itself to batch, where it carries out the task of producing a report.

```
        PGM

                DCLF        FILE(AR155DF)

                DCL         VAR(&CHARWORK) TYPE(*CHAR) LEN(5)
                DCL         VAR(&QRYSLT) TYPE(*CHAR) LEN(256)
                DCL         VAR(&JOBTYPE) TYPE(*CHAR) LEN(1)

                DCL         VAR(&ERRBYTES) TYPE(*CHAR) LEN(4) +
                              VALUE(X'00000000')
                DCL         VAR(&ERROR) TYPE(*LGL) VALUE('0')
                DCL         VAR(&MSGKEY) TYPE(*CHAR) LEN(4)
                DCL         VAR(&MSGTYP) TYPE(*CHAR) LEN(10)
                              VALUE('*DIAG')
                DCL         VAR(&MSGTYPCTR) TYPE(*CHAR) LEN(4) +
                              VALUE(X'00000001')
                DCL         VAR(&PGMMSGQ) TYPE(*CHAR) LEN(10)
                              VALUE('*')
                DCL         VAR(&STKCTR) TYPE(*CHAR) LEN(4) +
                              VALUE(X'00000001')

                MONMSG      MSGID(CPF0000) EXEC(GOTO CMDLBL(ERRPROC))

                RTVJOBA     TYPE(&JOBTYPE)
                IF          COND(&JOBTYPE *EQ '0') THEN(GOTO  CMDLBL(BATCH))
```

Figure 16.12: program that runs interactively and submits itself to a job queue (part 1 of 3).

```
        /* Program is running interactively */
                CHGVAR    VAR(&PANELID) VALUE(AR155)
                SNDRCVF
                IF        COND(&IN91) THEN(RETURN)
                CHGVAR    VAR(%SST(*LDA 1 3)) VALUE(&COMPANY)
                CHGVAR    VAR(%SST(*LDA 11 5)) VALUE(&CUST1)
                CHGVAR    VAR(%SST(*LDA 16 5)) VALUE(&CUST2)
                CHGVAR    VAR(%SST(*LDA 21 5)) VALUE(&CUST3)
                CHGVAR    VAR(%SST(*LDA 26 5)) VALUE(&CUST4)
                CHGVAR    VAR(%SST(*LDA 31 5)) VALUE(&CUST5)
                CHGVAR    VAR(%SST(*LDA 36 5)) VALUE(&CUST6)
                CHGVAR    VAR(%SST(*LDA 41 10)) VALUE(&OUTQ)
                CHGVAR    VAR(%SST(*LDA 51 3)) VALUE(&COPIES)

                SBMJOB    CMD(CALL PGM(AR155CL)) JOB(AR155)
                RETURN

BATCH: /* Program is running in batch mode */
                CHGVAR    VAR(&COMPANY) VALUE(%SST(*LDA 1 3))
                CHGVAR    VAR(&CUST1) VALUE(%SST(*LDA 11 5))
                CHGVAR    VAR(&CUST2) VALUE(%SST(*LDA 16 5))
                CHGVAR    VAR(&CUST3) VALUE(%SST(*LDA 21 5))
                CHGVAR    VAR(&CUST4) VALUE(%SST(*LDA 26 5))
                CHGVAR    VAR(&CUST5) VALUE(%SST(*LDA 31 5))
                CHGVAR    VAR(&CUST6) VALUE(%SST(*LDA 36 5))
                CHGVAR    VAR(&OUTQ) VALUE(%SST(*LDA 41 10))
                CHGVAR    VAR(&COPIES) VALUE(%SST(*LDA 51 3))
                CHGVAR    VAR(&QRYSLT) VALUE('HXCOMP =' *CAT %SST(*LDA +
                            1 3))
                CHGVAR    VAR(&CHARWORK) VALUE(&COMPANY)
                CHGVAR    VAR(&QRYSLT) VALUE('HXCOMP =' *CAT +
                            %SST(&CHARWORK 3 3))
                IF        COND(&CUST1 *NE 0) THEN(DO)
                CHGVAR    VAR(&CHARWORK) VALUE(&CUST1)
                CHGVAR    VAR(&QRYSLT) VALUE(&QRYSLT *BCAT &CHARWORK)
                ENDDO
                IF        COND(&CUST2 *NE 0) THEN(DO)
                CHGVAR    VAR(&CHARWORK) VALUE(&CUST2)
                CHGVAR    VAR(&QRYSLT) VALUE(&QRYSLT *BCAT &CHARWORK)
                ENDDO
                IF        COND(&CUST3 *NE 0) THEN(DO)
                CHGVAR    VAR(&CHARWORK) VALUE(&CUST3)
                CHGVAR    VAR(&QRYSLT) VALUE(&QRYSLT *BCAT &CHARWORK)
                ENDDO
                IF        COND(&CUST4 *NE 0) THEN(DO)
                CHGVAR    VAR(&CHARWORK) VALUE(&CUST4)
                CHGVAR    VAR(&QRYSLT) VALUE(&QRYSLT *BCAT &CHARWORK)
                ENDDO
```

Figure 16.12: program that runs interactively and submits itself to a job queue (part 2 of 3).

```
                IF      COND(&CUST5 *NE 0) THEN(DO)
                CHGVAR  VAR(&CHARWORK) VALUE(&CUST5)
                CHGVAR  VAR(&QRYSLT) VALUE(&QRYSLT *BCAT &CHARWORK)
                ENDDO
                CHGVAR  VAR(&QRYSLT) VALUE(&QRYSLT *BCAT ')')

                IF      COND(&OUTQ *EQ ' ') THEN(RTVUSRPRF  OUTQ(&OUTQ))
                IF      COND(&COPIES *LE 0) THEN(CHGVAR    VAR(&COPIES) +
                          VALUE(1))

                OVRPRTF FILE(AR155P1) OUTQ(&OUTQ) COPIES(&COPIES)
                OVRDBF  FILE(ARHISTPF) SHARE(*YES)
                OPNQRYF FILE((ARHISTPF)) QRYSLT(&QRYSLT) +
                          KEYFLD((HXDATE *DESCEND))
                CALL    PGM(AR155RG)
                CLOF    OPNID(ARHISTPF)
                DLTOVR  FILE(ARHISTPF)
                DLTOVR  FILE(AR155P1)
                RETURN

ERRPROC:        IF      COND(&ERROR) THEN(GOTO CMDLBL(ERRDONE))
                ELSE    CMD(CHGVAR VAR(&ERROR) VALUE('1'))

     /* Move all *DIAG messages to previous program queue */
                CALL    PGM(QMHMOVPM) PARM(&MSGKEY &MSGTYP +
                          &MSGTYPCTR &PGMMSGQ &STKCTR &ERRBYTES)

     /* Resend last *ESCAPE message */
ERRDONE:        CALL    PGM(QMHRSNEM) PARM(&MSGKEY &ERRBYTES)
                MONMSG  MSGID(CPF0000) EXEC(DO)
                SNDPGMMSG MSGID(CPF3CF2) MSGF(QCPFMSG) +
                          MSGDTA('QMHRSNEM') MSGTYPE(*ESCAPE)
                MONMSG  MSGID(CPF0000)
                ENDDO
                ENDPGM
```

Figure 16.12: Program that runs interactively and submits itself to a job queue (part 2 of 3).

To debug the batch occurrence of the program requires the Start Service Job (STRSRVJOB) command. STRSRVJOB has only one required parameter: the simple or qualified name of the job where the program is running. The simple name is the name specified in the JOB parameter of the SBMJOB command. The qualified name would consist of the simple name along with the user profile of the job and the six-digit job number assigned by the system. For example, a simple name might be AR155, and the qualified job name might be 179789/JOSEPH/AR155.

If you specify a simple name, you might want to use the second parameter—Duplicate Job Option (DUPJOBOPT). The default value—*SELECT—causes the system to present a selection display. The other permissible value is *MSG, which causes the system to issue an escape message if duplicate jobs are found. To debug the batch portion of this program, do the following steps:

1. Hold the job queue to which the batch program will be submitted (Figure 16.13). This prevents the program from beginning to run before you can issue the STRSRVPGM command.

```
hldjobq qbatch
```

Figure 16.13: Holding the job queue.

2. Call the program interactively, filling in the prompts with the correct values (Figure 16.14). When you press Enter, a new job is placed on the held job queue.

```
call ar155cl
```

Figure 16.14: Calling the program interactively.

3. Determine the qualified name of the submitted job. You can use various commands, such as WRKSBMJOB SBMFROM(*JOB) and WRKUSRJOB, to find the job on the job queue.

4. Issue the STRSRVPGM command, specifying the qualified name of the submitted job (Figure 16.15).

```
strsrvjob 179789/joseph/ar155
```

Figure 16.15: Issuing the STRASRVPGM command.

If you do this correctly, the system does not respond with a message.

```
strdbg ar155cl
```

Figure 16.16: Issuing the STRDBG command.

5. Issue the STRDBG command, specifying the name of the program to be debugged (Figure 16.16).

   You will be presented with the Display Module Source display. Press F12 to exit it, because you cannot enter debugging commands until the job becomes active.

6. Release the job queue to allow the serviced job to begin running. You will see the Start Serviced Job display (as shown in Figure 16.17).

```
Start Serviced Job

  System:   MCRISC
  Job:    AR155         User:   JOSEPH        Number:    179789

  The serviced job has been released from the job queue.  Press
  Enter to
  start the job or F10 to enter debug commands for that job.



  Press Enter to continue.

  F10=Command entry
  (C) COPYRIGHT IBM CORP. 1980, 1998.
```

Figure 16.17: The Start Serviced Job display.

Press F10 in order to enter a breakpoint. If you see the Command Entry display, enter the command DSPMODSRC (Display Module Source) and press Enter. The system responds by displaying the module source. Set a break point on the OPNQRYF command.

7. Now you're ready to begin execution of the program. Press F12 twice to leave the module source and command entry displays and return to the Start Serviced Job display. Press Enter to start execution of the serviced job.

8. Debug the program as you would if it were running in your own job. When you finish debugging, issue the ENDDBG command, followed by the ENDSRVJOB command.

THE DMPCLPGM COMMAND

The Dump CL Program (DMPCLPGM) command produces a report listing the contents of variables and the program message queue. Character variables are shown in both character and hexadecimal format.

Because it doesn't cause the program to abort, this report can be produced anytime during the execution of the program. DMPCLPGM has no parameters. The output produced goes to your job's default output queue. The program shown in Figure 16.18 illustrates use of DMPCLPGM. If it ends abnormally, the DMPCLPGM command runs and produces the report shown in Figure 16.19.

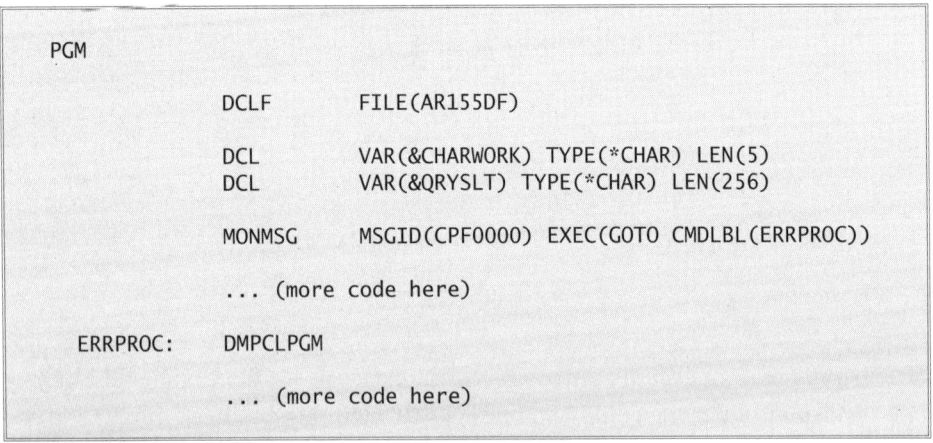

```
      PGM

                  DCLF       FILE(AR155DF)

                  DCL        VAR(&CHARWORK) TYPE(*CHAR) LEN(5)
                  DCL        VAR(&QRYSLT) TYPE(*CHAR) LEN(256)

                  MONMSG     MSGID(CPF0000) EXEC(GOTO CMDLBL(ERRPROC))

                  ... (more code here)

      ERRPROC:    DMPCLPGM

                  ... (more code here)
```

Figure 16.18: An example illustrating use of the DMPCLPGM command.

```
5769SS1 V4R3M0 980729          CL Program Dump          12/19/98  7:30:42      Page   1

Job name  . . . . . :  QPADEV0010  User name . . . . . :  JLIB     Job number  . . . :  179913
Program name  . . . :  AR155CL     Library . . . . . . :  JLIB      Statement . . . . :  5400
Module name . . . . :  AR155CL     Procedure name  . . :  AR155CL

                                        Messages

            Message                  Message              From                    To
     Time   ID        Sev   Type     Text                 Program      Inst       Program
     Inst
     073042 CPD3117   30    DIAG     Expression on QRYSLT pa QQQTKZ      *N        AR155CL      *N
                                     rameter missing parenth
                                     esis.
     073042 CPF9899   40    ESC      Error occurred during p QQQTKZ      *N        AR155CL      *N
                                     rocessing of command.

                                        Variables

     Variable   Type    Length   Value                    Value in Hexadecimal
                                 *...+....1....+....2....+  * . . . + . . . 1 . . . . + . . . . 2 . . . . +

     &CHARWORK  *CHAR     5      '00200'                  F0F0F2F0F0
     &COMPANY   *DEC    3 0      1
     &COPIES    *DEC    1 0      3
     &CUST1     *DEC    5 0      101
     &CUST2     *DEC    5 0      200
     &CUST3     *DEC    5 0      0
     &CUST4     *DEC    5 0      0
     &CUST5     *DEC    5 0      0
     &CUST6     *DEC    5 0      0
     &IN91      *CHAR     1      '0'                      F0
     &OUTQ      *CHAR    10      'QPRINT     '            D8D7D9C9D5E340404040
     &PANELID   *CHAR    10      'AR155      '            C1D9F1F5F54040404040
     &QRYSLT    *CHAR   256      'HXCOMP =001 *AND HXCUST=%'  C8E7C3D6D4D7407EF0F0F1405CC1D5C440C8E7C3E4E2E37E6C
                         +26     'VALUES( 00101 00200      '  E5C1D3E4C5E24D40F0F0F1F0F140F0F0F2F0F0404040404040
                         +51   '                          '  404040404040404040404040404040404040404040404040
                         +76   '                          '  404040404040404040404040404040404040404040404040
                         +101  '                          '  404040404040404040404040404040404040404040404040

                         +126  '                          '  404040404040404040404040404040404040404040404040
                         +151  '                          '  404040404040404040404040404040404040404040404040

                         +176  '                          '  404040404040404040404040404040404040404040404040
                         +201  '                          '  404040404040404040404040404040404040404040404040

                         +226  '                          '  404040404040404040404040404040404040404040404040
                         +251  '       '                     404040404040


                    * * * * *  E N D  O F  D U M P  * * * * *
```

Figure 16.19: The report produced by DMPCLPGM.

17

CL AND THE INTEGRATED LANGUAGE ENVIRONMENT

The Integrated Language Environment (ILE) provides a way for programs to use the resources they need without interfering with one another. It is a different philosophy from the Original Program Model (dating back to the IBM System/38). This chapter presents the basics of ILE and explains how to write CL code that fits into ILE-based applications.

TYPES OF OBJECT CODE

The i5 allows two types of executable code: procedures and programs. These reside in three object types—programs, service programs, and modules.

A procedure is compiled code that is not executable by itself. It must be linked with other code in order to form a program.

A program contains one or more procedures written in one or more ILE languages. Under ILE, it isn't accurate to speak of a CL program, an RPG program, a C program, or a COBOL program. A program may be made up of procedures written in any mixture of these languages. One of these procedures serves as the program entry point. In other words, when the program begins executing, this procedure is given control. To start execution of a program, use the CL CALL command or its equivalent in another language.

A CL module is created from one source member and contains one procedure. A module must be bound into a program or service program.

BINDING

The term *binding* refers to how executable code relates to other executable code. ILE supports three types of binding: bind by copy, bind by reference, and the dynamic call.

Binding by Copy

Binding by copy means that the executable code in a procedure is copied into the program object when the program is created. It is as if the called procedure's source code were part of the caller's source code. For example, refer to the two procedures, A and B, shown in Figures 17.1 and 17.2.

```
PGM

    DCL         &greeting       *CHAR       64
    DCL         &msg            *CHAR       64

    CALLPRC     PRC(B) PARM(&greeting)
    CHGVAR      &msg    (&greeting *TCAT '!')
    SNDPGMMSG   MSGID(CPF9897) MSGF(QCPFMSG) MSGDTA(&MSG) +
                    MSGTYPE(*COMP)
```

Figure 17.1: Procedure A is the caller.

```
PGM          PARM(&message)

   DCL          &message     *CHAR     64

   CHGVAR       &message  'Bonjour'
   ENDPGM
```

Figure 17.2: Procedure B is the called procedure.

If you bind the two by copy, the result would be as if you had written procedure A as in Figure 17.3 and there were no procedure B.

```
PGM

   DCL          &greeting    *CHAR     64
   DCL          &msg         *CHAR     64

   CHGVAR       &greeting  'Bonjour'
   CHGVAR       &msg    (&greeting *TCAT '!')
   SNDPGMMSG    MSGID(CPF9897) MSGF(QCPFMSG) MSGDTA(&MSG) +
                   MSGTYPE(*COMP)
```

Figure 17.3: A one-procedure equivalent to binding by copy.

If you were to change procedure B, replacing the string "Bonjour" with "Guten Morgen," the program created from these two procedures would continue to send the string "Bonjour!" as a completion message.

If you want the program to use the updated version of procedure B, you must either recompile the program, binding the new version of B by copy, or use another type of binding.

Binding by Reference

When you *bind by reference*, the system does not copy the called procedure's calculations into the program object. Instead, the program is told only how to interface with the called procedure. At runtime, the program retrieves the latest version of the called procedure, verifies that its interface has not changed and, if so, executes the called procedure.

If you bind procedures A and B by reference, and later change the string "Bonjour" to "Guten Morgen" in procedure B, the program generated from procedures A and B will report "Guten Morgen," even though it has not been recompiled.

The Dynamic Call

The dynamic call starts execution of a program. The calling process, which could be a procedure or a program, knows nothing of the interface of the called program. At run-time, the system must locate the called program and link it to the caller.

When a called program is modified and recompiled, the processes that call it will from then on use the new version of the called program.

COMPILATION

To create executable CL code, you use four commands:

- CRTCLMOD (Create CL Module).

- CRTSRVPGM (Create Service Program).

- CRTPGM (Create Program).

- CRTBNDCL (Create Bound CL Program).

The following sections consider each of these commands in more detail.

CRTCLMOD

CRTCLMOD creates a module from one CL source member. Even though the source member begins with the PGM command, the result is a module (not a program). The created module cannot be executed, but must be bound into a program or service program.

CRTSRVPGM

CRTSRVPGM creates a service program from one or more modules. There are two ways to tell CRTSRVPGM which modules you want to place into the service program.

- You may list modules in the MODULE parameter.

- You may use the BNDDIR parameter to list binding directories containing lists of module names.

A procedure in a service program may call procedures of other service programs. If so, you may use the BNDSRVPGM and BNDDIR parameters to permit the compiler to find them.

CRTPGM

CRTPGM creates an executable program from one or more modules. A program differs from a service program in that a program has an entry point and can be directly executed. This entry point is specified in the ENTMOD (Entry Module) parameter, which defaults to *FIRST. In other words, the first module listed in the MODULE parameter that has a program entry point becomes the entry point of the program.

The MODULE, BNDDIR, and BNDSRVPGM parameters work as they do with CRTSRVPGM. One of these procedures serves as the program entry point. Therefore, when the program begins executing, this procedure is given control. To start execution of a program, use the CL CALL command or its equivalent in another language.

A CL module is created from one source member and contains one procedure. A module must be bound into a program or service program.

CRTBNDCL

CRTBNDCL compiles a CL source member, producing an ILE program consisting of one procedure. This isn't the ideal way to compile CL. As a rule, you should use the CRTCLMOD command to build a module, and then bind that module into programs or service programs. The purpose of this command is to provide a way to create an ILE program instead of an OPM program when converting to ILE.

ACTIVATION GROUPS

An activation group is a division of a job. Just as jobs are not objects, activation groups are not objects. The purpose of activation groups is to provide a way to isolate resources to programs without interference from other programs.

Before you create a program or service program, you should decide which activation group it is to run in. Use the DFTACTGRP and ACTGRP parameters to inform the CL compiler of your choice of activation groups.

The Default Activation Group

The default activation group is the activation group that exists in every job. All OPM programs run in the default activation group, and ILE programs can run there as well.

When developing brand new applications, you should avoid the default activation group. The system treats this activation group differently from other activation groups. You should use the default activation group only when adding ILE programs to an application that includes OPM programs, and then only if necessary.

The alternative is to use named activation groups. You can name them yourself or you can ask the system to name them for you.

ACTGRP(IDENTIFIER)

If you want to assign a name of your choosing to an activation group, code that name in the ACTGRP parameter. For example, an interactive accounts payable inquiry program and the service programs it uses might run in activation group APINQ, while a general ledger inquiry program runs in GLINQ. Overrides, commitment control, and OPNQRYF commands issued in APINQ would not affect programs running in GLINQ.

*ACTGRP(*NEW)*

If you want the system to create an activation group and give it a unique name, code ACTGRP(*NEW). Be aware that this option can cause poor performance.

The system will create and destroy an activation group repeatedly as a program is activated and deactivated.

ACTGRP(*CALLER)

In order to tell the system that a program or service program should run in whichever activation group its caller runs in, specify ACTGRP(*CALLER). Be aware that the same program might behave in different ways, depending on whether its caller is running in the default activation group or not. The decision of which activation group to use is not always an easy one to make. Here are some guidelines that will help.

- If a program is called only once per job, specify ACTGRP(*NEW).

- If a program should share resources (e.g. commitment control, open data paths, overrides) of its caller, use *CALLER. However, avoid using *CALLER when the calling program is running in the default activation group.

- If a service program is closely tied to a few programs at most, and the procedures are application specific, specify *CALLER.

- If a service program is utilitarian in nature, run it in a named activation group. An example of a utilitarian service program would be one that contains string handling procedures. Such a service program does no input-output operations, and therefore does not share the types of resources that activation groups manage. If possible, choose a name that is descriptive of the tasks being performed. For a string-handling service program, you might specify ACTGRP(STRING).

Destroying Activation Groups

Use the Reclaim Activation Group (RCLACTGRP) parameter to explicitly destroy an activation group. This command accepts one parameter, which may have an activation group name or the special value *ELIGIBLE. An activation group is eligible for destruction if none of the programs in the group are currently active. Some reasons you might want to destroy an activation group are:

- A group of programs that runs in an activation group has completed and is unlikely to be re-executed.

- A program (or programs) tend to allocate a lot of memory. Destroying the activation group frees up the memory when it is no longer needed.

- A program is being run and debugged interactively. If you don't destroy the activation group after each recompilation, you will continue to debug the old version of the program.

PARAMETER DESCRIPTIONS

The following sections discuss in greater detail many of the parameters used by the compilation commands.

PGM: Program Name

The PGM parameter is the only one that is required. You must enter the qualified name of the program object (*PGM) being compiled. The library portion of this qualified name defaults to *CURLIB. If you use *CURLIB but your job has no current library (check with the DSPLIBL command), the program will be created in QGPL.

SRCFILE: Source File Name

The SRCFILE parameter is where you enter the qualified name of the source file that contains the code for the CL program. It defaults to QCLSRC in *LIBL. Don't use the default library of *LIBL. File QCLSRC can exist in many libraries (some of which could be higher than the right one in the library list).

SRCMBR: Source Member Name

The SRCMBR parameter names the source member within SRCFILE that contains the source code for the CL program being compiled. It defaults to *PGM, and that means the source member is assumed to have the same name as the compiled program will have (indicated in the PGM parameter).

For example, if PGM(SAMPLECL) SRCMBR(*PGM) is indicated, the source member name is assumed to be SAMPLECL.

Unless you have very peculiar requirements, you are better off using the same name for both the source member and the compiled program. Doing so simplifies the use of the CRTCLPGM and CRTBNDCL commands and avoids confusion.

TEXT: Text Description

All objects and file members should have text description on your system because it helps document objects and members. The TEXT parameter lets you enter up to 50 characters of text description for the *PGM object being created.

Because the default value is *SRCMBRTXT, the compiled program's text will match that of the source member (which you entered when you edited the source member with SEU).

DFTACTGRP: Default Activation Group

The DFTACTGRP parameter determines whether the compiled program will be part of the default activation group. *YES is the default value. If you use *YES, you cannot specify an activation group using the ACTGRP parameter.

OPTION: Compiler Listing Options

The OPTION parameter lets you enter one or more of the values listed in Table 17.1. Each value causes the system to produce some piece of output when the compiler runs. Table 17.1 lists the options.

Table 17.1: Compile Listing Options

Option	Description
*XREF	Produce a cross-reference listing of variables and labels in the program. Assumed unless *NOXREF is specified.
*NOXREF	Omit the cross-reference listing.
*SECLVL	For each compiler message, include the second-level text. This option is useful if some of the messages printed by the compiler do not make sense to you.
*NOSECLVL	Omit the second-level text. Assumed unless *SECLVL is specified.
*EVENTF	The compiler produces an event file for CODE/400.
*NOEVENTF	No CODE/400 event file is created. This is the default option.

USRPRF: Assumed User Profile

The USRPRF parameter specifies which user profiles are used for authorization to objects while the program is running. The default value is *USER, which means that the authority of the user who runs the program is in effect. The value of *OWNER means that the authorities of both the user running the program and the owner of the program are in effect. This is known as *adopted authority.*

For additional information on this topic, refer to Chapter 14, Security Considerations.

LOG: Log Commands

The LOG parameter decides whether each CL command included in the program will be logged to the job log. This parameter can have three different values: *JOB, *YES, or *NO. The default is *JOB.

- *JOB picks up the job's setting. The setting was initially set by the job description, and might have been changed later with the CHGJOB command. Check this job attribute with the DSPJOB command.

- *YES means that all commands in the CL program will be logged to the job log. Logging isn't only useful while debugging, but at all times. It lets you see the progress of a CL program as it executes.

- *NO means that no commands are logged to the job log.

REPLACE: Replace Existing Program

The REPLACE parameter indicates whether to replace an existing program of the same name when the compiler generates the new *PGM object. For example, you might be recompiling a program you created some time ago. REPLACE(*YES) does the following:

- Moves the existing program to library QRPLOBJ, where replaced objects accumulate until the library is cleared manually.

- Generates a new *PGM object in the correct library.

REPLACE(*NO) doesn't allow this automatic replacement. If the library already has a program of the same name, the CRTCLPGM or CRTBNDCL command fails, the old program is left untouched, and no program object is generated. REPLACE defaults to *YES.

TGTRLS: Target Release

If you have to support a system that is running under an older release of the operating system, you should use the TGTRLS parameter to force the system to create the CL program using the destination machine's version code instead of your system's. The compiled program can then be saved with the SAVOBJ command (also specifying the TGTRLS parameter with the same value) so that it can be restored onto the other system. TGTRLS accepts the following values:

- CURRENT: The program is created using your system's OS/400 version. When you save the compiled program, you must also specify *CURRENT. This value is the default.

- *PRV: The program is created using the OS/400 version immediately prior to your system's. For example, if your system is at V5R3M0, TGTRLS(*PRV) creates the program at V5R2M0. Note that the modification level (M0) does not matter.

- VNRNMN: The program is created using an older version of the operating system. For example, TGTRLS(V4R5M0) creates the program so that it can run on a V4R5M0 machine.

If you specify a previous release that is not supported on your system, the compilation aborts with escape message CPF0C35. The text of this message indicates the earliest supported release.

You might not be able to create a program to an older release if your program includes features that were not available at the time that release was current. For example, versions prior to V5R3M0 didn't support the SELECT command. If your CL program includes a SELECT statement, the CL program cannot be compiled using TGTRLS(V5R2M0).

AUT: Public Authority

The generated program can either be accessed by the public or it cannot. The AUT parameter indicates what level of access to the *PGM object you want to give the public.

The default value is *LIBCRTAUT. Other acceptable values are *EXCLUDE (no access), *USE (the public can call the program), or *ALL (the public can do anything, even delete the program).

You also can enter an authorization list name in the AUT parameter.

SRTSEQ: Sort Sequence

You may specify a sort sequence table to be used when comparing strings.

LANGID: Language ID

The language identifier should be used if SRTSEQ has the value *LANGIDSHR or *LANGIDUNQ.

DBGVIEW: Debugging View

You may specify how much debugging information will be stored with the compiled program. See Chapter 16 for more about the permissible values for this parameter.

ENBPFRCOL: Enable Performance Collection

The ENBPFRCOL parameter specifies how much performance data is collected for use with the Performance Explorer.

ACTGRP: Activation Group Name

The ACTGRP parameter indicates with which activation group the program will be associated once you call it. See the preceding section on activation groups.

OPTIMIZE: Optimization

*NONE (the default value) indicates that the program should not be optimized. You should use this value whenever possible; it allows you to debug the program. The *BASIC value allows you to display variable names during debugging, but you cannot change the values. The same is true with *FULL (except that the values displayed might not be the most current values).

A

SOME UTILITY COMMANDS

Thanks to its capability to extend its vocabulary, CL is a really flexible language. This appendix provides a number of utility commands that you can put to use immediately. Even if you don't need a particular command, the code provided for it will be useful for learning CL coding techniques.

To install a utility command, enter its code into a source physical file member and compile it. You should put the code in a library of your choice. The library should be available to you through the library list.

One solution is to create a library (name it UTILITY or something like that) and place it at the bottom of the system portion of the library list. To do so, you must change system value QSYSLIBL using the Work with System Values (WRKSYSVAL) command. See Figure A.1.

```
WRKSYSVAL qsyslibl
```

Figure A.1: Using WRKSYSVAL to change the default library list.

In the panel that shows up, enter an Option 2 (to change) and press Enter. Then type the name of the new library, after all the names already there, and press Enter again.

Note: Be aware that most, if not all, utility commands presented here make use of the first utility command, Forward Program Messages (FWDPGMMSG). You should make sure to install at least this command on your system.

MESSAGES

Virtually all CL programs must contain some kind of mechanism to forward program messages up the call stack. The idea is that, if a CL program ends, all the messages that have accumulated in its program-message queue should be sent to the CL program's caller. By doing so, the caller becomes aware that the CL program has failed, and can learn why by examining the messages received.

Forward Program Messages (FWDPGMMSG)

The FWDPGMMSG command solves one problem. Without the command, you would have to declare a number of variables in each CL program and remember to paste, near the program's end, a rather complicated piece of code. With FWDPGMMSG, there are no variables to declare and the end-of-program code is reduced to just two lines.

Here's how to use the command. Each CL program should have a program-level MONMSG that at least monitors for CPF0000. In case any machine messages show up, it's better if the MONMSG command monitors for MCH0000 at the same time. The EXEC parameter should contain a GOTO to label error (as shown in Figure A.2).

Don't forget the RETURN command right before the "error" label. And don't forget the MONMSG that follows FWDPGMMSG. It's needed in case FWDPGMMSG ends in error for some reason; without MONMSG, the CL program would get caught in an infinite loop.

```
PGM
   DCL ...
   DCL ...
   MONMSG (cpf0000 mch0000) EXEC(GOTO error)
   ...
   ... (body of program)
   ...
   RETURN
error:
   FWDPGMMSG
   MONMSG cpf0000

ENDPGM
```

Figure A.2: Integrating the FWDPGMMSG utility into a CL program.

Parameters

- MSGTYPE: Which messages to forward. Options are *DIAGESC (diagnostic and escape), *INFOCOMP (informational and completion), and *ALL.

- CVTESCAPE: Whether to convert escape messages to diagnostic messages. Options are *YES and *NO.

Figure A.3 contains the source code for command FWDPGMMSG.

```
/************************************************************************/
/*                                                                    */
/* To compile:                                                        */
/*                                                                    */
/*    CRTCMD   CMD(xxx/FWDPGMMSG) +                                   */
/*             PGM(xxx/FWDPGMMSGC) +                                  */
/*             SRCFILE(xxx/QCMDSRC) +                                 */
/*             TEXT('Forward Program Messages') +                     */
/*             ALLOW(*IPGM *IMOD *BPGM *BMOD)                         */
/*                                                                    */
/************************************************************************/
CMD  'Forward Program Messages'

   PARM msgtype *CHAR 9 DFT(*DIAGESC) RSTD(*YES) +
        VALUES(*DIAGESC *INFOCOMP *ALL) PROMPT('Message types')
```

Figure A.3: Source code for the command FWDPGMMSG (part 1 of 2).

```
    PARM cvtescape *CHAR 4 DFT(*NO) RSTD(*YES) VALUES(*YES *NO) +
         PROMPT('Convert *ESCAPE to *DIAG')
```

Figure A.3: Source code for the command FWDPGMMSG (part 2 of 2).

The command processing program of FWDPGMMSG is CL Program
FWDPGMMSGC. See Figure A.4.

```
/**********************************************************************/
/*                                                                    */
/* To compile:                                                        */
/*                                                                    */
/*    CRTCLPGM  PGM(xxx/FWDPGMMSGC) +                                 */
/*              SRCFILE(xxx/QCLSRC) +                                 */
/*              TEXT('CPP for FWDPGMMSG command')                     */
/*                                                                    */
/**********************************************************************/
PGM (&msgtype &cvtescape)

    DCL &apierrcde  *CHAR    8 X'0000000000000000'
    DCL &caller2    *CHAR   10
    DCL &cvtescape  *CHAR    4
    DCL &msgkey     *CHAR    4
    DCL &msgtype    *CHAR    9
    DCL &msgtypearr *CHAR   40
    DCL &nbrmsgtype *CHAR    4
    DCL &rcvvar     *CHAR  512
    DCL &struct     *CHAR   38
    DCL &topgmq     *CHAR   10 '*'
    DCL &topgmqlen  *CHAR    4 X'0000000A' /* Dec *EQ 10 */
    DCL &topgmqctr  *CHAR    4
    DCL &topgmqqual *CHAR   20 '*NONE      *NONE'
    /* Bridge over _CL_PEP if present */
    CALL qmhsndpm ('.' ' ' 'Dummy' X'00000005' '*INFO' '*'
X'00000002' +
                  &msgkey &apierrcde)
    CALL qmhrcvpm (&rcvvar X'00000200' 'RCVM0300' '*' X'00000002' +
                  '*ANY' &msgkey X'00000000' '*REMOVE' &apier-
rcde)
    CHGVAR &caller2 %SST(&rcvvar 492 10)
```

Figure A.4: FWDPGMMSGC is the command processing program for the FWDPGMMSG command (part 1 of 3).

```
    IF (&caller2 *EQ '_CL_PEP') DO
        CHGVAR %BIN(&topgmqctr) 3
    ENDDO

    ELSE DO
        CHGVAR %BIN(&topgmqctr) 2
    ENDDO
    /* Requested to preserve *ESCAPE messages */
    IF (&cvtescape *EQ '*NO') DO
        /* Move program messages */
        IF (&msgtype *EQ '*DIAGESC') DO
            CHGVAR &msgtypearr        '*DIAG'
            CHGVAR %BIN(&nbrmsgtype) 1
        ENDDO
        ELSE IF (&msgtype *EQ '*INFOCOMP') DO
            CHGVAR &msgtypearr        '*INFO    *COMP'
            CHGVAR %BIN(&nbrmsgtype) 2
        ENDDO
        ELSE IF (&msgtype *EQ '*ALL') DO
            CHGVAR &msgtypearr        '*INFO    *COMP    *DIAG'
            CHGVAR %BIN(&nbrmsgtype) 3
        ENDDO
        CALL qmhmovpm (' ' &msgtypearr &nbrmsgtype '*' &topgmqctr +
                    &apierrcde X'00000001' '*NONE     *NONE'
'*CHAR' +
                    '*' X'00000001')
        MONMSG cpf0000

        /* Resend escape message */
        IF (&msgtype *EQ '*DIAGESC' *OR +
            &msgtype *EQ '*ALL'          ) DO
            CHGVAR &struct (&topgmqctr *CAT &topgmqqual *CAT &topg-
mqlen +
                    *CAT &topgmq)
            CALL qmhrsnem (' ' &apierrcde &struct X'00000026' 'RSNM0100' +
                    '*' X'00000001')
            MONMSG cpf0000
        ENDDO
    ENDDO

    /* Requested to convert *ESCAPE messages */
    ELSE DO
        IF (&msgtype *EQ '*DIAGESC') DO
```

Figure A.4: FWDPGMMSGC is the command processing program for the FWDPGMMSG command (part 2 of 3).

297

```
      CHGVAR &msgtypearr          '*DIAG      *ESCAPE'
      CHGVAR %BIN(&nbrmsgtype) 2
   ENDDO
   ELSE IF (&msgtype *EQ '*INFOCOMP') DO
      CHGVAR &msgtypearr          '*INFO      *COMP'
      CHGVAR %BIN(&nbrmsgtype) 2
   ENDDO

   ELSE IF (&msgtype *EQ '*ALL') DO
      CHGVAR &msgtypearr          ('*DIAG      *ESCAPE   ' *CAT +
                                   '*INFO      *COMP')
      CHGVAR %BIN(&nbrmsgtype) 4
   ENDDO
   CALL qmhmovpm (' ' &msgtypearr &nbrmsgtype '*' &topgmqctr +
                 &apierrcde X'00000001' '*NONE      *NONE' +
                 '*CHAR' '*' X'00000001')
      MONMSG cpf0000
   ENDDO

 ENDPGM
```

Figure A.4: FWDPGMMSGC is the command processing program for the FWDPGMMSG command (part 3 of 3).

Send Status Message (SNDSTSMSG)

Sending a status message to the display station—so that the message appears on line 24 while your CL program keeps running—is a neat trick you can use to keep your users informed about what goes on.

Unfortunately, the technique requires you to have a good memory. You must remember to use SNDPGMMSG to send a message type *STATUS to call message queue *EXT. You also must use a predefined message. Additionally, no status messages might appear if the user changed jobs.

SNDSTSMSG keeps all these chores invisible to you. You supply the message in a text parameter, and you can override the user's desire to not see status messages.

Parameters

- MSG: The message appears as a status message. Up to 256 characters are allowed.

- FORCED: Whether to force (override) the user to see the status message. Options are *YES and *NO.

The source code for command SNDSTSMSG is shown in Figure A.5.

```
/******************************************************************/
/*                                                                */
/* To compile:                                                    */
/*                                                                */
/*     CRTCMD  CMD(xxx/SNDSTSMSG) +                               */
/*             PGM(xxx/STS001CL) +                                */
/*             SRCFILE(xxx/QCMDSRC) +                             */
/*             TEXT('Send Status Message')                        */
/*                                                                */
/******************************************************************/
CMD PROMPT('Send Status Message')

   PARM msg *CHAR 256 DFT(*NONE) SPCVAL((*NONE ' ')) EXPR(*YES) +
        PROMPT('Status message')

   PARM forced *CHAR 4 RSTD(*YES) DFT(*YES) VALUES(*YES *NO) +
        PROMPT('Forced display')
```

Figure A.5: Source code for the command SNDSTSMSG.

SNDSTSMSG's command processing program is CL Program STS001CL. See Figure A.6.

```
/*******************************************************************/
/*                                                                 */
/* To compile:                                                     */
/*                                                                 */
/*    CRTCLPGM  PGM(xxx/STS001CL) +                                */
/*              SRCFILE(xxx/QCLSRC) +                              */
/*              TEXT('CPP for SNDSTSMSG command')                  */
/*                                                                 */
/*******************************************************************/
PGM (&msg &forced)

   DCL &forced    *CHAR    4
   DCL &msg       *CHAR   256
   DCL &stsmsg    *CHAR    7

   MONMSG (cpf0000 mch0000) EXEC(GOTO error)

   /* Change job's STSMSG setting to *NORMAL */
   /* if FORCED(*YES) specified            */
   IF (&forced *EQ '*YES') DO
      RTVJOBA STSMSG(&stsmsg)
      CHGJOB STSMSG(*NORMAL)
   ENDDO

   /* Send the status message */
   SNDPGMMSG MSGID(cpf9897) MSGF(qcpfmsg) +
             MSGDTA(&msg) +
             TOPGMQ(*EXT) MSGTYPE(*STATUS)

   /* Restore job's STSMSG setting */
   IF (&forced *EQ '*YES') DO
      CHGJOB STSMSG(&stsmsg)
   ENDDO

   RETURN

   /* Forward error messages to caller */
 error:
   FWDPGMMSG
   MONMSG cpf0000

ENDPGM
```

Figure A.6: CL program STS001CL is the command-processing program for SNDSTSMSG.

Display Program Messages (DSPPGMMSG)

To see if a message has arrived at your message queue, you simply run the Display Message (DSPMSG) command. But to see if a program message has arrived at your call stack message queue, you're stuck. DSPPGMMSG lets you see those elusive messages.

Parameters

- NBRLVL: Enter the number of levels up the call stack of the program or procedure whose call stack messages you want to display. You can enter a number up to 99 or special values * (for current program) and *PRV (for the caller of the current program).

Figure A.7 contains the source code for command DSPPGMMSG.

```
/********************************************************************/
/*                                                                  */
/* To compile:                                                      */
/*                                                                  */
/*    CRTCMD  CMD(xxx/DSPPGMMSG) +                                  */
/*            PGM(xxx/DSPPGMMSGC) +                                 */
/*            SRCFILE(xxx/QCMDSRC) +                                */
/*            TEXT('Display Program Messages')                      */
/*                                                                  */
/********************************************************************/
CMD 'Display Program Messages'

   PARM nbrlvl *DEC 2 DFT(*) SPCVAL((* 0) (*PRV 1)) REL(*LE 99) +
        PROMPT('Number of levels up')
```

Figure A.7: Source code for the command DSPPGMMSG.

DSPPGMMSG requires display file DSPPGMMSGD. See Figure A.8.

```
          ***********************************************************************
          *
          * To compile:
          *
          *    CRTPF  FILE(xxx/DSPPGMMSGD) +
          *           SRCFILE(xxx/QDDSSRC) +
          *           TEXT('Display file for DSPPGMMSG command')
          *
          ***********************************************************************
     A                                          DSPSIZ(24 80 *DS3)
     A                                          PRINT
     A                                          ALTHELP(CA01)
     A                                          CA03
     A                                          CA12
     A                                          HELP
          *_____
     A          R MSGSR                         SFL
     A                                          SFLMSGRCD(04)
     A            SFLMSGKEY                      SFLMSGKEY
     A            SFLPGMQ                        SFLPGMQ(276)
          *_____
     A          R MSGSC                         SFLCTL(MSGSR)
     A                                          OVERLAY
     A                                          SFLDSP
     A                                          SFLDSPCTL
     A                                          SFLINZ
     A N80                                      SFLEND
     A                                          SFLSIZ(0021)
     A                                          SFLPAG(0020)
     A            SFLPGMQ                        SFLPGMQ(276)
          *_____
     A          R HEADER
     A                                          OVERLAY
     A                                     1  2'Display Program Messages'
     A                                          DSPATR(HI)
     A                                     1 47'Job:'
     A            QJOB           28   0  1 52
     A            QPGM           78   0  2  2
     A                                     3  2'
     A
     A
     A                                          DSPATR(UL)
     A                                          COLOR(BLU)
```

Figure A.8: Display file DSPPGMMSGD.

The command-processing program for DSPPGMMSG is CL program DSPP-GMMSGC. See Figure A.9.

```
/*******************************************************************/
/*                                                               */
/* To compile:                                                   */
/*                                                               */
/*    CRTCLPGM   PGM(xxx/DSPPGMMSGC) +                           */
/*               SRCFILE(xxx/QCLSRC) +                           */
/*               TEXT('CPP for DSPPGMMSG command')              */
/*                                                               */
/*******************************************************************/
PGM (&nbrlvl)

    DCLF dsppgmmsgd

    DCL &apierrcde  *CHAR    8 X'0000000000000000'
    DCL &callstkctr *CHAR    4
    DCL &jobnam     *CHAR   10
    DCL &jobnbr     *CHAR    6
    DCL &jobusr     *CHAR   10
    DCL &msgkey     *CHAR    4
    DCL &mod        *CHAR   10
    DCL &nbrlvl     *DEC     2
    DCL &pgm        *CHAR   10
    DCL &prc        *CHAR  256
    DCL &rcvvar     *CHAR 1000

    MONMSG (cpf0000 mch0000) EXEC(GOTO error)

    /* Prepare the call stack counter */
    CHGVAR %BIN(&callstkctr) (&nbrlvl + 1)

    /* Retrieve the caller's name */
    CALL qmhsndpm (' ' ' ' 'Dummy' X'00000005' '*INFO' '*' &cal
                 stkctr +&msgkey &apierrcde)

    MONMSG cpf24a3 EXEC(DO)
       SNDPGMMSG MSGID(cpf9898) MSGF(qcpfmsg) +
                 MSGDTA('Number of levels exceeds the current' *BCAT +
                    'depth of the call stack') +
                 MSGTYPE(*ESCAPE)
    ENDDO
```

Figure A.9: DSPPGMMSGC is the command-processing program for DSPPGMMSG (part 1 of 2).

```
        CALL qmhrcvpm (&rcvvar X'00000200' 'RCVM0300' '*' &callstkctr +
                      '*ANY' &msgkey X'00000000' '*REMOVE' &apierrcde)

        CHGVAR &pgm %SST(&rcvvar 472  10)
        CHGVAR &mod %SST(&rcvvar 482  10)
        CHGVAR &prc %SST(&rcvvar 492 256)

        /* Set up message subfile */
        RTVJOBA JOB(&jobnam) USER(&jobusr) NBR(&jobnbr)
        CHGVAR &qjob (&jobnbr *CAT '/' *CAT &jobusr *TCAT '/' *CAT &jobnam)

        IF (&mod *EQ '*N' *AND +
           &prc *EQ '*N'       ) DO
           CHGVAR &qpgm      ('Pgm=' *CAT &pgm)
           CHGVAR &sflpgmq &pgm
        ENDDO
        ELSE DO
           CHGVAR &qpgm      ('Prc=' *CAT &prc *TCAT '/' *CAT &mod *TCAT '/' +
                             *CAT &pgm)
           CHGVAR &sflpgmq (&prc *CAT &mod *CAT &pgm)
        ENDDO

        SNDF    RCDFMT(msgsc)
        SNDRCVF RCDFMT(header)

        RETURN

    error:
        FWDPGMMSG
        MONMSG cpf0000

    ENDPGM
```

Figure A.9: DSPPGMMSGC is the command-processing program for DSPPGMMSG (part 2 of 2).

PROGRAMMING AIDS

The following sections describe some shortcuts for handling common problems.

Start PDM (PDM)

If you work with PDM, you will appreciate the Start PDM (PDM) command. It provides a shortcut, for both WRKOBJPDM and WRKMBRPDM, and has some "convenience" features.

Parameters

- SRCLIB: Enter the name of the library containing the source code with which you want to work. If not given, it defaults to *USRPRF. In that case, the library name is assumed to be a dollar sign ($) plus the first nine characters of the user profile name.

- SRCFILE: SRCFILE is the name of the source file. If not given, it defaults to SOURCE. You also can enter *OBJ if you need to work with objects instead of source members. In that case, PDM is equivalent to WRKOBJPDM for all objects in the library.

- ADDLIBLE: Use ADDLIBLE to decide whether to add to the library list the library specified in SRCLIB. The default is *CURLIB, which makes that library the current library. Other valid values are *TOP (top of user portion of library list), *BOTTOM (bottom), *SYSLIBL (add to system portion of library list), and *NONE (do not add to library list).

For example, if you want to work with SOURCE file source in your own library ($ + your user profile name), simply type "PDM" at the command line and press Enter. Figure A.10 contains the source code for command PDM.

```
/**********************************************************************/
/*                                                                    */
/* To compile:                                                        */
/*                                                                    */
/*     CRTCMD   CMD(xxx/PDM) +                                         */
/*              PGM(xxx/PDMC) +                                        */
/*              SRCFILE(xxx/QCMDSRC) +                                 */
/*              TEXT('Start PDM') +                                    */
/*              ALLOW(*IPGM *IMOD *INTERACT *EXEC)                     */
/*                                                                    */
/**********************************************************************/
```

Figure A.10: Source code for the command PDM (part 1 of 2).

```
CMD 'Start PDM'

    PARM srclib *NAME 10 DFT(*USRPRF) SPCVAL((*USRPRF)) EXPR(*YES) +
        PROMPT('Source library')

    PARM srcfile *NAME 10 DFT(SOURCE) SPCVAL((*OBJ)) EXPR(*YES) +
        PROMPT('Source file')

    PARM addlible *CHAR 8 RSTD(*YES) DFT(*CURLIB) +
        VALUES(*CURLIB *TOP *BOTTOM *SYSLIBL *NONE) EXPR(*YES) +
        PMTCTL(pc1) PROMPT('Add to library list')
pc1: +
        PMTCTL CTL(srclib) COND((*NE '*LIB'))
        PMTCTL CTL(srcfile) COND((*NE '*OBJ')) LGLREL(*AND)
```

Figure A.10: Source code for the command PDM (part 2 of 2).

The PDM command runs CL Program PDMC. See Figure A.11.

```
/****************************************************************************/
/*                                                                        */
/* To compile:                                                            */
/*                                                                        */
/*    CRTCLPGM   PGM(xxx/PDMC) +                                          */
/*               SRCFILE(xxx/QCLSRC) +                                    */
/*               TEXT('CPP for PDM command')                             */
/*                                                                        */
/****************************************************************************/
PGM (&srclib &srcfile &addlible)
    DCL &addlible   *CHAR    8
    DCL &curlib     *CHAR   10
    DCL &srcfile    *CHAR   10
    DCL &srclib     *CHAR   10
    MONMSG cpf0000 EXEC(GOTO error)
    /* Work with all user libraries */
    IF (&srclib *EQ '*LIB') DO
        WRKLIBPDM LIB(*ALLUSR)
    ENDDO


    ELSE DO
        /* Work with user's own library */
        IF (&srclib *EQ '*USRPRF') DO
```

Figure A.11: PDMC is the command-processing program of command PDM (part 1 of 3).

```
        RTVUSRPRF RTNUSRPRF(&srclib)
        CHGVAR &srclib ('$' *CAT &srclib)
ENDDO


/* Verify existence of library */
CHKOBJ &srclib *LIB

/* Work with objects in library */
IF (&srcfile *EQ '*OBJ') DO
    WRKOBJPDM LIB(&srclib) OBJ(*ALL) OBJTYPE(*ALL) OBJATR(*ALL)
ENDDO
/* Work with members in source file */
ELSE DO
   /* Verify existence of source file */
   CHKOBJ &srclib/&srcfile *FILE

   /* Add library to library list */
   IF (&addlible *EQ '*CURLIB') DO
      RTVJOBA CURLIB(&curlib)
      CHGCURLIB CURLIB(&srclib)
   ENDDO
   ELSE IF (&addlible *EQ '*TOP') DO
      ADDLIBLE LIB(&srclib) POSITION(*FIRST)
   ENDDO
   ELSE IF (&addlible *EQ '*BOTTOM') DO
      ADDLIBLE LIB(&srclib) POSITION(*LAST)
   ENDDO
   ELSE IF (&addlible *EQ '*SYSLIBL') DO
      CHGSYSLIBL LIB(&srclib) OPTION(*ADD)
   ENDDO

   /* Work with source members */
   WRKMBRPDM FILE(&srclib/&srcfile)

   /* Remove library from library list */
   IF (&addlible *EQ '*CURLIB') DO
      IF (&curlib *EQ '*NONE') DO
         CHGVAR &curlib '*CRTDFT'
      ENDDO
      CHGCURLIB CURLIB(&curlib)
   ENDDO
   ELSE IF (&addlible *EQ '*TOP'    *OR +
            &addlible *EQ '*BOTTOM'    ) DO
      RMVLIBLE LIB(&srclib)
   ENDDO
```

Figure A.11: PDMC is the command-processing program of command PDM (part 2 of 3).

```
        ELSE IF (&addlible *EQ '*SYSLIBL') DO
           CHGSYSLIBL LIB(&srclib) OPTION(*REMOVE)
        ENDDO
     ENDDO
  ENDDO

  RETURN

error:
  FWDPGMMSG
  MONMSG cpf0000

ENDPGM
```

Figure A.11: PDMC is the command-processing program of command PDM (part 3 of 3).

Initialize Library (INZLIB)

INZLIB prepares a library for a new programming project. If the library doesn't exist, INZLIB creates it; otherwise, it clears it. Then it can create empty-source physical files.

Parameters

- LIB: Name of the library.
- TEXT: Text description for the library. It defaults to *NOCHG; if the library already exists, *NOCHG doesn't alter the text description.
- SRCFILE: What source files to create. You can create either a single source file (and name it here; it's "SOURCE" by default), or use special value *IBMSTD to create multiple source files following IBM's naming convention (QCLSRC, QDDSSRC, etc.).
- RCDLEN: Record length for the source files. The default is 92.
- TYPE: Type of library, either *PROD (production) or *TEST.
- AUT: Public authority. Valid values are *LIBCRTAUT, *CHANGE, *ALL, *USE, *EXCLUDE, or an authorization list name.
- ASP: Auxiliary storage pool number.

- CRTAUT: Default public authority for all objects created within the library. Valid values are *SYSVAL (default), *CHANGE, *ALL, *USE.

- CRTOBJAUD: What level of auditing to provide for objects created. Valid values are *SYSVAL (default), *NONE, *USRPRF, *CHANGE, *ALL.

Source code for the command INZLIB is shown in Figure A.12.

```
/*******************************************************************/
/*                                                                 */
/* To compile:                                                     */
/*                                                                 */
/*     CRTCMD   CMD(xxx/INZLIB) +                                  */
/*              PGM(xxx/INZLIBC) +                                 */
/*              SRCFILE(xxx/QCMDSRC) +                             */
/*              TEXT('Initialize Library') +                       */
/*              AUT(*EXCLUDE)                                       */
/*                                                                 */
/*******************************************************************/
CMD 'Initialize Library'

    PARM lib *NAME 10 MIN(1) EXPR(*YES) PROMPT('Library')

    PARM text *CHAR 50 DFT(*NOCHG) SPCVAL((*BLANK ' ') (*NOCHG)) +
         EXPR(*YES) PROMPT('Text description')

    PARM srcfile *NAME 10 DFT(source) SPCVAL((*IBMSTD)) EXPR(*YES) +
         PROMPT('Source files')

    PARM rcdlen *DEC 5 DFT(92) RANGE(13 32766) +
         PROMPT('Source file record length')

    PARM type *CHAR 5 RSTD(*YES) DFT(*PROD) VALUES(*PROD *TEST) +
         EXPR(*YES) PMTCTL(*PMTRQS) PROMPT('Library type')

    PARM aut *NAME 10 DFT(*LIBCRTAUT) +
         SPCVAL((*LIBCRTAUT) (*CHANGE) (*ALL) (*USE) (*EXCLUDE)) +
         EXPR(*YES) PMTCTL(*PMTRQS) PROMPT('Authority')

    PARM asp *DEC 2 DFT(1) RANGE(1 16) PMTCTL(*PMTRQS) +
         PROMPT('Auxiliary storage pool ID')
```

Figure A.12: Source code for command INZLIB (part 1 of 2).

```
    PARM crtaut *NAME 10 DFT(*SYSVAL) +
        SPCVAL((*SYSVAL) (*CHANGE) (*ALL) (*USE)) +
        EXPR(*YES) PMTCTL(*PMTRQS) PROMPT('Create authority')

    PARM crtobjaud *CHAR 10 RSTD(*YES) DFT(*SYSVAL) +
        VALUES(*SYSVAL *NONE *USRPRF *CHANGE *ALL) EXPR(*YES) +
        PMTCTL(*PMTRQS) PROMPT('Create object auditing')
```

Figure A.12: Source code for command INZLIB (part 2 of 2).

Command INZLIB executes CL Program INZLIBC. See Figure A.13.

```
/***************************************************************/
/*                                                           */
/* To compile:                                               */
/*                                                           */
/*    CRTCLPGM  PGM(xxx/INZLIBC) +                           */
/*              SRCFILE(xxx/QCLSRC) +                        */
/*              TEXT('CPP for INZLIB command') +            */
/*              AUT(*EXCLUDE)                                 */
/*                                                           */
/***************************************************************/
PGM (&lib &text &srcfile &rcdlen &type &aut &asp &crtaut &crtobjaud)

    DCL &asp        *DEC    2
    DCL &aut        *CHAR   10
    DCL &crtaut     *CHAR   10
    DCL &crtobjaud  *CHAR   10
    DCL &exists     *LGL    1
    DCL &false      *LGL    1 '0'
    DCL &lib        *CHAR   10
    DCL &rcdlen     *DEC    5
    DCL &srcfile    *CHAR   10
    DCL &text       *CHAR   50
    DCL &true       *LGL    1 '1'
    DCL &type       *CHAR   5

    MONMSG (cpf0000 mch0000) EXEC(GOTO error)

    /* Reject attempt to initialize IBM library */
    IF (%SST(&lib 1 1) *EQ 'Q') DO
        SNDPGMMSG MSGID(cpf9898) MSGF(qcpfmsg) +
                MSGDTA('INZLIB not allowed on IBM-supplied' *BCAT +
                    'libraries') +
```

Figure A.13: INZLIBC is the command-processing program for command INZLIB (part 1 of 3).

```
                    MSGTYPE(*ESCAPE)
ENDDO

/* Create library if necessary */
CHGVAR &exists &true

CHKOBJ &lib *LIB
MONMSG cpf9801 EXEC(DO)
   CHGVAR &exists &false
   RCVMSG MSGTYPE(*EXCP) RMV(*YES)
ENDDO

IF &exists DO
   CLRLIB &lib
   SNDPGMMSG MSGID(cpf9898) MSGF(qcpfmsg) +
             MSGDTA('Library' *BCAT &lib *BCAT 'cleared') +
             MSGTYPE(*INFO)
ENDDO
ELSE DO
   IF (&text *EQ '*NOCHG') DO
      CHGVAR &text ' '
   ENDDO
   CRTLIB &lib TYPE(&type) TEXT(&text) AUT(&aut) ASP(&asp) +
          CRTAUT(&crtaut) CRTOBJAUD(&crtobjaud)
   SNDPGMMSG MSGID(cpf9898) MSGF(qcpfmsg) +
             MSGDTA('Library' *BCAT &lib *BCAT 'created') +
             MSGTYPE(*INFO)
ENDDO

/* Change text description if necessary */
IF (&exists *AND &text *NE '*NOCHG') DO
   CHGOBJD &lib *LIB TEXT(&text)
   SNDPGMMSG MSGID(cpf9898) MSGF(qcpfmsg) +
             MSGDTA('Library text description changed') +
             MSGTYPE(*INFO)
ENDDO

/* Create source files */
IF (&srcfile *EQ '*IBMSTD') DO
   /* CL */
   CRTSRCPF &lib/qclsrc    RCDLEN(&rcdlen) TEXT('CL source')
   CRTSRCPF &lib/qcllesrc RCDLEN(&rcdlen) TEXT('ILE CL source')
   /* COBOL */
   CRTSRCPF &lib/qlblsrc   RCDLEN(&rcdlen) TEXT('COBOL source')
   CRTSRCPF &lib/qcbllesrc RCDLEN(&rcdlen) TEXT('ILE COBOL source')
   /* Commands */
   CRTSRCPF &lib/qcmdsrc RCDLEN(&rcdlen) TEXT('Command source')
```

Figure A.13: INZLIBC is the command-processing program for command INZLIB (part 2 of 3).

```
      /* DDS */
      CRTSRCPF &lib/qddssrc RCDLEN(&rcdlen) TEXT('DDS source')

      /* Menus */
      CRTSRCPF &lib/qmnusrc RCDLEN(&rcdlen) TEXT('Menu source')

      /* Panel groups */
      CRTSRCPF &lib/qpnlsrc RCDLEN(&rcdlen) TEXT('Panel group source')

      /* Query Management */
      CRTSRCPF &lib/qqmqrysrc  RCDLEN(&rcdlen) TEXT('QM query source')
      CRTSRCPF &lib/qqmformsrc RCDLEN(&rcdlen) TEXT('QM form source')

      /* REXX */
      CRTSRCPF &lib/qrexsrc) RCDLEN(&rcdlen) TEXT('REXX source')

      /* RPG */
      CRTSRCPF &lib/qrpgsrc   RCDLEN(&rcdlen) TEXT('RPG III source')
      CRTSRCPF &lib/qrpglesrc RCDLEN(&rcdlen) TEXT('RPG IV source')

      SNDPGMMSG MSGID(cpf9898) MSGF(qcpfmsg) +
              MSGDTA('Standard IBM source files created') +
              MSGTYPE(*INFO)
   ENDDO

   ELSE DO
      CRTSRCPF &lib/&srcfile RCDLEN(&rcdlen) TEXT('Programming Source')
      SNDPGMMSG MSGID(cpf9898) MSGF(qcpfmsg) +
              MSGDTA('Source file' *BCAT &srcfile *BCAT 'created') +
              MSGTYPE(*INFO)
   ENDDO

   /* Normal completion */
   SNDPGMMSG MSGID(cpf9898) MSGF(qcpfmsg) +
           MSGDTA('INZLIB completed successfully') +
           MSGTYPE(*COMP)

   RETURN

   /* Forward error message to caller */
 error:
   FWDPGMMSG
   MONMSG cpf0000

 ENDPGM
```

Figure A.13: INZLIBC is the command-processing program for command INZLIB (part 3 of 3).

Format CL Source (FMTCLSRC)

Appendix B shows how you can format your CL source code in order to make it easier to read and maintain. It involves some manual tinkering, but the results are well worth the effort. If you would rather have the computer format the CL code for you, however, you can use the FMTCLSRC command. The results are not as good, but you don't have to do anything manually.

Parameters

- SRCFILE: Qualified name of the source file containing the code to format. The library portion can be *LIBL, *CURLIB, or a specific name.

- SRCMBR: Name of the source member to format.

- OUTSRCFILE: Qualified name of the source file that is to contain the formatted code. It defaults to *SRCFILE, which means that the formatted code is to be placed in the same source file.

- OUTSRCMBR: Name of the source member where the formatted code is to be placed. It defaults to *SRCMBR, which means that the formatted code goes back into the original member; in other words, the member is updated.

- INDCOL: Number of columns to indent. FMTCLSRC indents code found within a DO/ENDDO pair or a PGM/ENDPGM pair. This parameter tells FMTCLSRC how many columns to indent per level. The default is 2.

- INSERRMRK: Insert error marker. If indentation causes data to be lost past the right margin of the source record, INSERRMRK inserts a line to warn about the error and stops program execution immediately. A message is sent identifying the record in error.

- DSPERR: Whether to invoke SEU to display the source member, if it ends in error.

Note: In order for FMTCLSRC to work correctly, the CL code must be "preformatted" in any of three ways: (1) the way SEU and the command prompter do; (2) the way FMTCLSRC does; (3) a mixture of both (some CL statements go one way and some the other).

Source code for the command FMTCLSRC is shown in Figure A.14.

```
/********************************************************************/
/*                                                                  */
/* To compile:                                                      */
/*                                                                  */
/*    CRTCMD  CMD(xxx/FMTCLSRC) +                                   */
/*            PGM(xxx/FMTCLSRCC) +                                  */
/*            SRCFILE(xxx/QCMDSRC) +                                */
/*            TEXT('Format CL Source') +                            */
/*            ALLOW(*ALL)                                           */
/*                                                                  */
/********************************************************************/
CMD 'Format CL Source'

   PARM srcfile q1 MIN(1) PROMPT('Source file')

q1: +
     QUAL *NAME 10 MIN(1) EXPR(*YES)
     QUAL *NAME 10 DFT(*LIBL) SPCVAL((*LIBL) (*CURLIB)) EXPR(*YES) +
         PROMPT('Library')

   PARM srcmbr *NAME 10 MIN(1) EXPR(*YES) PROMPT('Source member')

   PARM outsrcfile q2 PROMPT('Output source file')

q2: +
     QUAL *NAME 10 DFT(*SRCFILE) SPCVAL((*SRCFILE)) EXPR(*YES)
     QUAL *NAME 10 DFT(*LIBL) SPCVAL((*LIBL) (*CURLIB)) EXPR(*YES) +
         PROMPT('Library')

   PARM outsrcmbr *NAME 10 DFT(*SRCMBR) SPCVAL((*SRCMBR)) EXPR(*YES) +
       PROMPT('Output source member')

   PARM indcol *DEC 1 DFT(2) RANGE(1 4) +
       PROMPT('Indent columns per level')
   PARM inserrmrk *LGL 1 DFT(*YES) SPCVAL((*YES '1') (*NO '0')) +
       PROMPT('Insert error marker')

   PARM dsperr *LGL 1 DFT(*YES) SPCVAL((*YES '1') (*NO '0')) +
       PMTCTL(pc1) PROMPT('Display error in member')

pc1: +
     PMTCTL CTL(inserrmrk) COND((*EQ '1'))
```

Figure A.14: Source code for the FMTCLSRC command.

FMTCLSRC executes CL Program FMTCLSRCC. See Figure A.15.

```
/********************************************************************/
/*                                                                  */
/* To compile:                                                      */
/*                                                                  */
/*    CRTCLPGM   PGM(xxx/FMTCLSRCC) +                               */
/*               SRCFILE(xxx/QCLSRC) +                              */
/*               TEXT('CPP for FMTCLSRC command')                   */
/*                                                                  */
/********************************************************************/
PGM (&qsrcf &srcmbr &qoutsrcf &outsrcmbr &indcol &inserrmrk &dsperr)

       DCL &batch       *CHAR    1 '0'
       DCL &dsperr      *LGL     1
       DCL &error       *CHAR    1 'E'
       DCL &indcol      *DEC     1
       DCL &inserrmrk   *LGL     1
       DCL &jobtype     *CHAR    1
       DCL &outsrcf     *CHAR   10
       DCL &outsrcflib  *CHAR   10
       DCL &outsrcmbr   *CHAR   10
       DCL &qoutsrcf    *CHAR   20
       DCL &qsrcf       *CHAR   20
       DCL &rtncde      *CHAR    1
       DCL &seqnbr      *CHAR    6
       DCL &srcf        *CHAR   10
       DCL &srcflib     *CHAR   10
       DCL &srcmbr      *CHAR   10
       DCL &srctype     *CHAR   10

       MONMSG (cpf0000 mch0000) EXEC(GOTO error)
       /* Break qualified names */

       CHGVAR &srcf        %SST(&qsrcf    1 10)
       CHGVAR &srcflib     %SST(&qsrcf   11 10)
       CHGVAR &outsrcf     %SST(&qoutsrcf 1 10)
       CHGVAR &outsrcflib  %SST(&qoutsrcf 11 10)

       /* Input source member must exist */
       CHKOBJ &srcflib/&srcf *FILE MBR(&srcmbr)
```

Figure A.15: FMTCLSRCC is the source processing program for command FMTCLSRC (part 1 of 3).

```
/* Input source member must be type CLP, CLP38, or CLLE */
RTVMBRD &srcflib/&srcf &srcmbr SRCTYPE(&srctype)

IF (&srctype *NE 'CLP'   *AND +
    &srctype *NE 'CLP38' *AND +
    &srctype *NE 'CLLE'      ) DO
   SNDPGMMSG MSGID(cpf9898) MSGF(qcpfmsg) +
             MSGDTA('Source type is not CLP, CLP38 or CLLE') +
             MSGTYPE(*ESCAPE)
   RETURN
ENDDO

/* Resolve special values for output source file */
IF (&outsrcf *EQ '*SRCFILE') DO
   CHGVAR &outsrcf &srcf
   CHGVAR &outsrcflib &srcflib
ENDDO

IF (&outsrcmbr *EQ '*SRCMBR') DO
   CHGVAR &outsrcmbr &srcmbr
ENDDO

/* Create temporary output source file */
CHKOBJ qtemp/scratch *FILE
MONMSG cpf9801 EXEC(DO)
   RCVMSG MSGTYPE(*LAST)
   CRTSRCPF qtemp/scratch RCDLEN(92) TEXT('For FMTCLSRC')
ENDDO

CHKOBJ qtemp/scratch *FILE MBR(scratch)
MONMSG cpf9815 EXEC(DO)
   ADDPFM qtemp/scratch scratch SRCTYPE(clp)
ENDDO

CLRPFM qtemp/scratch scratch
/* Format CL source */
OVRDBF source_in  TOFILE(&srcflib/&srcf) MBR(&srcmbr)
OVRDBF source_out TOFILE(qtemp/scratch)  MBR(scratch)
CALL fmtclsrcr (&rtncde &seqnbr &inserrmrk &indcol)

IF (&rtncde *EQ &error) DO
   IF (&dsperr *AND &inserrmrk) DO
      RTVJOBA TYPE(&jobtype)
      IF (&jobtype *NE &batch) DO
         STRSEU SRCFILE(qtemp/scratch) SRCMBR(scratch)
      ENDDO
   ENDDO
ENDDO
```

Figure A.15: FMTCLSRCC is the source processing program for command FMTCLSRC (part 2 of 3).

```
        SNDPGMMSG MSGID(cpf9898) MSGF(qcpfmsg) +
                MSGDTA('Formatting ended in error at' *BCAT +
                        'sequence number' *BCAT &seqnbr) +
                MSGTYPE(*ESCAPE)
    RETURN
ENDDO


DLTOVR (source_in source_out)

/* Copy scratch source to desired output file */
CHKOBJ &outsrcflib/&outsrcf *FILE MBR(&outsrcmbr)
MONMSG cpf9801 EXEC(DO)
    CRTSRCPF &outsrcflib/&outsrcf RCDLEN(92)
ENDDO

MONMSG cpf9815 EXEC(DO)
    ADDPFM &outsrcflib/&outsrcf &outsrcmbr SRCTYPE(clp)
ENDDO

CLRPFM &outsrcflib/&outsrcf &outsrcmbr
CPYSRCF FROMFILE(qtemp/scratch) TOFILE(&outsrcflib/&outsrcf) +
        FROMMBR(scratch)          TOMBR(&outsrcmbr) +
        MBROPT(*REPLACE) +
        SRCOPT(*SEQNBR *DATE) SRCSEQ(1.00 1.00)
CLRPFM qtemp/scratch scratch

SNDPGMMSG MSGID(cpf9898) MSGF(qcpfmsg) +
        MSGDTA('CL source formatted successfully') +
        MSGTYPE(*COMP)

    RETURN

error:
    FWDPGMMSG
    MONMSG cpf0000

ENDPGM
```

Figure A.15: FMTCLSRCC is the source processing program for command FMTCLSRC (part 3 of 3).

The RPG IV program FMTCLSRCR, shown in Figure A.16, does the work of refor-matting the source code.

```
**********************************************************************
*
* To compile:
*
*    CRTBNDRPG  PGM(xxx/FMTCLSRCR) +
*               SRCFILE(xxx/QRPGLESRC) +
*               TEXT('Called from FMTCLSRCC') +
*               ACTGRP(*CALLER)
*
**********************************************************************
Fsource_in IF   F  132        DISK
Fsource_out0 A F  132         DISK


**********************************************************************

D before_pgm      S              1A
D curlvlnbr       S              9P 0
D do_1#           C                        CONST('THEN(DO)')
D do_2#           C                        CONST('EXEC(DO)')
D do_3#           C                        CONST('CMD(DO)')
D enddo#          C                        CONST('ENDDO')
D endfile         S              1A
D endpgm#         C                        CONST('ENDPGM ')
D errcode         S              1A
D errseqnbr       S              6A
D first12         S             12A
D found           S              9P 0
D indcol          S              1P 0
D indented        S            160A
D inserrmrk       S              1A
D inx             S              9P 0
D is_do           S              1A
D is_end          S              1A
D is_label        S              1A
D label_is        S             11A
D len             S              9P 0
D line_trunc      C                        CONST('*** ERROR *** LINE +
D                                           TRUNCATED ***')
D lstchrprv       S              1A
D normal          C                        CONST(X'20')
D pgm#            C                        CONST('PGM ')
```

Figure A.16: RPG program FMTCLSRCR (part 1 of 8).

```
D red              C                    CONST(X'28')
D wrkarr           S              1A    DIM(160)

      ***********************************************************

Isource_in NS
I                                  1    6  curseqnbr
I                                 13   92  srcline
      ***********************************************************
     * Mainline.

C      *ENTRY       PLIST
C                   PARM                      errcode
C                   PARM                      errseqnbr
C                   PARM                      inserrmrk
C                   PARM                      indcol

C                   EXSR      inzpgm
C                   EXSR      prcpgm
C                   EXSR      trmpgm

C                   RETURN


     *_____
     * ABORT:  Abort formatting (error found).

C      abort        BEGSR

     * Insert error marker in output source member, if requested.
C                   IF        inserrmrk = *ON
C                   EVAL      srcline = indented
C                   EXCEPT    update
C                   EXCEPT    errormark
C                   ENDIF

C                   EVAL      errcode   = 'E'
C                   EVAL      errseqnbr = curseqnbr

     * Terminate program immediately.
C                   EVAL      *INLR = *ON
C                   RETURN

C                   ENDSR
     *_____
     * CHKDO:  Check if current line is DO or PGM.
     *         Output:  IS_DO is either *ON or *OFF.
```

Figure A.16: RPG program FMTCLSRCR (part 2 of 8).

```
C     chkdo           BEGSR

C                     EVAL       is_do = *ON

* Set IS_DO to *ON if DO found in IF, ELSE, MONMSG, or if PGM.
C     do_1#           SCAN       srcline          found
C                     IF         found = 0
C     do_2#           SCAN       srcline          found
C                     IF         found = 0
C     do_3#           SCAN       srcline          found
C                     IF         found = 0
C                     IF         %SUBST(srcline:1:4) <> pgm#
C                     EVAL       is_do = *OFF
C                     ENDIF
C                     ENDIF
C                     ENDIF
C                     ENDIF
C                     ENDSR


*_____
* CHKEND:  Check if current line is ENDDO or ENDPGM.
*          Output:  IS_END is either *ON or *OFF.

C     chkend          BEGSR

C                     EVAL       is_end = *ON

* Set IS_END to *ON if ENDDO or ENDPGM found.
C     enddo#          SCAN       srcline          found
C                     IF         found = 0
C     endpgm#         SCAN       srcline          found
C                     IF         found = 0
C                     EVAL       is_end = *OFF
C                     ENDIF
C                     ENDIF

C                     ENDSR


*_____
* CHKLABEL:  Check if current line contains a label.
*            Output:  IS_LABEL is either *ON or *OFF.
C     chklabel        BEGSR
* Set IS_LABEL to *ON if ':' found in first 12 characters
* and the first two characters are not '/*'.
C                     EVAL       first12 = %SUBST(srcline:1:12)
```

Figure A.16: RPG program FMTCLSRCR (part 3 of 8).

320

```
C        ':'             SCAN       first12        found
C                        IF         found = 0  OR
C                                   %SUBST(srcline:1:2) = '/*'
C                        EVAL       is_label = *OFF
C                        ELSE
C                        EVAL       is_label = *ON
C                        ENDIF

C                        ENDSR

      *_____
      * INSLEADSPC:  Insert leading spaces for current level number.

C        insleadspc     BEGSR

      * Insert leading spaces (indent code).
C                        EVAL       wrkarr = *BLANK
C                        EVAL       inx = curlvlnbr * indcol + 1
C                        MOVEA      srcline        wrkarr(inx)
C                        EVAL       indented = *BLANK
C                        MOVEA      wrkarr         indented

      * If indentation pushes code beyond column 80, abort program.
C                        IF         %SUBST(indented:81) <> *BLANK
C                        EXSR       abort
C                        ELSE
C                        EVAL       srcline = indented
C                        ENDIF

C                        ENDSR

      *_____
      * INZPGM:  Initialize program.

C        inzpgm         BEGSR

C                        EVAL       curlvlnbr  = 0

C                        EVAL       before_pgm = *ON

C                        ENDSR

      *_____
      * PRCPGM:  Process program.

C        prcpgm         BEGSR
```

Figure A.16: RPG program FMTCLSRCR (part 4 of 8).

```
C                    EVAL      endfile = *OFF
* Process one record at a time.
C                    DOU       endfile = *ON
C                    READ      source_in
01
C                    EVAL      endfile = *IN01
C                    IF        endfile = *OFF
C                    EXSR      prcrcd
C                    ENDIF
C                    ENDDO

C                    ENDSR


*_____
* PRCRCD:   Process record.

C    prcrcd          BEGSR

* If record contains a label, write label by itself on a line,
* then write the rest in the next line.
C                    EXSR      chklabel
C                    IF        is_label = *ON   AND   before_pgm =
*ON
C                    EXSR      rmvlabel
C                    EVAL      is_label = *OFF
C                    ENDIF

C                    IF        is_label = *ON
C                    EVAL      label_is =
%TRIM(%SUBST(srcline:1:12))
C                    EXCEPT    label
C                    EXSR      rmvlabel
C                    ENDIF

* Don't write another line if the original line only contained
* a label.
C                    IF        (is_label = *ON   AND
C                              srcline <> *BLANK)   OR
C                              is_label = *OFF
* Remove all leading spaces.
C                    EXSR      rmvleadspc

* If current line is ENDDO/ENDPGM, decrease level number.
C                    EXSR      chkend
```

Figure A.16: RPG program FMTCLSRCR (part 5 of 8).

```
C                       IF        is_end = *ON  AND  curlvlnbr > 0
C                       EVAL      curlvlnbr = curlvlnbr - 1
C                       ENDIF

 * Insert appropriate number of leading spaces (indent code)
 * and then write the indented code.
C                       EXSR      insleadspc

C                       EXCEPT    update

C                       ENDIF

 * Store the last character in LSTCHRPRV.
 * This makes it possible to recognize continuation lines.
C        ' '            CHECKR    srcline      len
C                       IF        len > 0
C                       EVAL      lstchrprv = %SUBST(srcline:len:1)
C                       ELSE
C                       EVAL      lstchrprv = *BLANK
C                       ENDIF

 * If current line is DO or PGM, increase level number.
C                       EXSR      chkdo
C                       IF        is_do = *ON
C                       EVAL      curlvlnbr = curlvlnbr + 1
C                       ENDIF

 * Current line is no longer before the PGM statement.
C                       IF        %SUBST(srcline:1:3) = pgm#
C                       EVAL      before_pgm = *OFF
C                       ENDIF

C                       ENDSR


 *_____
 * RMVLABEL:  Remove label from current program line.

C     rmvlabel          BEGSR

 * Blank out the place where the label would be.
C                       EVAL      srcline = '              '  +
C                                           %SUBST(srcline:14)

C                       ENDSR
```

Figure A.16: RPG program FMTCLSRCR (part 6 of 8).

323

```
     *_____
     * RMVLEADSPC:  Remove all leading spaces from program line,
     *              provided it is a command or command continuation.

     C     rmvleadspc   BEGSR

     * Remove all leading spaces, unconditionally.
     C                  EVAL      srcline = %TRIML(srcline)

     * If current line is a continuation line, indent 13 spaces.
     C                  IF        lstchrprv = '+'  OR
     C                            lstchrprv = '-'
     C                  EVAL      srcline = '             ' + srcline
     C                  ENDIF

     C                  ENDSR

     *_____
     * TRMPGM:  Terminate program.

     C     trmpgm       BEGSR

     C                  EVAL      *INLR = *ON

     C                  ENDSR

     *_____
     * WRTLABEL:  Write label.

     C     wrtlabel     BEGSR

     * To write the label, extract it from the current line and write.
     C                  EXSR      rmvlabel
     C                  EXCEPT    label             .

     C                  ENDSR

     ************************************************************************

     Osource_outEADD           update
     O                         srcline           92

     O            EADD         label
     O                         label_is          23
```

Figure A.16: RPG program FMTCLSRCR (part 7 of 8).

```
     0          EADD          errormark
     0                        red             +12
     0                        line_trunc      +1
     0                        normal          +1
```

Figure A.16: RPG program FMTCLSRCR (part 8 of 8).

Compare Source Members (*CMPSRCMBR*)

Sometime during the process of developing an application, you might run into a common problem: having two versions of the same program. Perhaps you took a copy of the code home with you or perhaps a fellow programmer worked on it while you were away on vacation. Whatever the reason, it's possible to have two source members represent the same application program.

CMPSRCMBR helps you compare the versions. It asks for two source file names and two source members, and then does a line-by-line comparison. All differences are marked either on the screen or on the printer. If you select the screen, you can then position the cursor on a particular line, type an x and press Enter in order to see the entire line. You also can press function keys to invoke SEU and edit either source member.

This utility is similar in nature to IBM's Compare Physical File Member (CMPPFM) command, but differs in function.

Parameters

- SRCFILE1: Enter the qualified name of the first source file.

- SRCMBR1: Enter the name of the first source member.

- SRCFILE2: Enter the qualified name of the second source file. The default value, *SRCFILE1, indicates that SRCFILE1 and SRCFILE2 are the same file.

- SRCMBR2: Enter the name of the second source member. The default value, *SRCMBR1, indicates that SRCMBR1 and SRCMBR2 are the same member.

- MARKER: Type a single character to be used to mark the differences between the two members. The default value is | for a vertical line.

- IGNLEADSPC: Whether to ignore leading spaces in the lines of code. This option is valuable in free-format languages such as CL or COBOL. Options are *YES (ignore leading spaces), *NO (do not ignore), and *AUTO (whether to ignore or not depends on the source type).

- IGNCASE: Whether to ignore differences of case (uppercase or lowercase).

- IGNSRCTYPE: Whether to ignore differences of source type. Options: *NO (attempts to compare CLP and RPG yield an error message); *YES (anything goes).

- OUTPUT: Whether to present the differences on the screen or printer. The source code for command CMPSRCMBR is listed in Figure A.17.

```
/******************************************************************/
/*                                                                */
/* To compile:                                                    */
/*                                                                */
/*    CRTCMD  CMD(xxx/CMPSRCMBR) +                                */
/*            PGM(xxx/CMPSRCMBRC) +                               */
/*            SRCFILE(xxx/QCMDSRC) +                              */
/*            TEXT('Compare Source Members') +                    */
/*            ALLOW(*IPGM *IMOD *INTERACT *EXEC)                  */
/*                                                                */
/******************************************************************/
CMD   'Compare Source Members'

   PARM srcfile1 q1 MIN(1) PROMPT('Source file 1')
q1: +
     QUAL *NAME 10 MIN(1) EXPR(*YES)
     QUAL *NAME 10 DFT(*LIBL) SPCVAL((*LIBL) (*CURLIB)) EXPR(*YES) +
         PROMPT('Library')

   PARM srcmbr1 *NAME 10 MIN(1) EXPR(*YES) PROMPT('Source member 1')

   PARM srcfile2 q1 MIN(1) PROMPT('Source file 2')
```

Figure A.17: Source code for the CMPSRCMBR command (part 1 of 2).

```
        PARM srcmbr2 *NAME 10 DFT(*SRCMBR1) SPCVAL((*SRCMBR1)) EXPR(*YES) +
             PROMPT('Source member 2')

        PARM marker *CHAR 1 DFT(|) PROMPT('Marker character')

        PARM ignleadspc *CHAR 5 RSTD(*YES) DFT(*AUTO) +
             VALUES(*YES *NO *AUTO) PROMPT('Ignore leading spaces')

        PARM igncase *CHAR 4 RSTD(*YES) DFT(*YES) VALUES(*YES *NO) +
             PROMPT('Ignore case')

        PARM ignsrctype *CHAR 4 RSTD(*YES) DFT(*NO) VALUES(*YES *NO) +
             PROMPT('Ignore source type mismatch')

        PARM output *CHAR 6 RSTD(*YES) DFT(*) VALUES(* *PRINT) +
             PROMPT('Output')
```

Figure A.17: Source code for the CMPSRCMBR command (part 2 of 2).

The CMPSRCMBR utility uses display file CMPSRCMBRD (shown in Figure A.18).

```
        ********************************************************************
        *
        * To compile:
        *
        *     CRTDSPF   FILE(xxx/CMPSRCMBRD) +
        *               SRCFILE(xxx/SOURCE) +
        *               TEXT('Display file for CMPSRCMBR command')
        *
        ********************************************************************
        A                                          DSPSIZ(24 80 *DS3)
        A                                          PRINT
        A                                          CA03(03 'Exit')
        A                                        CA07(07 'Edit member 1')
        A                                        CA08(08 'Edit member 2')
        A                                          CA12(12 'Cancel')
        *_____
        A          R FKEYS
        A                            23  2'F3=Exit    F7=Edit Member1  -
```

Figure A.18: Display file CMPSRCMBRD (part 1 of 3).

```
A                                      F8=Edit Member2   F12=Cancel'
A                                      COLOR(BLU)
   *_____
A           R DIFFRCD                  SFL
A             SEQNBR1       6A  O  5  2
A             SRCDTA1P     30A  O  5  9
A             OPTION        1A  B  5 40COLOR(WHT)
A             SEQNBR2       6A  O  5 42
A             SRCDTA2P     30A  O  5 49
A             SRCDTA1      80A  H
A             SRCDAT1       6   H
A             SRCDTA2      80A  H
A             SRCDAT2       6   H
A             MARKERS      80A  H
   *_____
A           R DIFFCTL                  SFLCTL(DIFFRCD)
A                                      BLINK
A                                      OVERLAY
A  80                                  SFLDSP
A                                      SFLDSPCTL
A N80                                  SFLCLR
A N81                                  SFLEND(*MORE)
A                                      SFLSIZ(0018)
A                                      SFLPAG(0017)
A             SFLRCDNBR     4  OH      SFLRCDNBR(CURSOR *TOP)
A                                    1 30'Compare Source Members'
A                                      DSPATR(HI)
A                                    2 28'Enter option X to display'
A                                      COLOR(BLU)
A                                    3  2'M1:'
A             QSRCMBR1     33  O    3  6
A                                    3 40'|'
A                                      COLOR(BLU)
A                                    3 42'M2:'
A             QSRCMBR2     33  O    3 46
A                                    4  2'SeqNbr'
A                                      DSPATR(HI)
A                                    4  9'Source Data'
A                                      DSPATR(HI)
A                                    4 40'V'
A                                      COLOR(BLU)
A                                    4 42'SeqNbr'
```

Figure A.18: Display file CMPSRCMBRD (part 2 of 3).

```
A                                           DSPATR(HI)
A                                         4 49'Source Data'
A                                           DSPATR(HI)
  *_____
A            R NODIFF
A                                           OVERLAY
A                                         6  5'(No differences found)'
  *_____
A            R SHOWDIFF
A                                         1 30'Compare Source Members'
A                                           DSPATR(HI)
A                                         4  2'Member 1:'
A              QSRCMBR1      33A  O   4 13
A                                         5  2'Seq.Nbr.:'
A              SEQNBR1        6A  O   5 13
A                                         5 22'(Updated'
A              SRCDAT1        6   O   5 31
A                                         5 38')'
A              SRCDTA1       80A  O   6  1COLOR(TRQ)
A              MARKERS       80A  O   8  1COLOR(RED)
A              SRCDTA2       80A  O  10  1COLOR(TRQ)
A                                        11  2'Seq.Nbr.:'
A              SEQNBR2        6A  O  11 13
A                                        11 22'(Updated'
A              SRCDAT2        6   O  11 31
A                                        11 38')'
A                                        12  2'Member 2:'
A              QSRCMBR2      33A  O  12 13
A                                        23  2'Press Enter to continue.'
A                                           COLOR(BLU)
```

Figure A.18: Display file CMPSRCMBRD (part 3 of 3).

CMPSRCMBR also uses printer file CMPSRCMBR1 (shown in Figure A.19).

```
***********************************************************************
    *
    * To compile:
    *
    *   CRTPRTF  FILE(xxx/CMPSRCMBR1) +
    *            SRCFILE(xxx/SOURCE) +
    *            TEXT('Printer file for CMPSRCMBR command')
    *
***********************************************************************
    A            R HEADER                    SKIPB(4)
    A                                       1DATE EDTCDE(Y)
    A                                      +2TIME
    A                                      88'Compare Source Members'
    A                                      189'Page'
    A                                      +1PAGNBR EDTCDE(3)
    A                                        SPACEA(3)
    A                                        1'Source Member:'
    A              QSRCMBR1      33A        +2
    A                                      100'Source Member:'
    A              QSRCMBR2      33A        +2
    A                                        SPACEA(2)
    A                                        1'Seq. Nbr.'
    A                                       11'Source Data'
    A                                      100'Seq. Nbr.'
    A                                      110'Source Data'
    A                                        SPACEA(2)
    *_____
    A            R DETAIL
    A              SEQNBR1        6A         1
    A              SRCDTA1       80A        11
    A              SEQNBR2        6A        100
    A              SRCDTA2       80A        110
    A                                        SPACEA(1)
    A              MARKERS1      80A        11
    A              MARKERS2      80A        110
    A                                        SPACEA(2)
```

Figure A.19: Printer file CMPSRCMBR1.

CL Program CMPSRCMBRC, the command-processing program, is shown in Figure A.20.

```
/**********************************************************************/
/*                                                                    */
/* To compile:                                                        */
/*                                                                    */
/*    CRTCLPGM  PGM(xxx/CMPSRCMBRC) +                                  */
/*              SRCFILE(xxx/QCLSRC) +                                  */
/*              TEXT('CPP for CMPSRCMBR command')                     */
/*                                                                    */
/**********************************************************************/
PGM (&q_srcf1 &srcmbr1 &q_srcf2 &srcmbr2 &marker &ignleadspc &igncase +
     &ignsrctype &output)

    DCL &batch      *CHAR   1 '0'
    DCL &chksrctype *CHAR   4
    DCL &igncase    *CHAR   4
    DCL &ignleadspc *CHAR   5
    DCL &ignsrctype *CHAR   4
    DCL &jobtype    *CHAR   1
    DCL &marker     *CHAR   1
    DCL &output     *CHAR   6
    DCL &qsrcmbr1   *CHAR  33
    DCL &qsrcmbr2   *CHAR  33
    DCL &q_srcf1    *CHAR  20
    DCL &q_srcf2    *CHAR  20
    DCL &rtncde     *CHAR   1
    DCL &srcf1      *CHAR  10
    DCL &srcf2      *CHAR  10
    DCL &srcflib1   *CHAR  10
    DCL &srcflib2   *CHAR  10
    DCL &srcmbr1    *CHAR  10
    DCL &srcmbr2    *CHAR  10
    DCL &srctype1   *CHAR  10
    DCL &srctype2   *CHAR  10


    MONMSG (cpf0000 mch0000) EXEC(GOTO error)

    /* Break qualified names */
    CHGVAR &srcf1    %SST(&q_srcf1  1 10)
    CHGVAR &srcflib1 %SST(&q_srcf1 11 10)
    CHGVAR &srcf2    %SST(&q_srcf2  1 10)
    CHGVAR &srcflib2 %SST(&q_srcf2 11 10)
        CHGVAR &srcmbr2 &srcmbr1
```

Figure A.20: CL Program CMPSRCMBRC is the command processing program for the CMPSRCMBR command (part 1 of 3).

```
/* Resolve special value SRCMBR2(*SRCMBR1) */
IF (&srcmbr2 *EQ '*SRCMBR1') DO
ENDDO

/* Check existence of both source members */
CHKOBJ &srcflib1/&srcf1 *FILE MBR(&srcmbr1)
CHKOBJ &srcflib2/&srcf2 *FILE MBR(&srcmbr2)

/* Check equality of source types */
IF (&chksrctype *EQ '*YES') DO
   RTVMBRD &srcflib1/&srcf1 MBR(&srcmbr1) SRCTYPE(&srctype1)
   RTVMBRD &srcflib2/&srcf2 MBR(&srcmbr2) SRCTYPE(&srctype2)
   IF (&srctype1 *NE &srctype2) DO
      SNDPGMMSG MSGID(cpf9898) MSGF(qcpfmsg) +
               MSGDTA('Source types of members 1 and 2' *BCAT +
                      'do not match') +
               MSGTYPE(*ESCAPE)
      RETURN
   ENDDO
ENDDO

/* Change to OUTPUT(*PRINT) if in batch */
RTVJOBA TYPE(&jobtype)
IF (&jobtype *EQ &batch) DO
   CHGVAR &output '*PRINT'
ENDDO

/* Resolve IGNLEADSPC(*AUTO) according to source type */
IF (&ignleadspc *EQ '*AUTO') DO
   RTVMBRD &srcflib1/&srcf1 MBR(&srcmbr1) SRCTYPE(&srctype1)
   IF (&srctype1 *EQ 'RPG'       *OR +
       &srctype1 *EQ 'RPGLE'     *OR +
       &srctype1 *EQ 'SQLRPG'    *OR +
       &srctype1 *EQ 'SQLRPGLE'  *OR +
       &srctype1 *EQ 'PF'        *OR +
       &srctype1 *EQ 'LF'        *OR +
       &srctype1 *EQ 'DSPF'      *OR +
       &srctype1 *EQ 'PRTF'           ) DO
      CHGVAR &ignleadspc '*NO'
   ENDDO
   ELSE DO
      CHGVAR &ignleadspc '*YES'
   ENDDO
ENDDO
```

Figure A.20: CL Program CMPSRCMBRC is the command processing program for the CMPSRCMBR command (part 2 of 3).

```
   /* Compare */
repeat:
   OVRDBF file1 TOFILE(&srcflib1/&srcf1) MBR(&srcmbr1)
   OVRDBF file2 TOFILE(&srcflib2/&srcf2) MBR(&srcmbr2)

   CHGVAR &qsrcmbr1 (&srcflib1 *TCAT '/' *CAT &srcf1 *TCAT '(' *TCAT +
                     &srcmbr1 *TCAT ')')
   CHGVAR &qsrcmbr2 (&srcflib2 *TCAT '/' *CAT &srcf2 *TCAT '(' *TCAT +
                     &srcmbr2 *TCAT ')')

   CALL cmpsrcmbrr (&qsrcmbr1 &qsrcmbr2 &marker &ignleadspc &igncase +
                    &output &rtncde)

   DLTOVR (file1 file2)

   IF (&rtncde *EQ '1') DO
      STRSEU SRCFILE(&srcflib1/&srcf1) SRCMBR(&srcmbr1) OPTION(2)
      GOTO repeat
   ENDDO
   ELSE IF (&rtncde *EQ '2') DO
      STRSEU SRCFILE(&srcflib2/&srcf2) SRCMBR(&srcmbr2) OPTION(2)
      GOTO repeat
   ENDDO

   RETURN

error:
   FWDPGMMSG
   MONMSG cpf0000

ENDPGM
```

Figure A.20: CL Program CMPSRCMBRC is the command processing program for the CMPSRCMBR command. (part 3 of 3).

The grunt work is the job of RPG IV Program CMPSRCMBRR. See Figure A.21.

```
 *****************************************************************
 *
 * To compile:
 *
 *    CRTBNDRPG  PGM(xxx/CMPSRCMBRR) +
 *               SRCFILE(xxx/SOURCE) +
 *               TEXT('Called from CMPSRCMBRC')
 *
 *****************************************************************
Ffile1     IF   F   92        DISK
Ffile2     IF   F   92        DISK
FcmpsrcmbrdCF   E             WORKSTN SFILE(DIFFRCD:SFLRRN) USROPN
Fcmpsrcmbr1O    E             PRINTER OFLIND(*IN11) USROPN
 *****************************************************************
D i              S             9P 0
D igncase        S             4A
D ignleadspc     S             4A
D lower          C               CONST('abcdefghijklmnopqrstuvwxyz')
D marker         S             1A
D markers        S             80A
D output         S             6A
D rtncde         S             1A
D sflrrn         S             4P 0
D tempsrcdta     S               LIKE(srcdta1)
D upper          C               CONST('ABCDEFGHIJKLMNOPQRSTUVWXYZ')
D yes            C               CONST('*YES')
 *****************************************************************
Ifile1     NS
I                                1    6  seqnbr1
I                                7   12  srcdat1
I                               13   92  srcdta1
 *_____
Ifile2     NS
I                                1    6  seqnbr2
I                                7   12  srcdat2
I                               13   92  srcdta2
 *****************************************************************
 * Mainline.
 *
C                   EXSR      initialize
C                   EXSR      process
C                   IF        output = '*'
C                   EXSR      display
C                   ENDIF
```

Figure A.21: RPG program CMPSRCMBRR (part 1 of 5).

```
C                     EXSR      terminate
 *------------------------------------------------
 * DISPLAY:  Process display file if OUTPUT(*).
 *
C       display      BEGSR

 * Determine whether to display the subfile record format.
C                     IF        sflrrn > 0
C                     EVAL      *IN80 = *ON
C                     ELSE
C                     EVAL      *IN80 = *OFF
C                     ENDIF

 * Repeat until a function key is pressed.
C                     DOW       *IN03 = *OFF   AND
C                               *IN07 = *OFF   AND
C                               *IN08 = *OFF   AND
C                               *IN12 = *OFF
C                     WRITE     fkeys
C                     IF        *IN80 = *OFF
C                     WRITE     nodiff
C                     ENDIF
C                     EXFMT     diffctl

C                     SELECT
C                     WHEN      *IN03 = *ON   OR   *IN12 = *ON
C                     EVAL      rtncde = 'X'
C                     WHEN      *IN07 = *ON
C                     EVAL      rtncde = '1'
C                     WHEN      *IN08 = *ON
C                     EVAL      rtncde = '2'
C                     OTHER
 * Process options or exit program, depending on subfile contents.
C                     IF        *IN80 = *ON
C                     EXSR      prc_optns
C                     ELSE
C                     EVAL      *IN03 = *ON
C                     ENDIF
C                     ENDSL
C                     ENDDO
C                     ENDSR
 *-------------------------------------------------
 * INITIALIZE:  Initialize program.
```

Figure A.21: RPG program CMPSRCMBRR (part 2 of 5).

```
     *
     C     initialize  BEGSR
     C     *ENTRY      PLIST
     C                 PARM                  qsrcmbr1
     C                 PARM                  qsrcmbr2
     C                 PARM                  marker
     C                 PARM                  ignleadspc
     C                 PARM                  igncase
     C                 PARM                  output
     C                 PARM                  rtncde

     * Open and initialize appropriate output file.
     C                 IF          output = '*'
     C                 OPEN        cmpsrcmbrd
     C                 EVAL        *IN80 = *OFF
     C                 EVAL        *IN81 = *OFF
     C                 WRITE       diffctl
     C                 EVAL        sflrrn = 0
     C                 EVAL        sflrcdnbr = 1
     C                 ELSE
     C                 OPEN        cmpsrcmbr1
     C                 WRITE       header
     C                 ENDIF
     C                 ENDSR
     *_____
     * PRC_OPTNS:  Process subfile options.
     *
     C     prc_optns   BEGSR
     C                 EVAL        *IN99 = *OFF

     * Repeat until no more options.
     C                 DOU         *IN99 = *ON
     C                 READC       diffrcd                      99
     C                 IF          *IN99 = *OFF
     C                 EXFMT       showdiff
     C                 EVAL        option = ' '
     C                 UPDATE      diffrcd
     C                 ENDIF
     C                 ENDDO
     C                 ENDSR
     *_____
     * PRINT:  Print one line of differences.
     *         Note:  This subroutine is executed even if OUTPUT(*).
     *
     C     print       BEGSR
```

Figure A.21: RPG program CMPSRCMBRR (part 3 of 5).

```
C                   EVAL      markers  = *BLANK
C                   EVAL      markers1 = *BLANK
C                   EVAL      markers2 = *BLANK

 * Insert marker character for each character that is different
 * in both source members.
C 1   DO 80 i C     IF  SUBST(srcdta1:i:1) <> %SUBST(srcdta2:i:1)
C                   EVAL      %SUBST(markers:i:1) = marker
C                   ENDIF
C                   ENDDO

 * Process printer file overflow.
C                   IF        output = '*PRINT'
C                   IF        *IN11 = *ON
C                   WRITE     header
C                   EVAL      *IN11 = *OFF
C                   ENDIF
C                   ENDIF

 * Prepare display file or printer file.
C                   IF        output = '*'
C                   EVAL      srcdta1p = %SUBST(srcdta1:1)
C                   EVAL      srcdta2p = %SUBST(srcdta2:1)
C                   EVAL      sflrrn = sflrrn + 1
C                   WRITE     diffrcd
C                   ELSE
C                   EVAL      markers1 = markers
C                   EVAL      markers2 = markers
C                   WRITE     detail
C                   ENDIF
C                   ENDSR
 *_____
 * PROCESS:  Process both input files.
 *
C     process       BEGSR

 * Repeat until no more records.
C                   DOU       *IN01 = *ON OR *IN02 = *ON
C                   READ      file1                              01
C                   READ      file2                              02
C                   IF        NOT (*IN01 = *ON OR *IN02 = *ON)

 * Trim leading blanks if IGNLEADSPC(*YES).
C                   IF        ignleadspc = yes
C                   EVAL      tempsrcdta = %TRIML(srcdta1)
```

Figure A.21: RPG program CMPSRCMBRR (part 4 of 5).

```
C                   EVAL      srcdta1 = tempsrcdta
C                   EVAL      tempsrcdta = %TRIML(srcdta2)
C                   EVAL      srcdta2 = tempsrcdta
C                   ENDIF

 * Turn to uppercase if IGNCASE(*YES).
C                   IF        igncase = yes
C     lower:upper   XLATE     srcdta1           tempsrcdta
C                   EVAL      srcdta1 = tempsrcdta
C     lower:upper   XLATE     srcdta2           tempsrcdta
C                   EVAL      srcdta2 = tempsrcdta
C                   ENDIF

 * If there's a difference, mark it in the output file.
C                   IF        srcdta1 <> srcdta2
C                   EXSR      print
C                   ENDIF


C                   ENDIF
C                   ENDDO
C                   ENDSR
 *_____
 * TERMINATE:  Terminate program.
 *
C     terminate     BEGSR
C                   IF        output = '*'
C                   CLOSE     cmpsrcmbrd
C                   ELSE
C                   CLOSE     cmpsrcmbr1
C                   ENDIF
C                   EVAL      *INLR = *ON
C                   ENDSR
```

Figure A.21: RPG program CMPSRCMBRR (part 5 of 5).

PROGRAMMING SHORTCUTS

One common task is having to create a work file in QTEMP that has an external file definition. In cases like that, the simplest approach is to create the work file in the same library where you have created the programs that use the file, and then create a duplicate of the file in QTEMP using the CRTDUPOBJ command.

Create Work File (CRTWRKF)

CRTWRKF simplifies the duplication task by requiring only the name of the "model" work file. Even the library name defaults to *LIBL, allowing you to avoid hard-coding library names or going through gyrations to obtain it without hard-coding. CRTWRKF always creates the file in QTEMP, using the same name of the model.

Parameters

- MODEL: Enter the qualified name of the model work file. The library portion defaults to *LIBL, but can be changed to *CURLIB or a specific library name.

Figure A.22 contains the source code for command CRTWRKF.

```
/**********************************************************************/
/*                                                                  */
/* To compile:                                                      */
/*                                                                  */
/*    CRTCMD  CMD(xxx/CRTWRKF) +                                    */
/*            PGM(xxx/CRTWRKFC) +                                   */
/*            SRCFILE(xxx/QCMDSRC) +                                */
/*            TEXT('Create Work File') +                            */
/*            ALLOW(*ALL)                                           */
/*                                                                  */
/**********************************************************************/
CMD 'Create Work File'

   PARM model q1 MIN(1) PROMPT('Model physical file')
q1: +
     QUAL *NAME 10 MIN(1)
     QUAL *NAME 10 DFT(*LIBL) SPCVAL((*LIBL) (*CURLIB)) +
          PROMPT('Library')
```

Figure A.22: Source code for command CRTWRKF.

The command processing program is CL program CRTWRKFC. See Figure A.23.

```
/***********************************************************************/
/*                                                                     */
/* To compile:                                                         */
/*                                                                     */
/*     CRTCLPGM   PGM(xxx/CRTWRKFC) +                                  */
/*                SRCFILE(xxx/QCLSRC) +                                */
/*                TEXT('CPP for CRTWRKF command')                      */
/*                                                                     */
/***********************************************************************/
PGM (&qmodel)

    DCL &model      *CHAR    10
    DCL &modellib   *CHAR    10
    DCL &qmodel     *CHAR    20
    DCL &rtnlib     *CHAR    10

    MONMSG (cpf0000 mch0000) EXEC(GOTO error)

    /* Break qualified name */
    CHGVAR &model    %SST(&qmodel  1 10)
    CHGVAR &modellib %SST(&qmodel 11 10)

    /* Verify existence of model file */
    CHKOBJ &modellib/&model *FILE

    /* Create work file */
    DLTF qtemp/&model
    MONMSG cpf0000 EXEC(DO)
       RCVMSG MSGTYPE(*EXCP) RMV(*YES)
    ENDDO

    RTVOBJD &modellib/&model *FILE RTNLIB(&rtnlib)

    CRTDUPOBJ OBJ(&model) FROMLIB(&rtnlib) OBJTYPE(*FILE) +
              TOLIB(qtemp) NEWOBJ(*OBJ) DATA(*NO)

    RETURN

error:
   FWDPGMMSG
   MONMSG cpf0000

ENDPGM
```

Figure A.23: CL program CRTWRKFC is the command processing program for the CRTWRKF command.

Duplicate Object (DUPOBJ)

The Create Duplicate Object (CRTDUPOBJ) command is useful, but it has an important shortcoming that has yet to be addressed by IBM: the FROMLIB parameter does not support special value *LIBL or *CURLIB, thereby making it impossible to use library list support to locate the object one wants to duplicate.

DUPOBJ solves this problem and at the same time uses the standard qualified-name format for the old and new object names (something CRTDUPOBJ doesn't use).

Parameters

- OBJ: Enter the qualified name of the object you want to duplicate. The library portion may contain *LIBL, *CURLIB, or a specific library name.

- OBJTYPE: Enter the type of object, such as *PGM for program or *FILE for file.

- NEWOBJ: Enter the qualified name of the new, duplicate object. The default value for the object name is *OBJ (use the same name as the original object). The library portion defaults to *OBJLIB (use the same library as the original object), but also allows *CURLIB or a specific library name.

- DATA: Whether to copy the data, if the original object is *FILE.

Source code for command DUPOBJ is shown in Figure A.24.

```
/*******************************************************************/
/*                                                                 */
/* To compile:                                                     */
/*                                                                 */
/*     CRTCMD   CMD(xxx/DUPOBJ) +                                  */
/*              PGM(xxx/DUPOBJC) +                                 */
/*              SRCFILE(xxx/QCMDSRC) +                             */
/*              TEXT('Duplicate Object') +                         */
/*              ALLOW(*ALL)                                        */
/*                                                                 */
/*******************************************************************/
CMD 'Duplicate Object'

    PARM obj q1 MIN(1) PROMPT('Object')
```

Figure A.24: Source code for the DUPOBJ command (part 1 of 2).

```
q1: +
      QUAL *NAME 10 MIN(1) EXPR(*YES)
      QUAL *NAME 10 DFT(*LIBL) SPCVAL((*LIBL) (*CURLIB)) EXPR(*YES) +
          PROMPT('Library')

   PARM objtype *CHAR 8 MIN(1) EXPR(*YES) PROMPT('Object type')

   PARM newobj q2 PROMPT('New object')

q2: +
      QUAL *NAME 10 DFT(*OBJ) SPCVAL((*OBJ)) EXPR(*YES)
      QUAL *NAME 10 DFT(*OBJLIB) SPCVAL((*OBJLIB) (*CURLIB)) +
          EXPR(*YES) PROMPT('Library')

   PARM data *CHAR 4 RSTD(*YES) DFT(*YES) VALUES(*YES *NO) PMTCTL(pc1) +
       PROMPT('Copy data')
pc1: +
      PMTCTL CTL(objtype) COND((*EQ *FILE))
```

Figure A.24: Source code for the DUPOBJ command (part 2 of 2).

Figure A.25 contains the source code for CL Program DUPOBJC.

```
/****************************************************************************/
/*                                                                        */
/* To compile:                                                            */
/*                                                                        */
/*    CRTCLPGM  PGM(xxx/DUPOBJC) +                                        */
/*              SRCFILE(xxx/QCLSRC) +                                     */
/*              TEXT('CPP for DUPOBJ command')                           */
/*                                                                        */
/****************************************************************************/
PGM (&q_obj &objtype &q_newobj &data)

    DCL &atr         *CHAR   10
    DCL &data        *CHAR    4
    DCL &exists      *LGL     1
    DCL &newobj      *CHAR   10
    DCL &newobjlib   *CHAR   10
    DCL &obj         *CHAR   10
    DCL &objlib      *CHAR   10
    DCL &objtype     *CHAR    8
```

Figure A.25: CL program DUPOBJC is the command processing program for the DUPOBJ command (part 1 of 3).

```
DCL &q_newobj    *CHAR   20
DCL &q_obj       *CHAR   20
MONMSG (cpf0000 mch0000) EXEC(GOTO error)

/* Break qualified names */
CHGVAR &obj        %SST(&q_obj     1 10)
CHGVAR &objlib     %SST(&q_obj    11 10)
CHGVAR &newobj     %SST(&q_newobj  1 10)
CHGVAR &newobjlib  %SST(&q_newobj 11 10)

/* Retrieve library containing old object */
RTVOBJD &objlib/&obj &objtype RTNLIB(&objlib) OBJATR(&atr)

/* Resolve NEWOBJ() special values */
IF (&newobj *EQ '*OBJ') DO
   CHGVAR &newobj &obj
ENDDO

IF (&newobjlib *EQ '*OBJLIB') DO
   CHGVAR &newobjlib &objlib
ENDDO
ELSE IF (&newobjlib *EQ '*CURLIB') DO
   RTVJOBA CURLIB(&newobjlib)
   IF (&newobjlib *EQ '*NONE') DO
      CHGVAR &newobjlib 'qgpl'
   ENDDO
ENDDO

/* Reject duplication request if names are the same */
IF (&obj    *EQ &newobj    *AND +
   &objlib *EQ &newobjlib       ) DO
   SNDPGMMSG MSGID(cpf9898) MSGF(qcpfmsg) +
            MSGDTA('Old and new objects cannot have the' *BCAT +
                  'same name') +
            MSGTYPE(*ESCAPE)
ENDDO

/* Check existence of new library */
CHKOBJ &newobjlib *LIB
MONMSG cpf9801 EXEC(DO)
   SNDPGMMSG MSGID(cpf9898) MSGF(qcpfmsg) +
            MSGDTA('Library' *BCAT &newobjlib *BCAT +
                  'does not exist') +
            MSGTYPE(*ESCAPE)
ENDDO
```

Figure A.25: CL program DUPOBJC is the command processing program for the DUPOBJ command (part 2 of 3).

```
      /* Reject duplication request if new object exists */
      CHGVAR &exists            '1'
      CHKOBJ &newobjlib/&newobj &objtype
      MONMSG cpf0000 EXEC(DO)
         CHGVAR &exists '0'
      ENDDO

      IF &exists DO
         SNDPGMMSG MSGID(cpf9898) MSGF(qcpfmsg) +
                   MSGDTA('New object' *BCAT &newobjlib *TCAT '/' *CAT +
                          &objlib *BCAT 'already exists') +
                   MSGTYPE(*ESCAPE)
      ENDDO

      /* Ignore DATA(*YES) if object is not physical file */
      IF (&objtype *EQ '*FILE' *AND +
          &atr     *NE 'PF'          ) DO
         CHGVAR &data '*NO'
      ENDDO

      /* Create duplicate object */
      IF (&objtype *EQ '*FILE' *AND +
          &data    *EQ '*YES'        ) DO
         CRTDUPOBJ OBJ(&obj) FROMLIB(&objlib) OBJTYPE(*FILE) +
                   TOLIB(&newobjlib) NEWOBJ(&newobj) DATA(*YES)
      ENDDO
      ELSE DO
         CRTDUPOBJ OBJ(&obj) FROMLIB(&objlib) OBJTYPE(&objtype) +
                   TOLIB(&newobjlib) NEWOBJ(&newobj)
      ENDDO

      SNDPGMMSG MSGID(cpf9898) MSGF(qcpfmsg) +
                MSGDTA('Object' *BCAT &objlib *TCAT '/' *CAT &obj *BCAT +
                       'type' *BCAT &objtype *BCAT 'duplicated as' *BCAT +
                       &newobjlib *TCAT '/' *CAT &newobj) +
                MSGTYPE(*COMP)

      RETURN

   error:
      FWDPGMMSG
      MONMSG cpf0000

   ENDPGM
```

Figure A.25: CL program DUPOBJC is the command processing program for the DUPOBJ command (part 3 of 3).

Save and Restore Library List (SAVLIBL, RSTLIBL)

While a program is running, sometimes it's necessary to make changes to the library list or a program you call needs to have a particular setup for the library list, so the program changes the list with CHGLIBL, ADDLIBLE, or RMVLIBLE as soon as it starts. The problem, then, is restoring the library list to its previous state. The problem is compounded when the second program, in turn, calls a third program that also needs a particular setup for the library list.

The Save Library List (SAVLIBL) and Restore Library List (RSTLIBL) commands solve this problem. SAVLIBL saves the current setup for the library list in a *LIFO data queue, and RSTLIBL restores the library list by reading from the same data queue the setup it had originally. Between SAVLIBL and RSTLIBL you may have any number of CHGLIBL, ADDLIBLE, or RMVLIBLE commands. Figure A.26 provides a typical scenario.

```
      Program A              Program B              Program C
      ---------              ---------              ---------
      PGM                    PGM                    PGM

          CALL  b                SAVLIBL                SAVLIBL

      ENDPGM                     ADDLIBLE ...           RMVLIBLE ...

                                 /* Processing */       /* Processing */

                                 CALL  c                RSTLIBL

                                 /* Processing */   ENDPGM

                                 RSTLIBL

                             ENDPGM
```

Figure A.26: An example of using the SAVLIBL and RSTLIBL commands.

Program A calls B. Program B saves the library list, and then changes it in several ways before starting its own tasks. It also calls program C.

Program C saves the library list (second save) before changing it, does some processing, and then restores the library list (the way program B had it). When control returns to program B, the library list is then back the way the program expects it to be. Program B continues processing, and then restores the library list (to its original save) before returning control to program A. Program A can then continue its own processing with an intact library list.

Parameters

None.

Figure A.27 contains the source code for command SAVLIBL.

```
/****************************************************************/
/*                                                            */
/* To compile:                                                */
/*                                                            */
/*    CRTCMD  CMD(xxx/SAVLIBL) +                              */
/*            PGM(xxx/SAVLIBLC) +                             */
/*            SRCFILE(xxx/QCMDSRC) +                          */
/*            TEXT('Save Library List') +                     */
/*            ALLOW(*ALL)                                     */
/*                                                            */
/****************************************************************/
CMD 'Save Library List'
```

Figure A.27: Source code for command SAVLIBL.

SAVLIBL executes CL Program SAVLIBLC. See Figure A.28.

```
/**********************************************************************/
/*                                                                    */
/* To compile:                                                        */
/*                                                                    */
/*     CRTCLPGM  PGM(xxx/SAVLIBLC) +                                  */
/*               SRCFILE(xxx/QCLSRC) +                                */
/*               TEXT('CPP for SAVLIBL command')                      */
/*                                                                    */
/**********************************************************************/
PGM

   DCL &curlib    *CHAR   10
   DCL &dtaqe     *CHAR   300
   DCL &dtaqelen  *DEC     5 300
   DCL &usrlibl   *CHAR   275

   MONMSG (cpf0000 mch0000) EXEC(GOTO error)

   /* Create library list stack if necessary */
   CHKOBJ qtemp/liblstack *DTAQ
   MONMSG cpf9801 EXEC(DO)
      RCVMSG MSGTYPE(*LAST) RMV(*YES)
      CRTDTAQ qtemp/liblstack TYPE(*STD) MAXLEN(300) SEQ(*LIFO) +
             TEXT('Library list stack')
   ENDDO

   /* Save library list into stack */
   RTVJOBA CURLIB(&curlib) USRLIBL(&usrlibl)
   IF (&curlib *EQ '*NONE') DO
      CHGVAR &curlib '*CRTDFT'
   ENDDO

   CHGVAR &dtaqe (&curlib *CAT &usrlibl)

   CALL qsnddtaq ('LIBLSTACK' 'qtemp' &dtaqelen &dtaqe)

   RETURN

error:
   FWDPGMMSG
   MONMSG cpf0000
ENDPGM
```

Figure A.28: CL program SAVLIBLC is the command processing program for command SAVLIBL.

347

Source code for the command RSTLIBL is shown in Figure A.29.

```
/**********************************************************************/
/*                                                                    */
/* To compile:                                                        */
/*                                                                    */
/*    CRTCMD  CMD(xxx/RSTLIBL) +                                      */
/*            PGM(xxx/RSTLIBLC) +                                     */
/*            SRCFILE(xxx/QCMDSRC) +                                  */
/*            TEXT('Restore Library List') +                         */
/*            ALLOW(*ALL)                                            */
/*                                                                    */
/**********************************************************************/
CMD 'Restore Library List'
```

Figure A.29: Source code for the RSTLIBL command.

RTVLIBL executes CL program RSTLIBLC. See Figure A.30.

```
/**********************************************************************/
/*                                                                    */
/* To compile:                                                        */
/*                                                                    */
/*    CRTCLPGM  PGM(xxx/RSTLIBLC) +                                  */
/*              SRCFILE(xxx/QCLSRC) +                                */
/*              TEXT('CPP for RSTLIBL command')                     */
/*                                                                    */
/**********************************************************************/
PGM

    DCL &cmd        *CHAR  300
    DCL &cmdlen     *DEC   (15 5) 300
    DCL &curlib     *CHAR  10
    DCL &dtaqe      *CHAR  300
    DCL &dtaqelen   *DEC   5      300
    DCL &usrlibl    *CHAR  275
    DCL &wait       *DEC   5      0

    MONMSG (cpf0000 mch0000) EXEC(GOTO error)

    /* Reject request if SAVLIBL not executed before */
    CHKOBJ qtemp/liblstack *DTAQ
```

Figure A.30: CL program RSTLIBLC is the command-processing program for the RSTLIBL command (part 1 of 2).

```
      MONMSG cpf9801 EXEC(DO)

         SNDPGMMSG MSGID(cpf9898) MSGF(qcpfmsg) +
                  MSGDTA('RSTLIBL not allowed before SAVLIBL') +
                  MSGTYPE(*ESCAPE)
      ENDDO

      /* Restore library list */
      CALL qrcvdtaq ('LIBLSTACK' 'qtemp' &dtaqelen &dtaqe &wait)

      /* Reject request if nothing to restore */
      IF (&dtaqe *EQ ' ') DO
         SNDPGMMSG MSGID(cpf9898) MSGF(qcpfmsg) +
                  MSGDTA('Library list stack is empty') +
                  MSGTYPE(*ESCAPE)
      ENDDO

      CHGVAR &curlib  %SST(&dtaqe  1 10)
      CHGVAR &usrlibl %SST(&dtaqe 11 275)

      CHGCURLIB &curlib
      CHGVAR &cmd ('CHGLIBL (' *BCAT &usrlibl *TCAT ')')
      CALL qcmdexc (&cmd &cmdlen)

      RETURN

   error:
      FWDPGMMSG
      MONMSG cpf0000

   ENDPGM
```

Figure A.30: CL program RSTLIBLC is the command-processing program for the RSTLIBL command (part 2 of 2).

DATA QUEUES

Sending data to a data queue requires the use of QSNDDTAQ, an API you have to call passing several Parameters. Like most APIs, however, the Parameters are sometimes obscure and, being a CALL, you don't get any online help to tell you how many Parameters there are, what they are, and in which order you have to code them.

Send to Data Queue (SNDDTAQ)

SNDDTAQ is a "front-end" command that simplifies the use of QSNDDTAQ for CL programs. Being a command, you can prompt it, fill in the input fields, and then press Enter.

Parameters

- DTAQ: Qualified name of the data queue. The library portion defaults to *LIBL.

- DATA: Enter the data you want to send to the data queue. You can supply a maximum of 9999 bytes or the maximum permissible by the data queue, whichever is less.

- KEY: Enter the value of the key for this entry of the data queue, if the data queue is type *KEYED. The default value is *NONE.

- KEYLEN: Enter the length of the key.

Source code for command SNDDTAQ is shown in Figure A.31.

```
/******************************************************************/
/*                                                              */
/* To compile:                                                  */
/*                                                              */
/*    CRTCMD  CMD(xxx/SNDDTAQ) +                                */
/*            PGM(xxx/SNDDTAQC) +                               */
/*            SRCFILE(xxx/QCMDSRC) +                            */
/*            TEXT('Send to Data Queue')                        */
/*            ALLOW(*ALL)                                       */
/*                                                              */
/******************************************************************/
CMD 'Send to Data Queue'

   PARM dtaq q1 MIN(1) PROMPT('Data queue')
q1: +
      QUAL *NAME 10 MIN(1)
      QUAL *NAME 10 DFT(*LIBL) SPCVAL((*LIBL)) PROMPT('Library')
```

Figure A.31: Source code for the SNDDTAQ command (part 1 of 2).

```
    PARM data *CHAR 9999 DFT(*NONE) PROMPT('Data')

    PARM datalen *DEC 5 DFT(1) PROMPT('Data length')

    PARM key *CHAR 999 DFT(*NONE) PMTCTL(*PMTRQS) +
        PROMPT('Key value, if keyed')

    PARM keylen *DEC 3 DFT(0) PMTCTL(*PMTRQS) +
        PROMPT('Key length, if keyed')
```

Figure A.31: Source code for the SNDDTAQ command (part 2 of 2)

SNDDTAQ executes CL program SNDDTAQ. See Figure A.32.

```
    /***************************************************************/
    /*                                                             */
    /* To compile:                                                 */
    /*                                                             */
    /*    CRTCLPGM  PGM(xxx/SNDDTAQC) +                            */
    /*              SRCFILE(xxx/QCLSRC) +                          */
    /*              TEXT('CPP for SNDDTAQ command')                */
    /*                                                             */
    /***************************************************************/
    PGM (&qdtaq &data &datalen &key &keylen)

        DCL &data      *CHAR 9999
        DCL &datalen   *DEC     5
        DCL &dtaq      *CHAR    10
        DCL &dtaqlib   *CHAR    10
        DCL &key       *CHAR   999
        DCL &keylen    *DEC     3
        DCL &qdtaq     *CHAR    20


        MONMSG (cpf0000 mch0000) EXEC(GOTO error)

        /* Break qualified name */
        CHGVAR &dtaq    %SST(&qdtaq  1 10)
        CHGVAR &dtaqlib %SST(&qdtaq 11 10)

        /* Check existence of data queue */
        CHKOBJ &dtaqlib/&dtaq *DTAQ
```

Figure A.32: CL program SNDDTAQC is the command-processing program for the SNDDTAQ command (part 1 of 2).

```
/* Send to data queue */
IF (&data *EQ '*NONE') DO
   CHGVAR &data ' '
ENDDO

IF (&key *EQ '*NONE') DO
   CALL qsnddtaq (&dtaq &dtaqlib &datalen &data)
ENDDO
ELSE DO
   CALL qsnddtaq (&dtaq &dtaqlib &datalen &data &keylen &key)
ENDDO

RETURN

error:
   FWDPGMMSG
   MONMSG cpf0000

ENDPGM
```

Figure A.32: CL program SNDDTAQC is the command-processing program for the SNDDTAQ command (part 2 of 2).

Receive from Data Queue (RCVDTAQ)

RCVDTAQ Is a front-end command for API QRCVDTAQ. You can use RCVDTAQ in CL programs to simplify the use of QRCVDTAQ.

Parameters

- DTAQ: Qualified name of the data queue. The library portion defaults to *LIBL.

- DATA: Enter the name of a CL variable declared as TYPE(*CHAR) LEN(9999), which is to contain the data received from the data queue.

- DATALEN: Enter the name of a CL variable declared as TYPE(*DEC) LEN(5 0), which is to contain the length of the data received from the data queue.

- WAIT: Enter the number of seconds RCVDTAQ is to wait for an entry to become available in the data queue. The default value is *NONE (do not wait). Special value *NOMAX makes RCVDTAQ wait as long as necessary.

- ORDER: For *KEYED data queues, enter a code that indicates in which order to receive entries from the data queue. Valid values are *NONE, *EQ, *NE, *LT, *LE, *GT, and *GE.

- KEY: Enter the value of the key for the entry you want to receive.

- KEYLEN: Enter the length of the key value.

- SENDER: Enter the name of a CL variable, declared as TYPE(*CHAR) LEN(44), which is to contain the sender information of the data-queue entry just received.

Source code for command RCVDTAQ is shown in Figure A.33.

```
/*******************************************************************/
/*                                                                 */
/* To compile:                                                     */
/*                                                                 */
/*     CRTCMD  CMD(xxx/RCVDTAQ) +                                  */
/*             PGM(xxx/RCVDTAQC) +                                 */
/*             SRCFILE(xxx/QCMDSRC) +                              */
/*             TEXT('Receive from Data Queue') +                  */
/*             ALLOW(*IPGM *IMOD *BPGM *BMOD)                      */
/*                                                                 */
/*******************************************************************/
CMD 'Receive from Data Queue'

    PARM dtaq q1 MIN(1) PROMPT('Data queue')
q1: +
        QUAL *NAME 10 MIN(1)
        QUAL *NAME 10 DFT(*LIBL) SPCVAL((*LIBL)) PROMPT('Library')

    PARM data *CHAR 9999 RTNVAL(*YES) PROMPT('Data (9999)')

    PARM datalen *DEC 5 RTNVAL(*YES) PROMPT('Data length (5 0)')

    PARM wait *DEC 5 DFT(*NONE) SPCVAL((*NONE 0) (*NOMAX -1)) +
        PROMPT('Wait seconds')

    PARM order *CHAR 5 RSTD(*YES) DFT(*NONE) +
        VALUES(*NONE *EQ *NE *LT *LE *GT *GE) PMTCTL(*PMTRQS) +
        PROMPT('Retrieval order, if keyed')
```

Figure A.33: Source code for the RCVDTAQ command (part 1 of 2).

```
    PARM key *CHAR 999 DFT(*NONE) PMTCTL(*PMTRQS) +
        PROMPT('Key value, if keyed')

    PARM keylen *DEC 3 DFT(0) PMTCTL(*PMTRQS) +
        PROMPT('Key length, if keyed')

    PARM sender *CHAR 44 RTNVAL(*YES) PROMPT('Sender (44)')
```

Figure A.33: Source code for the RCVDTAQ command (part 2 of 2).

RCVDTAQ executes CL program RCVDTAQC. See Figure A.34.

```
/***************************************************************************/
/*                                                                         */
/* To compile:                                                             */
/*                                                                         */
/*     CRTCLPGM  PGM(xxx/RCVDTAQC) +                                       */
/*               SRCFILE(xxx/QCLSRC) +                                     */
/*               TEXT('CPP for RCVDTAQ command')                          */
/*                                                                         */
/***************************************************************************/
PGM (&qdtaq &data &datalen &wait &order &key &keylen &sender)

    DCL &data       *CHAR 9999
    DCL &data_x     *CHAR 9999
    DCL &datalen    *DEC    5
    DCL &datalen_x  *DEC    5
    DCL &dtaq       *CHAR  10
    DCL &dtaqlib    *CHAR  10
    DCL &key        *CHAR 999
    DCL &keylen     *DEC    3
    DCL &order      *CHAR   5
    DCL &order2     *CHAR   2
    DCL &qdtaq      *CHAR  20
    DCL &sender     *CHAR  44
    DCL &sender_x   *CHAR  44
    DCL &wait       *DEC    5

    MONMSG (cpf0000 mch0000) EXEC(GOTO error)
```

Figure A.34: CL program RCVDTAQC is the command-processing program for the RCVDTAQ command (part 1 of 2).

```
     /* Break qualified name */
     CHGVAR &dtaq    %SST(&qdtaq  1 10)
     CHGVAR &dtaqlib %SST(&qdtaq 11 10)

     /* Check existence of data queue */
     CHKOBJ &dtaqlib/&dtaq *DTAQ

     /* Receive from data queue */
     IF (&order *EQ '*NONE') DO
        CHGVAR &order2 'EQ'
     ENDDO
     ELSE DO
        CHGVAR &order2 %SST(&order 2 2)
     ENDDO

     CALL qrcvdtaq (&dtaq &dtaqlib &datalen_x &data_x &wait &order2 +
                   &keylen &key X'044F' &sender_x)

     CHGVAR &datalen &datalen_x
     MONMSG mch3601
     CHGVAR &data     &data_x
     MONMSG mch3601
     CHGVAR &sender   &sender_x
     MONMSG mch3601

     RETURN

error:
   FWDPGMMSG
   MONMSG cpf0000

ENDPGM
```

Figure A.34: CL program RCVDTAQC is the command-processing program for the RCVDTAQ command (part 2 of 2).

Clear Data Queue (CLRDTAQ)

API QCLRDTAQ clears a data queue of all data. The CLRDTAQ command is a front-end to this API.

Parameters

- DTAQ: Enter the qualified name of the data queue to be cleared. The library portion defaults to *LIBL.

Source code for command CLRDTAQ is shown in Figure A.35.

```
/******************************************************************/
/*                                                              */
/* To compile:                                                  */
/*                                                              */
/*    CRTCMD  CMD(xxx/CLRDTAQ) +                                */
/*            PGM(xxx/CLRDTAQC) +                               */
/*            SRCFILE(xxx/QCMDSRC) +                            */
/*            TEXT('Clear Data Queue') +                        */
/*            ALLOW(*ALL)                                       */
/*                                                              */
/******************************************************************/
CMD 'Clear Data Queue'

   PARM dtaq q1 MIN(1) PROMPT('Data queue')
q1: +
     QUAL *NAME 10 MIN(1)
     QUAL *NAME 10 DFT(*LIBL) SPCVAL((*LIBL)) PROMPT('Library')
```

Figure A.35: Source code for the CLRDTAQ command.

CLRDTAQ executes CL program CLRDTAQC. See Figure A.36.

```
/******************************************************************/
/*                                                              */
/* To compile:                                                  */
/*                                                              */
/*    CRTCLPGM  PGM(xxx/CLRDTAQC) +                             */
/*              SRCFILE(xxx/QCLSRC) +                           */
/*              TEXT('Clear Data Queue')                        */
/*                                                              */
/******************************************************************/
PGM (&qdtaq)

   DCL &dtaq      *CHAR   10
   DCL &dtaqlib   *CHAR   10
   DCL &qdtaq     *CHAR   20

   MONMSG (cpf0000 mch0000) EXEC(GOTO error)

   /* Break qualified name */
   CHGVAR &dtaq   %SST(&qdtaq  1 10)
```

Figure A.36: CL program CLRDTAQC is the command-processing program for the CLRDTAQ command (part 1 of 2).

```
        CHGVAR &dtaqlib %SST(&qdtaq 11 10)

        /* Check existence of data queue */
        CHKOBJ &dtaqlib/&dtaq *DTAQ

        /* Clear data queue */
        CALL qclrdtaq (&dtaq &dtaqlib)

        RETURN

    error:
        FWDPGMMSG
        MONMSG cpf0000

    ENDPGM
```

Figure A.36: CL program CLRDTAQC is the command-processing program for the CLRDTAQ command (part 2 of 2).

Retrieve Data Queue Description (RTVDTAQD)

RTVDTAQD retrieves the information you used to create a given data queue. This information is important if you want to delete the data queue and recreate it at a later time. Utility command RTVDTAQD (see below) does this precisely.

Parameters

- DTAQ: Enter the qualified name of the data queue. The library portion defaults to *LIBL.

- MAXLEN: Name of a CL variable, declared as TYPE(*DEC) LEN(5 0), which is to contain the maximum length of an entry to the data queue.

- SEQ: Name of a CL variable, declared as TYPE(*CHAR) LEN(6), that is to contain the sequence of the data queue. The values obtained may be *FIFO, *LIFO, or *KEYED.

- KEYLEN: Name of a CL variable, declared as TYPE(*DEC) LEN(3 0), that is to contain the length of the key to the data queue.

- TEXT: Name of a CL variable, declared as TYPE(*CHAR) LEN(50), that is to contain the text description of the data queue.

- FORCE: Name of a CL variable, declared as TYPE(*CHAR) LEN(4), that is to contain an answer to "Force data to auxiliary storage?" Values obtained may be either *YES or *NO.

- SENDERID: Name of a CL variable, declared as TYPE(*CHAR) LEN(4), that is to contain an answer to "Include sender ID in data queue entries?" Values obtained may be *YES or *NO.

Note: CL program RTVDTAQDC (the CPP for the rtvdtaqd command) uses a variable named &STRUCT as a fictitious data structure (data structures are not supported in CL). Check out the DCLs in this program, and see how the indentation helps reinforce the idea of a data structure and its related subfields.

Source code for command RTVDTAQD is shown in Figure A.37.

```
/***************************************************************************/
/*                                                                         */
/* To compile:                                                             */
/*                                                                         */
/*    CRTCMD   CMD(xxx/RTVDTAQD) +                                         */
/*             PGM(xxx/RTVDTAQDC) +                                        */
/*             SRCFILE(xxx/QCMDSRC) +                                      */
/*             TEXT('Retrieve Data Queue Description') +                   */
/*             ALLOW(*IPGM *BPGM *IMOD *BMOD)                              */
/*                                                                         */
/***************************************************************************/
CMD 'Retrieve Data Queue Description'

   PARM dtaq q1 MIN(1) PROMPT('Data queue')
q1: +
      QUAL *NAME 10 MIN(1)
      QUAL *NAME 10 DFT(*LIBL) SPCVAL((*LIBL)) PROMPT('Library')

   PARM maxlen *DEC 5 RTNVAL(*YES) PROMPT('Maximum entry length (5 0)')

   PARM seq *CHAR 6 RTNVAL(*YES) PROMPT('Sequence (6)')

   PARM keylen *DEC 3 RTNVAL(*YES) PROMPT('Key length (3 0)')

   PARM text *CHAR 50 RTNVAL(*YES) PROMPT('Text ''description'' (50)')

   PARM force *CHAR 4 RTNVAL(*YES) +
        PROMPT('Force to auxiliary storage (4)')

   PARM senderid *CHAR 4 RTNVAL(*YES) PROMPT('Include sender ID (4)')
```

Figure A.37: Source code for the RTVDTAQD command.

RCVDTAQD executes CL program RTVDTAQDC. See Figure A.38.

```
/***********************************************************************/
/*                                                                    */
/* To compile:                                                        */
/*                                                                    */
/*     CRTCLPGM  PGM(xxx/RTVDTAQDC) +                                 */
/*               SRCFILE(xxx/QCLSRC) +                                */
/*               TEXT('CPP for RTVDTAQD command')                     */
/*                                                                    */
/***********************************************************************/
PGM (&qdtaq &maxlen &seq &keylen &text &force &senderid)

    DCL &dtaq         *CHAR  10
    DCL &dtaqlib      *CHAR  10
    DCL &force        *CHAR  4
    DCL &force_x      *CHAR  4
    DCL &keylen       *DEC   3
    DCL &keylen_x     *DEC   3
    DCL &maxlen       *DEC   5
    DCL &maxlen_x     *DEC   5
    DCL &qdtaq        *CHAR  20
    DCL &senderid     *CHAR  4
    DCL &senderid_x   *CHAR  4
    DCL &seq          *CHAR  6
    DCL &seq_x        *CHAR  6
    DCL &struct       *CHAR  69  /* Data structure */
    DCL    &bytrtn    *CHAR  4   /* Binary */
    DCL    &bytavl    *CHAR  4   /* Binary */
    DCL    &maxl      *CHAR  4   /* Binary */
    DCL    &keyl      *CHAR  4   /* Binary */
    DCL    &seq1      *CHAR  1
    DCL    &snd1      *CHAR  1
    DCL    &force1    *CHAR  1
    DCL    &text50    *CHAR  50
    DCL &struct_len   *CHAR  4   /* Binary */
    DCL &text         *CHAR  50
    DCL &text_x       *CHAR  50

    MONMSG (cpf0000 mch0000) EXEC(GOTO error)

    /* Break qualified name */
    CHGVAR &dtaq    %SST(&qdtaq  1 10)
    CHGVAR &dtaqlib %SST(&qdtaq 11 10)

    /* Validata data queue name */
    CHKOBJ &dtaqlib/&dtaqlib *DTAQ
```

Figure A.38: RTVDTAQDC is the command-processing program for the RTVDTAQD command
(part 1 of 2).

```
    /* Retrieve attributes */
    CHGVAR %BIN(&struct_len) 69

    CALL qmhqrdqd (&struct &structlen 'RDQD0100' &qdtaq)

    IF (&seq1 *EQ 'F') +
       CHGVAR &seq_x '*FIFO'
    ELSE IF (&seq1 *EQ 'L') +
       CHGVAR &seq_x '*LIFO'
    ELSE +
       CHGVAR &seq_x '*KEYED'
    CHGVAR &seq &seq_x
    MONMSG mch3601

    CHGVAR &maxlen_x %BIN(&maxl)
    CHGVAR &maxlen    &maxlen_x
    MONMSG mch3601

    CHGVAR &keylen_x %BIN(&keyl)
    CHGVAR &keylen    &keylen_x
    MONMSG mch3601

    IF (&snd1 *EQ 'Y') +
       CHGVAR &senderid_x '*YES'
    ELSE +
       CHGVAR &senderid_x '*NO'
    CHGVAR &senderid &senderid_x
    MONMSG mch3601

    IF (&force1 *EQ 'Y') +
       CHGVAR &force_x '*YES'
    ELSE +
       CHGVAR &force_x '*NO'
    CHGVAR &force &force_x
    MONMSG mch3601

    CHGVAR &text_x &text50
    CHGVAR &text    &text_x
    MONMSG mch3601

    RETURN

error:
   FWDPGMMSG
   MONMSG cpf0000

ENDPGM
```

Figure A.38: RTVDTAQDC is the command-processing program for the RTVDTAQD command
(part 2 of 2).

Reorganize Data Queue (RGZDTAQ)

Data queues expand in size automatically whenever necessary (i.e., when sending data to a data queue that is full). When you receive (and therefore delete) entries from an expanded data queue, however, the data queue doesn't shrink back to its former size. It is possible, then, to have data queues that are gigantic in size and yet are empty or nearly empty.

RGZDTAQ deletes a data queue and creates it again (thereby reclaiming the wasted space). Because it makes use of the RTVDTAQD utility command, you must install RTVDTAQD if you want to use RGZDTAQ.

Parameters

- DTAQ: Qualified name of the data queue to be reorganized. The library portion defaults to *LIBL.

- PROMPT: Whether to prompt for the CRTDTAQ command when RGZDTAQ reaches the point where it has to recreate the data queue. The default value is *NO. If you use *YES, RGZDTAQ will stop at the prompt for CRTDTAQ and wait for you to change values and press Enter.

- AUT: Public authority for the data queue. The default value is *LIBCRTAUT. You can use other special values or an authorization list name.

Source code for command RGZDTAQ is shown in Figure A.39

```
/*************************************************************************/
/*                                                                     */
/* To compile:                                                         */
/*                                                                     */
/*     CRTCMD   CMD(xxx/RGZDTAQ) +                                     */
/*              PGM(xxx/RGZDTAQC) +                                    */
/*              SRCFILE(xxx/QCMDSRC) +                                 */
/*              TEXT('Reorganize Data Queue') +                        */
/*              ALLOW(*ALL)                                            */
/*                                                                     */
```

Figure A.39: Source code for the RGZDTAQ command (part 1 of 2).

```
/******************************************************************/
CMD 'Reorganize Data Queue'

   PARM dtaq q1 MIN(1) PROMPT('Data queue')
q1: +
      QUAL *NAME 10 MIN(1)
      QUAL *NAME 10 DFT(*LIBL) SPCVAL((*LIBL)) PROMPT('Library')

   PARM prompt *CHAR 4 RSTD(*YES) DFT(*NO) VALUES(*YES *NO) +
        PROMPT('Prompt for CRTDTAQ command')

   PARM aut *NAME 10 DFT(*LIBCRTAUT) SPCVAL((*LIBCRTAUT) (*CHANGE) +
        (*ALL) (*USE) (*EXCLUDE)) PROMPT('Authority')
```

Figure A.39: Source code for the RGZDTAQ command (part 2 of 2).

CL Program RGZDTAQC, as shown in Figure A.40, is the command-processing program for the RGZDTAQ command.

```
/******************************************************************/
/*                                                              */
/* To compile:                                                  */
/*                                                              */
/*    CRTCLPGM  PGM(xxx/RGZDTAQC) +                             */
/*              SRCFILE(xxx/QCLSRC) +                           */
/*              TEXT('CPP for RGZDTAQ command')                 */
/*                                                              */
/******************************************************************/
PGM (&qdtaq &prompt &aut)

   DCL &aut        *CHAR   10
   DCL &cmd        *CHAR   500
   DCL &dtaq       *CHAR   10
   DCL &dtaqlib    *CHAR   10
   DCL &force      *CHAR   4
   DCL &keylen     *DEC    3
   DCL &keylen_c   *CHAR   3
   DCL &maxlen     *DEC    5
   DCL &maxlen_c   *CHAR   5
   DCL &prompt     *CHAR   4
```

Figure A.40: CL program RGZDTAQC is the command-processing program for the RGZDTAQ command (part 1 of 3).

```
DCL &qdtaq        *CHAR    20
DCL &senderid     *CHAR     4
DCL &seq          *CHAR     6
DCL &text         *CHAR    50

MONMSG (cpf0000 mch0000) EXEC(GOTO error)

/* Break qualified name */
CHGVAR &dtaq      %SST(&qdtaq  1 10)
CHGVAR &dtaqlib %SST(&qdtaq 11 10)

/* Verify existence of data queue */
CHKOBJ &dtaqlib/&dtaq *DTAQ

/* Validate authorization list name */
IF (&aut *NE '*LIBCRTAUT' *AND +
    &aut *NE '*CHANGE'    *AND +
    &aut *NE '*ALL'       *AND +
    &aut *NE '*USE'       *AND +
    &aut *NE '*EXCLUDE'        ) DO
   CHKOBJ &aut *AUTL
ENDDO

/* Retrieve data queue description */
RTVDTAQD &dtaqlib/&dtaq MAXLEN(&maxlen) SEQ(&seq) KEYLEN(&keylen) +
        TEXT(&text) FORCE(&force) SENDERID(&senderid)

/* Build command string */
CHGVAR &maxlen_c &maxlen
CHGVAR &keylen_c &keylen

CHGVAR &cmd ('CRTDTAQ DTAQ('               *CAT +
             &dtaqlib *TCAT '/' *CAT &dtaq *TCAT +
             ') MAXLEN('                   *CAT +
             &maxlen_c                     *CAT +
             ') SEQ('                      *CAT +
             &seq                          *TCAT +
             ') TEXT('                     *CAT +
             &text                         *TCAT +
             ') FORCE('                    *CAT +
             &force                        *TCAT +
             ') SENDERID('                 *CAT +
             &senderid                     *TCAT +
```

Figure A.40: CL program RGZDTAQC is the command-processing program for the RGZDTAQ command (part 2 of 3).

```
                    ') AUT('                      *CAT +
                    &aut                          *TCAT +
                    ')')

        IF (&keylen *GT 0) DO
           CHGVAR &cmd (&cmd *BCAT 'KEYLEN(' *CAT &keylen_c *CAT ')')
        ENDDO

        IF (&prompt *EQ '*YES') DO
           CHGVAR &cmd ('?' *BCAT &cmd)
        ENDDO

        CALL qcmdchk (&cmd 500)
        MONMSG cpf6801 EXEC(GOTO normal_end)

        /* Delete and re-create data queue */
        ALCOBJ ((&dtaqlib/&dtaq *DTAQ *EXCL)) WAIT(0)
        MONMSG cpf0000 EXEC(DO)
           SNDPGMMSG MSGID(cpf9898) MSGF(qcpfmsg) +
                     MSGDTA('Cannot allocate data queue' *BCAT &dtaq *BCAT +
                            'in' *BCAT &dtaqlib) +
                     MSGTYPE(*ESCAPE)
        ENDDO

        DLTDTAQ &dtaqlib/&dtaq

        DLCOBJ ((&dtaqlib/&dtaq *DTAQ *EXCL))
        MONMSG cpf0000

        CALL qcmdexc (&cmd 500)

        SNDPGMMSG MSGID(cpf9898) MSGF(qcpfmsg) +
                  MSGDTA('Data queue' *BCAT &dtaq *BCAT 'in' *BCAT +
                         &dtaqlib *BCAT 'reorganized') +
                  MSGTYPE(*COMP)

normal_end:
   RETURN

error:
   FWDPGMMSG
   MONMSG cpf0000

ENDPGM
```

Figure A.40: CL program RGZDTAQC is the command-processing program for the RGZDTAQ command (part 3 of 3).

OTHER COMMANDS

The following sections describe other useful commands.

Comment (COMMENT)

Although it is an oddity, COMMENT performs a useful function. With COMMENT you can enter up to 512 characters of comment into a program and, optionally, have the program send you the comment as a message whenever the program reaches the COMMENT command.

Because CL never logs IFs, CHGVARs, or the Parameters in a CALL, the COMMENT command is most useful when you want to force the program to log variable values into the job log. COMMENT solves that problem. Figure A.41 shows an example of the use of COMMENT.

```
COMMENT TEXT('&CODE =' *BCAT &code) MSGOPT(*STATUS)
```

Figure A.41: An example showing how to use the COMMENT command.

When the program reaches the point shown in Figure A.41, it sends a *STATUS message to your display station that reveals the value of variable &CODE. In addition, that value is logged to the job log.

Parameters

- TEXT: The text of the comment. You can enter up to 512 characters, and you can use concatenation operators and substring functions to compose the comment on the fly.

- MSGOPT: Message option. It indicates who receives a message in addition to writing the text into the job log. Valid values are *NONE (no one gets a message; that's the default), *STATUS (sends a status message to *EXT), *USER (sends message to the user's message queue), *WRKSTN (sends message to the workstation's message queue), and *SYSOPR (sends message to QSYSOPR).

Source code for the COMMENT command is in Figure A.42.

```
/************************************************************************/
/*                                                                    */
/* To compile:                                                        */
/*                                                                    */
/*     CRTCMD   CMD(xxx/COMMENT) +                                    */
/*              PGM(xxx/COMMENTC) +                                   */
/*              SRCFILE(xxx/QCMDSRC) +                                */
/*              TEXT('CL Program Comment') +                          */
/*              ALLOW(*ALL)                                           */
/*                                                                    */
/************************************************************************/
CMD 'CL Program Comment'

    PARM text *CHAR 512 EXPR(*YES) PROMPT('Comment text')

    PARM msgopt *CHAR 7 RSTD(*YES) DFT(*NONE) +
         VALUES(*NONE *STATUS *USER *WRKSTN *SYSOPR) +
         PROMPT('Message option')
```

Figure A.42: Source code for the comment command.

COMMENT executes CL program COMMENTC. See Figure A.43.

```
/************************************************************************/
/*                                                                    */
/* To compile:                                                        */
/*                                                                    */
/*     CRTCLPGM  PGM(xxx/COMMENTC) +                                  */
/*               SRCFILE(xxx/QCLSRC) +                                */
/*               TEXT('CPP for COMMENT command')                     */
/*                                                                    */
/************************************************************************/
PGM (&text &msgopt)

    DCL &msgopt     *CHAR    7
    DCL &text       *CHAR    512
    DCL &user       *CHAR    10
    DCL &wrkstn     *CHAR    10
```

Figure A.43: CL program COMMENTC is the command-processing program for the comment command (part 1 of 2).

```
     MONMSG (cpf0000 mch0000) EXEC(GOTO ERROR)

     /* Send as a status message */
     IF (&msgopt *EQ '*STATUS') DO
        SNDPGMMSG MSGID(cpf9897) MSGF(qcpfmsg) +
                  MSGDTA(&text) +
                  TOPGMQ(*EXT) MSGTYPE(*STATUS)
     ENDDO

     /* Send message to user profile */
     ELSE IF (&msgopt *EQ '*USER') DO
        RTVJOBA USER(&user)
        SNDMSG MSG(&text) TOUSR(&user) MSGTYPE(*INFO)
     ENDDO

     /* Send message to workstation */
     ELSE IF (&msgopt *EQ '*WRKSTN') DO
        RTVJOBA JOB(&wrkstn)
        SNDMSG MSG(&text) TOMSGQ(&wrkstn) MSGTYPE(*INFO)
        /* If message queue not found, send to qsysopr */
        MONMSG (cpf0000) EXEC(DO)
           SNDMSG MSG(&text) TOUSR(*SYSOPR) MSGTYPE(*INFO)
        ENDDO
     ENDDO

     /* Send message to qsysopr */
     ELSE IF (&msgopt *EQ '*SYSOPR') DO
        SNDMSG MSG(&text) TOUSR(*SYSOPR) MSGTYPE(*INFO)
     ENDDO

     RETURN

   error:
     FWDPGMMSG
     MONMSG cpf0000

   ENDPGM
```

Figure A.43: CL program COMMENTC is the command-processing program for the comment command (part 2 of 2).

Display Object Information (DSPOBJINF)

The Display Object Description (DSPOBJD) command displays lots of information about an object, but the information is scattered among several panels (some of which have multiple pages). DSPOBJINF consolidates, all into a single panel, what (debatably) can be considered the most important information. Besides, the command allows the user to enter a new object name right into the panel. Therefore, there's no need to go back to the command line.

Parameters

- OBJ: Qualified name of the object whose information you want to display. The library portion defaults to *LIBL. *CURLIB also is acceptable.

- OBJTYPE: Type of object, such as *PGM or *DTAARA.

- MBR: Name of the member, within a file, whose information you want to display. It defaults to *NONE (display only file-level information). *FIRST also is acceptable.

Source code for the DSPOBJINF is shown in Figure A.44. DSPOBJINF uses display file OBJ024DF. See Figure A.45.

```
/********************************************************************/
/*                                                                  */
/* To compile:                                                      */
/*                                                                  */
/*     CRTCMD  CMD(xxx/DSPOBJINF) +                                 */
/*             PGM(xxx/OBJ024CL) +                                  */
/*             SRCFILE(xxx/QCMDSRC) +                               */
/*             TEXT('Display Object Information') +                 */
/*             ALLOW(*IPGM *IMOD *INTERACT *EXEC)                   */
/*                                                                  */
/********************************************************************/
CMD PROMPT('Display Object Information')

   PARM obj q1 MIN(1) PROMPT('Object')
q1: +
       QUAL *NAME 10 MIN(1) EXPR(*YES)
       QUAL *NAME 10 DFT(*LIBL) SPCVAL((*LIBL) (*CURLIB)) EXPR(*YES) +
           PROMPT('Library')

   PARM objtype *CHAR 7 MIN(1) EXPR(*YES) PROMPT('Object type')

   PARM mbr *NAME 10 DFT(*NONE) SPCVAL((*NONE) (*FIRST)) EXPR(*YES) +
       PROMPT('File member')
```

Figure A.44: The DSPOBJINF command.

```
*********************************************************************
*
* To compile:
*
*    CRTPF   FILE(xxx/OBJ024DF) +
*            SRCFILE(xxx/QDDSSRC) +
*            TEXT('Display file for DSPOBJINF command')
*
*********************************************************************
A                                          DSPSIZ(24 80 *DS3)
A                                          PRINT
A                                          CA03(03 'Exit')
A                                          CF06(06 'Display source')
A                                          CA07(07 'Edit source')
A                                          CF09(09 'Display object authoritie-
A                                            s')
A                                          CA12(12 'Cancel')
*_____
A          R INFO
A                                        1 28'Display Object Information'
A                                          DSPATR(HI)
A                                        2  4'Object:'
A            OBJ          10A  B         2 12CHANGE(30)
A                                          COLOR(TRQ)
A                                        2 24'Library:'
A            OBJLIB       10A  B         2 33CHANGE(30)
A                                          COLOR(TRQ)
A                                        2 45'Type:'
A            OBJTYPE       7A  B         2 51CHANGE(30)
A                                          COLOR(TRQ)
A                                        2 60'Member:'
A            MEMBER       10A  B         2 68CHANGE(30)
A                                          COLOR(TRQ)
A                                        3 60'(name, *NONE, *FIRST)'
A N99                                    4  2'General Information
A
A                                          DSPATR(UL)
A                                          COLOR(YLW)
A N99                                    5  2'Text'
A N99        TEXT         50A  O         5  8COLOR(TRQ)
A N99                                    5 60'Attr'
```

Figure A.45: The DSPOBJINF command uses this display file (part 1 of 4).

369

```
A N99          OBJATR      10A  0  5 65COLOR(TRQ)
A N99                              6  2'Owner'
A N99          OWNER       10A  0  6  8COLOR(TRQ)
A N99                              6 20'Created by'
A N99          CRTUSER     10A  0  6 31COLOR(TRQ)
A N99                              6 43'sys'
A N99          CRTSYSTEM    8A  0  6 47COLOR(TRQ)
A N99                              6 57'when'
A N99          CRTDATE      7A  0  6 62COLOR(TRQ)
A N99          CRTTIME      6A  0  6 70COLOR(TRQ)
A N99                              8  2'Storage
A                                    DSPATR(UL)
A                                    COLOR(YLW)
A N99                              8 30'Save
A                                    DSPATR(UL)
A                                    COLOR(YLW)
A N99                              8 60'Last Change/Use
A                                    DSPATR(UL)
A                                    COLOR(YLW)
A N99                              9  2'Size'
A N99          SIZE        15Y 00  9  8EDTCDE(1 *)
A                                    COLOR(TRQ)
A N99                              9 30'When'
A N99          SAVDATE      7A  0  9 36COLOR(TRQ)
A N99          SAVTIME      6A  0  9 44COLOR(TRQ)
A N99                              9 60'Chg'
A N99          CHGDATE      7A  0  9 66COLOR(TRQ)
A N99          CHGTIME      6A  0  9 74COLOR(TRQ)
A N99                             10  2'ASP'
A N99          ASP          2S 00 10  8COLOR(TRQ)
A N99                             10 30'Size'
A N99          SAVSIZE     15Y 00 10 36COLOR(TRQ)
A                                    EDTCDE(1 *)
A N99                             10 60'UseDt'
A N99          USEDATE      7A  0 10 66COLOR(TRQ)
A N99          USETIME      6A  0 10 74COLOR(TRQ)
A N99                             11  2'Ovf'
A N99          OVFASP       1A  0 11  8COLOR(TRQ)
A N99                             11 30'Cmd'
A N99          SAVCMD      10A  0 11 36COLOR(TRQ)
A N99                             11 60'UseCt'
A N99          USECOUNT     5Y 00 11 66EDTCDE(1)
A                                    COLOR(TRQ)
A N99                             12  2'Free'
A N99          STG         10A  0 12  8COLOR(TRQ)
```

Figure A.45: The DSPOBJINF command uses this display file (part 2 of 4).

```
A N99                                 12 30'SeqN'
A N99           SAVSEQNBR     4S 00 12 36COLOR(TRQ)
A N99                                 12 60'Rstor'
A N99           RSTDATE       7A  O 12 66COLOR(TRQ)
A N99           RSTTIME       6A  O 12 74COLOR(TRQ)
A N99                                 13  2'Cpr'
A N99           CPR           1A  O 13  8COLOR(TRQ)
A N99                                 13 30'Vol'
A N99           SAVVOL20     20A  O 13 36COLOR(TRQ)
A N99                                 13 60'Reset'
A N99           RESETDATE     7A  O 13 66COLOR(TRQ)
A N99           RESETTIME     6A  O 13 74COLOR(TRQ)
A N99                                 14 30'Dev'
A N99           SAVDEV       10A  O 14 36COLOR(TRQ)
A N99                                 15  2'Source
A                                        DSPATR(UL)
A                                        COLOR(YLW)
A N99                                 15 30'Savf'
A N99           SAVF         10A  O 15 36COLOR(TRQ)
A N99           SAVFLIB      10A  O 15 47COLOR(TRQ)
A N99                                 15 60'Other Data
A                                        DSPATR(UL)
A                                        COLOR(YLW)
A N99                                 16  2'File'
A N99           SRCF         10A  O 16  8COLOR(TRQ)
A N99                                 16 30'Lbl'
A N99           SAVLABEL     17A  O 16 36COLOR(TRQ)
A N99                                 16 60'Dmain'
A N99           OBJDMN        2A  O 16 66COLOR(TRQ)
A N99                                 17  2'Lib'
A N99           SRCFLIB      10A  O 17  8COLOR(TRQ)
A N99                                 17 60'SysLv'
A N99           SYSLVL        9A  O 17 66COLOR(TRQ)
A N99                                 18  2'Mbr'
A N99           SRCMBR       10A  O 18  8COLOR(TRQ)
A N99 98                              18 30'File Member     -
A                                                           '
A                                        COLOR(YLW)
A                                        DSPATR(UL)
A N99                                 19  2'Date'
A N99           SRCDATE       7A  O 19  8COLOR(TRQ)
A N99           SRCTIME       6A  O 19 16COLOR(TRQ)
A N99 98                              19 30'Rcds'
A N99 98        ACTRCDS      10Y 00 19 36COLOR(TRQ)
A                                        EDTCDE(1 *)
```

Figure A.45: The DSPOBJINF command uses this display file (part 3 of 4).

```
A N99 98                               19 60'FAttr'
A N99 98        FILEATTR         3A  O 19 66COLOR(TRQ)
A N99 98                               20 30'Dltd'
A N99 98        DLTRCDS        10Y 00 20 36COLOR(TRQ)
A                                         EDTCDE(1 *)
A N99 98                               20 60'FType'
A N99 98        FILETYPE         5A  O 20 66COLOR(TRQ)
A N99 98                               21 60'SrcTp'
A N99 98        SRCTYPE        10A  O 21 66COLOR(TRQ)
A                                      23  2'F3=Exit   F6=Show source  F7=Edit-
A                                         source   F9=DSPOBJAUT  F12=Cancel'
A                                         COLOR(BLU)
A               MESSAGE         75A  O 24  2DSPATR(HI)
```

Figure A.45: The DSPOBJINF command uses this display file (part 4 of 4).

DSPOBJINF executes CL program OBJ024CL. See Figure A.46.

```
/***************************************************************/
/*                                                           */
/* To compile:                                               */
/*                                                           */
/*    CRTCLPGM  PGM(xxx/OBJ024CL) +                          */
/*              SRCFILE(xxx/QCLSRC) +                        */
/*              TEXT('CPP for DSPOBJINF command')            */
/*                                                           */
/***************************************************************/
PGM (&qobj &objtype &member)

    DCL &chgts       *CHAR   13
    DCL &crtts       *CHAR   13
    DCL &false       *LGL     1 '0'
    DCL &objaud      *CHAR   10
    DCL &qobj        *CHAR   20
    DCL &resetts     *CHAR   13
    DCL &rstts       *CHAR   13
    DCL &rtnlib      *CHAR   10
    DCL &savvol      *CHAR   71
    DCL &savts       *CHAR   13
```

Figure A.46: A CL program that carries out the work of the DSPOBJINF utility (part 1 of 5).

```
    DCL &srcts      *CHAR    13
    DCL &true       *LGL     1  '1'
    DCL &usets      *CHAR    13

    DCLF obj024df

    MONMSG (cpf0000 mch0000) EXEC(GOTO error)

    /* Break qualified name */
    CHGVAR &obj     %SST(&qobj  1 10)
    CHGVAR &objlib %SST(&qobj 11 10)

    GOTO retrieve

    /* Show information */
display:
    SNDRCVF RCDFMT(info)

    CHGVAR &message ' '

    /* If F3 or F12 pressed, end program */
    IF (&in03 *OR &in12) +
       RETURN

    /* If new object name entered, get info */
    IF &in30 DO
       /* Verify existence of object */
retrieve:
       CHGVAR &in99 &false

       IF (&objlib *EQ ' ') DO
          CHGVAR &objlib '*LIBL'
       ENDDO

       IF (&member *EQ ' ') DO
          CHGVAR &member '*NONE'
       ENDDO

       CHKOBJ &objlib/&obj &objtype
       MONMSG cpf0000 EXEC(DO)
          CHGVAR &message ('Object/library not found.')
          CHGVAR &in99    &true
          GOTO display
       ENDDO
```

Figure A.46: A CL program that carries out the work of the DSPOBJINF utility (part 2 of 5).

```
IF (&objtype *EQ '*FILE' *AND +
    &member  *NE '*NONE'      ) DO
   CHGVAR &in98 &true
   CHKOBJ &objlib/&obj *FILE MBR(&member)

   MONMSG cpf9815 EXEC(DO)
      CHGVAR &message ('Member' *BCAT &member *BCAT 'not found.')
      CHGVAR &in99    &true
      GOTO display
   ENDDO
ENDDO
ELSE DO
   CHGVAR &in98 &false
ENDDO

/* Gather information about object */
RTVOBJD &objlib/&obj &objtype RTNLIB(&rtnlib) OBJATR(&objatr) +
        TEXT(&text) OWNER(&owner) ASP(&asp) OVFASP(&ovfasp) +
        CRTDATE(&crtts) CHGDATE(&chgts) SAVDATE(&savts) +
        RSTDATE(&rstts) CRTUSER(&crtuser) CRTSYSTEM(&crtsystem) +
        OBJDMN(&objdmn) USEDATE(&usets) USECOUNT(&usecount) +
        RESETDATE(&resetts) STG(&stg) CPR(&cpr) SIZE(&size) +
        SAVSIZE(&savsize) SAVCMD(&savcmd) SAVSEQNBR(&savseqnbr) +
        SAVVOL(&savvol) SAVDEV(&savdev) SAVF(&savf) +
        SAVFLIB(&savflib) SAVLABEL(&savlabel) SRCF(&srcf) +
        SRCFLIB(&srcflib) SRCMBR(&srcmbr) SRCDATE(&srcts) +
        SYSLVL(&syslvl) OBJAUD(&objaud)
CHGVAR &crtdate   %SST(&crtts   1 7)
CHGVAR &crttime   %SST(&crtts   8 6)
CHGVAR &chgdate   %SST(&chgts   1 7)
CHGVAR &chgtime   %SST(&chgts   8 6)
CHGVAR &savdate   %SST(&savts   1 7)
CHGVAR &savtime   %SST(&savts   8 6)
CHGVAR &rstdate   %SST(&rstts   1 7)
CHGVAR &rsttime   %SST(&rstts   8 6)
CHGVAR &resetdate %SST(&resetts 1 7)
CHGVAR &resettime %SST(&resetts 8 6)
CHGVAR &srcdate   %SST(&srcts   1 7)
CHGVAR &srctime   %SST(&srcts   8 6)

IF (&objtype *EQ '*FILE' *AND +
    &member  *NE '*NONE'      ) DO
   RTVMBRD FILE(&objlib/&obj) MBR(&member) RTNMBR(&member) +
           FILEATR(&fileattr) FILETYPE(&filetype) +
```

Figure A.46: A CL program that carries out the work of the DSPOBJINF utility (part 3 of 5).

```
                        SRCTYPE(&srctype) NBRCURRCD(&actrcds) +
                        NBRDLTRCD(&dltrcds)
            ENDDO

            ELSE DO
               CHGVAR &fileattr ' '
               CHGVAR &filetype ' '
               CHGVAR &srctype  ' '
               CHGVAR &actrcds  0
               CHGVAR &dltrcds  0
            ENDDO

            CHGVAR &objlib   &rtnlib
            CHGVAR &savvol20 %SST(&savvol 1 20)

            /* Warn if object is library */
            IF (&objtype *EQ '*LIB') DO
               CHGVAR &message ('Object is library; size info not accurate.')
            ENDDO
         ENDDO

         /* If F6 pressed, display source code */
         IF &in06 DO
            STRSEU SRCFILE(&srcflib/&srcf) SRCMBR(&srcmbr) OPTION(5)
            MONMSG cpf0000 EXEC(DO)
               RCVMSG MSGTYPE(*EXCP) RMV(*YES)
               CHGVAR &message ('Error while attempting to display source.')
            ENDDO
         ENDDO

         /* If F7 pressed, edit source code */
         IF &in07 DO
            STRSEU SRCFILE(&srcflib/&srcf) SRCMBR(&srcmbr) OPTION(2)
            MONMSG cpf0000 EXEC(DO)
               RCVMSG MSGTYPE(*EXCP) RMV(*YES)
               CHGVAR &message ('Error while attempting to edit source.')
            ENDDO
         ENDDO

         /* If F9 pressed, display object authorities */
         ELSE IF &in09 DO
            DSPOBJAUT OBJ(&objlib/&obj) OBJTYPE(&objtype)
            MONMSG cpf0000 EXEC(DO)
               RCVMSG MSGTYPE(*EXCP) RMV(*YES)
```

Figure A.46: A CL program that carries out the work of the DSPOBJINF utility (part 4 of 5).

```
          CHGVAR &message ('Error while attempting to display object' +
                          *BCAT 'authorities.')
      ENDDO
    ENDDO

    GOTO display

  error:
    FWDPGMMSG
    MONMSG cpf0000

  ENDPGM
```

Figure A.46: A CL program that carries out the work of the DSPOBJINF utility (part 5 of 5).

Count Objects (CNTOBJ)

CNTOBJ answers the question, "How many objects named so-and-so, of data type so-and-so, do I have?" It also tells you how much room those objects occupy.

Parameters

- OBJ: Qualified name of the objects to be counted. The object portion can contain the value *ALL, to count all objects, or it can contain a generic name or a specific name. The library portion can contain *LIBL, *CURLIB, or a specific library name.

- OBJTYPE: Type of object, such as *FILE or *PGM. It also accepts special value *ALL, for all types of objects.

The source code for command CNTOBJ is shown in Figure A.47.

```
/***********************************************************************/
/*                                                                   */
/* To compile:                                                       */
/*                                                                   */
/*    CRTCMD  CMD(xxx/CNTOBJ) +                                      */
/*            PGM(xxx/CNTOBJC) +                                     */
/*            SRCFILE(xxx/QCMDSRC) +                                 */
/*            TEXT('Count Objects') +                               */
/*            ALLOW(*IPGM *IMOD *INTERACT *EXEC)                     */
/*                                                                   */
/***********************************************************************/
CMD 'Count Objects'

    PARM obj q1 MIN(1) PROMPT('Object')

q1: +
      QUAL *GENERIC 10 SPCVAL((*ALL)) MIN(1) EXPR(*YES)
      QUAL *NAME 10 DFT(*LIBL) SPCVAL((*LIBL) (*CURLIB)) EXPR(*YES) +
          PROMPT('Library')

    PARM objtype *CHAR 8 DFT(*ALL) EXPR(*YES) PROMPT('Object type')
```

Figure A.47: CNTOBJ command source code.

CNTOBJ requires display file CNTOBJD. See Figure A.48.

```
*****************************************************************
      *
      * To compile:
      *
      *    CRTPF  FILE(xxx/CNTOBJD) +
      *           SRCFILE(xxx/QDDSSRC) +
      *           TEXT('Display file for CNTOBJ command')
      *
*****************************************************************
      A                                DSPSIZ(24 80 *DS3)
      A                                PRINT
      A                                CA03(03 'Exit')
      A                                CA08(08 'Work with objects')
      A                                CA12(12 'Cancel')
      *=============================================================
```

Figure A.48: The display file used by the Count Objects utility (part 1 of 2).

```
A             R PANEL
A                                         BLINK
A                                      1 34'Count Objects'
A                                         DSPATR(HI)
A                                      3  2'Objects counted:'
A                                      5 21'Objects:'
A             QUALOBJ      21   0     5 34
A                                      7 21'Object type:'
A             OBJTYPE       8   0     7 34
A                                      9  2'                        -
A                                         -
A                                                                   '
A                                         DSPATR(UL)
A                                         COLOR(BLU)
A                                     11  2'Results:'
A             COUNTER      15Y 00    11 21EDTCDE(1)
A                                         DSPATR(HI)
A                                     11 41'objects found.'
A             TOTALSIZE    15Y 00    13 21EDTCDE(1)
A                                     13 41'total bytes used.'
A                                     23  2'F3=Exit  F8=Work with objects   F-
A                                        12=Cancel'
A                                         COLOR(BLU)
```

Figure A.48: The display file used by the Count Objects utility (part 2 of 2).

The command-processing program for the Count Objects utility is CL program CNTOBJC. See Figure A.49.

```
/*******************************************************************/
/*                                                               */
/* To compile:                                                   */
/*                                                               */
/*    CRTCLPGM  PGM(xxx/CNTOBJC) +                               */
/*              SRCFILE(xxx/QCLSRC) +                            */
/*              TEXT('CPP for CNTOBJ command')                   */
/*                                                               */
/*******************************************************************/
PGM (&q_obj &objtype)

    DCL &blink      *CHAR    1 X'2A'
    DCL &msg        *CHAR    80
    DCL &normal     *CHAR    1 X'20'
```

Figure A.49: CNTOBJC is the command-processing program of CNTOBJ (part 1 of 2).

```
     DCL &obj       *CHAR   10
     DCL &objlib    *CHAR   10
     DCL &q_obj     *CHAR   20

     DCLF cntobjd

     MONMSG (cpf0000 mch0000) EXEC(GOTO error)

     /* Send status message to user */
     CHGVAR &msg ('Gathering information.' *CAT &blink *CAT +
                  'Please wait.' *CAT &normal)
     SNDPGMMSG MSGID(cpf9897) MSGF(qcpfmsg) MSGDTA(&msg) TOPGMQ(*EXT) +
               MSGTYPE(*STATUS)

     /* Break qualified name received from command */
     CHGVAR &obj    %SST(&q_obj  1 10)
     CHGVAR &objlib %SST(&q_obj 11 10)

     /* Build qualified name to present on the screen */
     CHGVAR &qualobj (&objlib *TCAT '/' *CAT &obj)

     /* Gather the necessary information */
     CALL cntobjc1 (&obj &objlib &objtype &counter &totalsize)

     /* Display results */
display:
     SNDRCVF

     /* If user presses F8, run WRKOBJPDM */
     IF &in08 DO
        WRKOBJPDM LIB(&objlib) OBJ(&obj) OBJTYPE(&objtype) OBJATR(*ALL)
        GOTO display
     ENDDO

     /* End program in any other case */
     RETURN

     /* Forward error messages to caller */
error:
     FWDPGMMSG
     MONMSG cpf0000

ENDPGM
```

Figure A.49: CNTOBJC is the command-processing program of CNTOBJ (part 2 of 2).

CL Program CNTOBJC1, shown in Figure A.50, retrieves object information.

```
/*******************************************************************/
/*                                                                 */
/* To compile:                                                     */
/*                                                                 */
/*     CRTCLPGM  PGM(xxx/CNTOBJC1) +                               */
/*               SRCFILE(xxx/QCLSRC) +                             */
/*               TEXT('Called from CNTOBJC')                       */
/*                                                                 */
/*******************************************************************/
PGM (&obj &objlib &objtype &counter &totalsize)

    DCL &counter    *DEC   15
    DCL &obj        *CHAR  10
    DCL &objlib     *CHAR  10
    DCL &objtype    *CHAR   8
    DCL &totalsize  *DEC   15


    DCLF qadspobj

    MONMSG (cpf0000 mch0000) EXEC(GOTO error)

    /* Build subfile of requested objects */
    DSPOBJD &objlib/&obj &objtype OUTPUT(*OUTFILE) +
            OUTFILE(qtemp/objects) OUTMBR(*FIRST *REPLACE)

    OVRDBF qadspobj TOFILE(qtemp/objects)

loop:
    RCVF
    MONMSG cpf0864 EXEC(GOTO endloop)

    /* Count objects in &COUNTER and total size in &TOTALSIZE */
    CHGVAR &counter   (&counter   + 1)
    CHGVAR &totalsize (&totalsize + &odobsz)
    GOTO loop

    /* When objects are exhausted, clear temporary outfile */
endloop:
    DLTOVR qadspobj
    CLRPFM qtemp/objects

    RETURN

    /* Forward error messages to caller */
error:
    FWDPGMMSG

    MONMSG cpf0000

ENDPGM
```

Figure A.50: This program gathers object information.

Convert Print to Physical File (*CVTPRTPF*)

Use the Convert Print to Physical File (CVTPRTPF) command to capture the printed output of a command or program to a database file. You must know the name of the printer file used by the program. Suppose you want to process the output generated by the Display Authorized Users (DSPAUTUSR) command. Unfortunately, DSPAUTUSR can output only to the display or printer because there is no outfile option. You can then code it as shown in Figure A.51.

```
CVTPRTPF   CMD(DSPAUTUSR  SEQ(*GRPPRF)   OUTPUT(*PRINT)) +
           PRTF(QPAUTUSR)   +
           TOFILE(QTEMP/USERS) +
           MBROPT(*FIRST *REPLACE)
```

Figure A.51: Using CVTPRTPF to capture print output from a command to a database file.

Or suppose program AR125R produces an accounts receivable report using printer file QSYSPRT. You can capture that report to disk with the code shown in Figure A.52.

```
CVTPRTPF   CMD(CALL PGM(AR125R)) +
           PRTF(QSYSPRT) +
           TOFILE(QTEMP/REPORT)
```

Figure A.52: Using CVTPRTPF to capture print output from a program.

CVTPRTPF consists of two objects, the CVTPRTPF command (Figure A.53) and CL program PRT004CL (Figure A.54).

```
/*******************************************************************/
/*                                                               */
/*    To compile:                                                */
/*                                                               */
/*       CRTCMD    CMD(xxx/CVTPRTPF) +                           */
/*                 PGM(xxx/PRT005CL) +                           */
/*                 SRCFILE(xxx/QCMDSRC) +                        */
/*                 TEXT('Convert printer output to disk file') + */
/*                 ALLOW(*IPGM *BPGM *IMOD *BMOD)                */
/*                                                               */
```

Figure A.53: Command CVTPRTPF (part 1 of 2).

```
/*   Example of usage:                                                      */
/*                                                                          */
/*          CVTPRTPF  CMD(DSPAUTUSR SEQ(*GRPPRF) OUTPUT(*PRINT))          +*/
/*                    PRTF(QPAUTUSR) +                                      */
/*                    TOFILE(QTEMP/USERS) +                                 */
/*                    MBROPT(*FIRST *REPLACE)                               */
*/                                                                          */
/**************************************************************************/
  CVTPRTPF:    CMD      PROMPT('Convert Print to Physical File')
               PARM     KWD(CMD) TYPE(*CMDSTR) LEN(3000) MIN(1) +
                           PROMPT('Command to produce output')
               PARM     KWD(PRTF) TYPE(*NAME) LEN(10) MIN(1) +
                           PROMPT('Printer file name')
               PARM     KWD(TOFILE) TYPE(Q1) MIN(1) PROMPT('To +
                           physical file')
               PARM     KWD(MBROPT) TYPE(E1) PROMPT('Member options')
  Q1:          QUAL     TYPE(*NAME) LEN(10) MIN(1)
               QUAL     TYPE(*NAME) LEN(10) DFT(*CURLIB) +
                           SPCVAL((*CURLIB)) PROMPT('Library')
  E1:          ELEM     TYPE(*NAME) LEN(10) DFT(*FIRST) +
                           SPCVAL((*FIRST)) PROMPT('Member to +
                           receive output')
               ELEM     TYPE(*CHAR) LEN(8) RSTD(*YES) DFT(*REPLACE) +
                           VALUES(*REPLACE *ADD) PROMPT('Replace or +
                           add records')
```

Figure A.53: Command CVTPRTPF (part 2 of 2).

```
/**************************************************************************/
/*                                                                          */
/*   To compile:                                                            */
/*                                                                          */
/*      CRTCLPGM  PGM(xxx/PRT004CL) +                                       */
/*                SRCFILE(xxx/QCLSRC) +                                     */
/*                TEXT('CPP for CVTPRTPF command')                          */
/*                                                                          */
/**************************************************************************/
  PGM        PARM(&cmd &prtf &qf &member)

     DCL       &cmd       *CHAR       3000
     DCL       &file      *CHAR       10
     DCL       &lib       *CHAR       10
     DCL       &mbr       *CHAR       10
```

Figure A.54:CL program PRT004CL is the CPP for CVTPRTPF (part 1 of 2).

```
DCL        &mbropt      *CHAR        8
DCL        &member      *CHAR        20
DCL        &prtf        *CHAR        10
DCL        &qf          *CHAR        20

  MONMSG   (cpf0000 mch0000)  EXEC(GOTO error)

CHGVAR     &file        %SST(&qf 1 10)
CHGVAR     &lib         %SST(&qf 11 10)
CHGVAR     &mbr         %SST(&member  3  10)
CHGVAR     &mbropt      %SST(&member  13  8)

CHKOBJ     OBJ(&lib/&file)  OBJTYPE(*FILE)
MONMSG     MSGID(CPF9810)   EXEC(DO)
  SNDPGMMSG    MSGID(CPF9898)    MSGF(QCPFMSG) +
               MSGDTA('Library' *BCAT 'not found') +
               MSGTYPE(*ESCAPE)
     RETURN
ENDDO
MONMSG     MSGID(CPF9801)   EXEC(DO)
  CRTPF       FILE(&lib/&file) RCDLEN(198)
ENDDO

CHKOBJ     OBJ(&lib/&file) OBJTYPE(*FILE)   MBR(&mbr)
MONMSG     MSGID(CPF9815) EXEC(DO)
  ADDPFM      FILE(&lib/&file) MBR(&mbr)
ENDDO

OVRPRTF    FILE(&prtf) HOLD(*YES)
CALL       PGM(QCMDEXC) PARM(&cmd 3000)
MONMSG     MSGID(CPF0000) EXEC(DO)
  FWDPGMMSG
  RETURN
ENDDO

CPYSPLF    FILE(&prtf) TOFILE(&lib/&file) JOB(*) +
           SPLNBR(*LAST) TOMBR(&mbr) MBROPT(&mbropt)
DLTSPLF    FILE(&prtf) JOB(*) SPLNBR(*LAST) +
           SELECT(*CURRENT)
DLTOVR     FILE(&prtf)
RETURN

error:
  FWDPGMMSG
  MONMSG  cpf0000
ENDPGM
```

Figure A.54:CL program PRT004CL is the CPP for CVTPRTPF (part 2 of 2).

B

CL CODING STYLE

Chapter 2 briefly explains some of the rationale behind "styling" your CL code. Let's be frank: Although the command prompter does much of the work all by itself, its output is ugly. And inconvenient. And difficult to read.

"Difficult to read" is, of course, the most important of those disadvantages. Program code is meant to be read by humans as well as compilers. A compiler doesn't care whether the program has comments, blank lines, is indented, or in general, is formatted properly; a human programmer does care.

Consider that, in the normal course of events, programs must be maintained. Either someone finds a bug in your CL programs or circumstances force you to add, change, or remove features. And it's usually a maintenance programmer (who is likely to be a rookie programmer) where the program-maintenance buck stops. It is important, therefore, to make the code as easy to understand as is humanly possible.

This appendix discusses several elements of good coding style for CL programs. Each element has its own section.

Starting Point: SEU + Command Prompter

Figure B.1 shows a typical program as it comes out of SEU. The programmer has formatted the code with the command prompter (by pressing F4 on every command).

```
    PGM
            DCL         VAR(&DLVRY) TYPE(*CHAR) LEN(10)
            DCL         VAR(&DSPNAME) TYPE(*CHAR) LEN(10)
            DCL         VAR(&GRPPRF) TYPE(*CHAR) LEN(10)
            DCL         VAR(&MSG) TYPE(*CHAR) LEN(80)
            DCL         VAR(&MSGQ) TYPE(*CHAR) LEN(10)
            DCL         VAR(&MSGQLIB) TYPE(*CHAR) LEN(10)
            DCL         VAR(&PGMRLIB) TYPE(*CHAR) LEN(10)
            DCL         VAR(&POSITION) TYPE(*DEC) LEN(3 0)
            DCL         VAR(&PROGRAMMER) TYPE(*LGL) LEN(1)
            DCL         VAR(&USRCLS) TYPE(*CHAR) LEN(10)
            DCL         VAR(&USRNAME) TYPE(*CHAR) LEN(50)
            DCL         VAR(&USRPRF) TYPE(*CHAR) LEN(10)
            DCL         VAR(&USRTXT) TYPE(*CHAR) LEN(50)
            MONMSG      MSGID(CPF0000)
    BEGIN:  RTVUSRPRF   USRPRF(*CURRENT) RTNUSRPRF(&USRPRF) +
                          GRPPRF(&GRPPRF) MSGQ(&MSGQ) +
                          MSGQLIB(&MSGQLIB) TEXT(&USRTXT) +
                          USRCLS(&USRCLS) DLVRY(&DLVRY)
    RTVJOBA JOB(&DSPNAM)
            CALL        PGM(QCLSCAN) PARM(&USRTXT X'050F' X'001F' ':' +
                          X'001F' '0' '0' ' ' &POSITION)
            IF          COND(&POSITION *GT 0) THEN(DO)

            CHGVAR      VAR(&POSITION) VALUE(&POSITION - 1)
            CHGVAR      VAR(&USRNAME) VALUE(%SST(&USRTXT 1 &POSITION))
            ENDDO

            ELSE        CMD(DO)
            CHGVAR      VAR(&USRNAME) VALUE(&USRTXT)
            ENDDO

            SNDPGMMSG   MSGID(CPF9898) MSGF(QCPFMSG) MSGDTA('Signing +
                          on' *BCAT &USRNAME *BCAT 'at' &DSPNAME +
                          *TCAT '..') TOPGMQ(*EXT) MSGTYPE(*STATUS)

            IF          COND(%SST(&DSPNAME 1 6) *EQ 'ACGDSP') THEN(DO)
            OVRPRTF     FILE(*PRTF) DEV(&DSPNAME *TCAT 'P1') +
```

Figure B.1: CL code formatted with the SEU command prompter (part 1of 2).

```
                            PAGESIZE(82 132) LPI(8) CPI(16.7) +

                            OVRFLW(80) FOLD(*NO) PAGRTT(0) OUTQ(*DEV) +
                            HOLD(*YES)
          ENDDO
                 CHGJOB     PRTKEYFMT(*PRTALL)
                 IF         COND(&GRPPRF *EQ 'QPGMR' *OR &GRPPRF *EQ +
                            'GRP_PGMR') THEN(DO)
                 CHGVAR     VAR(&PROGRAMMER) VALUE('1')
                 ENDDO
                 ELSE       CMD(DO)
                 CHGVAR     VAR(&PROGRAMMER) VALUE('0')
                 ENDDO
                 IF         COND(&PROGRAMMER *OR &USRCLS *EQ '*SYSOPR') +
                            THEN(DO)
          CHGSYSLIBL LIB(ALTQSYS) OPTION(*ADD)
                 ENDDO
                 IF         COND(&PROGRAMMER) THEN(DO)
                 CHGVAR     VAR(&PGMRLIB) VALUE('$' *CAT %SST(&USRPRF 1 9))
                 CRTLIB     LIB(&PGMRLIB) TEXT('Project library for' +
                            *BCAT &USRPRF)
                 CRTSRCPF   FILE(&PGMRLIB/SOURCE) TEXT('Main source file')
                 ADDLIBLE   LIB(&PGMRLIB) POSITION(*FIRST)
                 ENDDO
                 IF         COND(&DLVRY *NE '*BREAK') THEN(DO)
                 RCVMSG     MSGQ(&MSGQLIB/&MSGQ) MSGTYPE(*NEXT) +
                            MSGKEY(*TOP) RMV(*NO) MSG(&MSG)
                 IF         COND(&MSG *NE ' ') THEN(DO)
                 DSPMSG     MSGQ(&MSGQLIB/&MSGQ)
                 ENDDO
                 RCVMSG     MSGQ(&DSPNAME) MSGTYPE(*NEXT) MSGKEY(*TOP) +
                            RMV(*NO) MSG(&MSG)
                 IF         COND(&MSG *NE ' ') THEN(DO)
                 DSPMSG     MSGQ(&DSPNAME)
                 ENDDO
                 ENDDO
                 CALL       PGM(MGTLIB/&USRPRF)
                 IF         COND(&PROGRAMMER *OR &USRCLS *EQ '*SYSOPR') +
                            THEN(DO)
                 CALL       PGM(QSYS/QCMD)
                 ENDDO
          END:   ENDPGM
```

Figure B.1: CL code formatted with the SEU command prompter (part 2 of 2).

ADD COMMENTS

Comments explain what the code does and, if possible, why. It's important to add comments anywhere the code's purpose is not self-evident. Keep in mind that the maintenance programmer is not likely to have your experience, and you might not remember why, two years before, you coded a particular program the way you did.

Good comments are those that don't simply repeat what the code itself says. For example, if the code changes variable &COUNTER to zero, don't write a comment that says "Change &COUNTER to zero." That comment is useless. Write a more informative comment, such as "Initialize &COUNTER prior to entering loop." Figure B.2 shows the same program listed in Figure B.1. Comments are added for clarity.

```
/************************************************************************/
/*                                                                    */
/* Program: SIGNON                                                    */
/*                                                                    */
/* Purpose: Initial program to run when user signs on.               */
/*          It sets up job environment.                              */
/*                                                                    */
/************************************************************************/
            PGM
            DCL         VAR(&DLVRY) TYPE(*CHAR) LEN(10)
            DCL         VAR(&DSPNAME) TYPE(*CHAR) LEN(10)
            DCL         VAR(&GRPPRF) TYPE(*CHAR) LEN(10)
            DCL         VAR(&MSG) TYPE(*CHAR) LEN(80)
            DCL         VAR(&MSGQ) TYPE(*CHAR) LEN(10)
            DCL         VAR(&MSGQLIB) TYPE(*CHAR) LEN(10)
            DCL         VAR(&PGMRLIB) TYPE(*CHAR) LEN(10)
            DCL         VAR(&POSITION) TYPE(*DEC) LEN(3 0)
            DCL         VAR(&PROGRAMMER) TYPE(*LGL) LEN(1)
            DCL         VAR(&USRCLS) TYPE(*CHAR) LEN(10)
            DCL         VAR(&USRNAME) TYPE(*CHAR) LEN(50)
            DCL         VAR(&USRPRF) TYPE(*CHAR) LEN(10)
            DCL         VAR(&USRTXT) TYPE(*CHAR) LEN(50)
            MONMSG      MSGID(CPF0000)
/* Retrieve the user profile attributes */
  BEGIN:    RTVUSRPRF   USRPRF(*CURRENT) RTNUSRPRF(&USRPRF) +
```

Figure B.2: CL code with comments added (part 1 of 3).

```
                            GRPPRF(&GRPPRF) MSGQ(&MSGQ) +
                            MSGQLIB(&MSGQLIB) TEXT(&USRTXT) +
                            USRCLS(&USRCLS) DLVRY(&DLVRY)
            RTVJOBA    JOB(&DSPNAM)
/* Display "Signing on..." message */
            CALL       PGM(QCLSCAN) PARM(&USRTXT X'050F' X'001F' ':' +
                            X'001F' '0' '0' ' ' &POSITION)

            IF         COND(&POSITION *GT 0) THEN(DO)
            CHGVAR     VAR(&POSITION) VALUE(&POSITION - 1)
            CHGVAR     VAR(&USRNAME) VALUE(%SST(&USRTXT 1 &POSITION))
            ENDDO
            ELSE       CMD(DO)
            CHGVAR     VAR(&USRNAME) VALUE(&USRTXT)
            ENDDO
            SNDPGMMSG  MSGID(CPF9898) MSGF(QCPFMSG) MSGDTA('Signing +
                            on' *BCAT &USRNAME *BCAT 'at' &DSPNAME +
                            *TCAT '..') TOPGMQ(*EXT) MSGTYPE(*STATUS)
/* If signing on with Client Access, override printer files */
            IF         COND(%SST(&DSPNAME 1 6) *EQ 'ACGDSP') THEN(DO)
            OVRPRTF    FILE(*PRTF) DEV(&DSPNAME *TCAT 'P1') +
                            PAGESIZE(82 132) LPI(8) CPI(16.7) +
                            OVRFLW(80) FOLD(*NO) PAGRTT(0) OUTQ(*DEV) +

                            HOLD(*YES)
            ENDDO
/* Ensure print key formats output */
            CHGJOB     PRTKEYFMT(*PRTALL)
/* Determine if user is a programmer */
            IF         COND(&GRPPRF *EQ 'QPGMR' *OR &GRPPRF *EQ +
                            'GRP_PGMR') THEN(DO)
            CHGVAR     VAR(&PROGRAMMER) VALUE('1')
            ENDDO
            ELSE       CMD(DO)
            CHGVAR     VAR(&PROGRAMMER) VALUE('0')
            ENDDO
/* Place ALTQSYS at top of library list */

/* for programmers and system operators */
            IF         COND(&PROGRAMMER *OR &USRCLS *EQ '*SYSOPR') +
                            THEN(DO)
            CHGSYSLIBL LIB(ALTQSYS) OPTION(*ADD)
            ENDDO
/* If user is programmer, create programming library */
```

Figure B.2: CL code with comments added (part 2 of 3).

```
            IF         COND(&PROGRAMMER) THEN(DO)
            CHGVAR     VAR(&PGMRLIB) VALUE('$' *CAT %SST(&USRPRF 1 9))
            CRTLIB     LIB(&PGMRLIB) TEXT('PROJECT LIBRARY FOR' +
                         *BCAT &USRPRF)
            CRTSRCPF   FILE(&PGMRLIB/SOURCE) TEXT('MAIN SOURCE FILE')
            ADDLIBLE   LIB(&PGMRLIB) POSITION(*FIRST)
            ENDDO
/* IF ANY MESSAGES ARE FOUND IN THE USER'S MESSAGE QUEUE, */
/* DISPLAY THOSE MESSAGES BEFORE PROCEEDING               */
            IF         COND(&DLVRY *NE '*BREAK') THEN(DO)
            RCVMSG     MSGQ(&MSGQLIB/&MSGQ) MSGTYPE(*NEXT) +
                         MSGKEY(*TOP) RMV(*NO) MSG(&MSG)
            IF         COND(&MSG *NE ' ') THEN(DO)
            DSPMSG     MSGQ(&MSGQLIB/&MSGQ)
            ENDDO
            RCVMSG     MSGQ(&DSPNAME) MSGTYPE(*NEXT) MSGKEY(*TOP) +
                         RMV(*NO) MSG(&MSG)
            IF         COND(&MSG *NE ' ') THEN(DO)
            DSPMSG     MSGQ(&DSPNAME)
            ENDDO
            ENDDO


/* CALL PERSONALIZING PROGRAM */
            CALL       PGM(MGTLIB/&USRPRF)
            IF         COND(&PROGRAMMER *OR &USRCLS *EQ '*SYSOPR') +
                         THEN(DO)
            CALL       PGM(QSYS/QCMD)
            ENDDO
END:        ENDPGM
```

Figure B.2: CL code with comments added (part 3 of 3).

ADD BLANK LINES

Blank lines help break a long stream of commands into logical groups of commands that have related functions. A program without blank lines would be as bad as a book with all text set as a single paragraph! Figure B.3 shows how blank lines improve readability.

```
/********************************************************************/
/*                                                                  */
/* Program: SIGNON                                                  */
/*                                                                  */
/* Purpose: Initial program to run when user signs on.             */
/*          It sets up job environment.                            */
/*                                                                  */
/********************************************************************/
            PGM

            DCL        VAR(&DLVRY) TYPE(*CHAR) LEN(10)
            DCL        VAR(&DSPNAME) TYPE(*CHAR) LEN(10)
            DCL        VAR(&GRPPRF) TYPE(*CHAR) LEN(10)
            DCL        VAR(&MSG) TYPE(*CHAR) LEN(80)
            DCL        VAR(&MSGQ) TYPE(*CHAR) LEN(10)
            DCL        VAR(&MSGQLIB) TYPE(*CHAR) LEN(10)
            DCL        VAR(&PGMRLIB) TYPE(*CHAR) LEN(10)
            DCL        VAR(&POSITION) TYPE(*DEC) LEN(3 0)
            DCL        VAR(&PROGRAMMER) TYPE(*LGL) LEN(1)
            DCL        VAR(&USRCLS) TYPE(*CHAR) LEN(10)
            DCL        VAR(&USRNAME) TYPE(*CHAR) LEN(50)
            DCL        VAR(&USRPRF) TYPE(*CHAR) LEN(10)
            DCL        VAR(&USRTXT) TYPE(*CHAR) LEN(50)

            MONMSG     MSGID(CPF0000)

/* Retrieve the user profile attributes */
  BEGIN:    RTVUSRPRF  USRPRF(*CURRENT) RTNUSRPRF(&USRPRF) +
                       GRPPRF(&GRPPRF) MSGQ(&MSGQ) +
                       MSGQLIB(&MSGQLIB) TEXT(&USRTXT) +
                       USRCLS(&USRCLS) DLVRY(&DLVRY)

            RTVJOBA    JOB(&DSPNAM)

/* Display "Signing on..." message */
            CALL       PGM(QCLSCAN) PARM(&USRTXT X'050F' X'001F' ':' +
                       X'001F' '0' '0' ' ' &POSITION)

            IF         COND(&POSITION *GT 0) THEN(DO)
            CHGVAR     VAR(&POSITION) VALUE(&POSITION - 1)
            CHGVAR     VAR(&USRNAME) VALUE(%SST(&USRTXT 1 &POSITION))
            ENDDO

            ELSE       CMD(DO)
            CHGVAR     VAR(&USRNAME) VALUE(&USRTXT)
```

Figure B.3: Blank lines added to improve readability (part 1 of 3).

```
              ENDDO

              SNDPGMMSG  MSGID(CPF9898) MSGF(QCPFMSG) MSGDTA('Signing +
                           on' *BCAT &USRNAME *BCAT 'at' &DSPNAME +
                           *TCAT '..') TOPGMQ(*EXT) MSGTYPE(*STATUS)

  /* If signing on with Client Access, override printer files */
              IF         COND(%SST(&DSPNAME 1 6) *EQ 'ACGDSP') THEN(DO)
              OVRPRTF    FILE(*PRTF) DEV(&DSPNAME *TCAT 'P1') +
                           PAGESIZE(82 132) LPI(8) CPI(16.7) +
                           OVRFLW(80) FOLD(*NO) PAGRTT(0) OUTQ(*DEV) +
                           HOLD(*YES)
              ENDDO

  /* Ensure print key formats output */
              CHGJOB     PRTKEYFMT(*PRTALL)

  /* Determine if user is a programmer */
              IF         COND(&GRPPRF *EQ 'QPGMR' *OR &GRPPRF *EQ +
                           'GRP_PGMR') THEN(DO)
              CHGVAR     VAR(&PROGRAMMER) VALUE('1')
              ENDDO
              ELSE       CMD(DO)
              CHGVAR     VAR(&PROGRAMMER) VALUE('0')
              ENDDO

  /* Place ALTQSYS at top of library list */
  /* for programmers and system operators */
              IF         COND(&PROGRAMMER *OR &USRCLS *EQ '*SYSOPR') +
                           THEN(DO)
              CHGSYSLIBL LIB(ALTQSYS) OPTION(*ADD)
              ENDDO

  /* If user is programmer, create programming library */
              IF         COND(&PROGRAMMER) THEN(DO)
              CHGVAR     VAR(&PGMRLIB) VALUE('$' *CAT %SST(&USRPRF 1 9))
              CRTLIB     LIB(&PGMRLIB) TEXT('Project library for' +
                           *BCAT &USRPRF)
              CRTSRCPF   FILE(&PGMRLIB/SOURCE) TEXT('Main source file')
              ADDLIBLE   LIB(&PGMRLIB) POSITION(*FIRST)
              ENDDO

  /* If any messages are found in the user's message queue, */
  /* display those messages before proceeding               */
```

Figure B.3: Blank lines added to improve readability (part 2 of 3).

```
            IF          COND(&DLVRY *NE '*BREAK') THEN(DO)
            RCVMSG      MSGQ(&MSGQLIB/&MSGQ) MSGTYPE(*NEXT) +
                          MSGKEY(*TOP) RMV(*NO) MSG(&MSG)
            IF          COND(&MSG *NE ' ') THEN(DO)
            DSPMSG      MSGQ(&MSGQLIB/&MSGQ)
            ENDDO

            RCVMSG      MSGQ(&DSPNAME) MSGTYPE(*NEXT) MSGKEY(*TOP) +
                          RMV(*NO) MSG(&MSG)
            IF          COND(&MSG *NE ' ') THEN(DO)
            DSPMSG      MSGQ(&DSPNAME)
            ENDDO
            ENDDO

/* Call personalizing program */
            CALL        PGM(MGTLIB/&USRPRF)

            IF          COND(&PROGRAMMER *OR &USRCLS *EQ '*SYSOPR') +
                          THEN(DO)
            CALL        PGM(QSYS/QCMD)
            ENDDO

   END:     ENDPGM
```

Figure B.3: Blank lines added to improve readability (part 3 of 3).

PUT LABELS IN SEPARATE LINES

Labels (or "tags," the destinations of GOTO commands) can be placed in lines of their own. The rationale will become clear as you read the following two sections. In Figure B.4, labels have been moved to lines of their own.

```
   /**********************************************************************/
   /*                                                                  */
   /* Program: SIGNON                                                  */
   /*                                                                  */
   /* Purpose: Initial program to run when user signs on.             */
   /*          It sets up job environment.                            */
   /*                                                                  */
   /**********************************************************************/
```

Figure B.4: Labels have been moved to lines of their own (part 1 of 4).

```
              PGM

              DCL       VAR(&DLVRY) TYPE(*CHAR) LEN(10)
              DCL       VAR(&DSPNAME) TYPE(*CHAR) LEN(10)
              DCL       VAR(&GRPPRF) TYPE(*CHAR) LEN(10)
              DCL       VAR(&MSG) TYPE(*CHAR) LEN(80)
              DCL       VAR(&MSGQ) TYPE(*CHAR) LEN(10)
              DCL       VAR(&MSGQLIB) TYPE(*CHAR) LEN(10)
              DCL       VAR(&PGMRLIB) TYPE(*CHAR) LEN(10)
              DCL       VAR(&POSITION) TYPE(*DEC) LEN(3 0)
              DCL       VAR(&PROGRAMMER) TYPE(*LGL) LEN(1)
              DCL       VAR(&USRCLS) TYPE(*CHAR) LEN(10)
              DCL       VAR(&USRNAME) TYPE(*CHAR) LEN(50)
              DCL       VAR(&USRPRF) TYPE(*CHAR) LEN(10)
              DCL       VAR(&USRTXT) TYPE(*CHAR) LEN(50)

              MONMSG    MSGID(CPF0000)

/* Retrieve the user profile attributes */
BEGIN:
              RTVUSRPRF USRPRF(*CURRENT) RTNUSRPRF(&USRPRF) +
                          GRPPRF(&GRPPRF) MSGQ(&MSGQ) +
                          MSGQLIB(&MSGQLIB) TEXT(&USRTXT) +
                          USRCLS(&USRCLS) DLVRY(&DLVRY)

              RTVJOBA   JOB(&DSPNAM)

/* Display "Signing on..." message */
              CALL      PGM(QCLSCAN) PARM(&USRTXT X'050F' X'001F' ':' +
                          X'001F' '0' '0' ' ' &POSITION)

              IF        COND(&POSITION *GT 0) THEN(DO)
              CHGVAR    VAR(&POSITION) VALUE(&POSITION - 1)
              CHGVAR    VAR(&USRNAME) VALUE(%SST(&USRTXT 1 &POSITION))
              ENDDO
              ELSE      CMD(DO)
              CHGVAR    VAR(&USRNAME) VALUE(&USRTXT)
              ENDDO

              SNDPGMMSG MSGID(CPF9898) MSGF(QCPFMSG) MSGDTA('Signing +
                          on' *BCAT &USRNAME *BCAT 'at' &DSPNAME +
                          *TCAT '..') TOPGMQ(*EXT) MSGTYPE(*STATUS)

/* If signing on with Client Access, override printer files */
              IF        COND(%SST(&DSPNAME 1 6) *EQ 'ACGDSP') THEN(DO)
```

Figure B.4: Labels have been moved to lines of their own (part 2 of 4).

```
                OVRPRTF     FILE(*PRTF) DEV(&DSPNAME *TCAT 'P1') +
                            PAGESIZE(82 132) LPI(8) CPI(16.7) +
                            OVRFLW(80) FOLD(*NO) PAGRTT(0) OUTQ(*DEV) +
                            HOLD(*YES)
                ENDDO

/* Ensure print key formats output */
                CHGJOB      PRTKEYFMT(*PRTALL)

/* Determine if user is a programmer */
                IF          COND(&GRPPRF *EQ 'QPGMR' *OR &GRPPRF *EQ +
                            'GRP_PGMR') THEN(DO)
                CHGVAR      VAR(&PROGRAMMER) VALUE('1')
                ENDDO
                ELSE        CMD(DO)
                CHGVAR      VAR(&PROGRAMMER) VALUE('0')
                ENDDO

/* Place ALTQSYS at top of library list */
/* for programmers and system operators */
                IF          COND(&PROGRAMMER *OR &USRCLS *EQ '*SYSOPR') +
                            THEN(DO)
                CHGSYSLIBL  LIB(ALTQSYS) OPTION(*ADD)
                ENDDO

/* If user is programmer, create programming library */
                IF          COND(&PROGRAMMER) THEN(DO)
                CHGVAR      VAR(&PGMRLIB) VALUE('$' *CAT %SST(&USRPRF 1 9))
                CRTLIB      LIB(&PGMRLIB) TEXT('Project library for' +
                            *BCAT &USRPRF)
                CRTSRCPF    FILE(&PGMRLIB/SOURCE) TEXT('Main source file')
                ADDLIBLE    LIB(&PGMRLIB) POSITION(*FIRST)
                ENDDO

/* If any messages are found in the user's message queue, */
/* display those messages before proceeding              */
                IF          COND(&DLVRY *NE '*BREAK') THEN(DO)
                RCVMSG      MSGQ(&MSGQLIB/&MSGQ) MSGTYPE(*NEXT) +
                            MSGKEY(*TOP) RMV(*NO) MSG(&MSG)
                IF          COND(&MSG *NE ' ') THEN(DO)
                DSPMSG      MSGQ(&MSGQLIB/&MSGQ)
                ENDDO

                RCVMSG      MSGQ(&DSPNAME) MSGTYPE(*NEXT) MSGKEY(*TOP) +
                            RMV(*NO) MSG(&MSG)
```

Figure B.4: Labels have been moved to lines of their own (part 3 of 4).

```
              IF        COND(&MSG *NE ' ') THEN(DO)
              DSPMSG    MSGQ(&DSPNAME)
              ENDDO
              ENDDO

/* Call personalizing program */
              CALL      PGM(MGTLIB/&USRPRF)

              IF        COND(&PROGRAMMER *OR &USRCLS *EQ '*SYSOPR') +
                           THEN(DO)
              CALL      PGM(QSYS/QCMD)
              ENDDO

END:
              ENDPGM
```

Figure B.4: Labels have been moved to lines of their own (part 4 of 4).

REMOVE LEADING BLANKS

The command prompter begins all commands at column 14. Is there a reason for wasting 13 columns? Unless you can find a reason, you'd be better off removing all that wasted space. Your program lines will have more room and, therefore, require less continuations. In Figure B.5, wasted leading blanks have been removed.

```
/********************************************************************/
/*                                                                  */
/* Program: SIGNON                                                  */
/*                                                                  */
/* Purpose: Initial program to run when user signs on.             */
/*          It sets up job environment.                            */
/*                                                                  */
/********************************************************************/
PGM

DCL       VAR(&DLVRY) TYPE(*CHAR) LEN(10)
DCL       VAR(&DSPNAME) TYPE(*CHAR) LEN(10)
DCL       VAR(&GRPPRF) TYPE(*CHAR) LEN(10)
DCL       VAR(&MSG) TYPE(*CHAR) LEN(80)
```

Figure B.5: Leading blanks have been removed (part 1 of 4).

```
DCL        VAR(&MSGQ) TYPE(*CHAR) LEN(10)
DCL        VAR(&MSGQLIB) TYPE(*CHAR) LEN(10)
DCL        VAR(&PGMRLIB) TYPE(*CHAR) LEN(10)
DCL        VAR(&POSITION) TYPE(*DEC) LEN(3 0)
DCL        VAR(&PROGRAMMER) TYPE(*LGL) LEN(1)
DCL        VAR(&USRCLS) TYPE(*CHAR) LEN(10)
DCL        VAR(&USRNAME) TYPE(*CHAR) LEN(50)
DCL        VAR(&USRPRF) TYPE(*CHAR) LEN(10)
DCL        VAR(&USRTXT) TYPE(*CHAR) LEN(50)

MONMSG     MSGID(CPF0000)

/* Retrieve the user profile attributes */
BEGIN:
RTVUSRPRF  USRPRF(*CURRENT) RTNUSRPRF(&USRPRF) +
GRPPRF(&GRPPRF) MSGQ(&MSGQ) +
MSGQLIB(&MSGQLIB) TEXT(&USRTXT) +
USRCLS(&USRCLS) DLVRY(&DLVRY)

RTVJOBA    JOB(&DSPNAM)

/* Display "Signing on..." message */
CALL       PGM(QCLSCAN) PARM(&USRTXT X'050F' X'001F' ':' +
X'001F' '0' '0' ' ' &POSITION)

IF         COND(&POSITION *GT 0) THEN(DO)
CHGVAR     VAR(&POSITION) VALUE(&POSITION - 1)
CHGVAR     VAR(&USRNAME) VALUE(%SST(&USRTXT 1 &POSITION))
ENDDO
ELSE       CMD(DO)
CHGVAR     VAR(&USRNAME) VALUE(&USRTXT)
ENDDO

SNDPGMMSG  MSGID(CPF9898) MSGF(QCPFMSG) MSGDTA('Signing +
on' *BCAT &USRNAME *BCAT 'at' &DSPNAME +
*TCAT '..') TOPGMQ(*EXT) MSGTYPE(*STATUS)

/* If signing on with Client Access, override printer files */
IF         COND(%SST(&DSPNAME 1 6) *EQ 'ACGDSP') THEN(DO)
OVRPRTF    FILE(*PRTF) DEV(&DSPNAME *TCAT 'P1') +
PAGESIZE(82 132) LPI(8) CPI(16.7) +
OVRFLW(80) FOLD(*NO) PAGRTT(0) OUTQ(*DEV) +
HOLD(*YES)
ENDDO
```

Figure B.5: Leading blanks have been removed (part 2 of 4).

```
/* Ensure print key formats output */
CHGJOB      PRTKEYFMT(*PRTALL)

/* Determine if user is a programmer */
IF          COND(&GRPPRF *EQ 'QPGMR' *OR &GRPPRF *EQ +
'GRP_PGMR') THEN(DO)
CHGVAR      VAR(&PROGRAMMER) VALUE('1')
ENDDO
ELSE        CMD(DO)
CHGVAR      VAR(&PROGRAMMER) VALUE('0')
ENDDO

/* Place ALTQSYS at top of library list */
/* for programmers and system operators */
IF          COND(&PROGRAMMER *OR &USRCLS *EQ '*SYSOPR') +
THEN(DO)
CHGSYSLIBL LIB(ALTQSYS) OPTION(*ADD)
ENDDO

/* If user is programmer, create programming library */
IF          COND(&PROGRAMMER) THEN(DO)
CHGVAR      VAR(&PGMRLIB) VALUE('$' *CAT %SST(&USRPRF 1 9))
CRTLIB      LIB(&PGMRLIB) TEXT('Project library for' +
*BCAT &USRPRF)
CRTSRCPF    FILE(&PGMRLIB/SOURCE) TEXT('Main source file')
ADDLIBLE    LIB(&PGMRLIB) POSITION(*FIRST)
ENDDO

/* If any messages are found in the user's message queue, */
/* display those messages before proceeding               */
IF          COND(&DLVRY *NE '*BREAK') THEN(DO)
RCVMSG      MSGQ(&MSGQLIB/&MSGQ) MSGTYPE(*NEXT) +
MSGKEY(*TOP) RMV(*NO) MSG(&MSG)
IF          COND(&MSG *NE ' ') THEN(DO)
DSPMSG      MSGQ(&MSGQLIB/&MSGQ)
ENDDO

RCVMSG      MSGQ(&DSPNAME) MSGTYPE(*NEXT) MSGKEY(*TOP) +
RMV(*NO) MSG(&MSG)
IF          COND(&MSG *NE ' ') THEN(DO)
DSPMSG      MSGQ(&DSPNAME)
ENDDO
ENDDO

/* Call personalizing program */
```

Figure B.5: Leading blanks have been removed (part 3 of 4).

```
CALL        PGM(MGTLIB/&USRPRF)

IF          COND(&PROGRAMMER *OR &USRCLS *EQ '*SYSOPR') +
THEN(DO)
CALL        PGM(QSYS/QCMD)
ENDDO

END:
ENDPGM
```

Figure B.5: Leading blanks have been removed (part 4 of 4).

INDENT THE CODE

The importance of this step cannot be over emphasized. Because the command prompter leaves *all* command names beginning at column 14, you cannot tell, at a glance, whether you're looking at a line that is within a DO/ENDDO group. Indenting solves that problem.

You can take advantage of the chance to remove unnecessary blank spaces such as those found between the command name and the first parameter. Also, you can keep all labels in column 1 and have continuation lines start at the same column the first parameter starts.

For each level of the DO/ENDDO block, indent three columns. Keep the right margin at column 71 (the same as SEU). Of course, you don't have to do so if you are thinking of abandoning SEU. Figure B.6 shows the indented code.

```
/**************************************************************/
/*                                                          */
/* Program: SIGNON                                          */
/*                                                          */
/* Purpose: Initial program to run when user signs on.      */
/*          It sets up job environment.                     */
/*                                                          */
/**************************************************************/
PGM
```

Figure B.6: Indented CL source code (part 1 of 4).

```
        DCL VAR(&DLVRY) TYPE(*CHAR) LEN(10)
        DCL VAR(&DSPNAME) TYPE(*CHAR) LEN(10)
        DCL VAR(&GRPPRF) TYPE(*CHAR) LEN(10)
        DCL VAR(&MSG) TYPE(*CHAR) LEN(80)
        DCL VAR(&MSGQ) TYPE(*CHAR) LEN(10)
        DCL VAR(&MSGQLIB) TYPE(*CHAR) LEN(10)
        DCL VAR(&PGMRLIB) TYPE(*CHAR) LEN(10)
        DCL VAR(&POSITION) TYPE(*DEC) LEN(3 0)
        DCL VAR(&PROGRAMMER) TYPE(*LGL) LEN(1)
        DCL VAR(&USRCLS) TYPE(*CHAR) LEN(10)
        DCL VAR(&USRNAME) TYPE(*CHAR) LEN(50)
        DCL VAR(&USRPRF) TYPE(*CHAR) LEN(10)
        DCL VAR(&USRTXT) TYPE(*CHAR) LEN(50)

        MONMSG MSGID(CPF0000)


        /* Retrieve the user profile attributes */
     BEGIN:
        RTVUSRPRF USRPRF(*CURRENT) RTNUSRPRF(&USRPRF) GRPPRF(&GRPPRF) +
                MSGQ(&MSGQ) MSGQLIB(&MSGQLIB) TEXT(&USRTXT) +
                USRCLS(&USRCLS) DLVRY(&DLVRY)


        RTVJOBA JOB(&DSPNAM)

        /* Display "Signing on..." message */
        CALL PGM(QCLSCAN) PARM(&USRTXT X'050F' X'001F' ':' X'001F' '0' '0' +
            ' ' &POSITION)

        IF COND(&POSITION *GT 0) THEN(DO)
           CHGVAR VAR(&POSITION) VALUE(&POSITION - 1)
           CHGVAR VAR(&USRNAME) VALUE(%SST(&USRTXT 1 &POSITION))
        ENDDO
        ELSE CMD(DO)
           CHGVAR VAR(&USRNAME) VALUE(&USRTXT)

        ENDDO

        SNDPGMMSG MSGID(CPF9898) MSGF(QCPFMSG) +
                MSGDTA('Signing on' *BCAT &USRNAME *BCAT 'at' &DSPNAME +
                    *TCAT '..') +
                TOPGMQ(*EXT) MSGTYPE(*STATUS)


        /* If signing on with Client Access, override printer files */
        IF COND(%SST(&DSPNAME 1 6) *EQ 'ACGDSP') THEN(DO)
```

Figure B.6: Indented CL source code (part 2 of 4).

```
            OVRPRTF FILE(*PRTF) DEV(&DSPNAME *TCAT 'P1') PAGESIZE(82 132) +
                    LPI(8) CPI(16.7) OVRFLW(80) FOLD(*NO) PAGRTT(0) +
                    OUTQ(*DEV) HOLD(*YES)
      ENDDO

      /* Ensure print key formats output */
      CHGJOB PRTKEYFMT(*PRTALL)

      /* Determine if user is a programmer */
      IF COND(&GRPPRF *EQ 'QPGMR' *OR &GRPPRF *EQ 'GRP_PGMR') THEN(DO)
         CHGVAR VAR(&PROGRAMMER) VALUE('1')
      ENDDO
      ELSE CMD(DO)
         CHGVAR VAR(&PROGRAMMER) VALUE('0')
      ENDDO

      /* Place ALTQSYS at top of library list */
      /* for programmers and system operators */
      IF COND(&PROGRAMMER *OR &USRCLS *EQ '*SYSOPR') THEN(DO)
         CHGSYSLIBL LIB(ALTQSYS) OPTION(*ADD)
      ENDDO

      /* If user is programmer, create programming library */
      IF COND(&PROGRAMMER) THEN(DO)
         CHGVAR VAR(&PGMRLIB) VALUE('$' *CAT %SST(&USRPRF 1 9))
         CRTLIB LIB(&PGMRLIB) TEXT('Project library for' *BCAT &USRPRF)
         CRTSRCPF FILE(&PGMRLIB/SOURCE) TEXT('Main source file')
         ADDLIBLE LIB(&PGMRLIB) POSITION(*FIRST)
      ENDDO

      /* If any messages are found in the user's message queue, */
      /* display those messages before proceeding              */
      IF COND(&DLVRY *NE '*BREAK') THEN(DO)
         RCVMSG MSGQ(&MSGQLIB/&MSGQ) MSGTYPE(*NEXT) MSGKEY(*TOP) +
                RMV(*NO) MSG(&MSG)
         IF COND(&MSG *NE ' ') THEN(DO)
            DSPMSG MSGQ(&MSGQLIB/&MSGQ)
         ENDDO

         RCVMSG MSGQ(&DSPNAME) MSGTYPE(*NEXT) MSGKEY(*TOP) RMV(*NO) +
                MSG(&MSG)
         IF COND(&MSG *NE ' ') THEN(DO)
            DSPMSG MSGQ(&DSPNAME)
         ENDDO
      ENDDO
```

Figure B.6: Indented CL source code (part 3 of 4).

```
      /* Call personalizing program */
      CALL PGM(MGTLIB/&USRPRF)

      IF COND(&PROGRAMMER *OR &USRCLS *EQ '*SYSOPR') THEN(DO)
         CALL PGM(QSYS/QCMD)
      ENDDO

   END:
   ENDPGM
```

Figure B.6: Indented CL source code (part 4 of 4).

TURN IDENTIFIERS TO LOWERCASE

CL allows you to code anything in uppercase or lowercase. Yet the command prompter turns everything it can (except quoted constants and comments) into uppercase.

Text written in all uppercase (capital letters) is hard to read; that's why lowercase letters were invented. Use them! One approach is to turn to lowercase all identifiers used within the program (variable names, labels, and object names) and leave the rest (command names, keyword names, special values) in uppercase. As shown in Figure B.7, identifiers are in lowercase.

```
/******************************************************************/
/*                                                                */
/* Program: SIGNON                                                */
/*                                                                */
/* Purpose: Initial program to run when user signs on.           */
/*          It sets up job environment.                           */
/*                                                                */
/******************************************************************/
PGM

   DCL VAR(&dlvry) TYPE(*CHAR) LEN(10)
   DCL VAR(&dspname) TYPE(*CHAR) LEN(10)
   DCL VAR(&grpprf) TYPE(*CHAR) LEN(10)
   DCL VAR(&msg) TYPE(*CHAR) LEN(80)
   DCL VAR(&msgq) TYPE(*CHAR) LEN(10)
```

Figure B.7: Identifiers have been converted to lowercase (part 1 of 4).

```
    DCL VAR(&msgqlib) TYPE(*CHAR) LEN(10)
    DCL VAR(&pgmrlib) TYPE(*CHAR) LEN(10)
    DCL VAR(&position) TYPE(*DEC) LEN(3 0)
    DCL VAR(&programmer) TYPE(*LGL) LEN(1)
    DCL VAR(&usrcls) TYPE(*CHAR) LEN(10)
    DCL VAR(&usrname) TYPE(*CHAR) LEN(50)
    DCL VAR(&usrprf) TYPE(*CHAR) LEN(10)
    DCL VAR(&usrtxt) TYPE(*CHAR) LEN(50)


    MONMSG MSGID(cpf0000)

    /* Retrieve the user profile attributes */
begin:
    RTVUSRPRF USRPRF(*CURRENT) RTNUSRPRF(&usrprf) GRPPRF(&grpprf) +
            MSGQ(&msgq) MSGQLIB(&msgqlib) TEXT(&usrtxt) +
            USRCLS(&usrcls) DLVRY(&dlvry)


    RTVJOBA JOB(&dspnam)


    /* Display "Signing on..." message */
    CALL PGM(qclscan) PARM(&usrtxt X'050F' X'001F' ':' X'001F' '0' '0' +
                      ' ' &position)

    IF COND(&position *GT 0) THEN(DO)
       CHGVAR VAR(&position) VALUE(&position - 1)
       CHGVAR VAR(&usrname) VALUE(%SST(&usrtxt 1 &position))
    ENDDO
    ELSE CMD(DO)
       CHGVAR VAR(&usrname) VALUE(&usrtxt)
    ENDDO

    SNDPGMMSG MSGID(cpf9898) MSGF(qcpfmsg) +
            MSGDTA('Signing on' *BCAT &usrname *BCAT 'at' &dspname +
                  *TCAT '..') +
            TOPGMQ(*EXT) MSGTYPE(*STATUS)

    /* If signing on with Client Access, override printer files */
    IF COND(%SST(&dspname 1 6) *EQ 'ACGDSP') THEN(DO)
       OVRPRTF FILE(*PRTF) DEV(&dspname *TCAT 'P1') PAGESIZE(82 132) +
              LPI(8) CPI(16.7) OVRFLW(80) FOLD(*NO) PAGRTT(0) +
              OUTQ(*DEV) HOLD(*YES)
    ENDDO
```

Figure B.7: Identifiers have been converted to lowercase (part 2 of 4).

```
      /* Ensure print key formats output */
      CHGJOB PRTKEYFMT(*PRTALL)

      /* Determine if user is a programmer */
      IF COND(&grpprf *EQ 'QPGMR' *OR &grpprf *EQ 'GRP_PGMR') THEN(DO)
         CHGVAR VAR(&programmer) VALUE('1')
   ENDDO
   ELSE CMD(DO)
         CHGVAR VAR(&programmer) VALUE('0')
   ENDDO


      /* Place ALTQSYS at top of library list */
      /* for programmers and system operators */
      IF COND(&programmer *OR &usrcls *EQ '*SYSOPR') THEN(DO)
         CHGSYSLIBL LIB(altqsys) OPTION(*ADD)
   ENDDO

      /* If user is programmer, create programming library */
      IF COND(&programmer) THEN(DO)
         CHGVAR VAR(&pgmrlib) VALUE('$' *CAT %SST(&usrprf 1 9))
         CRTLIB LIB(&pgmrlib) TEXT('Project library for' *BCAT &usrprf)
         CRTSRCPF FILE(&pgmrlib/source) TEXT('Main source file')
         ADDLIBLE LIB(&pgmrlib) POSITION(*FIRST)
   ENDDO

      /* If any messages are found in the user's message queue, */
      /* display those messages before proceeding              */
      IF COND(&dlvry *NE '*BREAK') THEN(DO)
         RCVMSG MSGQ(&msgqlib/&msgq) MSGTYPE(*NEXT) MSGKEY(*TOP) +
               RMV(*NO) MSG(&msg)
         IF COND(&msg *NE ' ') THEN(DO)
            DSPMSG MSGQ(&msgqlib/&msgq)
         ENDDO

         RCVMSG MSGQ(&dspname) MSGTYPE(*NEXT) MSGKEY(*TOP) RMV(*NO) +
               MSG(&msg)
         IF COND(&msg *NE ' ') THEN(DO)
            DSPMSG MSGQ(&dspname)
         ENDDO
   ENDDO

      /* Call personalizing program */
      CALL PGM(mgtlib/&usrprf)

      IF COND(&programmer *OR &usrcls *EQ '*SYSOPR') THEN(DO)
```

Figure B.7: Identifiers have been converted to lowercase (part 3 of 4).

```
        CALL PGM(qsys/qcmd)
      ENDDO

  end:
  ENDPGM
```

Figure B.7: Identifiers have been converted to lowercase (part 4 of 4)

REMOVE UNNECESSARY KEYWORDS

After a day or two coding CL, it becomes bothersome to see all the VAR, TYPE, and LEN keywords in DCL commands or all the VAR and VALUE keywords in CHGVARS. They seem to clutter the program for no useful purpose.

CL allows you to remove some keywords (not all, however). Take advantage of this feature to clean up the code. For example, you can remove keywords from PGM, DCL, DCLF, MONMSG, CHGVAR, IF, GOTO, and CALL. As shown in Figure B.8, such keywords have been removed.

```
   /****************************************************************/
   /*                                                            */
   /* Program: SIGNON                                            */
   /*                                                            */
   /* Purpose: Initial program to run when user signs on.       */
   /*          It sets up job environment.                      */
   /*                                                            */
   /****************************************************************/
   PGM

     DCL &dlvry *CHAR 10
     DCL &dspname *CHAR 10
     DCL &grpprf *CHAR 10
     DCL &msg *CHAR 80
     DCL &msgq *CHAR 10
     DCL &msgqlib *CHAR 10
     DCL &pgmrlib *CHAR 10
     DCL &position *DEC (3 0)
```

Figure B.8: Unnecessary keywords have been removed (part 1 of 3).

```
        DCL &programmer *LGL 1
        DCL &usrcls *CHAR 10
        DCL &usrname *CHAR 50
        DCL &usrprf *CHAR 10
        DCL &usrtxt *CHAR 50

        MONMSG cpf0000

        /* Retrieve the user profile attributes */
begin:
        RTVUSRPRF USRPRF(*CURRENT) RTNUSRPRF(&usrprf) GRPPRF(&grpprf) +
                MSGQ(&msgq) MSGQLIB(&msgqlib) TEXT(&usrtxt) +
                USRCLS(&usrcls) DLVRY(&dlvry)

        RTVJOBA JOB(&dspnam)

        /* Display "Signing on..." message */
        CALL qclscan (&usrtxt X'050F' X'001F' ':' X'001F' '0' '0' ' ' +
                &position)

        IF (&position *GT 0) DO
           CHGVAR &position (&position - 1)
           CHGVAR &usrname %SST(&usrtxt 1 &position)
        ENDDO
        ELSE DO
           CHGVAR &usrname &usrtxt
        ENDDO

        SNDPGMMSG MSGID(cpf9898) MSGF(qcpfmsg) +
                MSGDTA('Signing on' *BCAT &usrname *BCAT 'at' &dspname +
                *TCAT '..') +
                TOPGMQ(*EXT) MSGTYPE(*STATUS)

        /* If signing on with Client Access, override printer files */
        IF (%SST(&dspname 1 6) *EQ 'ACGDSP') DO
           OVRPRTF *PRTF DEV(&dspname *TCAT 'P1') PAGESIZE(82 132) +
                LPI(8) CPI(16.7) OVRFLW(80) FOLD(*NO) PAGRTT(0) +
                OUTQ(*DEV) HOLD(*YES)
        ENDDO

        /* Ensure print key formats output */
        CHGJOB PRTKEYFMT(*PRTALL)

        /* Determine if user is a programmer */
        IF (&grpprf *EQ 'QPGMR' *OR &grpprf *EQ 'GRP_PGMR') DO
```

Figure B.8: Unnecessary keywords have been removed (part 2 of 3).

```
        CHGVAR &programmer '1'
    ENDDO
    ELSE DO
        CHGVAR &programmer '0'
    ENDDO

    /* Place ALTQSYS at top of library list */
    /* for programmers and system operators */
    IF (&programmer *OR &usrcls *EQ '*SYSOPR') DO
        CHGSYSLIBL altqsys OPTION(*ADD)
    ENDDO

    /* If user is programmer, create programming library */
    IF (&programmer) DO
        CHGVAR &pgmrlib ('$' *CAT %SST(&usrprf 1 9))
        CRTLIB &pgmrlib TEXT('Project library for' *BCAT &usrprf)
        CRTSRCPF &pgmrlib/source TEXT('Main source file')
        ADDLIBLE &pgmrlib POSITION(*FIRST)
    ENDDO

    /* If any messages are found in the user's message queue, */
    /* display those messages before proceeding              */
    IF (&dlvry *NE '*BREAK') DO
        RCVMSG MSGQ(&msgqlib/&msgq) MSGTYPE(*NEXT) MSGKEY(*TOP) +
              RMV(*NO) MSG(&msg)
        IF (&msg *NE ' ') DO
           DSPMSG &msgqlib/&msgq
        ENDDO

        RCVMSG MSGQ(&dspname) MSGTYPE(*NEXT) MSGKEY(*TOP) RMV(*NO) +
              MSG(&msg)
        IF (&msg *NE ' ') DO
           DSPMSG &dspname
        ENDDO
    ENDDO

    /* Call personalizing program */
    CALL mgtlib/&usrprf

    IF (&programmer *OR &usrcls *EQ '*SYSOPR') DO
        CALL qsys/qcmd
    ENDDO

end:
ENDPGM
```

Figure B.8: Unnecessary keywords have been removed (part 3 of 3).

ALIGN SIMILAR LINES (DCLS IN PARTICULAR)

Notice how much easier it is to read the block of DCLs in the program shown in Figure B.9. There are no distracting keywords and all DCLs are arranged into neat columns. Also aligned in columns are the parameters of consecutive CHGVAR commands.

```
/*****************************************************************/
/*                                                               */
/* Program: SIGNON                                               */
/*                                                               */
/* Purpose: Initial program to run when user signs on.          */
/*          It sets up job environment.                          */
/*                                                               */
/*****************************************************************/
PGM

    DCL &dlvry      *CHAR    10
    DCL &dspname    *CHAR    10
    DCL &grpprf     *CHAR    10
    DCL &msg        *CHAR    80
    DCL &msgq       *CHAR    10
    DCL &msgqlib    *CHAR    10
    DCL &pgmrlib    *CHAR    10
    DCL &position   *DEC     (3 0)
    DCL &programmer *LGL     1
    DCL &usrcls     *CHAR    10
    DCL &usrname    *CHAR    50
    DCL &usrprf     *CHAR    10
    DCL &usrtxt     *CHAR    50

    MONMSG cpf0000

    /* Retrieve the user profile attributes */
begin:
    RTVUSRPRF USRPRF(*CURRENT) RTNUSRPRF(&usrprf) GRPPRF(&grpprf) +
              MSGQ(&msgq) MSGQLIB(&msgqlib) TEXT(&usrtxt) +
              USRCLS(&usrcls) DLVRY(&dlvry)

    RTVJOBA JOB(&dspnam)

    /* Display "Signing on..." message */
    CALL qclscan (&usrtxt X'050F' X'001F' ':' X'001F' '0' '0' ' ' +
```

Figure B.9: Similar lines and parameters have been aligned (part 1 of 3).

```
                       &position)

IF (&position *GT 0) DO
   CHGVAR &position (&position - 1)
   CHGVAR &usrname  %SST(&usrtxt 1 &position)
ENDDO
ELSE DO
   CHGVAR &usrname &usrtxt
ENDDO


SNDPGMMSG MSGID(cpf9898) MSGF(qcpfmsg) +
          MSGDTA('Signing on' *BCAT &usrname *BCAT 'at' &dspname +
                 *TCAT '..') +
          TOPGMQ(*EXT) MSGTYPE(*STATUS)

/* If signing on with Client Access, override printer files */
IF (%SST(&dspname 1 6) *EQ 'ACGDSP') DO
   OVRPRTF *PRTF DEV(&dspname *TCAT 'P1') PAGESIZE(82 132) +
           LPI(8) CPI(16.7) OVRFLW(80) FOLD(*NO) PAGRTT(0) +
           OUTQ(*DEV) HOLD(*YES)
ENDDO

/* Ensure print key formats output */
CHGJOB PRTKEYFMT(*PRTALL)


/* Determine if user is a programmer */
IF (&grpprf *EQ 'QPGMR' *OR &grpprf *EQ 'GRP_PGMR') DO
   CHGVAR &programmer '1'
ENDDO
ELSE DO
   CHGVAR &programmer '0'
ENDDO


/* Place ALTQSYS at top of library list */
/* for programmers and system operators */
IF (&programmer *OR &usrcls *EQ '*SYSOPR') DO
   CHGSYSLIBL altqsys OPTION(*ADD)
ENDDO

/* If user is programmer, create programming library */
IF (&programmer) DO
   CHGVAR &pgmrlib ('$' *CAT %SST(&usrprf 1 9))
   CRTLIB &pgmrlib TEXT('Project library for' *BCAT &usrprf)
   CRTSRCPF &pgmrlib/source TEXT('Main source file')
   ADDLIBLE &pgmrlib POSITION(*FIRST)
```

Figure B.9: Similar lines and parameters have been aligned (part 2 of 3).

```
    ENDDO

    /* If any messages are found in the user's message queue, */
    /* display those messages before proceeding             */
    IF (&dlvry *NE '*BREAK') DO
       RCVMSG MSGQ(&msgqlib/&msgq) MSGTYPE(*NEXT) MSGKEY(*TOP) +
              RMV(*NO) MSG(&msg)
      IF (&msg *NE ' ') DO
         DSPMSG &msgqlib/&msgq
      ENDDO

       RCVMSG MSGQ(&dspname) MSGTYPE(*NEXT) MSGKEY(*TOP) RMV(*NO) +
              MSG(&msg)
      IF (&msg *NE ' ') DO
         DSPMSG &dspname
      ENDDO
    ENDDO
    /* Call personalizing program */
    CALL mgtlib/&usrprf

    IF (&programmer *OR &usrcls *EQ '*SYSOPR') DO
       CALL qsys/qcmd
    ENDDO

 end:
 ENDPGM
```

Figure B.9: Similar lines and parameters have been aligned (part 3 of 3).

Choose the Right Code Editor

Perhaps your reaction to all this styling discussion is to say: "No way! I'm not going to all that trouble!" If that is so, you have all the more reason to abandon SEU as your code editor. It might sound crazy, but it's not as crazy as sweating over ugly code or trying to fix it using such a klunky, kludgy klutz as SEU.

You can always move all your code development and maintenance to a PC or Macintosh that is somehow connected to your eServer system. There are, for example, enormous advantages to editing source code using a word processor on a Macintosh:

- You can program complicated macros in the word processor (something that is impossible to do with SEU).

- You can have several windows open at the same time. This becomes extremely important when you have to develop complicated software that requires you to look at, and change, several pieces of code at the same time. For example, you write a CL program that must call an RPG program. When you code the RPG program, you don't remember the parameter list. With a word processor it's easy to keep several (or many) windows open at once. With SEU, you are limited to two windows (both rather small), and you can edit code only in one of them.

- Do you want to break a line in two or join two lines? Even if you figure out how to code exit programs to drive built-in line commands, available in V4R2 or later, that's rather hard to do in SEU. Word processors do these tasks very easily. Depending on what you want to do, move the cursor and press Delete or Return.

- Indenting code is a breeze with a word processor. Create a macro that adds three leading spaces and you're done. SEU forces you to type RR3... RR; it's a much less convenient thing to do.

- A code editor designed for the specific purpose can do even more for you. Word processors are great (better than SEU), but they're not really made for the job. A source-code editor that "understands" CL and RPG, however, can make your job more enjoyable. An editor can help you avoid drudgery by, for example, coloring the code on the fly to enable you to highlight comments and special commands so you'll have no trouble spotting them. In addition to IBM's CODE and LPEX editors, several third-party editors are available.

C

SAMPLE SIGN-ON PROGRAM

```
PGM

    DCL &dlvry        *CHAR    10
    DCL &dspname      *CHAR    10
    DCL &grpprf       *CHAR    10
    DCL &msg          *CHAR    80
    DCL &msgq         *CHAR    10
    DCL &msgqlib      *CHAR    10
    DCL &pgmrlib      *CHAR    10
    DCL &position     *DEC      3
    DCL &programmer   *LGL      1
    DCL &usrcls       *CHAR    10
    DCL &usrname      *CHAR    50
    DCL &usrprf       *CHAR    10
    DCL &usrtxt       *CHAR    50

    MONMSG cpf0000

    /* Retrieve the user profile attributes */
    RTVUSRPRF *CURRENT RTNUSRPRF(&usrprf) GRPPRF(&grpprf) +
            MSGQ(&msgq) MSGQLIB(&msgqlib) +
            TEXT(&usrtxt) USRCLS(&usrcls) DLVRY(&dlvry)
```

Figure C.1: Sample Sign-on Program (part 1 of 3).

```
RTVJOBA JOB(&dspnam)

/* Display "Signing on..." message */
CALL qclscan (&usrtxt X'050F' X'001F' +
              ':' X'001F' +
              '0' '0' ' ' &position)

IF (&position *GT 0) DO
   CHGVAR &position (&position - 1)
   CHGVAR &usrname  %SST(&usrtxt 1 &position)
ENDDO
ELSE DO
   CHGVAR &usrname &usrtxt
ENDDO

SNDPGMMSG MSGID(cpf9898) MSGF(qcpfmsg) +
          MSGDTA('Signing on' *BCAT &usrname *BCAT 'at' +
                 &dspname *TCAT '..') +
          TOPGMQ(*EXT) MSGTYPE(*STATUS)

/* If signing on with Client Access, override printer files */
IF (%SST(&dspname 1 6) *EQ 'ACGDSP') DO
   OVRPRTF *PRTF DEV(&dspname *TCAT 'P1') +
           PAGESIZE(82 132) LPI(8) CPI(16.7) OVRFLW(80) +
           FOLD(*NO) PAGRTT(0) OUTQ(*DEV) HOLD(*YES)
ENDDO

/* Ensure print key formats output */
CHGJOB PRTKEYFMT(*PRTALL)

/* Determine if user is a programmer */
IF (&grpprf *EQ 'QPGMR'    *OR +
    &grpprf *EQ 'GRP_PGMR'      ) DO
   CHGVAR &programmer '1'
ENDDO
ELSE DO
   CHGVAR &programmer '0'
ENDDO

/* Place ALTQSYS at top of library list */
/* for programmers and system operators */
IF (&programmer          *OR +
    &usrcls *EQ '*SYSOPR'    ) DO
   CHGSYSLIBL altqsys OPTION(*ADD)
ENDDO
```

Figure C.1: Sample Sign-on Program (part 2 of 3).

```
   /* If user is programmer, create programming library */
   IF (&programmer) DO
      CHGVAR &pgmrlib ('$' *CAT %SST(&usrprf 1 9))
      CRTLIB &pgmrlib TEXT('Project library for' *BCAT &usrprf)
      CRTSRCPF &pgmrlib/source TEXT('Main source file')
      ADDLIBLE &pgmrlib POSITION(*FIRST)
   ENDDO

   /* If any messages are found in the user's message queue, */
   /* display those messages before proceeding */
   IF (&dlvry *NE '*BREAK') DO
      RCVMSG MSGQ(&msgqlib/&msgq) MSGTYPE(*NEXT) MSGKEY(*TOP) +
            RMV(*NO) MSG(&msg)
      IF (&msg *NE ' ') DO
         DSPMSG MSGQ(&msgqlib/&msgq)
      ENDDO

      RCVMSG MSGQ(&dspname) MSGTYPE(*NEXT) MSGKEY(*TOP) +
            RMV(*NO) MSG(&msg)
      IF (&msg *NE ' ') DO
         DSPMSG MSGQ(&dspname)
      ENDDO
   ENDDO

   /* Call personalizing program */
   CALL mgtlib/&usrprf

   IF (&programmer *OR        +
      &usrcls *EQ '*SYSOPR' ) DO
      CALL qsys/qcmd
   ENDDO

ENDPGM
```

Figure C.1: Sample Sign-on Program (part 3 of 3).

D

DEBUGGING *OPM* PROGRAMS

As discussed in chapter 16, the Integrated Language Environment (ILE) supports interactive debugging. Programmers who must debug OPM code can use the ILE interactive debugger as well or they may use the old OPM line-oriented debugger. This appendix describes the line debugger. A third debugger, ISDB, is not discussed here. It is also a full-screen debugger but, because the ILE interactive debugger can be used with OPM programs, it isn't needed.

THE STRDBG COMMAND

The Start Debug (STRDBG) command runs one of two debuggers over OPM programs.

- STRDBG OPMSRC(*YES) invokes the ILE source debugger for an OPM program.

- STRDBG OPMSRC(*NO) invokes the line-oriented debugger for an OPM program.

The following parameters of STRDBG are commonly used with OPM programs:

- PGM (Program) is where you enter the qualified name of the program object you want to debug. You can enter up to 10 program names. If your CL program calls another program, both programs can be debugged simultaneously. If you need to add a program to the debugging session after you have run STRDBG, you can run the Add Program (ADDPGM) command. Conversely, you can run Remove Program (RMVPGM) if you want to remove a program from the debugging session.

- DFTPGM (Default Program) is where you enter the name of the one program that will be considered the default program by other debugging commands. This parameter defaults to *PGM. The program named in the PGM parameter (or the first one if several were named there) is considered the default program.

- MAXTRC (Maximum Trace Records) is where you can indicate how many trace records the system is to keep in the trace file. The default value is 200.

- TRCFULL (Trace Full) is where you indicate what to do when the trace file is full. The default value of *STOPTRC causes the system to stop program execution at the next breakpoint. Continuing beyond this breakpoint causes the system to stop program execution at each subsequent statement within the range of statements being traced, and the new records are added to the trace file.

- The value *WRAP causes the system to write over the trace file once the file is full. This means that the first record to be added beyond the end of the trace file will overwrite the first record in the trace file.

- UPDPROD (Update Production Files) lets you indicate whether to allow files in production libraries to be updated by specifying *YES or *NO. If you specify *NO (default value) and the program being debugged attempts to write a record or change a record in a database file of a production library, an error message is issued. If the program being debugged has write or update statements to database files, you should enter the value *YES to avoid these error messages or leave it as *NO, but move the file to a test library.

- OPMSRC (OPM Source Debug), if *YES, specifies that an OPM program is to be debugged in full-screen mode. The OPM program must have been compiled with OPTION(*SRCDBG).

The following additional parameters are applicable to OPM, but are unlikely to be needed.

- DSPMODSRC (Display Module Source) determines whether or not the source debug program is shown when debugging begins. For OPM programs compiled with OPTION(*SRCDBG), the source debug program is shown. If all programs in the PGM parameter are OPM programs compiled OPTION(*NOSRCDBG), the source debug program display is not shown.

- UNMONPGM (Unmonitored Message Program) is the name of the program to be called when an OPM program being debugged generates an unmonitored escape message. This program must receive eight parameters. See the online help for STRDBG for more information.

THE LINE-ORIENTED DEBUGGER

With the Add Breakpoint (ADDBKP) command, you can instruct the system to stop the execution of the program being debugged at certain statements. You actually enter the source statement numbers and indicate what variable(s) should be displayed in each case.

Note: Remember that when you specify a breakpoint at a particular statement number, the system actually stops before it executes the statement.

The ADDBKP Command

The ADDBKP command contains many parameters, but not all of them are discussed here. The following parameters are the most important ones:

- STMT (Statement) allows you to enter the statement number where you want to add a breakpoint. You can enter up to 10 statement numbers each time you execute the ADDBKP command.

- PGMVAR (Program Variable) allows you to enter the name of up to 10 program variables you want the system to display when it reaches the breakpoint. You don't have to enter any program variables, however. When the breakpoint is reached, you can then run the Display Program Variable (DSPPGMVAR) command to display any program variable.

- Because CL variable names all begin with the ampersand (&) character, you must surround the variable name in single quotes (such as '&OUTQ') or the variable name will be rejected as if it were invalid.

- OUTFMT (Output Format) indicates how to show the variables. The default value is *CHAR, which displays the variable values in character format. You also can select *HEX to display them in hexadecimal format. For example, if variable &X has the value "A", *CHAR would show the letter "A" itself while *HEX would show C1 (its hexadecimal representation).

- PGM (Program) indicates to what program you are adding a breakpoint. It defaults to *DFTPGM, which adds the breakpoint to the default program for the debugging session.

For long variables of type *CHAR, you can use the START and LEN parameters to indicate what portion of the string to display. START is the starting position and LEN is how many characters to display. For example, if you have defined a 2000-byte character string, you can display positions 1245 to 1254 at a breakpoint by specifying START(1245) LEN(10). It will save you from having to press the Page Down key repeatedly.

Suppose you have a CL program that is failing, and you want to add a breakpoint at statement 2500 (note it is not statement 25.00 as listed by SEU, but statement 2500 as listed by the compiler). Before running this statement, you want to display variable &COUNTER (which is decimal). Run the command shown in Figure D.1.

```
ADDBKP STMT(2500) PGMVAR('&counter')
```

Figure D.1: Adding a breakpoint to a program for debugging.

Changing and Removing Breakpoints

After you add a breakpoint, you might want to change it later. For example, you might want to add or remove a variable. All you need to do is run the ADDBKP command again. This time ADDBKP will write over the old breakpoint, redefining it.

If you added an unnecessary breakpoint, it will be confusing (as well as bothersome) to have the program stop at it each time. You can remove it with the Remove Breakpoint (RMVBKP) command, which has only two parameters: STMT (statement number) and PGM (name of the program).

Displaying and Changing Variables

Variables can be displayed by specifying their names in breakpoints. However, you can use another method. You can display any program variable during a breakpoint stop by pressing the F10 key (which presents a command line) and running the Display Program Variable (DSPPGMVAR) command. The DSPPGMVAR command has many of the same parameters as the ADDBKP command.

You can also change the variable. While stopped at a breakpoint, you can run the Change Program Variable (CHGPGMVAR) command. When the program resumes execution, it will use the new value you supplied. This feature can be invaluable during debugging.

Conditional Breakpoints

Breakpoints don't have to stop the program each time the statement is reached. You can make the breakpoint conditional in two ways.

First, you can use the SKIP parameter of the ADDBKP command. For example, SKIP(30) means that the statement will not cause a breakpoint the first 30 times it is executed. This feature can be very useful if you want to examine program variables after a loop has repeated a certain number of times.

Second, you can use the BKPCOND (Breakpoint Condition) parameter of the ADDBKP command. The BKPCOND parameter requires a logical expression such as (*PGMVAR1 *GT 30). Figure D.2 shows an example.

```
ADDBKP STMT(1000) PGMVAR('&counter' '&outq') +
       BKPCOND(*PGMVAR1 *GT 30)
```

Figure D.2: An example of the BKPCOND parameter with logical expression as its parameter.

The program will stop at statement 1000 only if &COUNTER is greater than 30. *PGMVAR1 means "the first variable listed in the PGMVAR parameter." You can enter *PGMVAR2, *PGMVAR3, and all the way to *PGMVAR10.

The ADDTRC, DSPTRC, and RMVTRC Commands

The line debugger permits you to collect trace data, which tracks statements that have been executed by the program. This data is especially useful if the program contains many IFs and GOTOs (which can be confusing when you examine the source).

To start using the trace function, run the Add Trace (ADDTRC) command. With ADDTRC, you specify a range, or several ranges of statements that you want traced, and what variable(s) you want the trace file to track. Using ADDTRC is easy because you already know most of the parameters and they are the same as in the ADDBKP command.

Once you have used the ADDTRC command one or more times, you might not remember what statements are being traced. You can use the Display Trace (DSPTRC) command to get a quick answer to the question, "What statements am I tracing?"

If you decide to remove trace from one or more statement ranges, run the Remove Trace (RMVTRC) command.

The DSPTRCDTA and CLRTRCDTA Commands

Trace begins collecting data as the program runs. You can display this trace information anytime with the Display Trace Data (DSPTRCDTA) command. You can direct the information to the display station or printer and you are also given a chance to clear the trace data after you view it.

If you don't clear the trace data when you are finished displaying it with DSPTRCDTA, you can still erase the trace data at a later time with the Clear Trace Data (CLRTRCDTA) command.

E

THE ORIGINAL PROGRAM MODEL

The Original Program Model (OPM) is the name IBM gave to the model of program object that was available on the S/38 and on the AS/400 until the introduction of ILE. OPM is still widely used, but IBM is no longer enhancing OPM compilers and is discouraging the use of OPM. Nevertheless, programmers will have to continue to deal with OPM for some time to come.

Table E.1 lists some of the more obvious differences between OPM and ILE CL. Other differences, such as message handling, are too complex for inclusion here. For more information, consult the *ILE Concepts* manual.

Table E.1: OPM and ILE CL Comparisons

OPM	ILE
CL source members are compiled with the CRTCLPGM command.	CL source members are compiled with the CRTCLMOD and CRTBNDCL commands.
The TFRCTL command is permitted.	The TFRCTL command is not permitted.
Programs must run in the default activation group.	Programs may run in the default activation or in other activation groups.
The COPYRIGHT command is not supported.	COPYRIGHT is supported.
The CALLPRC command is not supported.	CALLPRC is supported and preferred where possible.
Parameters in called CL programs must match the parameter list supplied by the caller.	Parameters in called CL modules do not have to match the parameter list supplied by the caller, but referencing an unpassed parameter generates escape message MCH3601.

F

Even though it's difficult to find a System/38 in production, there is still a lot of S/38 code running on i5, iSeries, and AS/400 machines. The programmer who has to maintain S/38 code must understand the changes that IBM made to CL when the AS/400 was introduced. This chapter points out the most important differences.

OBJECTS

The i5 server defines many object types that did not exist on the S/38.

Object Type

Here's a partial list of object types the S/38 lacks:
*ALRTBL, *AUTL, *CFGL, *CLD, *CNNL, *COSD, *CSI, *CSPMAP, *CSPTBL, *CTLD (REPLACING *CUD), *DTADCT, *FLR, *FNTRSC, *FORMDF, *MENU, *MODD, *NWID, *OVL, *PAGDFN, *PAGSEG, *PDG, *PNLGRP, *PRDAVL, *PRDDFN, *PRDLOD, *QMFORM, *QMQRY, *QRYDFN, *RCT, *SCHIDX, *S36, *USRIDX, *USRQ, *USRSPC.

Object type *PRTIMG has been discontinued.

Qualified Names

The most visible difference between S/38 and AS/400 CL is in the way qualified names are written. If an object is named OBJ1 and it is located in library LIB1, the S/38 references that object as shown in Figure F.1.

```
OBJ1.LIB1
```

Figure F.1: S/38 code to specify a qualified name.

In other words, the order of the names is object first and then the library. A period separates the names. Figure F.2 shows how the AS/400 references this same object.

```
LIB1/OBJ1
```

Figure F.2: AS/400 code to specify a qualified name.

The order of the names has been reversed and the separator is now a slash instead of a period.

If you think of a PC subdirectory as a library and ignore the fact that the slash slants the wrong way, the reversal makes AS/400 qualified names more similar to PC qualified names on the PC. Qualified names begin with the most generic (the library name) and end with the most specific (the object name). It makes more sense than the other way around.

The separator character had to be changed because OS/400 allows periods in object names to support S/36 file names in the S/36 environment.

CHANGES IN COMMANDS

IBM changed commands for several reasons. The S/38 supported card devices, for example, while the AS/400 does not. This change makes the Create Card File (CRTCRDF) command and others obsolete. Command parameters also may have changed. Even the default values supplied may have changed. S/38 commands usually have QGPL as the default library for newly created objects. The AS/400 uses *CURLIB (the current library). All CRTXXX commands have parameter PUBAUT changed to AUT.

Some commands were renamed to conform to a more sensible naming convention. For example, S/38 commands have three verbs to describe the beginning of a task: BGN (begin), ENT (enter), and STR (start). The AS/400 uses STR exclusively.

Appendix A of the *S/38 Environment Programmer's Guide and Reference* contains a complete description of all the commands that were changed. For your convenience, Table F.1 contains a partial listing.

Table F.1: Conversion of S/38 Commands to AS/400	
System/38	**AS/400 Description**
APYPGMCHG	APYPTF
BGNCMTCTL	STRCMTCTL
BGNPASTHR	STRPASTHR
BRWPFM	DSPPFM
CHGCUD	CHGCTLxxx, where xxx is the type of controller.
CHGDEVD	CHGDEVxxx, where xxx is the type of device.
CHGDOCOWN	CHGDLOOWN
CHGSTGCFG	Use DST with a dedicated system.
CLNPRT	Not supported.

Table F.1: Conversion of S/38 Commands to AS/400, continued	
System/38	**AS/400 Description**
CNLJOB	ENDJOB
CNLJOBABN	ENDJOBABN
CNLNETF	DLTNETF
CNLRCV	ENDRCV
CNLRDR	ENDRDR
CNLRQS	ENDRQS
CNLSPLF	DLTSPLF
CNLWTR	ENDWTR
CPYFRMVDSK	CPYFRMPCD
CPYTOVDSK	CPYTOPCD
CRTCUD	CRTCTLxxx, where xxx is the type of controller.
CRTDEVD	CRTDEVxxx, where xxx is the type of device.
DCLDTAARA	NOT SUPPORTED
DFNKBDMAP	SETKBDMAP
DLTCUD	DLTCTLD
DLTDOC	DLTDLO
DSNFMT	STRSDA
DSPACTJOB	WRKACTJOB
DSPCTLSTS	WRKCFGSTS
DSPCUD	DSPCTLD
DSPDEVSTS	WRKCFGSTS
DSPDOCAUT	DSPUSRPMN

Table F.1: Conversion of S/38 Commands to AS/400, continued	
System/38	**AS/400 Description**
DSPJOBQ	WRKJOBQ
DSPJRNA	WRKJRNA
DSPJRNMNU	WRKJRN
DSPLINSTS	WRKCFGSTS
DSPMNU	GO
DSPMSGF	WRKMSGF
DSPOBJLCK	WRKOBJLCK
DSPOUTQ	WRKOUTQ
DSPOUTQD	WRKOUTQD
DSPPGMCHG	DSPPTF
DSPPGMMNU	STRPGMMNU
DSPRPYL	WRKRPYLE
DSPSBMJOB	WRKSBMJOB
DSPSBS	WRKSBSJOB
DSPSPLFA	WRKSPLFA
DSPSYS	WRKSBS
DSPSYSSTS	WRKSYSSTS
DSPWTR	WRKWTR
EDTSRC	STRSEU
EML3270	STREML3270
ENDJOB	ENDBCHJOB
ENDSRV	ENDSRVJOB

Table F.1: Conversion of S/38 Commands to AS/400, continued

System/38	AS/400 Description
ENTDBG	STRDBG
ENTPS	STROFC
FMTRJEDTA	CVTRJEDTA
GRTDOCAUT	DRTUSPRMN
JOB	BCHJOB
JRNAP	STRJRNAP
JRNPF	STRJRNPF
LODPGMCHG	LODPTF
LSTCMDUSG	PRTCMDUSG
LSTERRLOG	PRTERRLOG
MNGDIR	WRKDIR
PCHPGM	Use PTF support.
PRPAPAR	CRTAPAR
RCVDTAARA	Not supported. Use RTVDTAARA.
RMVPGMCHG	RMVPTF
RPLLIBL	CHGLIBL
RSTDOC	RSTDLO
RSTPGMPRD	RSTLICPGM
RVKDOCAUT	RVKUSRPMN
SAVDOC	SAVDLO
SNDDTAARA	Not supported. Use CHGDTAARA.
SRVJOB	STRSRVJOB

Table F.1: Conversion of S/38 Commands to AS/400, continued

System/38	AS/400 Description
TRMCPF	ENDSYS
TRMGRPJOB	ENDGRPJOB
TRMSBS	ENDSBS
VRYCTLU	VRYCFG
VRYDEV	VRYCFG
VRYLIN	VRYCFG

New Commands

i5/OS has many commands that the S/38 does not have. Table F.2 lists a few especially useful commands you can start using immediately:

Table F.2: New AS/400 Commands

New Command	Description
CHGCURLIB	Changes the current library setting in your job.
CHGLIBL	Takes the place of the RPLLIBL command. Adds a parameter to let you change the current library.
CHGPWD	Change the user's password. Starts an interactive program.
CHGSHRPOOL	Change shared memory pools among subsystems.
CHKPWD	Check the user's password. If the password supplied in a parameter is not the user's password, CHKPWD issues an escape message.
CHKRCDLCK	Check record locks. If the routing step holds any record locks, the CHKRCDLCK issues an escape message.
CPROBJ	Compress Object. Objects of type *MENU (IBM-supplied), *PNLGRP and device *FILE can be compressed to about 50 percent of their original size to decrease DASD usage. The system decompresses them manually when needed.

Table F.2: New AS/400 Commands, continued

New Command	Description
CPYFRMQRYF	Copy From Query File. Allows you to copy the output "file" produced by OPNQRYF to an actual database file, which can then be processed in any form.
CPYLIB	Copy Library. Creates a duplicate of an entire library, including the objects contained in it.
CRTMNU	Create a *MENU object. Menus created with CRTMNU (or SDA) are easily maintained.
DSCJOB	Disconnect Job. A disconnected job does not use system resources. The job can be connected again by having the user sign on to the system using the same display device. The system reconnects and recovers completely.
DSPWSUSR	Display Workstation User. This command can be executed by selecting Option 7 from the SysRq menu. It identifies the user who is signed on to a display device.
EDTLIBL	Edit Library List. Lets you edit the library list interactively.
DTOBJAUT	Edit Object Authority. Lets you edit object authorities interactively.
FNDSTRPDM	Find String using PDM. Scans a member, group of members, or an entire source file for a character string. Each match can be listed,or the source member can be edited or compiled immediately.
LODRUN	Load tape and run application. Facilitates installation of software that has been distributed with diskettes or tapes.
PRTDEVADR	Print Device Addresses. Prints a chart listing the devices that have been configured in a workstation controller.
RTVCFGSRC	Retrieve Configuration Source. Creates a CL source member with all the CRTxxx commands that would duplicate the existing configuration of devices, controllers, lines, and classes.
RTVCFGSTS	Retrieve configuration status. Retrieves the status code of a device, controller or line to a CL variable.
RTVLIBD	Retrieve library description. Retrieves the library type (*PROD or *TEST), the ASP, text description, and the default create authority—all to CL variables.

Table F.2: New AS/400 Commands, continued	
New Command	**Description**
RTVMBRD	Retrieve member description. Retrieves information about file members to CL variables.
RTVOBJD	Retrieve object description. Retrieves data about an object to CL variables.
SLTCMD	Select command. Presents a display listing the commands in a library (all commands or generic name), and lets you select the one you want to run. Great for finding the appropriate command. Warning! It's too easy to type incorrectly and end up executing DLTCMD (Delete Command) instead. Be very, very careful.
STRCPYSCN	Start copy screen. As the display device changes images, they are copied to another display device, to a printer, or to a database file.
WRKXXX	"Work with" commands. WRKxxx commands allow you to get a displayed list of objects by type, using the *ALL or generic name. For example, WRKF shows a list of files; WRKDTAARA shows a list of data areas. Numbered options are available to perform different tasks on each object listed, such as 4=Delete or 7=Rename.

SYSTEM VALUES

The i5 has many system values that were not available on the S/38.

New System Values

Table F.3 gives you an idea of what is new.

Table F.3: AS/400 New System Values	
System Value	**Description**
QAUTOCFG	Automatic configuration.
QCONSOLE	Name of the system console.
QPRTDEV	Name of the system printer.

435

Table F.3: AS/400 New System Values, continued	
System Value	**Description**
QSTRUPPGM).	Name of the start-up program IPL.
QIPLDATTIM	Date and time of next automatic IPL.
QRMTIPL	Allow/disallow remote IPL.
QIPLTYPE	Type of IPL to perform.
QIPLSTS	Type of last IPL performed.
QPWRRSTIPL	Automatic IPL after power is restored.
QSTRPRTWTR	Start printer writers at IPL.
QSECURITY	Security level.
QKBDTYPE	Keyboard type.
QSPCENV	Special environment.
QDEVNAMING	Default device naming scheme.
QPFRADJ	Perform automatic performance adjustment at IPL.
QPWDEXPITV	Interval for password expiration.
QDSPSGNINF	Display sign-on information.
QMODEL	AS/400 model.

Changed System Values

A few system values have changed default values or type or length: QSYSLIBL, QMAXSIGN, QAUTOIMPL, QCTLSBSD, QSCPFCONS, QBASPOOL, QMCHPOOL, QUPSMSGQ, QUPSDLYTIM.

Obsolete System Values

A few S/38 system values are no longer supported: QCSNAP, QBADPGFRM, QSIGNLVL, QSRVONLY, QCHGLOGSIZ, QSRVLOGSIZ, QSYSOPRDEV, QAUXSTGTH, QSCPF-SIGN.

THE S/38 ENVIRONMENT

i5/OS has a facility called the S/38 Environment (S/38E), which is supported by the existence of library QSYS38. Library QSYS38 contains the S/38E commands as they were on the real S/38. To enter the S/38E, execute the command shown in Figure F.3.

```
CALL QCL
```

Figure F.3: The command to enter the S/38 environment.

Description

The system presents the S/38E Command Entry screen (which works like the native AS/400 Command Entry, not like the S/38 Command Entry). The command prompter also works as it does in native (not as it did on the S/38). From this screen, you can enter S/38 commands using S/38 syntax.

If you write a CL program (using the EDTSRC command), the source member type will be CLP38 by default, and SEU will recognize S/38 command syntax. When you run the CRTCLPGM command afterwards, this special syntax will be recognized, too.

CL programs written and compiled in the S/38E can be executed outside of the environment by running the call command. The system automatically recognizes the program as an S/38E CL program.

Converting to eServer i5 or iSeries

Sooner or later you will want to convert your S/38E CL programs to native CL programs. This task is simplified by the Convert CL Source (CVTCLSRC) command. CVTCLSRC has three parameters:

- FROMFILE: Enter the qualified name of the source file that contains the S/38 CL source.

- TOFILE: Enter the qualified name of the source file that will contain the converted CL code.

- FROMMBR: Enter the name of one or more members in FROMFILE that will be converted to native CL. The members are written into TOFILE and they keep the same names.

No ILE

The Integrated Language Environment (ILE) was not introduced on the S/38. Although they are not called such, all programs are OPM-type programs. Therefore, the S/38 doesn't support modules, static binding, activation groups, and other ILE concepts.

G

FOR S/36 PROGRAMMERS

As with the System/38, there are few System 36 shops in existence anymore. But you may inherit old S/36 code and as such may have to convert OCL to CL. This appendix will help you understand the differences. CL didn't exist on the System/36. All program control was written in Operation Control Language (OCL).

CL is rather simple. The challenge to updating it is to figure out CL equivalents to tricks and techniques in OCL.

INTERPRETED VERSUS COMPILED LANGUAGES

Because OCL is an interpreted language, it is never compiled. You write the code and execute it. The system must read the source code and interpret it each time the source program is executed.

For programmers, interpreted languages are comfortable, but they usually are slow and CPU-intensive. However, compiled languages like CL must be translated into machine language before they can be executed. This translation is performed by the compiler and it's done only once.

Compiled programs run faster than interpreted ones, but they do require that extra step of compilation before they can be used.

THE S/36 ENVIRONMENT

The S/36 Environment (S/36E) is a special function of i5/OS that lets you run S/36 software with little modification. The S/36E also allows you to operate the i5 as if it were an S/36 (within limits). You can execute most of the S/36 control commands (such as D U, C P, and so on), run procedures manually, and enter OCL manually.

The S/36E is provided by the existence of three libraries: QSSP (which contains the S/36E IBM-supplied procedures, programs, and OCL interpreter), #LIBRARY (which you can use to place your own procedures), and QS36F (which will contain all your S/36E data files).

Entering and Leaving the S/36E

You can enter the S/36E in two ways. First, the security officer might have assigned you to the S/36E. In this case, every time you sign on, you automatically enter the S/36E by specifying SPCENV(*S36) in your user profile or specifying SPCENV(*SYSVAL) and changing system value QSPCENV to *S36.

Second, you can run the Start S/36 (STRS36) command. When you do, your interactive job will remain as it was, but the S/36E functions will now be available. You can still run i5/OS commands. The only visible difference is that the command line of the menu no longer supports lowercase characters. Everything you type goes in capital letters just as it does on a S/36.

You leave the S/36E by signing off or by running the End S/36 (ENDS36) command.

Running S/36E Procedures

If you are in the S/36E, you can run S/36E procedures by typing the procedure name (with parameters, if necessary) and pressing Enter (if you are in the appropriate library).

If you aren't in the S/36E, you can still run S/36E procedures by executing the Start S/36 Procedure (STRS36PRC) command, which can be executed manually or included in a CL program.

CL Equivalents S/36 OCL

The following sections describe substitution expressions, procedure control expressions, and OCL statements.

Substitution Expressions

?n? Procedure parameters can be referenced only by their positional number in the S/36. CL program parameters are referenced by their name. For example, you never speak of the fifth parameter (?5?) of a CL program, but of parameter &OPTION.

?n'value'?, ?nT'value'?, ?nF'value'? These substitution expressions are ways to assign a value to a procedure parameter. They are performed in native CL with the Change Variable (CHGVAR) command. For example, ?3'A'? means that if parameter 3 has no value, 'A' must be assumed. In CL you must code an IF statement to check on the variable that is taking the place of the third parameter (let's call it &PARM3, for example). If &PARM3 is zero or blank (depending on its data type), you CHGVAR &PARM3 to give it a value of 'A'.

?R?, ?nR?, ?R'mic'?, ?nR'mic'? These substitution expressions stop the procedure in the middle and get an input value from the user. The value is assigned to a temporary parameter (?R? and ?R'MIC'?) or to a regular positional parameter (?NR? and ?NR'MIC'?).

This expression can be mimicked in CL with the Send User Message (SNDUS-RMSG) command. Consider the CL code shown in Figure G.1.

```
SNDUSRMSG MSG('Enter missing parameter') +
          MSGTYPE(*INQ) +
          MSGRPY(&reply)
```

Figure G.1: Using SNDUSRMSG to replace ?R?.

SNDUSRMSG interrupts the CL program execution and shows the message indicated. Because it is an inquiry message (*INQ), it asks for a reply, which is stored in variable &REPLY. &REPLY must be of type *CHAR, with a maximum length of 132.

?Cn? and ?C'value'? OCL uses these substitution expressions to calculate the length of a procedure parameter or a character constant. Neither expression has a direct translation into CL. CL has no way to calculate lengths. But, then again, it rarely needs to because CL variables are fixed-length data. In contrast, OCL procedure parameters are variable-length data.

?CD? Return codes are usually not needed in CL. Most OCL procedures reference ?CD? only as a way to determine what key is pressed from a prompt-ed- screen format. When a display is presented by a CL program (using the SNDRCVF command), all the indicators of the display file can be referenced in the CL program by using variable names beginning with &IN, followed by two digits.

If the display file's DDS indicates that pressing F3 turns on indicator 03, you can check variable &IN03 with an IF command in the CL program. If it is true (equal to '1'), indicator 03 is on, which in turn means that the user pressed F3. If the indicator is off ('0'), the user pressed a different key.

Return codes also are used in OCL procedures to check the completion of certain steps such as the compilation of a member. In CL, you can perform this function with the MONMSG command. If a command within a CL program fails, the MONMSG command can trap the message issued by the failing command.

?CLIB? and ?SLIB? To determine the name of the current library, CL programs use the RTVJOBA command as shown in Figure G.2.

```
DCL     &lib     *CHAR    10

    RTVJOBA CURLIB(&lib)
```

Figure G.2: Using RTVJOBA to replace ?CLIB?.

There is no equivalent to the ?SLIB? substitution expression because i5/OS jobs do not have session libraries.

?DATE? and ?TIME? To retrieve the system date and the system time, use the RTVSYSVAL command. The system date can be retrieved from system value QDATE (or its portions retrieved from system values QMONTH, QDAY, and QYEAR). QDATE must be retrieved into a six-character variable. QMONTH, QDAY, and QYEAR must be retrieved into a two-character variable.

To retrieve the system time, use the RTVSYSVAL command to retrieve system value QTIME (into a six- or nine-character variable), or QHOUR, QMINUTE, and QSECOND (into a two-character variable). If you use a nine-character variable to retrieve QTIME, you will get the system time with an accuracy down to milliseconds.

To retrieve the current job's date (not the system date), use the RTVJOBA command as shown in Figure G.3.

```
DCL     &date     *char 6

    RTVJOBA DATE(&date)
```

Figure G.3: Using RTVJOBA to replace ?DATE?.

443

?F'S,name'?, ?F'S,name,date'?, ?F'A,name'? and ?F'A,name,date'? i5
database files do not have allocated space; they have only actual space used. You can
retrieve this information using the RTVMBRD command, as shown in Figure G.4.

```
DCL     &used    *dec    10

    RTVMBRD FILE(...) MBR(...) NBRCURRCD(&used)
```

Figure G.4: Using RTVMBRD to replace ?F'A,name'?.

After RTVMBRD executes, variable &USED will have the number of records in the
file member. RTVMBRD also returns other information, such as:

- The number of deleted records.

- The number of bytes occupied by the file member's data and access path.

- The library in which the file is found.

- Member creation date.

?L'position,length'? Retrieving any portion of the LDA is easy in CL. You use
the RTVDTAARA command using data area name *LDA. Figure G.5 shows how to
retrieve LDA positions 101 to 150.

```
    RTVDTAARA DTAARA(*LDA (101 50)) RTNVAR(&data)
```

Figure G.5: Using RTVDTAARA to replace ?L'position,length'?.

You also can use the CHGVAR command. See Figure G.6.

```
    CHGVAR &NEWVAR %SST(*LDA 101 50)
```

Figure G.6: Using CHGVAR to replace ?L'position,length'?.

444

&NEWVAR is the new variable's name. The value being assigned to it is %SST(*LDA 101 50), which is a shortcut to access the LDA. Under i5/OS, jobs do not have a system LDA.

?Mmic? and ?M'mic,position,length'? To retrieve the text of a predefined message, use the RTVMSG command. See Figure G.7.

```
RTVMSG MSGID(...) MSGF(...) MSG(&message)
```

Figure G.7: Using RTVMSG to replace ?Mmic?.

You must specify the message ID ("mic") in the MSGID parameter and the name of the message file in the msgf parameter. Variable &MESSAGE contains the entire message text.

?MENU? i5 jobs do not have "current menus." Therefore, the ?MENU? expression has no meaning.

?PRINTER? You can retrieve the name of the current printer name or the current output queue name with the RTVJOBA command. See Figure G.8.

```
RTVJOBA OUTQ(&outq) OUTQLIB(&outqlib) PRTDEV(&prtdev)
```

Figure G.8: Using RTVJOBA to replace ?PRINTER?.

You don't have to retrieve both &PRTDEV and the &OUTQ and &OUTQLIB pair. However, &OUTQ and &OUTQLIB are more likely to be relevant than &PRTDEV.

?PROC? Under i5/OS there is no "top level CL program." Therefore, the ?PROC? substitution expression has no equivalent.

?SYSLIST? The i5/OS architecture does not have a system list device. This substitution expression has no equivalent.

?USER? You can retrieve the name of the user running a CL program with the RTVUSRPRF command. See Figure G.9.

```
DCL       &user    *CHAR    10

    RTVUSRPRF USRPRF(*CURRENT) RTNUSRPRF(&user)
```

Figure G.9: Using RTVUSRPRF to replace ?USER?.

?VOLID? and ?VOLID'location'? There is no equivalent because none is needed. In almost all cases, the programmer must retrieve the volume ID of a diskette or tape only to code a SAVE, SAVELIBR, INIT, or other procedure that specifies the correct volume ID. Because all i5/OS commands that manipulate diskettes or tapes allow a volume ID of *MOUNTED, the system will accept whatever diskette or tape is already mounted, regardless of the volume ID.

?WS? To retrieve the name of the requesting workstation, run the RTVJOBA command. See Figure G.10.

```
DCL     &dspnam    *CHAR    10
RTVJOBA JOB(&dspnam)
```

Figure G.10: Using RTVJOBA to replace ?WS?.

This coding technique works only for interactive jobs. Batch jobs have no way to retrieve the name of the workstation that submitted the job.

Procedure Control Expressions

IF ACTIVE-procname CL has no equivalent for this condition test and in most cases the test is not needed. You can simulate this expression by allocating a data area object with the ALCOBJ command when a CL program begins running. If another CL program needs to know if the first one is running, it only has to attempt to allocate the same data area. If the ALCOBJ command fails, it means that the first program is running.

IF BLOCKS-size Not needed with i5/OS, this type of test is superfluous because the database never needs contiguous space on disk.

IF CONSOLE-YES The i5 is a console-less machine. Although there is a display station that the system considers the system console (connected to port 0, address 0 of the first workstation controller), all other display stations can do everything the system console does, except communicate with the CPU during an attended IPL. Therefore, it does not matter whether or not a procedure is running from the system console. If you need to know, however, Figure G.11 shows you how.

```
RTVSYSVAL qconsole &console
   RTVJOBA   JOB(&dspnam)

   IF (&console *EQ &dspnam) DO
   ...
```

Figure G.11: Using RTVSYSVAL and RTVJOBA to replace IF CONSOLE-YES.

In this program segment, both &CONSOLE and &DSPNAM are character variables that are 10 bytes long. Because the name of the system console is stored in system value QCONSOLE at all times, you just need to code an IF statement to determine if the current display station is the console.

IF DATAF1-name To determine if a file exists, use the CHKOBJ command. If CHKOBJ fails with an escape message of CPF9801, the file does not exist.

IF DATAI1-name and IF DATAT-name There is no equivalent. Simply attempt to make use of the file in the tape or diskette, and make sure to code a MONMSG immediately afterwards to trap an error message if the file is not there.

IF DSPLY-type There is no equivalent and none is needed. Under i5/OS, display files can take care of themselves. The program that uses them does not need to know what size is supported by the display device.

IF EVOKED-YES Use the RTVJOBA command as shown in Figure G.12.

```
·  DCL      &subtype    *CHAR    1

    RTVJOBA SUBTYPE(&subtype)
```

Figure G.12: Using RTVJOBA to replace IF EVOKED-YES.

If the job is running evoked, &SUBTYPE will contain the letter E.

IF INQUIRY-YES Because i5/OS doesn't have an inquiry mode, there is no equivalent for this condition test.

IF JOBQ-YES Use RTVJOBA as shown in Figure G.13.

```
    DCL     &jobtype    *CHAR    1
    RTVJOBA TYPE(&jobtype)
```

Figure G.13: Using RTVJOBA to replace IF JOBQ-YES.

If the job is running in batch mode (i.e., "from the job queue"), &TYPE will have the character '0' (zero).

IF LOAD-'member,library' and IF SUBR-'member,library' Load and subroutine members are compiled members in the S/36 architecture. The i5 equivalent is an object of a certain type. For example, a load member of type RPG (a compiled RPG program) is a *PGM object to the i5. A load member of type FMT (a compiled screen format) is a *FILE object to the i5.

Use the CHKOBJ command to check the existence of the object. If CHKOBJ fails with a message of CPF9801, the object does not exist.

IF MRTMAX-procname Because CL programs are never MRT, this condition test has no meaning.

IF PROC-'member,library' Procedure members are to the S/36 what CL programs objects (*PGM) are to the i5. Use the CHKOBJ command to check the existence of the object. If CHKOBJ fails with message CPF9801, the program does not exist.

IF SECURITY-ACTIVE i5/OS security works differently from S/36 security. S/36 security is considered active when the system requires entry of a password upon sign-on. On the i5, security is active when system value QSECURITY has a value of '20' or greater. Use the RTVSYSVAL command as shown in Figure G.14.

```
DCL        &security    *CHAR   2

RTVSYSVAL qsecurity &security
IF (&security *GE '20') ...
```

Figure G.14: Using RTVSYSVAL QSECURITY to replace IF SECURITY-ACTIVE.

IF SECURITY-level When the i5 is working at security level 30 or higher, individual objects of any kind can be secured. Therefore, this kind of test is unnecessary. There is no equivalent.

IF SOURCE-'member,library' Checking the existence of a source member is easy with the CHKOBJ command. Source members are not directly attached to a library—as they are on the S/36—but to a source physical file, which in turn is contained in a library (a three-level hierarchy). Use CHKOBJ as shown in Figure G.15.

```
DCL    &lib    *CHAR    10
DCL    &mbr    *CHAR    10
DCL    &srcf   *CHAR    10

CHKOBJ &lib/&srcf *FILE MBR(&mbr)
MONMSG cpf9815 EXEC(...)
```

Figure G.15: Using CHKOBJ and MONMSG to replace IF SOURCE-'member,library'.

&LIB and &SRCF indicate the name of the library and source file. &MBR is the name of the source member. If the member doesn't exist in the source file indicated, message CPF9815 is issued.

IF SWITCH-setting Use the %SWITCH function as shown in Figure G.16.

```
IF %SWITCH(X100XXXX) ...
```

Figure G.16: Using %SWITCH to replace IF SWITCH-setting.

This example checks that switch 2 is on and switches 3 and 4 are off. All other switches are irrelevant.

IF string1=string2 and IF string1/string2 Use the IF command and the *EQ comparison operator to compare two variables.

IF string1>string2 Use the IF command and the *GT comparison operator.

IF VOLID-volumeid The i5 usually does not care what the diskette's or tape's volume ID is because all commands that manipulate diskettes or tapes accept a special value of *MOUNTED. You can check for this condition, however, with the CHKDKT or CHKTAP command (for diskette or tape, respectively). Figure G.17 shows an example using a diskette.

```
CHKDKT DEV(...) VOL('MINE')
MONMSG ...
```

Figure G.17: Using CHKDKT and MONMSG to replace IF VOLID-volumeid.

The system issues CPF6165 if the diskette drive is not ready or CPF6162 if the volume ID is not 'MINE'. For tapes, use CHKTAP and monitor for CPF6760 and CPF6720 respectively.

// * 'message' Use the SNDPGMMSG command to send a message to inform the user about the progress of a CL program. Specify TOPGMQ(*EXT)

MSGTYPE(*STATUS). You can code either your own predefined message or use message ID CPF9898 in message file QCPFMSG. Then write the free-form message text in the MSGDTA parameter without the ending period. See Figure G.18.

```
SNDPGMMSG MSGID(cpf9898) MSGF(qcpfmsg) +
          MSGDTA('Now deleting files') +
          TOPGMQ(*EXT) MSGTYPE(*STATUS)
```

*Figure G.18: Using SNDPGMMSG to replace // * 'message'.*

The command shown in Figure G.18 sends the message "Now deleting files." The period is automatically included. The message is sent to the display station and it always appears on line 24.

// ** 'message' Use the SNDUSRMSG command to send a message to the system operator, which suspends execution of the CL program. Figure G.19 shows you how.

```
SNDUSRMSG MSG('Mount next tape') +
          MSGTYPE(*INQ) +
          VALUES('C' 'G') DFT('G') +
          TOMSGQ(qsysopr) MSGRPY(&reply)
```

*Figure G.19: Using SNDUSRMSG to replace // **'message'.*

Although it looks complicated, the command offers more than // **. The VALUES parameter indicates that the system operator will be forced to choose between a reply of C or G. DFT('G') means that if the system operator presses Enter without typing a reply, G will be assumed by default. The reply will be assigned to variable &REPLY (which must be a one-character variable). You can then use an IF command to cancel the program if the operator entered C or go (continue) if the operator entered G.

// CANCEL Use the RETURN command to stop processing a CL program. The RETURN command always returns control to the program that called your

CL program. If you started the CL program manually (or by selecting a menu option), control returns to the keyboard.

// EVALUATE Use the CHGVAR command to assign a value to a variable.

// GOTO and // TAG In CL, the // GOTO statement becomes a GOTO command. GOTO always transfers control to a CL program label, which is the name of the label immediately followed by a colon (:). As of V5R3, CL includes DOWHILE, DOUNTIL, and DOFOR commands to control looping.

// PAUSE 'message' Refer to the description of the // ** statement. You can use the same technique with TOMSGQ(*) instead of TOMSGQ(QSYSOPR).

// RESET procname There is no exact equivalent to the // RESET statement. You can use the TFRCTL command to some extent. Refer to Chapter 7 for a detailed description of this command.

// RETURN Use the RETURN command; they are exact equivalents. However, there is no equivalent for // RETURN *ALL.

OCL Statements

// ALLOCATE and // DEALLOC Use the ALCOBJ command to allocate the device description object for the diskette or tape device. Refer to Chapter 11 for more information about ALCOBJ.

// ATTR Only the PRIORITY parameter has an equivalent: the CHGJOB command. Specify the priority value in the RUNPTY parameter.

// CANCEL PRT Use the DLTSPLF command to delete spooled files.

// CHANGE Use the CHGSPLFA command to change spooled-file attributes.

// DATE Use the CHGJOB command to change the job's date by specifying a new date in the date parameter.

// DEBUG Debugging works very differently on the i5. For more information about the debugging facilities, refer to Chapter 16.

// EVOKE There is no direct equivalent because there is no such thing as an evoked job in native mode. Use the SBMJOB command to submit the job to a job queue that is different from the one you use for normal job queue jobs.

// FILE The function of // FILE is unnecessary in CL programs. When a program is called, it automatically knows what files to use. CL programs need to supply file information only when it becomes necessary to override the defaults. Use the OVRDBF command in these cases.

For example, the file might be located in a library that you either don't have in your library list or that is lower in the library list than another library that also contains the same file. Use the OVRDBF command with the FILE and TOFILE parameters as shown in Figure G.20.

```
OVRDBF FILE(filea) TOFILE(&lib/fileb)
```

Figure G.20: Using OVRDBF to replace // FILE.

FILEA is the name by which the program knows the file (equivalent to // FILE NAME-). FILEB is the actual name of the file on disk (equivalent to // FILE LABEL-).

// FORMS Use the CHGJOB command to change your job's printer settings. Not all settings are supported on the i5. For example, the number of characters per inch is automatically set when a file that needs special settings is used. This function works automatically because the printer file object (*FILE) already contains the setting.

// IMAGE Because the IBM 3262 printer is not supported on the i5, the // IMAGE statement is irrelevant.

// INCLUDE Use the CALL command to call another program or the CALLPRC command to invoke a procedure.

// INFOMSG Use the CHGJOB command and specify STSMSG(*NONE) to suppress status messages, STSMSG(*NORMAL) to allow them, and STSMSG(*USRPRF) to return the STSMSG to its default value.

// JOBQ Use the SBMJOB command to submit a job to a job queue. Refer to chapter 12 for more information about batch processing.

// LIBRARY There is no direct equivalent. The library list support allows you to indicate the libraries you will be using in your job. If you use // LIBRARY to change the current library, use the CHGCURLIB command in native.

// LOAD and // RUN Both statements are replaced with the CALL command. The CALL command performs both functions.

// LOCAL Use the CHGVAR or the CHGDTAARA command to change the local data area by specifying a data area name of *LDA. There is no system LDA under i5/OS.

// LOG Use the CHGJOB command with LOGCLPGM(*YES) or LOGCLPGM(*NO) to turn logging of CL program statements to the job log on and off.

// MEMBER The // MEMBER statement is not needed. The SNDPGMMSG command includes a parameter (MSGF) for indicating the name of the message file where the predefined messages are located.

// MENU Use the GO command to display a menu.

// MSG Use the SNDMSG command to send a message to another user, display station, or message queue (including QSYSOPR for the system operator).

// NOHALT The // NOHALT statement is not supported. Use the system reply list support instead. See Chapter 6 for more information. You also can use MONMSG to trap error conditions in your CL programs as soon as they occur.

// OFF Use the SIGNOFF command to sign off the system.

// POWER OFF Use the PWRDWNSYS command to shut down the system.

// PRINTER Because the printer file object (*FILE) already includes all the printer settings the // PRINTER statement isn't necessary. If you need to override settings, use the OVRPRTF command.

// PROMPT Use the SNDRCVF command to make the system present a display to the workstation. The display file used must be declared to the CL program with the DCLF command.

// REGION There is no equivalent and none is needed.

// RESERVE There is no equivalent and none is needed because the i5 doesn't require contiguous space on disk.

// START PRT Use the STRPRTWTR or RLSWTR command to start a printer. Use the CHGWTR command to change printer writer settings.

// STOP PRT Use the ENDWTR or HLDWTR command to stop a printer.

// SWITCH Use the CHGJOB command with the SWS parameter to change the switches.

// SYSLIST There is no such thing as the system list device on the i5.

// VARY Use the VRYCFG command to vary on or off a device.

// WAIT Use the DLYJOB command to force a CL program to wait until a specific time or for a certain length of time.

Most-Used OCL Procedures

Table G.1 lists S/36 procedures with their i5/OS equivalents.

Table G.1: S/36 Procedures with i5/OS Equivalents	
S/36 Procedure	**i5/OS Equivalent**
ALOCFLDR	Not needed.
ALOCLIBR	Not needed.
BALPRINT	Not supported.
BLDFILE	CRTPF
BLDINDEX	CRTLF
BLDLIBR	CRTLIB
BLDMENU	CRTMNU
CACHE	Not needed.
CATALOG	DSPLIB, DSPDKT, DSPTAP
CHNGEMEM	RNMM
COBOLC	CRTCBLPGM, CRTCBLMOD, CRTBNDCBL
COMPRESS	Not needed.
CONDENSE	Not needed.
COPYDATA	CPYF
COPYI1	DUPDKT
COPYPRT	CPYSPLF, CPYF TOFILE(QSYSPRT), DSPSPLF
CREATE	CRTMSGF
DATE	CHGJOB DATE(...)
DELETE	DLTF, DLTLIB
DFU	GO DFU

Table G.1: S/36 Procedures with i5/OS Equivalents, continued	
S/36 Procedure	**i5/OS Equivalent**
DISABLE	ENDSBS
ENABLE	STRSBS
ENTER	CHGDTA
ERR	SNDPGMMSG
FORMAT	CRTDSPF
FROMLIBR	CPYF, SAVOBJ, CPYTODKT, CPYTOTAP
HELP	Press Help key.
HISTORY	DSPLOG, DSPJOBLOG
INT	INZDKT, CLRDKT, RNMDKT
INQUIRY	DSPDTA
IPL	PWRDWNSYS RESTART(*YES)
JOBSTR	LODRUN
KEYSORT	Not needed
LIBRLIBR	CPYSRCF, CRTDUPOBJ
LINES	OVRPRTF
LIST	Not supported. Use RUNQRY.
LISTDATA	DSPPFM
LISTLIBR	DSPLIB, DSPPFM, CPYSRCF TOFILE(*PRINT)
LOG	CHGJOB LOGCLPGM(...)
NOHALT	Not supported. Use system reply list.
PASSTHRU	STRPASTHR
PASSWORD	CHGPWD

Table G.1: S/36 Procedures with i5/OS Equivalents, continued	
S/36 Procedure	**i5/OS Equivalent**
PRINT	CHGJOB PRTDEV(...) OUTQ(...)
PRINTKEY	CHGJOB PRTKEYFMT(...) CHGUSRPRF PRTKEYFMT(...)
QRYRUN	RUNQRY
REMOVE	RMVM, DLTPGM, DLTF
RENAME	RNMOBJ
RESPONSE	Not supported. Use system reply list.
RESTFLDR	RSTDLO
RESTLIBR	RSTOBJ
RESTORE	RSTOBJ
RPGC	CRTRPGPGM, CRTRPGMOD, CRTBNDRPG
SAVE	SAVOBJ
SAVEFLDR	SAVDLO
SAVELIBR	SAVLIB
SDA	STRSDA
SECEDIT	CRTUSRPRF, CHGUSRPRF, DLTUSRPRF, EDTOBJAUT
SEU	STRSEU
SORT	FMTDTA, OPNQRYF
SWITCH	CHGJOB SWS(...)
SYSLIST	Not supported.
TAPECOPY	DUPTAP
TOLIBR	CPYF, RSTOBJ, CPYFRMDKT, CPYFRMTAP

Table G.1: S/36 Procedures with i5/OS Equivalents, continued	
S/36 Procedure	**i5/OS Equivalent**
TAPEINIT	INZTAP
UPDATE	CHGDTA

Control Commands

Table G.2 lists S/36 commands with their i5/OS equivalents.

Table G.2: S/36 Commands and i5/OS Equivalents	
S/36 Command	**i5/OS Equivalent**
ASSIGN	Not supported.
CANCEL:	
C P	DLTSPLF
C J	ENDJOB
C S	ENDJOB
C jobname	ENDJOB
CHANGE:	
G COPIES	CHGSPLFA COPIES(...)
G DEFER	CHGSPLFA SCHEDULE(...)
G FORMS	CHGSPLFA FORMTYPE(...)
G ID	CHGSPLFA PRTDEV(...)
G P	CHGSPLFA PRTSEQ(...)
G PRTY	CHGSPLFA OUTPTY(...)
G SEP	CHGSPLFA FILESEP(...)
G JOBQ	CHGJOB JOBPTY(...)
GJOBS	CHGJOBQE MAXACT(...)

Table G.2: S/36 Commands and i5/OS Equivalents, continued

S/36 Command	i5/OS Equivalent
CONSOLE	Not supported.
HOLD:	
H P	HLDSPLF
H J	HLDJOB
INFOMSG	CHGJOB STSMSG(...)
JOBQ	SBMJOB
MENU	GO
MODE	
MSG	SNDMSG, DSPMSG
OFF	SIGNOFF
POWER	PWRDWNSYS
PRTY	CHGJOB (RUNPTY(...)
RELEASE:	
L P	RLSSPLF
L J	RLSJOB
REPLY	Reply message in DSPMSG panel.
RESTART	CHGSPLFA RESTART(...)
START:	
S P	STRPRTWTR, RLSWTR, CHGWTR
S JOB	RLSJOB
S J	x
S SERVICE	Not needed.
S S	STRSBS
S W	VRYCFG

Table G.2: S/36 Commands and i5/OS Equivalents, continued

S/36 Command	i5/OS Equivalent
STATUS:	
D S	DSPJOB
D J	WRKJOBQ
D P	WRKOUTQ, WRKSPLF
D W	WRKCFGSTS *DEV
D WRT	WRKWTR
D U	WRKACTJOB, WRKSBSJOB
STOP:	
P P	ENDWTR, HLDWTR
P JOB	HLDJOB
P J	HLDJOBQ
P SERVICE	Not needed.
P S	ENDSBS *ALL, ENDSYS
P W	VRYCFG
TIME	DSPSYSVAL QTIME, DSPSYSVAL QDATE
VARY	VRYCFG

FORGETTING S/36 TECHNIQUES

Because you come from an S/36 background, you probably have an S/36 mindset and a tendency to use S/36 coding techniques when you program the i5. After all, computers are computers, and what applies to one machine also should apply to another.

Although the preceding statement might be true to some degree, you should forget certain S/36 coding techniques because they are not efficient in the i5.

Control Record in a File

The S/36 supports data files that have more than one record type. This capability is often used to keep control information about the file in a control record (usually the first record of the file). For example, a customer master file could have a control record that keeps track of the last customer number that was assigned. When a user needs to create a new customer record, you read the first record to find out the last customer number used, add 1, update the control record, and then add the new customer record using the newly calculated customer number.

DB2 physical files don't support multiple record types. Each physical file can have only one record format. You could keep the control information in a separate physical file, but the i5's data area object (*DTAARA) is a better solution.

The preceding customer file example could be designed differently on the i5. You could create a decimal data area and give it the same name as the customer file as shown in Figure G.21.

```
CRTDTAARA DTAARA(custmast) TYPE(*DEC) LEN(6 0) VALUE(0) +
          TEXT('Last customer number assigned')
```

Figure G.21: An example of using a data area to replace a control record in a file.

This command creates data area CUSTMAST so it keeps a decimal value of six digits (no decimals) and it is initialized to zero. From now on—each time a user needs to add a customer record—you can read the data area, add 1, update the data area, and then add the record using the calculated customer number. Your RPG or COBOL programs can read and update data areas directly. If you are using another language, you can create a CL program that does the reading (RTVDTAARA) and updating (CHGDTAARA) for you. You then call this CL program from your HLL program.

Creating and Deleting Work Files

Programmers often need to store information in temporary work files. For example, you might need to gather records from several files before you print a report. In this case, you would have to build a temporary file on the S/36, add the records, use the file, and delete it when you were done.

On an i5, you should create a work file permanently, with DDS, in the same library in which you are placing the database files for the application. Before you begin writing to the work file, you should make a copy of this file in library QTEMP, and then use the QTEMP copy instead of the original file. Run the OVRDBF command with TOFILE(QTEMP/FILENAME) so that your programs use the QTEMP copy you just created. When your job is done, the QTEMP copy will be deleted automatically by the system.

To simplify the process, use the Create Work File (CRTWRKF) command provided in Appendix A. This command creates a copy of a model file in QTEMP. See Figure G.22.

```
PGM

    CRTWRKF mylib/workfile
    OVRDBF workfile TOFILE(qtemp/workfile)

    /* Now all references to WORKFILE automatically refer */
    /* to the copy in QTEMP—not to the original file      */

ENDPGM
```

Figure G.22: The correct way to create and use a work file on the i5.

Using the LDA to Pass Data

The S/36 has no way other than the LDA to pass data back and forth between procedures and programs or between two different programs. Therefore, you are probably accustomed to using the LDA for everything. Because the LDA also exists under i5/OS (it is 1024 characters long instead of 512), you might think you don't have to change your ways.

Remember that the LDA resides on disk and that each read/write necessitates a disk I/O operation. Both on the S/36 and i5, the LDA is slow for this reason. The LDA is not a good medium to pass numeric data because the LDA is alphanumeric.

Fortunately, i5/OS lets you pass information between programs through program parameters. Suppose you have a program, named VEND01, that can—depending on the data you pass to it—either list a vendor's information on the printer or display it on the screen. On the S/36, you probably would code the procedure as shown in Figure G.23.

```
//   LOCAL OFFSET-1,DATA-'L023582'
//   LOAD VEND01
//     FILE NAME-VNDMST,DISP-SHR
//   RUN
```

Figure G.23: S/36 code to pass information to a program through LDA.

The procedure (shown in Figure G.23) would list the information for vendor 023582. Program VEND001 uses LDA position 1 for the option (display or list) and positions 2-7 for the vendor number. Translated to CL, statement by statement and keeping the LDA, the procedure would look like the code shown in Figure G.24.

```
CHGDTAARA DTAARA(*LDA (1 7)) VALUE('L023582')
CALL vend01
```

Figure G.24: CL code to pass information to a program through LDA.

While at times requiring more code, using parameters is more efficient. See Figure G.25.

```
    DCL &option      *CHAR   1
    DCL &vendor      *DEC    6

    CHGVAR &option 'L'
    CHGVAR &vendor 023582

    CALL vend01 (&option &vendor)
```

Figure G.25: CL code to pass information to a program through parameters.

Executing Dynamically Built Statements

Because OCL is an interpreted language, the OCL programmer can easily build a statement and execute it. See Figure G.26.

```
    //   INCLUDE ?1? ?2?
```

Figure G.26: S/36 code to dynamically build a statement.

The OCL statement shown in Figure G.26 executes the procedure named in parameter 1 and passes the parameters listed in parameter 2. Because it is a compiled language, CL cannot do this as easily. Compiled languages execute faster, but they aren't able to build ad hoc statements and execute them as simply.

To do the same thing in CL, you must use a call to QCMDEXC. For example, consider the CL program shown in Figure G.27.

```
    PGM (&cmd &parms)

        DCL &cmd       *CHAR   10
        DCL &parms     *CHAR   200
        DCL &cmdstr    *CHAR   211
        DCL &length    *DEC    (15 5)
```

Figure G.27: CL code to dynamically build a statement (part 1 of 2).

```
        CHGVAR &cmdstr (&cmd *BCAT &parms)
        CHGVAR &length 211

        CALL qcmdexc (&cmdstr &length)

 ENDPGM
```

Figure G.27: CL code to dynamically build a statement (part 2 of 2).

The program receives two parameters: &CMD (the name of the command to be executed) and &PARMS (the entire parameter list). In the CL program, the command string is built in variable &CMDSTR by concatenating &CMD and &PARMS with the *BCAT operation (which leaves a blank in between). While 211 is assigned to &LENGTH, which is required by program QCMDEXC, 211 also is the length of &CMDSTR.

Using // FILE LABEL-xxx

The LABEL parameter of the // FILE statement is often used in S/36 OCL when a program must reference a file by a name that' is different from the actual name of the file on disk. CL has no direct equivalent to the // FILE statement. When you want to execute a program, you CALL it and the system automatically knows what files are needed and how they are needed. Still, sometimes you will need to override the automatic process.

Use the Override with Database File (OVRDBF) command. Specify in the FILE statement the name by which the program knows the file, and specify the actual name of the file in the TOFILE parameter, qualified with a library name as necessary, as shown in Figure G.28.

```
        OVRDBF FILE(customer) TOFILE(custmstr)
        CALL pgm1
```

Figure G.28: Using OVRDBF with TOFILE to replace // FILE label-xxx.

In this case, program PGM1 knows the file as CUSTOMER, but the file actually exists with a name of CUSTMSTR.

You might be using the LABEL parameter so that the same program can process two or more different files that have the same record layout. In this case, you can use two or more files with the same name (residing in different libraries) or use a single file with multiple members. In both cases, you would still want to use the OVRDBF command to point to the correct file or member.

For example, you might have a cash-receipts history system that keeps the cash receipts for each month in a different file, such as CASHR01 or CASHR02, and up to CASHR12 for all 12 months of the year. When you code this application on the i5, you can use a single file, CASHREC, and use a different member for each month (members CASHR01 through CASHR12). To process the records for June (month number six), code the OVRDBF command (as shown in Figure G.29) before the first program that uses the file.

```
OVRDBF cashrec MBR(cashr06)
```

Figure G.29: Using OVRDBF with MBR to replace // FILE label-xxx.

Abusing // PRINTER

Printing special forms on the S/36 requires that you code a // PRINTER statement in your procedures so that the printer file used in your HLL program is set to the proper forms size, forms name, number of characters per inch, lines per inch, lines per form, and overflow line number. If you forget to code the // PRINTER statement or code it incorrectly, the special forms will be printed incorrectly.

The i5 solves the potential coding problem by storing the printer settings inside the printer-file object itself. When you create a printer file with the CRTPRTF command, you can specify all these settings and many more. Because none is needed, you don't have to worry about an equivalent for the // PRINTER statement.

However, if you ever need to temporarily override the settings of a printer file, you can use the Override with Printer File (OVRPRTF) command. You should get into the habit of creating printer files for each special form you need to print.

Make sure you include all the attributes to bring about a correctly formatted output.

Indirect Reference Using ??N??

OCL substitution expressions can be nested. You can code something like ?L'?2?,?3?'? and the system knows how to interpret it. Of these substitution expressions, one of the most bizarre is ??N?? to indirectly reference a parameter by its position number.

This technique is used in loops within procedures in order to process a different parameter on each pass of the loop. For example, you can code a procedure that prints up to 30 source members. To use it, the user enters the name of each source member in a separate parameter. The procedure then goes into a loop (where parameter 64 controls the loop by varying between 1 and 30). Then a statement (such as the one shown in Figure G.30) is used to run LISTLIBR on each member.

```
// EVALUATE P64=0
// TAG NEXT
// EVALUATE P64=?64?+1
// IF ??64??= RETURN
LISTLIBR ??64??,SOURCE,JLIB
// GOTO NEXT
```

Figure G.30: S/36 code to loop within a procedure.

If the loop is on the 16th iteration, ?64? has a value of 16. Therefore, ??64?? is equal to ?16?, which retrieves the value of the 16th parameter (the name of the 16th source member). Because parameters are not referenced by number, but by variable name, this powerful technique is missing in CL. You can simulate an array in CL by declaring a variable long enough to contain the names of all source members. Because 30 members are allowed (each one in a different parameter), and each can be 10 characters long on the i5, declare &MBRLIST as 300 characters. Then use the CHGVAR command as shown in Figure G.31.

```
CHGVAR &mbrlist (&mbr01 *CAT &mbr02 *CAT &mbr03 *CAT &mbr04 *CAT +
                 &mbr05 *CAT &mbr06 *CAT &mbr07 *CAT &mbr08 *CAT +
                 &mbr09 *CAT ... etc.)
```

Figure G.31: CL code to use CHGVAR to set up a variable to simulate an array.

In the CL program loop (which uses a control variable such as &N that varies from 1 to 30), code the statements shown in Figure F.32.

```
CHGVAR &offset (&n * 10 - 9)
   CHGVAR &member %SST(&mbrlist &offset 10)
```

Figure G.32: Code to loop within the CL program.

&OFFSET is calculated to know where in &MBRLIST the name of the current source member is. Then %SST is used to extract 10 characters from &MBRLIST starting at &OFFSET. For the 16th member, &OFFSET is 151. Variable &MEMBER will then contain the name of the current member.

Using #GSORT

i5/OS provides three ways to sort files using:

- A logical file built over the physical file to be sorted.

- The OPNQRYF command.

- The FMTDTA command.

Of the preceding three methods, Format Data (FMTDTA) is the closest to #GSORT. The command even uses the same H, O, I, and F specifications in the same format. If you know #GSORT, you can start using FMTDTA almost immediately.

The most important differences between #GSORT and FMTDTA is that FMTDTA requires that you code the sort specifications in a separate source member. FMTDTA is closer to the SORT procedure than to an in-line #GSORT (which is used by many procedures). Because you cannot pass parameters to the sort specification member, you cannot perform dynamic sort specifications by substitution expressions as you can on the S/36.

If you need more dynamic processing, use the Open Query File (OPNQRYF) command. While a complete discussion about OPNQRYF is well beyond the scope of this book, Figure F.33 shows the basic process.

```
OVRDBF  file1 SHARE(*YES)
   OPNQRYF FILE((file1)) QRYSLT(...) KEYFLD(...)
   CALL    pgm1
   CLOF    file1
   DLTOVR  file1
```

Figure G.33: Using OPNQRYF to replace #GSORT.

The OVRDBF command with SHARE(*YES) is necessary. FILE1 is the name of the file that you need to sort.

OPNQRYF is next; it again references FILE1. In QRYSLT, you code an expression that indicates which records to select. KEYFLD lets you code the fields by which OPNQRYF will sort. The key difference between #GSORT and OPNQRYF is that #GSORT references fields by beginning and ending position, while OPNQRYF uses field names. The file must have been created from data description specifications (DDS) that describe all fields contained in the record.

CLOF closes the file (which was left open by OPNQRYF) and DLTOVR removes the override provided by OVRDBF.

You also can sort a physical file by creating a logical file over it. This method is similar to using OPNQRYF, except that the logical file is a permanent object. Logical files should be used only for sorts that are likely to occur many times. For example, a customer master file is likely to be sorted by name or in descending order of total amount due.

INDEX

NOTE: Boldface indicates illustrations and code; t indicates a table.

E

Edit Object Authority (EDTOBJAUT) command, 240, 241

editors, code, 410–411

EDTOBJAUT. *See* Edit Object Authority (EDTOBJAUT) command

ELSE command, 66–68, **66**, **67**
DO with, 67–68, **67**

embedded quotes, 190–191, **191**

End Debug (ENDDBG) command, 258

End Program (ENDPGM) command, 9–10, **10**, 79, **80**

End Receive (ENDRCV) command, 170, 172

End Subroutine (ENDSUBR) command, 73–75

ENDDBG. *See* End Debug (ENDDBG) command

ENDDO command, 63–65, **63**, **64**, **65**

ENDPGM. *See* End Program (ENDPGM) command

ENDRCV. *See* End Receive (ENDRCV) command

ENDSELECT command, 68

ENDSUBR. *See* End Subroutine (ENDSUBR) command

EQ, 61

error handling
error messages in, 100–101
Create Data Area (CRTDTAARA) command and, 196, **196**
Monitor Message (MONMSG) command in, 101–103, **101**, **102**, **103**
command-level (global), 104, **104**
program-level (global), 103–104, **103**
MONMSG and global error trapping in, 8–9
selective prompting and, 224
specific vs. generic monitoring in, 105–106, **105**

error messages, 100–101

escape messages, 86*t*
for CHKOBJ, 198–199*t*

eServer iSeries, 1

Evaluation (EVAL) command, 263–266, **265**, **266**

expressions, 54–55
logical, 59–61, **60**, 61*t*, **61**
quotes used in, 191–192
S/36, procedure control, 446–452, **447–451**
S/36, substitution, 441–446, **441–446**

F

F4 key to format statements, 11–15, **11**, **13**, **14**, 18

FIFO data queues, 144

FILE LABEL–xxx use, S/36, 466–467, **466**

file management, 169–187
Add Logical File Member (ADDLFM) command in, 176
Add Physical File Member (ADDPFM) command in, 176, 177, **177**
Change Logical File Member (CHGLFM) command in, 176
Change Physical File Member (CHGPFM) command in, 176
Clear Physical File Member (CLRPFM) command in, 176
Close (CLOSE) command in, 175, **175**
control records in files in, S/36, 462–463, **462**
Convert Print to Physical File (CVTPRTF) command in, 187, 381, **382–383**
Create Duplicate Object (CRTDUPOBJ) command in, 183
Create Physical File (CRTPF) command in, 170, **171**, 176
Create Work File (CRTWRKF) command in, 183, **183**, 339–340, **339–340**, 463
database file member processing in, 176–177. *See also* database management
Declare File (DCLF) command in, 169–171, **171**
Delete File (DLTF) command in, 101, 176, **197**
Display (DSPxxx) commands in, 184–186
Display File Field Description (DSPFFD) command in, 184
Display Overrides (DSPOVR) command in, 179
End Receive (ENDRCV) command in, 170, 172
Format Data (FMTDTA) command in, 469–470
Open Query File (OPNQRYF) command in, 469–470, **470**
outfiles and, 184–186
override commands in, 178–179
Override with Database File (OVRDBF) command and, 172–173, **172**, 178–179, **178**, 466–467, **466**
Override with Display File (OVRDSPF) command in, 179

R

NOTE: Boldface indicates illustrations and code; t indicates a table.

System i Books from MC Press

APIs at Work, 2nd edition

ISBN: 978-158347-069-5
Author: Bruce Vining, Doug Pence, and Ron Hawkins
http://www.mc-store.com/5085.html

IBM i5/iSeries Primer, 4th edition

ISBN: 978-158347-039-8
Authors: Ted Holt, Kevin Forsythe, Doug Pence, and Ron Hawkins
http://www.mc-store.com/5070.html

Free-Format RPG IV

ISBN: 978-158347-055-8
Author: Jim Martin
http://www.mc-store.com/5073.html

The Modern RPG IV Language, 4th edition

ISBN: 978-158347-064-0
Author: Robert Cozzi, Jr.
http://www.mc-store.com/5080.html

The Programmer's Guide to iSeries Navigator

ISBN: 978-158347-047-3
Author: Paul Tuohy
http://www.mc-store.com/5075.html

See more titles at http://www.mc-store.com